Attitudes, Beliefs, and Choices

Are Yours

Creating the Life

You Desire?

Alexandra Delis-Abrams, Ph.D.

Printed in China

Dedication

Dear Alissa and Corianna,

At the time this book is preparing for its birth Alissa, you just had your third-year birthday, and Corianna, your third-month birthday. *Attitudes, Beliefs, and Choices* has been dedicated to you both, as well as subsequent grandchildren, as a legacy from your YiaYia.

For more than thirty years, I have been hot on a pursuit of Self-realization. What that means is simply remembering who I am, and what my purpose is in this lifetime.

What I have handed down to you is a compilation of wisdom I've derived through and extracted from, my childhood, young adult life, work, formal education, seminars, workshops, trainings, books, articles, events, travels, businesses, groups, therapy, family, service, volunteering, and encounters with a wide variety of people in the world. I've written notes on paper towels, napkins, scratch paper, notebooks of variable sizes, and business cards for such a long time, many have yellowed. In addition to the attempt to interpret my poor penmanship, it is a miracle I was able to read them. Tucked away in files, I began the arduous task of retrieving what I felt was important enough to include in this work. Undoubtedly, I have left out something, so there will be a few things for you to discover on your own, that will nurture your personal and spiritual growth.

I've grown to know myself through my joys and accomplishments, as well as my struggles, pain, and disappointments. Just as you are with the perfect set of parents to learn your life lessons here in Earth school, so you will be drawn to the perfect circumstances, people, and opportunities to accomplish your mission here. Remember, there are no accidents.

A few closing thoughts.

- The game of life, if aware it's being played on the game board of Love, may be a more deeply enriching adventure for you.

- Start, then continue to question your beliefs, as they are valueless unless you test them and live by them.

- Be open to life, embrace your wholeness, and know lasting happiness is within. Follow your heart and be true to yourself.

- You always have choices. You always have options. Make them conscious ones, as every choice changes the world a little bit. Your free will is a gift you were given at birth. Use it to your advantage.

- Be open to your intuition, the infallible teacher of truth, and you will be brilliantly guided throughout your journey.
- Laughter is healthy for your body, mind and soul. As you mature into adulthood, keep laughing as much as you are now as children.

It's infectious.

I pray the Great Spirit will give me a long and healthy life, for me to participate with you, so we can play, learn, and love together. Thank you for giving me the identity of "grandmother," which is an awesome opportunity to express and live what I've learned along the way.

I love you absolutely!

YiaYia

CONTENTS

Suggestions From The Attitude Doc
For Using This Book:

The book is set up alphabetically with each section being a different "feeling" word. It can be read cover-to-cover or as a tool to help you with a particular feeling.

Peruse the contents pages to discover the word that best fits your mood at the moment, as well as its opposite. Or you may want to close your eyes and allow your finger to move down the page and stop where it does, which will mean that is the word to read and reflect on. Trust the process.

At the end of each section is a "Reflection Time." Its purpose is self-reflection, and it requires your honesty.

Have fun with the process. The book is a reference for the adult reader in seeking personal and spiritual growth, a family communication tool, and a foundation for a child's life.

Enjoy the journey!

My Attitude of Gratitude...

is not exclusive to this book, because it is the fullness of my life experiences, and those I have participated with, that has brought me to the words that are on these pages.

The creation and production of this book does not start and end in any particular order. Everyone was genuinely important to this project, including Max, our Aussie Shepherd. He stayed with me each night until the wee hours, tucked under my husband's desk, leaning his head up against the side of it—his favorite position. Thank you Max, my loyal friend.

Gene, my husband of forty years, continually provided support, including dinner brought in to my office on many occasions, so I would eat something. "The door to the bird cage has always been open in our marriage," were his profound words when he was asked about the success of our long-term marriage. For this, I thank you immensely—for honoring my need for freedom. This bird was free to fly AND to stay. What an important lesson, and what a gift.

My immediate family, Jeff, Christopher, Linda, Danielle, and Michael, extended family, and friends, seem to know the full plate I attempt, and sometimes successfully manage to juggle, with my assorted projects and activities. I feel especially blessed that my three big sisters are my dear friends. Although my folks have been gone for more than thirty years, and my in-laws for only a few, I feel their pride and affection. To you all, an enormous thank you. I feel all of your unconditional love.

The Wood River Valley and The Light on the Mountain Spiritual Center are a meaningful source of community and family. I love the many mountain ranges of this valley that exude strength and power, right here in my back yard. They are a constant reminder of their Source.

The Self-Realization Fellowship has been my anchor since 1971, when I "accidentally" found the Lake Shrine, home of the Gandhi World Peace Memorial, in Pacific Palisades, California. Paramahansa Yogananda and his teachings have provided me with Truth, and the answers to the questions I've sought most of my life:

"Who am I?"

"Where did I come from?"

"What am I doing here?"

"Where am I going?"

Every time I felt blocked, or was searching for something and needed a particular reference or photo, I asked for guidance to find it, and I got it. Thank you, Creative Intelligence, Source, Greater Force, Spirit, Life, Indwelling Spirit, Divine Designer, God, Formless Stuff of the Universe, Conscious Mind, Light, Love, Oneness—for partnering with me in this project, as well as life. Thank you for infusing me with undaunted determination to achieve my aspirations. We're a team.

My friend and colleague, Dr. Theresa Dale, innovator of the protocol, Neuro-physical Reprogramming, which I have used in my practice for over ten years, will always be the recipient of my appreciation. Since 1987, when I started practicing, I've always been open to more efficient methods of being of service to my clients and willing to change when something more effective presented itself. I need not look any longer. NPR, which you will read about, is brilliant. Thank you TD.

I've called myself a "stretch" rather than a "shrink" because my clients and students become vast, rather than diminished in their thinking. Molly Misetich is my "stretch." She knows me so well and is one of my special confidants to whom I turn when the "stretch" is in need of a "stretch." I'm most appreciative for her loyal friendship, service, and talents she brings to my business. Thanks Molly.

To all of those who participated in the content of this book by sharing their stories, I send hugs along with my affection. I tremendously respect your challenges and am indebted for your contributions.

My thanks to the team of editors and administrative gals who have handed the baton from one to another. My friend, Gail Burkett was the first to offer her editing skills. Then came Molly Misetich, Kathleen Urbany, Betty Shaw, Janit Karias, and Sue Martin. Thanks to you all for being terrific cheerleaders. To Marcia Mode-Stavros, "efharisto," for being there with the perfect words at the perfect time of need. To my team involved with the design of this book, Rod Kelly, Jonathon Smith, KK Lipsey, Molly Misetich, and Jeff Abrams, a huge thanks for your gifts.

My thanks is extended to Narda Pitkethly for sharing Katie Rogers with me. Her Alabama accent will live long in my heart. She truly moved this project forward with her editing and writing skills. For so long I've been ignorant as to how many ways there are to sit on a normal computer chair. "Katie, you must write a book." You live what this book is all about—vibrant energy, amazing support, and a positive attitude. Ya'll are the best.

Finally, I acknowledge and thank those of you who have chosen to read this book and for being open to recognize the power of our attitudes, beliefs and choices. Have fun on your journey.

Throughout the book, I have made reference to friends, family members, clients, lecturers, interviewees, various authors, and others. I used fictitious names as well as actual names when given permission to do so. Material has been taken from keynote addresses, conferences, interviews from my dissertation, sessions with clients, and even anonymous e-mails, to which no specific reference is available. It is my intention to do honor to all persons and theories included, and I have sometimes listed their books and writings, not necessarily because I derived material from them, but as a courtesy. On the other hand, I did not list all of the books, but only those that I mention directly, from persons such as Deepak Chopra or Gary Zukav who appear several times in the book.

"Dear God, So far today, God, I've done alright. I haven't lost my temper, haven't been greedy, grumpy, nasty, or over-indulgent. I'm really glad about that. But in a few minutes, God, I'm going to get out of bed and from then on I'm probably going to need a lot more help. Thank you."

Unknown

A is for feeling... Acknowledged

Definition: recognized, accepted, accredited, validated

Opposite: overlooked, ignored, disregarded

To feel acknowledged is to feel honored. It means to know you did something of value, or you are someone who has worth. To feel acknowledged is to feel accepted and loved.

The search for acknowledgement can be like the infamous search for the Holy Grail. Many are looking for it in the wrong place. Robert A. Johnson, noted Jungian analyst, says in his book, *He,* "It [the Grail] doesn't exist in physical reality. It is inner reality...It is not a specific place...It comes with a certain level of consciousness." While questing for this experience, one expects to find the happiness outside oneself. Johnson says, "This never works because the Grail isn't a place. What we're really looking for is inner acknowledgement, self-approval of who we are, as we are. To accept ourselves as we are is the same as giving a gift to ourselves – the greatest gift of all. Only then can we accept others."

"Just" a Mother

How do we instill this concept of self-acceptance in our children? Or better yet, what is the best way to acknowledge children yet instill self-worth? There are times when we won't get the acknowledgement we feel we want, need, and deserve. Try what my granddaughter, Alissa, did one day when we were working on a puzzle together. When I didn't say "good girl" to her after she put in a matching piece, she said, "Good girl!" to herself. Self-acknowledgement is empowering.

When I received my degree from graduate school and had to bend down so the hood could be placed over my head, I felt so proud of my accomplishment. I can still feel myself, as I received my hood, with an enormous smile on my face that came directly from my heart. Although I would have loved the whole world to acknowledge me, it was my husband Gene, a constant support in my life, who was there to witness this indelible moment. He acknowledged me with flowers and tender words. However, the true depth of my accomplish was the internal experience.

The yearning for acknowledgement begins in childhood. Our parents are our primary relationships, and those relationships become the foundation for our belief structure and attitudes about life. Many parents take it much too lightly. Women are often embarrassed when they are asked what kind of work they do, and their response is, "I'm just a mother." Have you ever said that? Have you ever heard it? The words "I'm just a mother" come from a woman who has a low opinion of self. "I didn't go to college, I don't have talent, I have no concrete means of earning a living. I'm JUST a mother." Realize that a child's life will be molded from the environment created by that parent. What an awesome responsibility!

If we start constructing a building on shaken ground, we may in time, have an unstable finished product. To acknowledge yourself as a magnificent spiritual being is rule number one in preparing a child for life. If it's not part of your nature, then you have to learn how to accept and love yourself, regardless of who betrayed or discounted you during your childhood.

Overachiever Identity

Male clients in particular, long for their father's approval. As a child they never heard, "I feel so proud of you, son. You are growing into a thoughtful and caring person. I love you. I love who you are. You add such meaning to my life." Unfortunately, few have heard their male parent ever speak those three powerful words – I love you. Mother's love is considered to be more or less unconditional, while there is an unspoken concept that you have to earn father's love. Merit appears to be analogous with a father's love. Self-worth and value are locked up with his words, looks, gestures, and actions. What is your experience of this statement?

Keep in mind it is your experience that is important. A son might grow up feeling left out, emotionally neglected, disregarded, and abandoned. It may very well affect his self-worth and success in all areas of his life. If one were to interview the father, he might express how much he loves his son and how incredibly proud he is of his accomplishments. It would never occur to the father that his son didn't feel accepted by him.

As a child, do you feel you have to earn your father's love by doing something to please him, or are you enough being who you are? As a parent, do you feel you have to earn your father's love?

One client, a professional woman with a strong identity as an overachiever, had tried desperately all of her life to be acknowledged by her father. She had attained success in many areas of her life, but in her belief system, she still lacked that one thing that would make the difference. If she accomplished one more goal she would earn Daddy's approval. She never gave herself acknowledgement until she was willing to change her beliefs about her past. "I need Daddy's approval to be accepted," was released and replaced with "Who I am, as I am, is enough."

Acknowledging Others

Is it difficult for you to acknowledge someone for something they've done, physically or altruistically? How about something they created or earned? How about simply for being? "I want to tell you how important you are in my life and how much you contribute to me. Thank you for being exactly who you are and someone I can share my heart with." Magic words—words that can turn a person's life around—words that can be instrumental in another person's choices—words that empower.

While you explore these questions for yourself, be aware if there is an obstacle that may be preventing you from communicating these words. Be honest now. Is it embarrassing? What will be implied if you share how important someone is to you? Like your child, a friend, an employee, a teacher? I'll venture to say you could do it in a heartbeat with your pet. Consider that your upbringing could be affecting you in this way.

Now that you've answered those questions, maybe you're actually ready to step forth, take a risk, and acknowledge someone in your life. So what's required? For that answer, I turn to Helice Bridges, author of *Who I Am Makes A Difference*, founder of Difference Makers, and globally recognized as the "First Lady of Acknowledgement." She is an internationally recognized professional speaker who delivers a message that "You Make a Difference." As of December 2003, through the Blue Ribbon Ceremony, over 5.5 million people worldwide have learned to bring out the greatness in themselves and others. Her incredible story is written in the best-selling book, *Chicken Soup for the Soul.*

Helice knows each of us makes a difference, and she uses her words to share that idea. Her objective is to reveal to others their own uniqueness, allowing their light to shine through. When this happens, judgment fades. Let the miracles happen.

In the simple eight-step "ceremony," she promotes self-esteem like no other. This simple act takes less time than it takes to take a shower or cook a two-minute egg.

Helice encourages us all to acknowledge others. First, a blue ribbon is placed above the heart of the person you want to acknowledge. On the ribbon, in gold writing are the words, "Who I Am Makes a Difference." It is placed upward toward all their dreams coming true, which you support. Let them know the difference they make in your life. Now give them two ribbons to honor someone else. After this brief ceremony, you will have deeply touched someone's life, while feeling warmth and goodness in yourself. Your relationship takes on new meaning and importance. Possibly you've moved through a barrier and your confidence level has escalated. Good for you!

Now, did that person get it? Did he or she truly hear your acknowledgement? You will know by his or her response. Be aware of it. "I got it. Thank you for sharing that with me. I really feel you're sincere, and I appreciate your thoughts. It means a lot to me. I feel validated." The person receiving the acknowledgment needs to allow the words to penetrate.

Talking Stick

Parents: We all want to know that who we are is special and unique and that we make a difference. Acknowledge your children for who they are, not necessarily for what they do. Recognize their essence, rather than the doing-ness of the personality. Speak the truth to your children. Tell them how they contribute to life, to your life, and what a difference they make, however small, no matter what conflict you may be experiencing with them at the time, no matter what – tell them. The earlier in childhood you start this practice, the easier the subsequent years will be.

Children: Acknowledge your parents. When was the last time you expressed appreciation to your parents for all they do for you? When my son, Jeff, was in elementary school he left me a note one day that said, "Thanks Mom for making my lunches." Such a small gesture – six words – but what an impact to my heart! Thirty years later, I am writing about it. Maybe your parents don't appear to do that much for you. Well, acknowledge them anyway, for being who they are, and watch what happens. Give your parents a break. It's their divine role to protect you, set boundaries, and care about you. Don't be so hard on them. Respect should be mutual. If it's not, talk about it. Borrow the idea of a "talking stick" from Native American culture and learn how to speak from your heart, as well as listen. Select a stone, stick, crystal – whatever you like will work perfectly. Have a heart connection with it and speak while holding it, while the others are silent until their turns come around.

Miss Annie, my friend who owns a preschool, told me a story of a three-year-old student who took home the idea of a "talking stone," and asked her father to sit on the imaginary "peace mat" with her and pick up the talking stone. Three years old! What a champion!

There is a metaphysical belief that we choose our parents. This belief says that before you became physical, at some level of consciousness, a contract was made and agreed upon between mother, father, and child. If we give merit to this belief, then our parents are the perfect ones to help us learn our life's lessons just as we are the perfect children for our parents to discover their lessons in Earth School. We're all students here on Earth in this fascinating school.

You chose your folks. They chose you. Act as if this belief is true. Take responsibility for it and then notice the quantum leap in your growth and relationship with them. Leave the victim energy behind and own your life. That's where you'll find power.

Employers: Acknowledge your employees. Have they been dedicated to you? Do they do their best every day? Do they make a difference in your business? Examine each individual, be honest, and you will find something. What, if anything, prevents you from engaging in this way? Would honoring them demean you in some way? Would it mean giving away your power? Would it lessen your effectiveness somehow? Would it diminish your righteousness? Could that be a good thing? Yes, unless you would rather be right than happy.

Do you get the idea? This is an important habit to establish in your life. When the act of acknowledging someone else becomes second nature, it becomes easy and comfortable to do. An important prerequisite is to be able to acknowledge yourself first, for who you are. Realize the Holy Grail is within you.

Maybe today was a great day and everything went well for you, or maybe it was not so great of a day, and things didn't go so well. Every day is a day of life. What attitude did you demonstrate throughout this day? What did you learn about yourself? Can you acknowledge yourself for who you are, regardless of the events of the day? Learn from it. You created it exactly how it turned out. Take responsibility for your thoughts, words, and actions. You can create the future from clarity of the present or from being a victim of your past. You are always faced with a choice and it is your responsibility to make a good one!

Reflection Time:

1. I invite you to engage in an experiment for thirty nights. Before you go to bed, look into the mirror and take some deep breaths while looking at your body. Start with a minute, then extend it to three or four. Notice a tendency to judge. That's a conditioned response. Acknowledge your body exactly the way it is. Speak the words, "I love you just the way you are." Notice your level of comfort or discomfort in saying this. Just notice your feelings and keep doing this every night. After a few days and when you're feeling brave, stand there in your birthday suit and perform the same exercise.

2. A variation of the above is to look into your eyes and connect with yourself. Recall the day and your interactions with people. Were you kind? Rude? Impatient? Tolerant? Acknowledge yourself for engaging with life – exactly the way you did. Notice a tendency to judge. Again, that's old conditioning. Be aware of other choices you could have made, and what might have been the consequences. Tomorrow is another day and another opportunity to choose and act.

3. Another variation is to look in the mirror and see your Self – the essence of who you are – your true Nature – filled with Light and Love. See yourself as a wave of a vast and powerful ocean with the same qualities. Expect miracles.

4. Make a list of the people in your life who rub you the wrong way. Be willing to evaluate that trait in that person that bugs you. Now be willing to notice if that trait happens to be in you. Now, notice characteristics about them that are positive. Also, notice those in you. Now stretch your perception and be willing to see your oneness with that person.

5. Take a walk in your neighborhood and choose to connect with everything your eyes light upon. Acknowledge it, him, her to yourself and the value added to your life.

"It is impossible for me to experience love and fear at the same time. It is also impossible for me to experience peace when I am fearful."

Foundation for Inner Peace, *A Course in Miracles*

A is for feeling... Afraid

Definition: frightened, anxious, scared, terrified
Opposite: courageous, brave, bold

What are your deepest fears? What are you truly afraid of? We have all felt afraid. Fear can build when we are home alone at night hearing the wind howl, when we hear of the latest cancer statistic, or when worrying if our child will experiment with crystal meth. Fear is a natural feeling and our job here is to overcome and take charge of it, rather than being ruled by it.

We have created many things to feel afraid of in today's world. We often feel afraid when we don't feel accepted, or if we have little or no self-confidence. When we are out of balance, it can be because of fear. At a deep level we fear we'll never make it in the world, or that no one will ever love us, and we must be destined to be alone. We can become convinced that we'll die before we have made a contribution. Our life purpose diminishes when we feel separate, unworthy, and incomplete, and starts to resemble an unfinished symphony.

We are afraid that we'll be judged for something we say or don't say, feel or don't feel, for the way we walk, express, interact, dress, laugh, or talk. We are often judged for being too happy, judged for being too quiet, judged for being too creative, judged for being too smart, judged for not being smart enough, for speaking with a heavy voice, for having thick eyebrows. You name it.

What gets many young people into trouble is the fear of being judged for being angry. It's not okay to be angry in our culture. We alienate people from us, and that takes us back again to the fear of being alone. What a vicious cycle fear constitutes! We haven't learned or been taught that anger is a feeling, that it is energy, and that it is natural. Rage is not natural, and that is what comes from denying anger, which all stems from being afraid.

Fear distorts our thinking and prevents us from being clear, centered, and stable. An acronym for fear that's been around for awhile is:

False Evidence Appearing Real

I had a client who wanted to get pregnant. She yearned to be a mother. Her doctor gave her some incomplete information and said, "We'll talk more after the X-rays have been read." So, in the meantime, my client's mind took total control over her well-being. She saw her chances of getting pregnant reduced and gave way to her emotions. Her thoughts were spiraling with FEAR, and she didn't even have the facts. After the X-rays were read and discussed with the doctor, lo and behold, the evidence in my client's mind was false. It was a dramatic shift in peace of mind and attitude. Besides feeling positive again about getting pregnant, she learned a valuable lesson about giving in to fear.

Being afraid keeps us from moving forward. One of fear's companions, guilt, keeps us stuck in the past. Feelings of being stuck can manifest in the large intestine in the form of constipation. What power we give emotions of fear and guilt! Fearful thoughts can turn into panic attacks–loss of breath, heart palpitations, racing thoughts, and anxiety. The body responds to the thought and acts accordingly.

We fear we're not enough, inadequate to the task, but we constantly try to prove the opposite to others, while wearing a mask of arrogance and smugness. One of the things that foster fear is our belief in lack, which is grounded in unworthiness of everything, including abundance. The result is significant self-sabotage.

We fear our feelings whether they are strong or soft. We fear our anger equal to our vulnerability. Feeling separate and fearful of intimacy can be damaging to any relationship. We become agoraphobic (fear of public places) as well as claustrophobic (fear of being closed in). Fear definitely devastates and sabotages us with every opportunity.

Teen Wolf

Young girls, out of their own subconscious fears, have been known to torment each other and act aggressively. The victims don't defend themselves because they're afraid of conflict and confrontation, or they lack self-confidence, which could ultimately lead to the worst thing–being alone. So because of the strong need to be included, they retreat like the omega wolf, with its tail between its legs. They forsake self-expression, create lack of confidence, and give their power away, all out of fear.

Often, these girls hold in their anger because they don't have the tools to express their feelings. They may not feel heard by parents, they may feel rejected by their peers, their grades may have suffered and depression is a result. Rather than feeling the depression and seeking immediate help, many turn to dulling those feelings, numbing out on whatever drug they can acquire, or they engage in casual sex to experience a connection.

"Club drugs," such as MDMA, or Ecstasy, are often used at nightclubs, but their use has spread to many other social settings. Current science is showing changes to critical parts of the brain from use of these drugs. The National Institute of Drug Abuse states that these drugs can also dramatically increase heart rate and blood pressure, along with altering the body's ability to regulate internal temperature, which can lead to hypothermia. If that's not enough, chronic use or high doses can cause memory loss, muscle breakdown and kidney and cardiovascular system failure.

The following is a tragic story about a woman who chose to deny her underlying feelings and act out by taking the drug Ecstasy. She hit a homeless man on a highway while under the influence of it. Rather than stopping immediately once she hit him, she continued to drive the car with his body lodged in her windshield. She said, "[I] couldn't think to do the right thing. I was scared and was crying." The man was apparently alive for several hours after he was hit and probably would have survived had he been taken to a hospital. A jury convicted her of murder.

What a tremendous loss of creativity, passion, service, and joy for this woman, not to mention the loss of a human life! It seemed she was caught up in a snowball effect of fearful decisions. Not only that, but she chose to drive while under the influence, and then felt so afraid, that she didn't know to stop after the accident occurred. Fear prevented the driver from making the right choice from beginning to end in this scenario.

Do you harbor fearful or trusting thoughts as you raise your young ones today? Granted, raising our little ones today may be more challenging, because our world is a different place than it was twenty years ago. Obviously, everything changes. But it is different than the world I knew. As a kid, growing up on the shores of Lake Erie, none of us knew about mood swings or being afraid to grow up. We played kick-the-can long after it got dark, jacks, hide 'n seek in the linens hanging out on the clothesline to dry. We taught ourselves to swim and play tennis, and everyone had a blast running through the changing colors of the water fountain at the nearby park. Our parents never worried about us shooting up or sniffing glue or household cleaners. It was more wholesome and carefree. How about you? Was your childhood fearful or fun-filled?

Optical Illusions

Our five senses are the driving force behind our fears. I recall driving down the Pacific Coast Highway and seeing what I thought was a dead animal on the road. My heart started beating faster and my mind started racing with the thoughts of how to rescue this animal. My palms got sweaty, and my mouth became dry. As I apprehensively approached the scene of my senses, there on the highway was an old dirt-embedded blanket. After a sigh of relief, I chuckled at the thought that my senses, once again, got the best of me. The mind is relentless in wanting to get the best of us.

When we engage in fear, we invariably make poor choices in our personal lives. I believe the influence of fear in our collective lives is portrayed in war. The following is a selection from the "Friends of Peace Pilgrim" newsletter, Volume 39, written by Christine Northrup, M.D., business owner, physician, surgeon, mother, author of *Women's Bodies, Women's Choices*, and speaker.

"The fear and anxiety caused by the possibility of war are the biggest health challenges we face right now. As a physician, I know full well that emotions such as fear and anger impede the healing process and, if held long enough, actually lock us into a vicious cycle that produces more pain, more fear, and more anxiety. This can wreak havoc on our minds, bodies and spirits."

Fear has become more intense in our society, it seems. It appears that people's lives are run by fear. We can give the media partial thanks for that. The news is not really new at all. It's always about something negative, horrific, catastrophic, or devastating. What wonders could manifest from a good news newspaper!

Just imagine what amazing changes could happen to our society if we taught qualities such as intuition, peace, calmness, self-control, will power, and concentration in our schools. We would have a body of children who knew they were capable of being the masters of their minds. The educational system would be founded on well-selected staff, teachers and administrators, and supported by a parent body that is totally aware of their own nature. Our children's minds are like plastic and can be molded into any shape with the help and support of a responsible, caring, and centered adult. To learn first, then to teach others, is how to harmoniously develop all the necessary factors to life.

September 11, "9/11," and the aftermath have provided us the opportunity to be fearful each day, with every breath we take, with everything we do. Do we really want to live our lives in this way? We do have a choice of choosing fear and doubt or love and trust. This is such a powerful truth. Become self-empowered and use it to replace fear. Engage your ability to introspect and discriminate. Under all circumstances, learn to trust the process.

Getting Over It

So, how do we overcome our fears? The number of books written on the subject of fear could fill many library shelves. Medications for fear are introduced to the market place frequently.

We are not alone in feeling afraid. Start by asking a loyal friend to act as a caring listener, knowing the space is safe, feeling trust and acceptance. Maybe a trusted teacher, coach, neighbor, or relative could act as a support. It grows from there. Understand what might be feeding the fear, or where the fear really came from in the first place.

Feeling afraid can be dissolved by actually feeling the fear, which means feeling the body sensations. Become aware. Feel the thought of fear in the body. Is there a color associated with feeling afraid? If so, what color is it and what does it feel like? What are your racing thoughts in those moments? Feel those thoughts and feelings that are connected with feeling afraid. Feel the beliefs you have about the perceived fear. Allow yourself to feel it fully. The fear just might disappear. In other words, LOVE the fear, knowing that it too is a part of you. Only then will it loosen its grasp.

If we were to feel and communicate our feelings, we would be expressing our truth and living a life of integrity, in lieu of being a slave to the mind with its fearful thoughts. When I am being true to myself, I am living with integrity. I am more equipped to examine a situation thoroughly and be pro-active in finding resolution. If I am out of integrity with myself, lacking clarity and balance, I will relinquish my power and give in to the fear and the doubt generated from my mind.

In whatever choice we make, we have the choice of feeling afraid or of feeling loved. We have that much power. When we know we have such power, we can consciously improve the quality of our life. To eliminate some of the destructive fear in your life, ignite the feeling of freedom instead. It is important to discern and be cautious. It's probably not the best idea to leave a camera on the front seat of an unlocked car while attending a sporting event. Use your good judgment, also known as common sense.

When I observe and stay centered, I am in control. Once, while driving on a state highway, traveling less than the minimum speed because of the winter road conditions, I suddenly hit "black ice." For those of you who don't live in a four season geographical area, black ice is ice that blends into the road so that it is invisible to the driver's eye. It is invisible until the tires of your car connect with it! I had the opportunity to experience it first hand. In the driver's manual, it tells us not to apply our brakes. I instinctively released my hands from the wheel and my foot from the brake, and completely surrendered. I observed the entire experience; I observed the car make a 360-degree turn! (My heart gets fluttery just writing about it.) My husband, who was a passenger, was astounded by my behavior. I was also. Fortunately there were no cars on the road. I was thankful for the angels that I knew were watching over me.

Life will continue to present situations that invite us to be fearful, but when we feel alive, secure and confident, we demonstrate a strength that not only empowers and inspires us, but others as well. We always have a choice. We can live each day with composure that exemplifies the power behind a roaring river or we can feel weak, frail, and fearful.

The Thought of Fear

This story is a parable from a Self-Realization Fellowship lecture about a saint and the ghost of death. While meditating late one night, a certain saint saw a ghost of the dread smallpox disease entering the village where he lived. "Stop!" he cried. The ghost replied, "I will take only three people." The saint nodded. The following day three persons died of smallpox; the next day several more died. Each day, more took their last breath. The saint meditated deeply on this great deception, feeling he was not told the truth. The ghost replied by saying, "I did speak the truth to you. I took only three. The rest killed themselves with the thought of fear."

Become the master of the moments of your life and learn to embrace fear. Love fear to death! Rather than resisting it, face fear and work on its dissolution. Our fears can serve us or sabotage us. When we learn and become aware of them, we are on the road to empowerment. Only then, will you truly be free, and truly be living.

Reflection Time:

1. Let's take a look at a hypothetical situation. You have a meeting with your employer and have a hunch you're going to be put on probation. Fear wells up in you and the thoughts start churning. Your sleep has been impaired and so has your digestion and interactions with family members. The worst-case scenario is that you get fired, because you feel you didn't do anything to deserve probation, and reject the action. Notice how your fearful thoughts are escalating and you haven't even had the meeting yet. False Evidence Appearing Real.

2. Let's say this scenario really happened to you. Better yet, recall any time when you felt that kind of fear. Take time to reflect and ask yourself if this is a pattern. Have you explored the details of it?

3. Examine the beliefs surrounding this situation. Breathe deeply and start to actually feel the beliefs and fear – feel it in the cells of your being – turn on a flow of colors, images of the past, body sensations, thoughts. Allow anything to come forward. Use no judgments. Feel it fully and chances are it will disappear–that's right, disappear. It could actually go away. The use of the breath along with feeling what you resist is a powerful combination for healing.

4. Now create a fear list and write down all the things that you are currently aware of feeling afraid of in your life.

5. Does this list serve your highest good in any way? Does a life filled with fear and doubt bring you the results you seek? Perhaps love and trust are the forces you would prefer.

6. Start tracking the feeling of fear in your past. Were your parents fearful people? How about those close to you? Teachers? Relatives? How about parents of your friends?

7. What is your commitment to seeking answers about your fears?

8. To what degree are you honest with yourself?

9. Challenge your fears. Fear of growing and of transformation can take you out of living in the moment. When you see yourself wanting what you do not have, instead of what you do have, confront it. Is the grass really greener on the other side?

10. Do the people you spend time with, spend time with fear?

"When you listen to the voice in your head, listen to it impartially. That is to say, do not judge. You'll soon realize: There is the voice, and here I am listening to it, watching it. This I am realization, this sense of your own presence, is not a thought. It arises from beyond the mind."

Eckhart Tolle, *The Power of Now*

A is for feeling... Aware

Definition: cognizant, observant, attentive, mindful

Opposite: blocked, oblivious, unaware, attached

What are you aware of this very moment? Stop reading and notice your environment. What do you hear, see, sense, and feel to the touch? Are you aware of your heart beating, your breath, your thoughts, and your feelings? Notice, observe, and be conscious and attentive to your inner and outer world.

To be aware is to be alert or awakened to a heightened sense of reality. To be aware is to be conscious of your inner self and outer environment. Being aware allows you to learn through your life experience.

The Shoe That Talked Rather Than Walked

Here's a story of how my awareness served me when I was in graduate school. It was imperative I fulfill an internship program. I searched for the perfect organization in which to work and gain hours to complete the requirement. There were many intriguing interviews, but none had spoken to me thus far. I knew I would eventually affiliate with the appropriate staff where I would learn important principles relative to my chosen career path and where my energies would be respected.

"Keep on keeping on," my inner voice said. "You'll create the perfect fit." (Sort of like the storage container bottoms and tops. Have you ever noticed they both have numbers on them? For example, a #2 bottom goes perfectly with a #2 top. A #4 top may fit a #2 bottom, but the fit really isn't that tight. After a short time, air seeps in and it is obvious, it's NOT a perfect fit, because the food dries up.) I wanted a #2 for my #2!

I had arranged for an appointment that sounded rather promising. Dressed for success, I arrived at the location, feeling confident and eager to embrace this opportunity. No sooner had I closed my car door and taken a few steps, that I felt an abrupt imbalance in my stride. Oh my goodness! I had broken the heel on my shoe! My lovely beige pump, which matched exquisitely with a stylish neutral suit, had completely broken in half. To say it was embarrassing to walk into my meeting with one shoe on and the other in my hand is an understatement.

During the interview, I was aware of a small window in the office being blown open and shut. Like air filling a sail, the breeze would thrust the window open, then moments later, would slam it shut with a vengeance. I was aware of the game nature was playing as I interacted with my interviewer, sharing my background and answering questions.

I graciously thanked my potential employer and hobbled my way to the car. I felt uneasy and somewhat discouraged about the experience. I knew my search for the perfect internship was not over. The meeting felt strained, uncomfortable, and stiff. The harmonious "vibes" just weren't there. The "feeling" was missing; there was no chemistry. It lacked excitement, connection, and heart. It wasn't even a #4 and a #2!

Once in the confines of my car, I gazed down at my shoe and found myself saying, "Well, shoe, what do you want me to know about this interview?" The message came intuitively, "You won't be supported here. Just as the window continually opened and shut, this group will be closed to you every time you open and attempt to express your uniqueness."

Paul Pearsall, Ph.D., author of *Making Miracles* writes, "Jung described what psychologists view as the classic example of a psychological synchronicity - or what he called 'creative acts...meaningful coincidences'."

So, what are you aware of this very moment? Be open to any message you might be getting about something. You may be making a decision about what you've just read, or a judgment that it is helpful or absolutely ridiculous. Talking to your shoe? Come on now.

Is Aunt Alex on Drugs?

Everybody becomes aware at her or his own perfect time. While sharing with some of my relatives about my book, I related the prior story about the shoe. That night my nephew's son asked his mom in all seriousness, "Is Aunt Alex on drugs?" (I always was the odd one in the family!)

Research is beginning to validate what the East has taught for thousands of years–to value quiet time, be aware, listen to your heart, and give in kindness. Stop. Be aware of the value you place on quiet time. Simply notice the answer, without judgment. If nothing comes to you, terrific. Just be aware of it, and notice if you receive an answer at another time–maybe an hour later, maybe a day later. Be mindful.

This kind of awareness was encouraged through the unique graduate program I participated in while studying for a degree in transpersonal counseling. As a class, we met for five days in a still and pristine environment, in Anza Borrego State Park in the San Diego area, and acknowledged Mother Nature as our teacher. A morning assignment was a mini vision quest of three hours; each student meandered on his or her own, connecting with any aspect of the great outdoors that drew his or her attention. It was a contemplative period of being open and merging with an element–a rock, shrub, sage, tumbleweed, a cloud, whatever–in the inner space of receptivity. We each pondered the message offered. What I received was always something of value. I addressed my flaws and my beliefs that no longer served me. It was such a powerful adventure, taking in my inner world, heightening my awareness of my relationship to myself and to life.

I encourage you to stretch your thoughts on awareness to include all your senses. For example: notice the many sensations while touching an ice cube, then being in a sauna; the sound of Mozart, and then Tibetan chanting; the smell of a rose, and the smell of smoke; the sight of a sunrise and a full moon; the taste of a lemon, then an apple. Consider the many aspects of your nature–physical, mental, emotional, and spiritual. Then, as you detach from your five senses and retreat within to your sixth sense, your intuition, you rely on your own innate wisdom, and benefit in all ways. Educate yourself by making use of your intuition. Better yet, use all of your senses to become aware.

Times are Changin'

We have entered into a most exhilarating time on the planet as we encounter the transition into a new, profound way of experiencing life. The balance of feminine and masculine energy (yin and yang) is now being explored, understood, and integrated into our nature as individuals—parents, teachers, managers, politicians, lawyers, and children.

Aspects of the yang, or masculine energy, are linear thinking, form, rigidity, structure, "centered in the mind," and doing-ness. How many of us would admit we function in this accelerated society as "doing machines?" The yin energy possesses characteristics of the right brain, which are creativity, formlessness, space, process-orientation, sensitivity, play, imagination, heart, flexibility, artistry, holistic thinking, intuition, and emotion. Take a moment and notice–be aware–of where you tend to identify. Make a few notes if you choose to, or just be aware and allow.

Our society is slowly opening to a new paradigm and recognizing the mind-body connection. Feelings are being honored as an important part of who we are. Research is proving the validity of this connection, which is vital to our happiness and quality of life. It is a challenge to be aware of the balance of our feminine and masculine energies. To experience our wholeness, we need to acknowledge the condition of our lives.

Too many of us grew up having to stifle feelings for our own survival. In lieu of being true to ourselves, we chose to please others at any cost. As we matured, we mastered denying our feelings. We can no longer make those same choices today and expect healthy lives. They no longer serve us as responsible adults. In addition, we are responsible for raising self-reliant and responsible children. We must prepare our future leaders more effectively by helping children maintain their joy, unconditional love, resiliency, playfulness, and total acceptance. Be aware of your relationship with the children in your life, as a teacher, parent, grandparent, aunt/uncle, neighbor, or caregiver. Track your most recent emotional experience with a child and notice how willing you were to allow the child to express feelings. Be attentive to how present you were with the child during that time. Simply notice–be aware.

Female vs. Male

Maybe I'm biased, but I believe it is mostly the women, through their awareness, who are spearheading these important changes, on the job as well as in the home. (Attention: male readers. Be aware if you are feeling defensive after reading the prior statement!) The proportion of women clients and seminar participants to male clients or participants is significantly higher. The need to be in control is a strong belief in men, as well as in women. Recently, sessions with two different women clients revealed the following similar beliefs:

- "I am what I produce."
- "My value is associated with what I do."
- "I must be doing something for others to be loved."
- "If I am helpful, I am guaranteed love."

When asked, "What kind of person would have this belief?" the discovery by the clients was revealing. Their answers: "A caregiver," "A person who doesn't value being," "A needy person," "An insecure person," "A person who isn't enough being who they are." Can you relate to any of these?

Hi-ho, Hi-ho...

When the purpose of our work is to be of service, we are giving to ourselves, as well as others. Our life is enriched tenfold, bringing true happiness. Going to the workplace with the desire to contribute, be helpful, make a difference, and express joy will enrich every aspect of life. Co-workers enjoy being around us instead of avoiding our presence. I recall a client who called for a session, sheepishly confessing, "I've become aware of the fact that nobody ever asks me out to lunch. I think my attitude needs adjustment." In our sessions, she explored her beliefs about her self-worth, relationships, and work. We discovered profound feelings of separation that led to insights that spurred a new awareness. She changed her behavior and it directly affected her reality. She went from a state of imbalance, where she rarely allowed time for fun, relaxation, and self-nurturing, to feeling grounded in wholeness.

Some of the results of attitude-shifting in the workplace, in school, or at home might be:

- A commitment to telling the truth.
- Communicating with intention and clarity.
- Responding rather than reacting. (Blame, shame, guilt, or fault, are all judgment, not responsibility.)
- Working in a livelihood you love. Work is more than a paycheck and holiday bonus.
- Being of service, cooperating, and working in harmony.
- Offering programs to employees that focus on self-improvement.
- Accomplishing a more balanced life style.
- Acknowledging love and joy as our essence and what we are all truly seeking.
- Treating our fellow beings with kindness and compassion.

Am I describing your working environment? How about your home environment?

It's very exciting to be aware of ourselves as whole beings as we learn to integrate this powerful force within us. This is the essence of the new millennium. Times are changing. To be better prepared for it, we might want to chip away at the old belief structure and evaluate what truly serves us and what is outdated and sabotaging. Are you aware of holding onto something old in your belief system?

Life has gifts to bring and lessons to teach us every day. When we are more open to its message, we increasingly become our own teacher and our own master. When we open to our awareness, we are on a challenging journey to truly master the moments of our life and make the best choices for our highest good. Even more, we become aware of the times we don't make the wisest choices and also of the times we do. Just remember that you feel more empowered when you have many, rather than fewer options, or choices. Offer your child, your partner, your friend, or your employee choices, and it will be appreciated.

This is self-discovery. It can be educational and fun if we practice awareness and learn to observe our thoughts, feelings, words, and actions. Take the next step, stretch some more, and observe yourself being non-attached to the outcome—strictly in observation, with no judgment or opinion. This is Zen thinking. Alternatively, we can choose to observe ourselves as being totally attached and plugged in, reacting to anything that pushes our buttons. Like the string of lights on a Christmas tree that becomes brilliant with color once plugged into the electrical socket, we can also light up with emotions that may be most inappropriate to the moment. We can get plugged into the situation, the spoken or unspoken word, and react. Be aware and observe.

Bird's Eye View

I recall an awareness I had while sitting in seat 9A waiting on the tarmac for a departure. Looking out the window, I noticed the activity on the ground in proximity of the airplane. The viewing range was quite limited. However, after the pilot was given the go-ahead and throttled forward into the air, I could see more and more of the surrounding area. By the moment, my awareness became expansive. I could see for miles and miles and miles. The higher we climbed, the more vast my vision and experience. My sight shifted from limited to expansive. It was one of those "aha" moments, a great metaphor for expanding my awareness and perspective.

As we keep expanding to include the events in our lives, rather than being affected by them, we actually learn to hold them in a way that is not damaging to our well-being. They become events, situations, circumstances, or merely the content in our life, each a neutral experience. We, in turn, become the context—that which holds and broadens our experiences.

There are degrees of awareness, so you can expand more and more fully into life. Dr. Deepak Chopra suggests we learn to develop "witness consciousness." My interpretation of this term is that you simply become an onlooker, instead of casting a critical thought towards another's behavior. Rather than harshly judging your response to a comment, simply be a spectator of yourself. When we are still and observe what is so, without reacting to it, we allow our innate wisdom to surface. We realize that this is not the entire picture. Be aware, breathe, and observe.

It's a fascinating process. This is one of the most important steps we can take in personal, professional, or spiritual growth. The more aware we become, the better parenting skills we exhibit, the more caring an employer we become, the more compassionate we are as a partner, the more connected we are to our friends etc., etc., etc. Get the idea? In other words, the more we recognize our wholeness and demonstrate those qualities, the happier we are as individuals; when we are happy, that energy influences the collective consciousness, and the world becomes a more peaceful and harmonious place to reside. So the more happy beings there are on the planet, the scales tip and reality shifts on a global level. Let the games begin!

Reflection Time:

Socrates professed there is great power in a question. Each chapter will conclude with Reflection Time, designed for you to get even more benefit from this book. Use a journal to record what you learn about how you got to be who you are. Respond to the questions in the following Reflection Time portion of the subsequent chapters by being relentlessly honest with yourself. And have fun!

1. Give yourself about twenty minutes of quiet time one morning–in a private room at home, a bench at the local park, the seashore, or even at a quaint restaurant to savor a croissant and your favorite beverage. Allow your thoughts to slow down. Observe your self, being open to receive truth. Put your attention on what may be turmoil in your life, and how to find the answers you're seeking. Breathe slowly, deeply, and notice your breath.

2. Start a journal and write in it every morning for twenty minutes. *The Creative Journal*, by Lucia Capacchione, is a magnificent reference for journaling as well as Julia Cameron's *The Artist's Way*.

3. Are you steamrolling (plowing) through life with a list of to-dos as your rudder, oblivious to your surroundings? Try experiencing life without a list.

4. Be receptive to the messages of life in whatever form they appear. Write them down to encourage the flow.

5. Notice if there is conflict in the relationship with your parents or with your child. Can you pinpoint what the conflict is rooted in? Communicate and explore.

6. How often have you passed by your desired exit on the freeway? Or maybe been given one too many speeding tickets in the same month? Notice how many nights that you've been home for dinner the past week. Is it time for an adjustment?

7. Engage in a discussion with a friend on the subject of awareness. Notice your different or similar points of view.

8. Study a page, or ad from a magazine for a few minutes, with the purpose of being aware and retaining the detail. Close the magazine and make a list of everything you can recall in your mind from what you observed.

9. Close your eyes and do a visualization of something you desire to be, do have. Be aware of creating detail in the picture. Feel it then be aware.

10. What is your "shoe" saying to you about your life?

"The disastrous feature of our civilization is that we've developed more materially than spiritually. There is imbalance."
Dr. Albert Schweitzer

B is for feeling... Balanced

Definition: centered, focused, clear, stable
Opposite: unaligned, disjointed

Press rewind in your memory bank and stop at a time when you were a child on a teeter-totter with someone. If they were heavier than you were, you were most likely up in the air more than you were on the ground. If they were lighter than you were, you were the one more often on the ground. Remember a time with another person when the weight was just right, evenly distributed? You went back and forth, up and down, up and down, in perfect balance.

It seems we have to learn to balance so much in our lives. How do I manage my time to grow my private practice, write, lecture, meditate, serve my community, nurture my marriage, read, interact with my children, hike, exercise, stimulate my brain, restore, rest, spend time with my dog, and have fun with friends? Whew! What a balancing act between personal and professional desires!

Another way to describe feeling balanced is being centered. Consider the analogy of the ceiling fan. When I feel centered, I am right there at the center of the fan connected to the source of the power. When I'm out of balance, I'm out on the blade, and once something unexpected arises, the chances are good to excellent that I'll get knocked off. The momentum throws me into my ego and into the illusion. In that imbalance I become a victim of the illusion. It appears oh-so-real and sometimes I can collapse into it, rather than remembering the truth of the present moment of NOW that exists within my center.

To seek balance is to yearn for stability and grounding. In a world of instability, this can be quite a challenge. Can we teach our children about balance while they are young and absorbing their environment? We need to be able to project love, humor, and understanding to our little ones in a manner that will help them recognize when they are out of balance, giving them the tools they need to bring balance back into their lives. We can help them understand that all aspects of their lives are important.

31

The more we honor balance in our lives, the more we experience peace of mind. What if...

- the ocean only had waves that came in and didn't go out.
- everything went up and not down.
- there was only activity and no rest.
- there was only receiving and no giving.
- we only inhaled and didn't exhale.

Our consciousness can't register these examples because everything is duality and balance. Try this simple exercise. Take in a breath and hold it. Keep holding it. Now keep holding it while taking in another breath, and another, and another. Point made.

Mariel Hemingway's book, *Finding My Balance*, is a must-read for all truth-seekers. She says, "The funny thing is that I am sure that what's center for me today was imbalance yesterday, or will be tomorrow. But forget that, I make a commitment to nothing except my willingness to be present on my own feet, inside my body, today – right now." To read her life story is inspiring and motivating in helping us find our own balance, as well as surrendering. "When you surrender, struggle ceases," she says as response to her life-threatening experience in the ocean. Her book is a magnificent portrayal of life.

The moment something unplanned occurs, it can throw us out of balance. We're out there on the blade and off we slide, caught up in the drama. These are the times for strong inner balance, taking the reins of the mind and pulling in. What is truly happening now? What is the next thing I need to do? We can teach this to our children only when we know how it is done. This is doable through balancing our 24-hour clock, and remembering at the same time that there is no time. Time is the past and the future. The present has no time because it is now.

In my workshops, I use a four-legged chair to demonstrate stability and to represent the different part of our nature: physical, mental, emotional, and spiritual. When each leg is solid and strong, the chair functions. However, when any one of the legs is splintered, weak, or broken to any degree, the chair is in a state of dysfunction. In other words, when each aspect of our nature is honored, nurtured, and respected, we manifest our own strength and security.

The field I chose to study and practice is called "transpersonal psychology." "Transpersonal" means "beyond the personal," bridging the world of spirit with the world of matter. Transpersonal psychology recognizes the physical, mental, emotional, and spiritual aspects of each of us as healing forces in our life. We have a body, a mind, feelings, and a spirit, or soul. Each must be honored. Light and shadow are part of our Earthly experience. We suffer when we deny the shadow in us, rather than honoring it. We suffer when we identify only with the ego, when we forget we are whole beings. Wholeness includes reason and feeling, being and doing, the anima and animus, or feminine and masculine, left and right brain, intuitive and five sensory orientations, etc. Get the idea? We are multi-sensory beings–vast, expansive, and powerful who have forgotten our true identity.

Instead, we've grown to identify our nature with the personality. We become addicted to what is outside of us, hanging onto the edge of the blade of the fan, doing what we can to stay there. We create a lifestyle that mimics this imbalance, trying to keep up with the illusion. We fill ourselves with negative thinking and self-talk that has us constantly striving for achievements to gain self-worth. What would happen if your life slowed down somewhat? What would your inner critic say? Keep in mind the purpose of the ego is to survive, and its voice can be oh-so-subtle.

Dr. Albert Schweitzer says, "It is not necessarily about joining a church or temple. It's about expressing our consciousness, peace, and joy. Get in touch and connect with this. Be in communication with your eternal self."

Balancing Act

Where in your life are you experiencing imbalance? Remember, if there is imbalance in one aspect of your life, it affects all of your life. The workplace seems to take a lot of precious energy for one reason or another. Pat Barrentine, one of the contributors of the book, *When The Canary Stops Singing: Women's Perspectives on Transforming Business*, says, "What is out of balance is that feelings are not welcome in the work setting." Are they welcomed in your work setting? Do you feel safe and secure to express your thoughts and feelings to your superior or co-worker? In addition she states,, "Some even go so far as to recommend a recognition of spiritual values in the workplace." They all share an orientation toward life characterized by a personal commitment to self-discovery, transformation, and spiritual growth. Finding our balance is finding our wholeness, which brings us closer to finding our truth.

Take some time; be brave and work with the Wheel of Life chart in this section's "Reflection Time." In the chart, the wheel represents your life. It's a tool to help determine how well your wheel rolls. When balanced, life rolls at a pace that resembles ease, grace, and calm. When out of balance, it doesn't. Dissect each spoke in the wheel and figure out your degree of balance.

There is an art to being balanced while we are doing. It requires a connection to our essence –staying in the center of the fan while it's spinning. The more grounded you are in the center, or the more identified in the source of the power, the more balanced, the more centered, the more in observation you are to the duality of life. Laughter and tears, pleasure and pain, success and failure, winning and losing, passion and emptiness, become events that you hold and observe rather than dramatize. When the weight is evenly distributed, we teeter-totter through life effortlessly, handling the ups and downs with ease and joy, rather than the struggle.

Reflection Time:

Study the Wheel of Life chart with regard to the following questions. It could also be an interesting experiment to explore with your family. Have fun with it.

1. Finances–Five laws of wealth are earning, spending, saving, investing, and tithing. Do you set goals for each? Do your beliefs on abundance support you or sabotage you?

2. Job/Career–Are you your job, your profession, or do you have a job/profession?   Would you describe yourself as a workaholic? Your partner? Your parents? Is the corporate ladder getting the best of you?   Are you doing what you love to do on a daily basis?

3. Physical–Are you a fast-food junkie, or have you educated yourself about nutrition? Your body deserves the best. It acts as your soul's "Toyota" and you should care for it better than you care for your car. Do you exercise regularly?

4. Mental–You have as many as 60,000 thoughts a day. Are the ones you think positive? Do they enhance your existence, or are they negative and self-defeating? You choose. Do you live in the past with regret, or live in the future with anticipation or worry? Your choice.

5. Emotional–Our feelings have either been suppressed or expressed as children. Were you "allowed" to express or did you have to suppress? We react in the manner we are accustomed, unless we self-examine and make changes in our thoughts, words, and action.

34

6. Family/Home Life–Are you spending plenty of quality time with your family? When was the last time you read your child a bedtime story, told her how precious she is to you, spent quality time talking with your son about sex, drugs, or girls? They grow up all too quickly and they need you NOW.

7. Social/Relationships–Dinner for two, a weekend fling in the mountains, a spa experience, camping with friends—you, as parents or professionals must make time for your relationship. Friendship is vital to any marriage. We must take time for relationships, whatever marital status we claim. As someone once said, a relationship is the most important ship you will ever be on.

8. Spiritual–Most important is the relationship you have with your Self–with the essence of who you are. Do you start your day with a twenty-minute meditation? Do you listen to your intuition, your sixth sense? How about time in nature, with no distractions–no cell phone, no pager, no tug from the world, just you in the natural world? Try it, you'll like it. "Go to the mountains, your cares will fall off like the autumn leaves," said John Muir (on a Sierra Club Calendar), crusader for preserving the wild and sacred places on Earth.

"Betrayal is so profound because it shakes our confidence and causes us to doubt ourselves."

Dennis S. Reina and Michelle L. Reina, *Trust & Betrayal in the Workplace*

B is for feeling... Betrayed

Definition: violated, abandoned, revealed, deceived

Opposite: trusted, assured, dependable

Have you ever felt betrayed? I have. It hurts. It can be devastating when I have put my faith and confidence in someone and they don't perform, or it didn't work out as I had hoped, planned, or assumed it was going to. I was let down and upset. We can feel alone and empty, and experience a loss of trust in humankind when we feel betrayed. The devastation can feel abusive and humiliating.

Betrayal can occur at any level. It happens in life everywhere. A loyal wife is betrayed through her husband's adulterous behavior. A student may feel betrayed when a teacher does not explain the reasoning behind the grade given on a final exam. The successful new salesperson feels betrayed when she overhears her co-workers gossiping about her at the water fountain. A friend assures another she'd never go out with the boy that just broke up with her, and two days later she sees them together holding hands. She feels betrayed.

Big-scale Betrayal

The higher echelon of several major corporations felt they were beyond the law and could do whatever they wanted to do with the funds. They believed they could use and manipulate funds for their own personal gain. Stories of their greed were uncovered in 2002. Because of their lack of integrity and their dishonesty, stockholders who placed their trust and faith in them suffered tremendous financial loss and emotional suffering. Many walk today in the path of bitterness and resentment. Their expectations are gone, along with their faith in humanity. Such disrespect under these circumstances seems unforgivable. There is no doubt that forgiveness is challenging, but it is a necessity for our own well-being.

Own It

How do we have faith and trust when this horrible thing called betrayal has occurred in our life? How do we rebuild trust? This is the challenge because not only have we lost trust in people after this violation, but also we mistrust ourselves. We feel vulnerable, weak, and open for another bout of anguish. We have to lick our wounds like a dog does when he's been hurt.

Before we can let go of any painful situation there is homework to be done if we want to learn from it and prevent it from reoccurring in our home movie. We must do our personal work and explore this opportunity from all vantage points. Yes, you feel like you've been victimized. Yes, you have lost trust. The important question is, how can you move on with life and use the experience to your benefit?

A thirteen-year-old client I had seen several times was ready to address the quality of her relationship with her father. She had confided in him and told him that she was depressed and requested that he not say anything to her mother. However, he betrayed her trust by telling her mother. This was the only time my client had ever chosen to open her heart and be vulnerable with him. The beliefs that she created from this were that she "would never tolerate disloyalty," "men will break your heart," and "men are unstable." Deep within these beliefs was a hurt child. Initially, she was not ready to explore this, but once engaged in the process, she knew it was important to release. She did so. Her body was happier, and she felt more in control in her life as she created a new way of seeing herself as an authentically self-empowered person. She released the identity of being betrayed, took total responsibility for it, and moved on.

On the other hand, the brother of another client, a Vietnam veteran, still holds onto self-pity, anger, hostility, and betrayal. He was angry as a child and the war gave him a place to "hang" his anger. You have to do the work. It doesn't just go away. To this day he is still 'F–ing' everything that doesn't fit in his system of thinking.

In lieu of owning it all, we can hold on to our lack of forgiveness and make another wrong, wrong, wrong. I heard Garth Brooks sing a song entitled, "We Buried the Hatchet but Left the Handle Sticking Out." What a title! Do you know anybody who is holding onto the handle? What would you say about their intention?

Guess who gets to be right when we make others wrong? A course of action, such as criticizing and judging, leads to an attitude that alienates us from others as well as brings inner suffering. Being ripped off, taken advantage of, betrayed, and/or screwed, is all linked with victimization.

This perpetuates darkness and leads to bitterness, which tends to make people become hard, cold, callous, and closed off from their heart. We all know the number one killer disease in our nation is heart disease. The heart gets blocked from the flow of love. The heart is about LOVE. We truly do sabotage our happiness through our attitudes, beliefs, and choices.

Look into your past and recall a person you may have betrayed. Retrieve the situation and details as fully as possible. There may even be more than one. Again, be honest! Your current dilemma is surfacing to allow you to clean up your past—believe it or not. Recollection and attention to the core incident can bring freedom, healing, self-forgiveness, and peace of mind.

I've counseled clients who hold onto the pain of their childhood and to the attitude that condemns their parents for not living up to their unfulfilled expectations. Now as parents, their own children don't even bring them the fulfillment they hope for, because of the lack of certain unachieved goals, so it becomes a double whammy. By the way, these happen to be goals set by the parent, not the child. Crazy-making...

To resolve your own unresolved issues concerning betrayal, first be willing to look at the situation honestly and from an objective point of view. Be open to hold the belief that this must be happening for your highest good, no matter what the appearance. I know from experience that this works. If you are willing to at least explore this point of view, you have taken a gigantic personal leap.

If you choose otherwise, betrayal will turn into toxic energy in your body, not the other person's (as you might wish). You will feel resentment, jealousy, anger, revenge, and regret, to name a few harmful feelings. We step into our own misery through thoughts generated from our experiences. We feed into a negative mindset that runs over and over, again and again, recreating the pain every time.

- If only people could be trusted.
- If only they'd hear my side of the story.
- If only things had worked out the way I wanted them to, then I'd be happy.
- If only I had taken that other job offer, I wouldn't have been put in this position.
- If only she'd change, I'd be a free man.

The list is endless! We have the power to create a new list. When we realize that our reality is created by our intentions, our life shifts and opens. What does intention have to do with betrayal?

Unconscious Intentions

Gary Zukav says in *The Seat of the Soul*, "If you truly desire to change the relationship with your husband, that change begins with the intention to change it. How it will change depends upon the intention that you set." It takes more than a wish or a desire. It takes the use of our will if we truly want to free ourselves from feeling betrayed. Start to take responsibility for it, which means own it, then recognize that it is happening in your reality, and on some level you have created the situation in order to learn from it.

Responsibility is not blame, shame, fault, or guilt. When we choose responsibility, we merely recognize we are the source of our experience. In not owning the situation, we give our power away, which is yet, another choice. When the light bulb goes on, and it goes on at different times for each of us, we realize the place of power lies only in taking responsibility for it all, even if it appears to be outside of us.

Gary says we know our intention by what we have in our reality. He talks about "unconscious intentions," which are intentions or beliefs we carry out and are not aware of. Embracing the concept of "unconscious intentions" may require stretching our perception, yet it is a truly deep and powerful approach to embracing the pain and the pleasure of our lives. Gary says, "If you are not aware of your intentions, the strongest one will win." For example, you may have an intention of being a strong team member at your work, and an unconscious intention that you're dissatisfied with your job and would be better off working elsewhere. Sooner or later, you are laid off. So obviously, your unconscious intentions set the wheels in motion, and the situation turned out exactly as you had "intended."

How do we become aware of our unconscious intentions? We begin by scrutinizing our truths, our beliefs, our desires, and our soul. One way is by recognizing what we've manifested in our lives. For example, a failed relationship. "Oh, I guess I didn't really want to be in this relationship." Another way would be to actually evaluate what your intentions are and be honest with yourself. The more you come to know yourself, the more your intentions will cease to be a mystery.

It has been scientifically proven that our cells hold memory–memory of pain or pleasure, fear or love, bitterness or freedom. Our thoughts are a form of energy. Read anything by Ernest Holmes, founder of a philosophy called Science of Mind. The core belief in this teaching is simply, "Change your thinking; change your life." A quote from a book of his called *This Thing Called You* states, "It makes no difference what your harvest may have been last year; today you can create a new future if you have the faith to believe that you can."

The Power of Breath

My friend, Allen Hallada, has a hot tip for those who want to move through the betrayal residue efficiently and quickly. Allen is a veterinarian and has been successfully teaching breathing techniques for several years to his patients' owners, as well as to others. He is helpful not only to the pet but also to the owner. "Pet owners, although they may love their pets unconditionally, still have their own stuff. Whether they realize it or not, an owner's unresolved negative emotions can affect a pet. My thought is that even an abused animal will forgive and not hold onto betrayal." Don't you want to do the same for your pet?

The breath is famously known to calm the mind. It is our first connection to the physical world and stands to reason why it would influence our behavior.

"I've found that a way through pain is learning to breathe. Breathing properly will help us to be more present in our own bodies, and to be better listeners and diagnosticians."

"Rather than reaching for the aspirin bottle and looking for the fix outside of oneself, I encourage people to learn to breathe properly. Indirectly, their pets benefit from their owners' awareness of their breath. Proper breath will facilitate feeling in the body and address those locked-up feelings. Repressed feelings often get stuck at the neck or diaphragm, and they freeze there, which stops personal and spiritual growth."

"The breathing techniques I teach are body-centered, which retrains the breathing program, in order to avoid fight-or-flight, fear-based breathing. Fight-or-flight-based breathing occurs at a rate of fourteen or more breaths per minute while body-centered belly breathing occurs at less then fourteen breaths."

Allen told me his own experience with the breathing program is amazing, and how much it contributes to his happiness in life. For one reason or another, when he is off it, the unconscious patterns arise and he goes into those feelings of victim consciousness, feeling sorry for himself and wondering why he's not getting what he wants in life. He observes the pain in his body and recognizes it as the wake-up call. "Get back to the breath," he reminds himself. Once he does, he feels like he hits his threshold again and is making wise choices. When he's doing the program, life flows–relationships are incredible and success just happens.

I started a Qi (Chi) Gong class after hearing about it for years. I am enthralled with its grace and power. Qi Gong is a 3000-year-old Chinese practice based on the use of all one's faculties: body, mind, and spirit. It recognizes the life energy, or "chi," that flows through a system of meridians in the body. Qi Gong is comprised of five elements: movement, breathing, concentration, relaxation, and attitude. It is said the required deep breathing oxygenates the body and massages the internal organs. The results of this ancient art are serenity and a feeling of being centered (just what we're looking for to heal betrayal). To quote from the website, "Every attitude one has contributes to either empowerment or dis-empowerment, truth or illusion, health and recovery, or its opposite, discomfort and disease. Usually nothing except one's own attitude can inhibit progress."

Life will shift when we choose to hold the belief that pain is often the prod for inner growth and reflection. Believe you will benefit from this saga, grow from it, and be a stronger person because of it. Choose to move on with clarity and trust. It may sound like a tall order. Reach out for support and don't give up! Re-claim your birthright! You deserve peace of mind.

Reflection Time:

1. Review your life with regard to betrayal. It would be beneficial to spend quiet and alone time for this review. A supportive friend could be drawn in at some point to offer key details. When I say supportive, I don't mean someone who will agree with you in being a victim, but instead a friend who sees the bigger picture and is willing to be there for you through caring, compassion, truth, and kindness.

2. Ask yourself, "What is this really about?" Deeply examine the content. Be aware. Be curious about the details.

3. Focus on your feelings. What was transpiring in your life at that time? What choices did you make?

4. Are you looking for someone to blame?

5. Is it too humiliating to own this experience?

6. Do you see a pattern here? If so, when did it start? (Here's a hint: go back to the earliest memory you can think of, when feelings of betrayal were present with regard to this event in your life.)

7. What answers come to you? Listen to them, write about them, honor them, feel them, release them, and learn from them. Have the courage to learn more about this complex being–you.

8. Try singing your feelings about being betrayed while in the shower. Notice anything afterwards?

9. Slip on your poet identity and write a spontaneous poem about this feeling.

10. Be honest as you ask yourself when was a time you betrayed another?

"...as one goes through life one learns that if you don't paddle your own canoe, you don't move."

Katharine Hepburn

B is for feeling... Brave

Definition: courageous, bold, hardy, confident, undaunted
Opposite: timid, fearful, cowardly

Brave is feeling confident and willing to take a risk. Webster's II Dictionary defines "brave" as "To face and endure with courage." Courage is the key word here. We must have the courage to persevere and follow through with a dream or passion. It takes strength of mind and morals to face difficulties and be willing to move forward with an attitude to support your purpose. We must have heart (which is the etymology of the word "brave") and be willing to take risks. When we face danger or are presented with a conflicting situation and we choose to embrace it with confidence, strength, and fortitude, we are coming from our heart. The mind brings in the conviction, if it's on the side of the heart, or it could talk you out of following through. It's good to discern and evaluate with your mind, then move into your heart with conviction and boldness.

Walking on the Edge

It takes a brave soul to walk into the unknown. A new friend, Paul Lewis, started his own company called Edgewalks, out of his experience working for the North Carolina Outward Bound School. I asked Paul to share some examples of going into the unknown.

Paul says, "Every time I meet my students, it is the unknown. I think it is the purest of the unknowns because even the students don't know what is going to unfold before them. Walking with them on their journeys, I find that they are awestruck by the simplicity. They are also amazed that they can live with very little and are literally walking into new territories. Carrying all they need for twenty-three days on their back introduces them back to their raw self, and they begin to like what they see, or don't like what they see."

"Walking in the wilderness is going into the two unknowns. There is obviously the wilderness as we see, feel, hear, smell, taste, etc. It is

43

here you begin to see the student's 'wilderness,' (their unknowns), and watch the magic happen when the two states of wilderness become one naturally. I have watched it happen when I look into their eyes as they sparkle, amongst surprised self-discovery. I have heard it via primal screams that celebrate life, and I certainly have felt it when tears fall like raindrops. None of this happens without the willingness to risk for growth. All of it happens when that risk is embraced with an intention to do good things and to go to good places—without and within."

My own experiences of backpacking in the Sierra Nevada mountains, with my Sierra Club buddy, Betty Jo, bring back memories of feeling brave. After we had set up our camp, she left to do some climbing, saying she'd be back soon. Well, the next time I saw her was about six hours later! I was feeling concerned, angry, and frustrated, as I was in a wilderness setting...alone! My trust level in the early seventies wasn't as high as it is today, some thirty years later. Finally, I overcame those feelings and replaced them with bravery.

Breaking Through

Molly Melching is a brave woman in the sense that she followed her heart in order to help people contribute to deep social transformation in Senegal, West Africa.

Many years ago, as a young woman, she went to study for her Master's Degree at Cheikh Anta Diop University in Dakar. Sensitive to the thousands of out-of-school children roaming the streets of the capital city of Dakar, Molly joined the Peace Corps on an individual placement and opened a center for street children. After six years, she moved this center to a small village near the city of Thiès. "The people there had nothing, but they were so optimistic. There was no rain the year I arrived; thus, no water, no crops, no food. It was the worst year of my life. However, this experience motivated me to develop a basic non-formal education program in national languages that helped the villagers to read and write, solve problems, and generally improve the health and environmental conditions of their community."

Her bravery and courage led her to continue her commitment to making life better in West Africa. Thirty years later, she is the director of Tostan, a Non-Governmental Organization based in Senegal. Tostan means "breakthrough" in Wolof, the most-widely spoken language in Senegal.

After having met Molly at a dinner party (she and her Senegalese husband, Malick Diagne, were visiting the States.) and learning of her life, I can understand why she must be revered as a hero to the many women who live in Senegal.   This was a most fascinating evening as our conversation was about life in Africa, particularly the age-old custom of female genital cutting (FGC). When the village participants of the Tostan program learned about their human rights and the health consequences of FGC, they then worked with the village leaders and their families to convince them to support their movement to abandon this harmful practice. The people in 1,271 villages have now abandoned the practice.

Gerry Mackie, a professor at Notre Dame University and expert on FGC says, "For many years there has been a great effort to encourage the abandonment of female genital cutting in practicing areas. With the exception of Tostan, program success has been elusive. In a few years, Tostan has led more than 600,000 people to abandon FGC."

Molly told us about one woman who did the cutting as a profession and this woman's brave and daring decision to discontinue this practice. She chose to change her attitude and create new beliefs about FGC.

I asked Molly if she would consider making a personal contribution to this book. She gladly offered the following:

"I took Oureye Sall to Germany for International Women's Day March 8, 2000. On the way home in the airplane, we sat next to a wealthy lady who was complaining about how her husband had left her for a younger woman. At one point she started sniffling in despair. I translated and told Oureye about the woman's woes. Oureye said, 'Tell her not to cry, Molly.'

She herself was married at eight to a man her parents had chosen for her, divorced by her husband at ten, remarried at fourteen to a man fifty-five years old who was just retiring! Obviously, at that age, girls have no choice but to accept. This early marriage or forced marriage is so frequent in Africa. 'I had to work to care for my children amidst poverty and illness, and look at me, I'm still singing and dancing.'

"This cheered the woman so (and really put her problems in perspective) that she gave Oureye the umbrella she was carrying as a small present!"

Molly went on to say, "Strangely enough I never really chose consciously to live in Senegal. When I arrived, I immediately felt that this is where I was 'supposed' to be, and from then on I never seriously entertained the idea of leaving. The hardest part was defending the fact that I was staying on and on and on to my family and friends who just did not understand.

"In the beginning it must have seemed very odd indeed to everyone since I didn't have a well-paying job or nice house. In retrospect however, I realize that all my experiences, no matter how small or insignificant, were necessary to lead me to where I and Tostan are today and to accomplish all the things that we have been able to achieve."

"Because I knew that I would be living here, I tried very hard to understand the different cultural values and beliefs. When I was frustrated, my motto was, 'It's not them, it's you who doesn't understand.' So I would try to find out what was behind the attitude or behavior before judging or becoming upset. This helped me to learn and ultimately grasp the deeper aspects of Senegalese culture. Without this understanding, I could never have attempted to work on issues relating to important social transformation."

It takes understanding to be brave - understanding that our fears inhibit our lives, that our beliefs are the foundation of our reality, that through understanding we grow, educate ourselves, and have relationships that are more meaningful, that we deserve to have happier lives, and a more fulfilling livelihood.

Being brave doesn't have to mean undertaking something as extreme as restructuring an entire culture's belief system. It can be as simple as asking someone out on a date, or taking those guitar lessons that you've always thought about. For example, in *The Feelings Storybook*, I wrote a story for the letter "B" about Bonnie. It depicts an illustration of a little girl feeling brave because she's going down the high slide. Every time she has played in the park in the past, she went down the low slide. This time she is ready for bigger experiences in her young life. She believes in herself and feels she can do anything. This is the gist of feeling brave—pushing our limits whether by an inch or by miles.

I heard author Molly Evans interviewed on National Public Radio. She said, "The people that stand up and scream and yell are the ones who make a difference." In other words, use your voice. Don't sit in your seat, squirming. It can be done in a way that is effective without being cruel. The name of her book? *Bushwhacker*.

Be Brave

Parents must teach courage when a child is young—early childhood. Teachers must teach it as early as pre-school. Miss Annie, Director of Kids House, told me one of her students came to school in the morning and said he was feeling shy. She spoke with him in a manner that made him feel understood and then asked, "Do you want to be shy today or brave?" He thought for a few moments and said, "I'm going to be brave, Miss Annie."

Encouraging words are important. Even with Max, our Aussie Shepherd, I try to use selective words when Max is afraid of the thunder or a questionable dog. Stephanie Huber, dog behaviorist and author of *Life in the Canine*, once told me that saying "okay" validates their fear, so I say, "Be brave," instead of "It's okay." Makes sense to me.

When we give our children the vocabulary to express their feelings while they are learning to talk, they grow into self-empowered young people and adults. I will stress this point over and over; transferring skills has to start early! It takes courage for a teenager to face his/her peers, when he's invited to get high or ditch school for the day. Courage is demonstrated when you say, "This doesn't work for me and I'm not going to participate." Where does a fourteen-year-old get that courage when she may be outnumbered? How does she feel brave enough to stand up for herself? It starts at home.

As this new generation learns and experiences confidence, self-worth, and self-mastery, it will form a new patina over the global consciousness. Feelings have to become a primary language rather than a foreign language.

But how do we teach something, or give away what we don't have? It's not an easy thing to do. How do we, as parents, instill virtues such as patience, respect, tolerance, and trustworthiness, if we don't live those values in our own life? What if we don't have an experience of them? Children learn what they live, the old adage goes . . .

- If a child lives with criticism, she learns to condemn.
- If a child lives with praise, he learns to appreciate.
- If a child lives with hostility, she learns to fight.
- If a child lives with tolerance, he learns to be patient.

Are you, as a parent, a role model for patience, tolerance, and understanding? Are you ready to condemn or praise? What lessons is your child learning through you? Do you try new things? Are you the one ready to stick your neck out? Were you that way as a child? If not, where did you learn it?

Do you support your child in speaking his/her mind, or do you inhibit his/her freedom of speech? Is your child free to say, "I understand what you're saying, but I don't see it that way."?

Your child doesn't always have to agree with you. Sure there is a risk in speaking your truth. You can lose friends, but then, were they really your friends? Truth speaking is not necessarily the way to win the popularity contest, but isn't integrity worth it?

I'll Ask, But I Really Don't Want To Know

I greatly admire an eleven-year old young man named Nic. His coach had spoken to his class of his frustration that there wasn't more time to allow the boys to play sports, and he wondered aloud what could be done to give them more time. The coach openly asked if anyone had a suggestion to his dilemma. Nic bravely spoke up, without arrogance or malice in his voice, and suggested that if the coach didn't talk so much, maybe they would have more time to play. No comment was made following this. However, during the next period, Nic was called to the principal's office without an explanation as to why. Much to his surprise and in no uncertain terms, Nic was instructed never to talk to a teacher that way again, and was told that an apology was in order.

Nic came home from school and told his mother, a single mom, about the episode. His remark was a natural and honest response to an inquiry. He gave an answer without fear of repercussion. Yet, the adult chose to take it personally without giving the youngster the freedom to express. "Well, there's another male I don't want to be like," Nic said. By this comment made to his mother, it's obvious the repercussion of his innocence had an effect on his belief system and life.

If you feel brave, you might live with integrity, knowing what is right through your intuition, and be willing to take action. If you see someone being hurt or bullied, you take action. You recognize differences as being different—not better and not worse. This builds character, because you feel confident moving through the mind's considerations. You by-pass that chatter and proceed with the action you know is correct and appropriate. This builds strength, persistence, follow-through, determination, and self-esteem.

From Russia with Love

My hairdresser, Margarita, has been in the U.S. only three years from Russia, and she is in the process of buying her own hair salon. She came here speaking only a few words of English, and did housecleaning to pay the bills. She did not formally go to school to learn the English language, but today speaks it like she did. When the opportunity to buy the business surfaced, her mind shrieked with fearful and doubtful thoughts, but her insides said, "Yes." She is one mother who is being a role model for her twelve-year old son, Vladamir, who brags to his friends about her. "My mom is strong and brave." I'm so proud of you Margarita—so proud to know you.

It takes courage to be brave, to speak your truth, to stand up for yourself, to leap into the great unknown, to trust, to listen to your inner wisdom. Be the role model who stands up for yourself. Be the hero in your child's life. Be the hero in your own life.

Reflection Time:
1. Can you think of a time when you felt brave? How did it feel?
2. How did you walk and hold your body? What was your self-talk?
3. Did you feel supported?
4. What was the status of your confidence/self-worth?
5. What visuals came up in your mind's eye?
6. What mentors influenced you? What were your lessons?
7. Can you recall a time when you chose to stuff your feelings and ignore what you really wanted to say?
8. After reflecting on each scenario, how did you feel afterwards?
9. In which scenarios did you feel nourished? Which were detrimental? When did you feel confident and strong, diminished and weak?
10. How were your relationships affected? Your work? Your self image? Your spirituality?

"To be nobody-but-yourself–in a world which is doing its best, night and day, to make you everybody else–means to fight the hardest battle which any human being can fight, and never stop fighting."
Buckminster Fuller ~ Architect, *Philosopher, and Poet*

C is for feeling... Challenged

Definition: assertive, provoked, venturous, daring, threatened

Opposite: accepting, complacent, indifferent, content

We face challenges every day in all aspects of life. It could be car trouble on the way to a meeting, computer glitches, lost inventory expected for a trade show, a feud with a lover, a difficult math problem, or tackling Mount Everest. What is important is our attitude to the challenge. Are we intrigued with the challenge, or do we let it beat us down? How we choose to believe and respond to these challenges is what will determine the outcome. In her book, *Heart of a Woman*, Maya Angelou says, "Whenever a crisis comes, say only two words–'Thank you.'" A challenge, therefore, could be gift, if you choose to see it that way.

Notice a difference between the two phrases, "I have a problem" versus "I'm being faced with a challenge." One is heavy and serious and the other is lighter and somewhat fascinating. Which one do you focus on when faced with a challenge?

Our son-in-law, Michael McClary, organizes a raft trip every summer for friends and family. One year we had extraordinary heat and winds that cracked trees during the middle of the night. In the morning as we assessed damages, we could hardly believe our eyes as we saw that a tree had punctured one of our rafts–the one that held nine people. That raft was history. After pondering the best course of action, we decided to "hitchhike" down the Boise River. So we did. Everything worked out as it always does. Most impressive was Michael's calm and calculating attitude (one of his many endearing qualities) during a challenging situation.

Buckminster Fuller, one of the greatest thinkers of our time, left us a wealth of knowledge about challenging experiences. "A lot of people think or believe or know they feel (experience)– but that's thinking or believing or knowing; not feeling (experiencing). Almost anybody can learn to think or believe or know, but not a single human being can be taught to feel (experience). Why? Because whenever you think or you believe or you know, you're a lot of other people, but the moment you feel (experience), you're nobody-but-yourself. To be nobody-but-yourself–in a world which is doing its best, night and day, to make you everybody else– means to fight the hardest battle which any human being can fight, and never stop fighting." Amazing words from his book, Critical Path.

Bucky also spoke about energy being contractive and expansive and that it doesn't move linearly. "It moves all around, spherically." He says we can feel this energy and can work with it, whether it is in ourselves or others. Reminds me of my Qi Gong (see "B is for feeling... Betrayed") classes and how we work and experience the "chi" (energy).

To just be ourselves—why does this have to be so challenging? If we were happy with who we are, the job would be natural and effortless, but mostly that is not the case.

Riding That Wave

Working with energy will be a challenge for thirteen-year-old Bethany Hamilton as she pursues her passion and talent as a surfer, now that she has only her right arm. While surfing in her home territory on the island of Kauai in Hawaii, she was bitten by a fourteen-foot tiger shark and had her left arm completely severed. She stayed calm and prayed to God. She also said that during the episode she wondered if she was going to lose her sponsors! She lost one-half of her blood volume, yet survived–I believe, due to attitude. While being interviewed, she was asked if she thought she would surf again. Her answer was, "Think? I know I will." I would say her response to this incident has been an inspiration to people around the globe. "It must have happened for a reason," was one of her comments shortly after she was on the beach. We were vacationing on the island of Kauai when the incident happened, so I emailed her the following thought: "Through this challenge, you will make a huge impact on people. No doubt greater than you ever would have by being a professional surfer." Approximately one month later, the television show 20/20, aired a short video clip of Bethany out on her board expressing her passion.

Charging through Challenges

Examples of overcoming challenges can be found in nature. Although the branches of the Douglas fir tree are upright and shaggy, and the bark is thick and furrowed, these giants' arms can easily break, yet they seem to heal their own wounds. Growing in a rugged climate, the Douglas fir will "twist and sculpt itself from a thousand indignities and come out gnarled and more spectacular. Twenty to fifty percent of its mass is underground and sometimes its roots will reach out and join the roots of a cut or shattered stump. The buddy trees will keep the stump alive for hundreds of years, its top scabbing over with bark and its growth continuing." The *Seattle Times* article, "Story of a Survivor," by William Dietrich goes on to say that these trees can routinely live for 500 to 700 years, and if not burned, blown, or cut, can exceed a millennium. One reached a record age of 1400 years!

Do we have something to learn from the Doug Fir? I should say so. The tree becomes more spectacular after the challenge. And don't you just love those buddy trees? We all need buddy trees to weather through our challenges. It is true that nobody can go to the gym for us, but having a support system is essential.

I've found that many young couples starting their family feel challenged as they attempt to balance life. The challenge is to nurture the relationship that brought them together in the first place, while respecting their individual needs and desires. Now along comes baby number one, and their time is diverted to the demands of a young dependent life. The pie gets cuts even smaller when a second child is born. There is a demand to rise beyond what the reality is presenting and expand one's ability to go beyond the appearance of the moment, or time, in one's life. Work, home care, good nutrition for the family, proper school, health cares, social life, spiritual education and more, become challenges in maintaining balance in this picture.

What is necessary in order to allow you to embrace a challenging situation rather than become frenzied and panicked by it? Keep in mind we suffer only because we resist the way it is. We resist what our reality is mirroring. So guess what? It keeps persisting and we feel pain to some degree. It could be in an area of finances, relationships, school, health, career, or maybe we feel forgotten, alone, or unsupported by life. There is a potential problem in everything that doesn't go the way we want it to go. We all have these moments from time to time. It's part of living on the planet.

Some of us have more challenging moments than others. I personally can't imagine what living in a concentration camp would be like; how many of us actually can? Few were able to survive and continue their lives with strength and optimism. One survivor, Victor Frankl, told his captors in the concentration camp, "You can take my wedding ring, but you can't take away the attitude I have about you doing that." His book, Man's Search for Meaning, is illuminating. He states that we can control our happiness, and how we react to these challenges in life is what brings us to mastery; how we react to them reflects our attitude, and attitude is everything in life. So, pick a good one!

In those cases when you're feeling sorry for yourself, feeling frightened, angry, despondent, whatever, I invite you to examine the circumstances. What kind of baggage are you carrying around pertaining to this challenge? Baggage may be part of the journey. By baggage, I mean the stuff we carry inside of us—the invisible satchel of undelivered communications, resentments, grudges, hurt feelings, make wrongs, resistances, or sour attitudes. It's the baggage that makes life a struggle. As we embrace our circumstances and take responsibility for them, we learn to shift our perspective, which gives us the opportunity to see life from a different angle.

What we become while trying to overcome these situations is what's important. Life offers us an array of conditions in which we have the power to choose the course of action to take. For example:

- Maybe you've just been given news about a physical challenge.
- Maybe you came home from work and found your home empty– gone the wife, the kids, and much of the furniture.
- Maybe you just received a letter saying you were not accepted to the college of your choice.
- Maybe you just found out your best friend has been having an affair with your husband.
- Maybe your girlfriends want you to do things against your better judgment.
- Maybe you are an early childhood teacher facing tightened budgets, slashed programs, over-crowded classrooms, and state standards.

Maybe, maybe, maybe. The list will go on and on. We won't escape the challenges that come our way, but we can escape the power they have over us.

Feelings arise underneath the challenges. We experience anger due to unfulfilled desires. Often anger will be a sign to deal with unresolved pain, which is being triggered by the event. It may be deep and the circumstances are manifesting to give us the chance to look at it. Don't take a pill to shove it down–embrace it, invite it in, and examine it. Ask yourself what you are afraid of. Fear is often irrational. Worry is a form of fear. If it's rational, do what you need to do to deal with it. The answers are all inside of you. Stop. Look. Listen. Allow the answers to come.

"Courage," in French, means "vision, accomplishment, and help for others on their journey." By having courage, we can rise above our challenge and practice personal discipline while improving ourselves and affecting the circumstances. We can overcome the obstacles while portraying courage and inner strength. Ask yourself, "What is the possible good that could come out of this situation?" This question will stimulate deeper understanding. You are asking a question of your inner self, which is part of the whole. The answers will come.

And sometimes, when we've managed to get through a challenge, another will come on its heels. This one may be even more challenging. It matters not, just use the same formula. Go within; in your core is your power. Life will keep doing what it does. Are we willing to bend in the wind like the aspens? Every day is different. One day we're the statue and the next the pigeon. Be present and do your best, feeling and observing life in the Now.

So, what are more options for balance and peace of mind while we're in these moments of feeling challenged? Start the exploration process by observing what is happening and how you're feeling. Be in the moment and be aware of everything. Determine a few beliefs about the situation and practice "witness consciousness," where you experience being the observer rather than a participant in the drama. Notice how your body is feeling. Ask if you're willing to see this situation as a challenge rather than a problem.

Again, rather than resisting, try feeling the feelings associated with the pain. Yes. Let the body really experience what it feels like to feel the way you're feeling about being challenged. The challenges will keep coming, you can be assured. What you do with them determines the quality of your life.

We have a choice. The choice is simple. We are victims of circumstances, or we can choose to take responsibility for them. I prepared a bookmark for my clients, with each side denoting the attributes of being a victim vs. responsible in life. This is a useful reminder for those times when we get stuck, and we all do.

Characteristics of a victim:

Self-pity, blame, martyr-like, self-righteous, envious, gossiping, judgmental, limited thinking, defensive, hold grudges, disparaging, scattered and conditional loving.

Characteristics of someone who takes responsibility:

In control, healthy, communicative, trusting, open-minded, whole, complete with self, balanced, empowered, aware, forgiving, and unconditionally loving.

Think of those role models who have chosen to take responsibility for their lives rather than succumbing to the victim mentality. Every one of my clients can be placed in this category. How many can you name?

In London, while waiting for my lorry to take me to the airport I had turned on the "tele" and was fortunate to hear the comments of a spokesperson for Nelson Mandela after he was released from prison. When asked if he was bitter about his experience, the spokesman's answer was, "He doesn't have time to be bitter and resentful. He has a country to build." It's fascinating to me how much information comes through our consciousness in one day, and why we retain what we do.

So bark out your challenge. Build your country. Climb your mountains. Tackle your prey. After all, it's only life.

Reflection time:

1. Bring up on the screen of your mind a situation or person that has been particularly challenging to you. What are your feelings about it?
2. Track it to discover when it started. What was happening in your life at the time?
3. Is your reaction a pattern?
4. Which characteristics are you exhibiting? (victim/responsibility)
5. Allow your mind to access all the thoughts, without judgment.
6. Now see this situation or person, feeling the issue and feelings linked to it.
7. Notice your point of view, as well as the results from that point of view.
8. Ask your inner self if there is another way you could perceive this same situation or person. Notice what comes forward. All the answers are inside. Trust your inner guidance.
9. Next, take some time to close your eyes and breathe deeply. Repeat in your mind when you inhale, the word, "calm." On the exhale, say to yourself, "down." In other words, your mantra becomes "calm down" as you breathe in and out.
10. What do you hold onto during challenging times?

"Always remember, I have sent you nothing but angels."
Neale Donald Walsh, *The Little Soul and The Sun*

C is for feeling... Compassion

Definition: tenderness, mercy, forgiveness, kindness
Opposite: oppression, cruelty, indifference, hatred

I believe compassion is a different feeling than sympathy. My idea of sympathy is feeling sorry for someone, but compassion is putting yourself in the place of another, and caring, relating, and understanding their deep suffering. Compassion is seeing that soul as your self and feeling for their plight.

Mother Theresa was and is an icon of compassion. She rescued abandoned babies, street urchins, and homeless people dying in the alleys. She developed innumerable shelters for those in need, including lepers, pregnant prostitutes, AIDS patients, and others. She was known to scoop up the most down and out, the "untouchables," the lowest in the caste system. When asked what has been her greatest happiness, she said, "The joy of loving Jesus. I would do anything for him." When she was asked what she does to help the children of the world, she simply said that she loved them.

A visit to India, where Mother Theresa began her mission work at age eighteen, stirred a myriad of feelings in me. I stretched my perception to include what my five senses were telling me. The sights of India were astonishing. I'd watch cows stroll across the street, people crossing anywhere, any direction, with no crosswalk lines to be seen. The smells were intoxicating every time I walked by a food vendor cart. The sounds can be described as "noisy." I found myself touching all the elegantly decorated and colorful saris with admiration.

Although I reacted to the onslaught of my senses, I merged into a more expanded consciousness to be able to "hold" this experience. I saw street life through a filter of compassion while I felt a deep respect for each soul's journey, which had brought them to that exact point in time and place. My soul linked up with the beauty in the people and the joy they exhibited for life. I played with the children who were absolutely delightful with their curiosity. As I changed film in my camera, they all gathered to observe this phenomenon. I interacted with the taxi drivers and learned of their challenges and heartaches. I befriended a woman in a general store, who was a teacher, and to this day we exchange greetings at holiday time. These are lasting memories that have contributed in making me who I am today.

On my last day in Bombay, I was riding in a taxi back to my room. The driver stopped for a red light. There on the corner was an outstandingly beautiful young Indian mother, dressed in her magnificently colorful sari. She held a young child on her hip. This woman's deep brown eyes connected with mine, as her arm reached out to me. It all happened too fast, but all I could do was place an orange in her hand, the only thing I had immediate access to. Our eyes remained connected after the driver accelerated with the turn of the green light. Tears burst forth and I sobbed all the way back to my hotel room. That experience is vivid in my mind to this day. My cells have imprinted it, and that was over twenty years ago. I felt such compassion for this sweet soul as she begged for food.

Compassion Comes in Many Forms

From India, we move to the mountains and an experience our son, Jeff, shared with me about a time he was riding his mountain bike through a magnificent pine forest. When he reached the crest of a hill, his feeling of exhilaration changed to devastation as he gazed upon a clear-cut. He sat next to one of the stumps and counted the rings, which added up to nearly the age of Jeff's grandfather at the time. He felt a deep and profound compassion for Mother Earth and for the trees–the lungs of the Earth.

On another note, at the time of this writing, with troops still in the Middle East, it seems as though our soldiers are feeling betrayed by our government, as they were told three times that they'd be going home. America On-line titled the story "Soldiers Stuck in Iraq." It is still unclear when they will return to their families. Meanwhile, U.S. soldiers are dying daily. One soldier was near tears, as he had to tell his wife he wouldn't be coming home as told. One soldier put Bush on his own Most Wanted List. Out of feeling betrayed, there is frustration, anger, hurt, grief, and indifference to name a few. The soldiers said they "will continue to do their job, but they no longer have their heart in the mission." I have such compassion for these soldiers; some have young children back home who need their mothers and fathers.

Elie Weisel, author of "Night," Holocaust survivor, and Nobel Peace Prize winner, spoke to the high school students, faculty, and community in Sun Valley. He brought a message of hope and inspiration. "Whatever situation, challenges, choices you make, never allow yourself to yield to

57

indifference." To remain silent and indifferent is "the greatest sin of all." His solution for the Middle East is for both countries to become intimately involved with each other and start building human relationships, bringing children from both sides. He also said that tolerance can be taught, and that we must learn from the past and "invoke hope." As we teach our children tolerance, we also teach about compassion.

There are many unkind acts committed on the planet that trigger our anger and thoughts of injustice. Acts towards animals are discovered daily, as well as those towards humans. We must take action by speaking up.

These acts are also opportunities to look deeper, beyond the appearance, to see the message for us individually and collectively. Too many bewildered and troubled souls have forgotten their true nature, then lash out into society and cause the innocent to suffer. How far must we reach within to feel compassion for these individuals?

Monkey Love

Consider the jungles of Africa where the chimps and gorillas try to exist in their part of the ecosystem. Jane Goodall and Dian Fossey are great examples of people who have compassion for the animal kingdom.

The Dian Fossey Gorilla Fund International thrives even after the death of this strong and compassionate woman. It is possible to adopt a gorilla for yourself or as a gift certificate to protect mountain gorillas. This can be done through the Dian Fossey Gorilla Fund International. You'll receive a photo of your gorilla and adoption papers. What a unique gift! Because of the compassion Dian Fossey showed towards the gorillas, and her public campaign she waged against gorilla poaching, the gorilla population continues to make steady gains. Unfortunately, she was mysteriously murdered in her cabin in 1985 and is not here to see the work of her love and labors.

I heard Jane Goodall speak many years ago and was inspired by the compassion and passion this woman demonstrates–so much so, that I became a member of the Jane Goodall Institute. Forty years from the inception, the Institute operates in Africa, Asia, Europe, and North America with programs in Belgium, Japan, and South Africa. Jane appears to be tireless and relentless as she pursues her quest to save the chimps. "Only when we understand can we care...only when we care will we help...only if we help shall they be saved," she declares. If this isn't the heart of compassion, I don't know what is!

In her book, *Reason For Hope,* I felt pain and incredible compassion for the chimps as I read about her visits to the research centers, along with the abuse and lack of respect she has seen over the years towards the chimps. "If she can see it, I guess I can read it and share that knowledge with others," I thought. She is a source of inspiration.

While staying with a friend in San Diego and surfing the tube late one evening, I miraculously came across the Achievement Network. Four women were interviewed. Jane Goodall was one. Students were in the audience and could ask questions of any of the women. "What was your proudest moment?" Jane's answer was when the chimps (Fifi and her family) accepted her for the first time. She spoke of a yearning, deep inside to live with the animals in their environment. Her obvious compassion was expressed as the video clip of her showed a visit to a laboratory, where her friends, the chimps, were being inoculated for malaria and hepatitis. One reached out a little hand to connect with her. The love that the two of them felt at that moment tugged at my heart and brought me to tears. "It's what keeps me up late at night and makes me determined to fight," Jane said. Because chimps are so like humans, they become projects for research, which she doesn't find respectful. I don't either. There has to be another way. Her time is spent traveling and lecturing to educate the public for chimp protection.

Another of the four interviewees was Sylvia Earl, Ph.D., who is an internationally renowned oceanographer. Oh, this woman was dynamic as she shared her expertise! When asked by one of the many aware and caring students about the status of the coral reefs, she responded by saying we are at a critical point and need to make decisions now to turn things around. "We don't know how to put back the coral reefs, or how to fix them." Why are the reefs in such danger? Boats, pollution, careless divers, you name it. Without reefs, the entire ecosystem of the Earth is in danger. Educate yourself on this and other environmental subjects at http://www.ecoisp.com/resources.asp Dr. Earl, I thank you for your dedication to Mother Earth.

Heart Connection

Compassion can be practiced everywhere you look in life. Rather than judging and labeling something, we can look inside of ourselves and reach out beyond those labels. We can feel compassion through living in our hearts rather than our minds.

I have my own furry friend that triggers compassion in me. July Fourth is anything but a day of freedom for Max, our Aussie Shepherd. He is so traumatized by the loud noises of the day that he won't relieve himself when taken for a walk with a leash. His body shakes and quivers as he seeks to find safety in the corner of my bedroom closet. I comfort him, gently stroking him and suggest he "be brave," and then I add the support of a homeopathic remedy to help relax him.

Understanding is important and necessary as we ask ourselves, "What is the gift in this troubling circumstance?" What can I learn from it?" Through my years of personal growth in academia, I've learned about a power in us, which is a strength that will help us heal from absolutely anything. It's called LOVE. I believe we have such experiences to provide lessons for our personal and spiritual growth. When we learn from them, we evolve and influence others.

As everything operates in perfection, we are always at the right place and the right time, like the man in this next story. He was observing an older couple in a restaurant. On the table in front of them was a hamburger and French fries. He noticed that they cut the sandwich in half and doled out the French fries equally. He then observed that the man started eating but the woman didn't. Feeling compassionate, and assuming they had some financial struggles, he approached them, and asked if he could buy them another meal so they could eat together. The woman said, "I'm fine. I'm just waiting for him to finish eating. We share everything and it was his time first for the teeth."

Is compassion a learned behavior? Are some of us more compassionate than others? What are the criteria for being compassionate? My granddaughter, Alissa, would often crawl over to a baby at the daycare center when he/she was crying. She offered her own form of compassion by putting her head on the shoulder of the crying child, or touching him/her, obviously wanting to comfort. She was only eight months old at that time–so young, so wise, so connected!

Ram Dass, one of the early pioneers in the human potential growth movement said, "Be a soul and you'll see a soul. The soul and the ego see suffering from two different perspectives." Certainly, young children see from the eyes of their soul. Do you? Ram Dass was the keynote speaker at the 2003 Sun Valley Mountain Wellness Festival, which occurs every Memorial Day weekend.

When asked, "What are the five most important questions to be considered as we move into the new millennium?" The Dalai Lama said,

- How do we address the widening gap between rich and poor?
- How do we protect the Earth?
- How do we educate our children?
- How do we help Tibet and other oppressed countries and people of the world?

- How do we bring spirituality (deep caring for one another) through all disciplines of life?

He went on to say that all five questions fall under the last one. "If we have true compassion in our hearts, our children will be educated wisely, we will care for the Earth, and those who 'have not' will be cared for."

Living with compassion will touch the deepest place in your heart and become more of the fabric of your life as you practice it. Just open yourself. Be willing to feel your own pain as you recognize it in another person or situation. Ask, "What can I do to alleviate it?"

The Little Soul and The Sun by Neale Donald Walsh, is a profound and thought-provoking child's fable and speaks to the notion that we are all connected, and when we have compassion for others, we are in essence having compassion for ourselves. It delivers a message that could transform the planet if we were all to adopt it. The question is, are you ready to hear it and take it into your life?

Reflection Time:

1. Explore a situation that elicits compassion, i.e. an abducted child; a lost cat; children living in nations at conflict, etc.

2. What message is speaking to you with regard to it?

3. How is this person or situation a reflection of you?

4. What judgments do you have about it?

5. Is your heart open to feel, or does your mind override it?

6. What lesson could you possibly learn through this circumstance?

7. What can you do about it?

8. Observe a homeless person or someone experiencing hard times and ask, "How is this person like me?" We may both be seeking happiness, good health, and prosperity; we may both feel pain and pleasure; we may both try to avoid suffering, feel impatient, or like cookies; we may both have goals and aspirations; we may both fear death, as well as fully live in each moment.

9. Use this exercise to explore your inner world. Journal about the insights, share with a friend, and meditate. Learn and grow. Learn and glow.

10. What is your attitude about being compassionate towards animals?

"The whole library of the universe is hidden within you. All the things you want to know are within yourself. To bring them out, think creatively."

Paramahansa Yogananda, *The Autobiography of A Yogi*

C is for feeling... Creative

Definition: artistic, poetic, aesthetic

Opposite: stuck, blocked, stiff

Being creative comes from a higher place within us as if we are plugged into something bigger than we are. When we feel creative, we experience our uniqueness and our originality.

R. L. Rowsey is the managing director of Company of Fools, a theater company based in Hailey, Idaho. His thoughts about creativity are as follows:

"Having a background in music, I started out using the piano to help me express myself. It's great for everyone, at any age, to have an outlet. Music is my passion. Some people cook well, write creatively, or have an eye for finding treasures while going into a thrift store. We're not all creative in the same way. Creativity comes from deep inside, whatever that means. It's inside us all, and how we apply it, is up to us. To support creativity in young people, it's important to give them the opportunity to be wrong – to try something new – to not get it 'right' the first time. Nobody has more creativity than anybody else does. Some just have more access to it than others do. Once you dive into it, you can celebrate it. I believe that when you put a group of people together, the creativity soars. Exploring together can heighten individual creativity as well as collective. Say your school is having a play, and you walk down the hall to audition. You hear a voice saying, 'Nah, you won't get any role.' Another voice could say, 'Why not just try?' It's a matter of which voice you listen to. Who are the most creative people you know? I'd say little babies, because when young, a blanket can be a castle or a cape or a kite. Make a decision to have your life filled with more castles and know there are some days when the clouds obstruct the castles. The clouds will come and go, but the castles are there all the time."

Is your life filled with castles, capes, and kites?

Daydream Believers

The late Leo Buscaglia, author of numerous titles (including *Love*), teacher, and inspirational speaker, referred to Einstein, Galileo, Edison, and Leonardo da Vinci as having been accused of being daydreamers. "We are told that we must leave our dreams behind with our childish thoughts... Without fantasies and dreams there can be no creativity, in invention." Allow yourself your daydreams and see what comes of them!

If your creativity feels blocked, I highly recommend Julia Cameron's incredible classic, *The Artist's Way*. It has a remarkable message that brings out the inner, playful child who flourishes while being connected to all.

Once a month our community has the opportunity to connect with the work of artists when our local galleries offer an "Art Walk." From six to nine P.M., you can cruise the streets of Ketchum (the business community adjacent to Sun Valley) and view the variety of art. One night I was so drawn to the work of Victoria Adams. It just grabbed my heart. She paints glorious landscapes that are so ethereal that it took me right into my heart. I wrote her, asking if she would comment about creativity and this is what she sent to me.

"I see my own creativity as being inextricably linked to my 'regular' life. I use the same processes to bake a pie as I do to make a painting. That is, I try to concentrate on a task and somewhere along the line I get pulled into the process and become absorbed. I play at it, listening to the suggestions my intuitive voice gives me. 'Let's try this, let's try that,' without editing very much. That voice has been encouraging me from the earliest days of my artistic endeavors. It takes awhile to even know it's there, which comes with awareness. When I'm making a painting, I'm constantly looking for areas that don't look right, that need fixing. When everything in the painting is 'fixed,' it's finished."

So, Victoria lives creativity. How fascinating! She takes risks and listens to the voice within to create works of art. What an honor to have her contribution to this book!

The Field of Flowers was created by Kathleen Mardian. "I wanted to construct art that would represent every child at Hemingway Elementary, and to have each child be able to say, 'See there...that's my flower. That's my part of the entire art piece and it's important.' It worked. They were all so eager to show off their own creation to friends, teachers, parents. What better way to show their unique expression than with flowers. There is a sweetness and a power to the brain child of originality, AND we all possess it. It's magical! Take time to get to know yourself in a new way."

"Creativity is as limitless as space. It permeates our everyday living, whether it's a walk with our dog, or a resounding song in the shower. It's an expression of feeling, of knowledge, of love and loneliness. Creativity allows you to release and expose your inner self. It is choice. Everyone is unique in their imaginative, inventive mind."

Children have the ability to create with enthusiasm because they are free to express themselves. This freedom seems to leave us as we progress through life, but children still have the unaffected gift of creativity. Through word, song, art, the possibilities are infinite. The children's art reflects their own attitudes and beliefs, whether it's an assigned work or creative expression.

Art and Journaling Go Together

Ruthann Saphier, is a friend of mine who embarked on a watercolor and journal-taking class. Although she had written in a journal for years, she had no known talent as an "artist." The purpose of the class was to record experiences with a paintbrush as well as linearly. I recently looked through one of her journals with admiration, inspiration, and excitement. She had taken a weekend trip to San Francisco and with colored pencils, sketched a memorable account of her visit. What a fun way to record an experience!

In 1896, a conversation took place between Johannes Brahms and Joseph Joachim, a famous Hungarian violinist. The discussion focused on the source of creativity and genius. Brahms said, "I immediately feel vibrations that thrill my whole being. These are the Spirit illuminating the soul power within, and in this exalted state, I see clearly what is obscure in my ordinary moods, then I feel capable of drawing inspiration from above, as Beethoven, Bach, and Mozart did."

Beyond Time and Space

When I'm feeling creative I can feel my juices running! Time stops for me. I lose sight of everything and anything. I would imagine all artists, musicians, craftspeople, and chefs who are living their passion and feeling their creativity can relate to this.

My husband Gene and I were driving home from a conference, when we started to converse about a project we wanted to develop. I started taking notes as we bounced off each other's ideas. We were so involved and "in the flow" that we took a wrong turn. Then once we got back on the interstate, we couldn't believe we were almost at our exit. How could this be? We laughed about it and were just amazed! Time had stood still, as we had experienced this idea of creativity—of being in our passion and in the flow of life. It was an awesome experience in creativity, spontaneity, and interaction, and we had fun in the process.

Many feel creativity belongs only to artists, musicians, architects, etc. This is a myth. We are all creative, just as R. L. Rowsey said. It is our essence. We simply need to access it through one of many vehicles.

Creative Solutions

For example, the kitchen is a terrific place to express one's self creatively. Elise and Evan MacMillan, fourteen and seventeen years of age respectively, blended their talents into a thriving business called The Chocolate Farm. The business evolved out of her homemade chocolate animals at a community youth marketplace in Denver, Colorado. The Chocolate Farm specializes in making chocolate farm animals. The demands for their products are high, as there are many people who claim to be chocoholics. The Chocolate Farm could bring in revenues in excess of one million dollars this year! How's that for a success story about creativity?

Speaking of chocolate, here is an interesting bit of trivia about one of our most decadent sweets. Chocolate is sourced from a seed that comes from the cacao tree. Rain forest pollinators are crucial to perpetuation of this tree. Midges are tiny flies that live in the rain forest. They are tiny enough to work their way into flowers to pollinate them. Without this action, seeds wouldn't become fertilized and chocolate would become an endangered product. Everything makes a difference. If it weren't for this fly, no bigger than the head of a pin, you wouldn't get your See's Candy. Chop off the rain forest and say good-bye chocolate.

Following is an email that was sent to me with a committed message of "It can't hurt to try."

"The Brazilian congress is now voting on a project that will reduce the Amazon forest to 50% of its size. The area to be deforested is four times the size of Portugal and would be mainly used for agriculture and pastures for live stock. All the wood is to be sold to international markets in the form of wood chips, by large multinational companies. The truth is that the soil in the Amazon forest is useless without the forest itself. Its quality is very acidic and the region is to susceptible to constant floods. At this time more than 160,000 square kilometers deforested with the same purpose are abandoned and in the process of becoming deserts." I was asked to affix my name to a list that had 467 names on it already. As the sender had said, 'No harm in trying.'"

Terry Tempest Williams, a naturalist, writer, and conservationist offers her advice on creativity, in light of her own passions, in an interview in Delicious Living, October, 2003. When asked what she thought we should be focusing on in terms of the environment, she said, "I feel like we are at a time of great creativity if we choose to embrace it as such and if we choose to engage the will of our imaginations and imagine another way of being in the world. Democracy requires our participation." Sound familiar?

We have to keep on keeping on. I heard about a school that is using dogs to help struggling first-graders with their reading. The children read to specially trained golden and Labrador retrievers. Teachers say the K-9 Kids project helps build the skills and self-esteem of the young readers. There is no shortage of creativity.

I tapped into one of those vehicles of creativity after reading a book called Use Both Sides of Your Brain by Tony Buzan. During the many classes and lectures I attended in graduate school, using mainly the left side of the brain, I felt inspired to use colored pens to record key words and phrases that were essential to the material in order to activate the right side. It was a fun method to record pertinent information.

Another friend of mine started a graphics design business that stemmed from her talent as a highly creative artist. She stressfully produced and diligently attempted to satisfy every client. She was successful in her pursuits; however, two years after selling her business, she had no desire to draw in any form. She commented, "When I do, it will be strictly for pleasure and not for monetary gain." Too many long hours were spent designing for the purpose of earning a living and the pressure to please. That channel for creativity served her for a time in her life, and now she is a licensed massage therapist, and offers psychic readings. Creativity is always flowing. It's up to us how we express it.

Learning calligraphy is yet another form to express creativity. I delved into it years ago and found myself totally immersed in the process. I could think of nothing else and became completely lost in the graceful and beautiful strokes while doing calligraphy.

Landscaping, designing clothing, interior decorating, fence building, photography, ceramics, teaching, writing—goodness, the list is simply endless! At one time, Danielle, our daughter, displayed her earrings by hooking them to a lovely piece of lace, which she hung on the wall. She also added a few unique shells to my soap dish in the guest bathroom, which is something I wouldn't have thought of. Creativity can poke its head up anywhere, in anyway, if you let it.

What are your creative gifts? For you to first discover them, it is necessary to remove the judgment factor from your life. It is a stopper for sure. Start to fall in love with life and be open to the miracles that happen every moment. Ask Life to reveal to you the ways in which you are creative, and I guarantee you, the answers will come. We are all unique, so therefore, our creativity will be expressed in a multitude of unique ways. Just get started.

Reflection Time:

1. Do you have an opinion about yourself with regard to creativity?
2. Do you spend any quiet, alone time during the day?
3. Have you discovered a creative outlet for yourself? How do you access it? How much time do you devote to its expression?
4. Are you judgmental with regard to your creative attempts?
5. What creative ideas do you have for recycling in your home?
6. What does creativity mean to you? In what form is something creative?
7. Recall any memory of the past when your creativity was stunted, denied, laughed at, squelched, or ridiculed.
8. What are your beliefs and attitudes about your own ability to be creative?
9. What is the most devastating thing that happened to you with regard to your creativity?
10. Fun contributes to the creation of an environment that nurtures and sustains personal motivations. Are you having fun yet?

"Security is mostly a superstition. It does not exist in nature...life is either a daring adventure or nothing."

Helen Keller

D is for feeling... Daring

Definition: bold, audacious, defiant, adventurous

Opposite: cowardly, timid, chicken-hearted

"I double dare you." Has anyone ever said this to you? Fulfilling a dare can give you a heightened sense of self, having done something that you might not usually do. You might even call it a "rush." Think of the term "daredevil." What images does this word conjure up for you?

I had a run-in with a daredevil when I was downhill skiing on a run that I should not have been on. I faced a slope full of moguls. As I contemplated what to do, I asked a man who was ripping and ready to go, his skis on fire, how to get down the thing. He said, "Just ride them mothers!" I wasn't a ball of fire, but it was daring for me, and yes, I made it!

I had another daring adventure when I was involved in a ropes course as part of a personal growth week in the Sierra Nevada mountains. I was invited to participate in various ropes techniques such as Tyrolian traverse, zip line, and rappelling down a mountain. The Tyrolean traverse is an old alpine climbing technique used to "span" a horizontal gap between two spires. Ropes are anchored at both points. I got into a harness hooked to the rope by a pulley, and then pulled myself, hand over hand, across the rather deep chasm to the other side. Halfway through, releasing my hands and hanging from the pulley was an option. It's quite exciting. The zip line is a cable that is tensioned and on an incline, and is used in a self-confidence activity. It is set up or down a slope, or across a gap, and it is usually built high off the ground. Students clip in via a harness and "zip" down the cable. It's a blast. Rappelling is the usual technique used to descend a cliff after climbing it by a series of ropes.

The entire experience was scary and exciting at the same time. The exercise was optional; we all had the opportunity to say, "Thanks, but no thanks." The group was inspiring, as we all chose to proceed, taking our thoughts and feelings with us. By the end of that day, I was so exhilarated and felt that no goal was too grandiose for me to tackle.

For a special birthday, my husband, Gene, chose to push through a few of his barriers, and go parasailing. Parasailing is where a large parachute is attached behind a boat so that the person "flies," while being dragged by the vessel. For him, it was quite daring. He's now talking about doing something similar called paragliding, but this time, he'll be running off a mountaintop, no boat, no nothing (except the parachute)! As I said, he's "talking" about it.

Gene's thoughts about this were triggered by a memorial service we had attended that had significant meaning for us. The gentleman who had made his transition was someone who could be called daring. He lived his life with passion and great joy. Although we did not know this person very well, we derived great value from the spoken words and sharing from family and friends. Can you think of a funeral you attended that triggered insight? As a result of attending, maybe you were inspired to change a behavior or pattern? Maybe you even decided to become more daring?

The Razor's Edge

I heard a saying that "If you're not on the razor's edge, you're taking up too much space." Can you speak from experience of being on the razor's edge? What would have to happen for you to stand out and take a risk, to make a difference, be bold, or be daring?

"I resign." Have you ever wanted to affix your signature to these words? I know of a young man who did exactly that, mainly because of the S-word. Stress can overpower our common sense, as well as our clarity. For this young man, sending in his resignation was a daring act, as he had a mortgage to pay, a family to feed, and credit card debt to pay off (the result of a garage full of "toys"). In some ways, this action may have been reckless. However, the stress level in his life was reaching epidemic levels. Was his a daring act? Reckless behavior? A spontaneous reaction? Or, did he respond to intuitive wisdom and guidance?

It's probably a good thing this young man did what he did, or else he may have developed severe physical problems, like those of a retired police chief I know. I asked him, "How did you handle your stress during your thirty-year career?" "Not well," he chuckled. "What does that mean?" I asked. "Colon surgery, gum surgery, TMJ [rebuilt jaw], two heart attacks, and a triple by-pass." WOW! It sounds like retirement saved his life for sure.

Sometimes we judge ourselves for a decision to pursue something unusual or daring. I had a tug of war with myself as I innocently signed

69

up for a winter wilderness class. I anticipated picking up a few pointers for my summer backpacking trips. There was an outing scheduled, and I was expected to attend. However, I was somewhat intimidated by the fact that I'd never gone in the backcountry during the season where everything on the ground is white. Plus, I was the only female amongst a group of ski patrol experts—I was clearly out of my league. But I went anyhow, in spite of the voice that spoke of that four letter word that can run our lives—FEAR. Yes, I chose to move forward with the array of mixed feelings and thrilled that I did. I cross-country skied with the guys to a hut that overlooked the most spectacular basin; I gazed on the sun-sparkling pristine snow; I ate lunch on a rocky outcropping, and I simply took in the magic of each moment. It was a darling adventure for me. Will I do it again? Probably not. But I'm certainly delighted that I pushed through my mental obstacles! The guys were of great support to me and contributed to a memory I'll never forget.

An Odyssey

Another daring journey I undertook was roaming the Greek islands on my own for several months. Our youngest was a senior now and my absence would be a lovely opportunity for more one-on-one with her father. However, while still in the idea stage, the conversation in my mind was ongoing. "You really shouldn't go for so long." The response, "But if I'm going to work on my language, it has to be a chunk of time." Then came, "You'll never get all your family responsibilities covered." In retort, I heard, "Just make your list and it will all get taken care of and will work out perfectly." Then, before I knew it, there I was observing the Greek Independence Day parade on March 25, 1985, singing the Greek National anthem as the celebration proceeded downtown through Athens! I felt visiting my father's homeland and exploring my roots was a daring act on my part. I'm grateful I took the initiative to add these treasured memories to my life.

While attending the Banff Mountain Film Festival, I learned of Erik Weihenmayer, avid mountain climber, who has scaled Mt. McKinley, ascended El Capitan, and surmounted Everest—and not seen any of it. Blind since the age of thirteen, he says, "If I had never lost my sight I don't know if I would have had to ever look very hard past baseball and basketball. I can kind of figure out the puzzle of the rock under my hands." Erik loves to climb and loves the teamwork involved. He loves the "feel." Erik is a goal-oriented person that appears to fulfill his dreams in spite of his blindness. The guy is daring in my opinion.

Not everyone on the planet has to live a daring live, but we can have daring moments, experiences, and behaviors, when we go beyond our self-imposed limits and do something slightly out of character, or something quite outrageous. Brave acts take us out of our pigeonhole and expand our consciousness. We feel more confident, more adventurous, and certainly more alive.

So what prevents you from being daring? Are you afraid others won't accept your actions or that you'll be judged? When we look honestly at why we don't live our lives more fully, we seem to have a hidden agenda of "What would people say?" Do you have an investment in being a "people-pleaser?"

Chills and Thrills

Some people can be recklessly daring. Being reckless can make the endorphins soar, which may motivate someone to perform a daring act. We have a fascination with speed and thrills.

Remember Evil Kinevel? He leaped across Hell's Canyon on his motorcycle. That was the year my son elected to emulate him at Halloween. I recall making his costume out of a white sheet and cutting out shiny red and blue stars that defined his long legs. A white helmet covered his curly blonde hair. Daredevils can inspire all types and ages!

Snowshoe Thompson carried the mail in the Sierra Nevada Mountains, through blizzards and treacherous conditions. He may have looked upon it as his job, but to me, it was daring.

I read a news article about a ninety-two-year-old man with artificial knees who set a record for being the oldest person to skydive alone.

A single mother raising her children alone is daring too, and noble, if you ask me.

And what about Pete Rieke, who climbed Mount Hood, an over 11,000 foot summit, paralyzed from the waist down, using a series of devices?

We all have our own ideas of what "daring" is. For example, it could be a daring decision for a parent to sign up for a sex education course. Donna Miller teaches a course on health education that focuses on discussing sexual issues with your children. Would you be daring enough to take a course like this with your child? Donna's classes are promoted strictly through word of mouth and are attended by both parent and child. The first night is for parents only who have no clue what they have signed up for. They are nervous and the old belief tapes are running. Donna says nobody is talking about these issues until it's often too late.

And what about Helen Keller, who is quoted at the beginning of this chapter? She was an inspiration to millions of people throughout the

71

world because of her courage and ability to overcome both blindness and deafness.   She had a phenomenal power of concentration and memory, and she was determined to succeed. What a role model!

So, determine what your own limits are, and then push them even further. Look at your life and ask yourself where the daredevil within you needs to make him or herself known. Hey... I double-dare you!

Reflection Time:
1. If there were nothing stopping you, what would you do in your life that was daring?
2. What is stopping you?
3. Are you willing to move through that obstacle? If your answer is no, why not?
4. Do you know anyone who is daring? Do you admire her/him? Why?
5. Do you know someone who did something daring and "failed?"
6. It could be daring to look into your own life and observe your past or your dissatisfaction with your job, mate, lifestyle, patterns, or motives. Be daring and examine what's working and what's not.
7. Does inertia blanket your natural ability to be daring? Confront any obstacles in your path. Take responsibility for creating your own life and joy.
8. What acts do you consider daring?
9. What would have to happen for you to embrace an identity of being daring?
10. Do you consider the expression of truth a daring act?

Out of the night that covers me,
Black as the Pit from pole to pole,
I thank whatever gods may be
For my unconquerable soul...

And yet the menace of the years
Finds, and shall find me, unafraid.

It matters not how strait the gate,
How charged with punishment the scroll,
I am the master of my fate;
I am the captain of my soul.
William E. Henley, "Invictus"

D is for feeling... Despondent

Definition: depressed, gloomy, sorrowful, despaired
Opposite: happy, valued, joyful

To be despondent is to feel a loss of confidence, to experience very low energy, to have thoughts of hopelessness, or to be deep in despair. Have you ever felt like crawling into bed, pulling those covers over your head and just wanting it to all go away? Accompanied by a feeling of emptiness and isolation, these feelings can be overpowering and oh-so-painful. It's like shrinking inside. Despondency feels small and insignificant.

I know a young woman who is feeling despondent in her life. She's working emotionally to heal from a dysfunctional family history, which is intensely challenging. In the meantime, she's attempting to further her education but feels unsuccessful at her financial quests. Her hands feel tied and she feels unsupported by Life. Her spirit, confidence, hope, and trust are at an all-time low. In her despondency, she is ill equipped to control her mind. Decisions need to be made for graduate school, as her current rent is due, and there is no money in the bank for either. She feels lost, alone, and in despair. It happens to a variety of people and unfortunately, the only answer our society is fixated with is medication.

As a preventative measure, I would inaugurate a program about how to discipline and become the master of the mind. For the millions afflicted

73

with despondency, there are methods of moving through this condition, but it takes education, self-discipline, support, and patience.

It's helpful to know that depression is also a sign of unexpressed anger and buried emotion. Taking action in some way is important. Review the period of time when these feelings were initiated. What was transpiring in your life then? What haven't you said to whom? Move the energy—dance, sing, and scream in the shower! I've done that many times. Move the energy! Be introspective and discover what's there. Be honest with yourself—feel it! Depression is a wake-up call. Don't press the "snooze" button on this alarm. Don't numb the feelings with another prescription. Be aware of your feelings. Acknowledge them. Take action. You'll be so much happier in the long run.

Many folks tend to complain to their "doc" about their condition. Complaints may be an action level above despondent, but before they know it, they've relinquished their power to a prescription which magically makes the pain go away—sort of. Pain often pops up somewhere else, and another medication is prescribed, until the numbness sets in, and this may continue on and on. This can continue for years.

I believe we need to get to the source of our moods. For our highest good, we need to face our struggles straight on, in order to resolve them. It all depends on how we want to live life. I recommend taking charge of life and not giving our power away to a pill—or anything else for that matter.

Despondency affects the lives of loved ones in a way that can be as devastating as the depression itself. Feelings of frustration, worry, resentment, and helplessness can eat away the joy of life. Xavier Amador, Ph.D., National Director for NAMI (National Association for the Mentally Ill), states "People who live with a depressed person are more prone to depression and have a higher risk for developing other emotional problems such as anxiety and phobias."

Psychoneuro-what?

In 1988, when I was doing research for my dissertation topic, "Laughter, Enthusiasm, and Joy as Healing Modalities," I first became aware of a new word that didn't exact roll off my tongue. It wasn't in the dictionary, and is not recognized by the thesaurus program in my computer. During a personal interview with the late Norman Cousins in his office at UCLA, I soon learned its meaning. "Psychoneuroimmunology" is "the study of the direct correlation between stress and the functioning of the physical body, including the immune system." Since it is easy to understand how powerful emotions can be referred to as stressors, the next obvious step is to correlate feelings and health.

Norman Cousins was one of the first to introduce living proof that laughter and a joyful heart, as well as anger and fear, influence our health. I am grateful for the contribution he made to my project and for the exceptional opportunity of interacting with him about the subject and his process.

The body-mind connection principle acquired more respect and validity thanks to the research by Dr. Candace Pert, author of Molecules in Motion, and Adjunct Professor of Physiology of Biophysics at Georgetown University Medical School. Although the traditional and prevalent concept suggests the mind is located within the brain, scientific research is rapidly creating a new paradigm, revealing evidence that the mind is actually traveling throughout the body in the form of the immune system.

When we feel happy, our immune cells feel happy and we enjoy good health. When we feel sad, depressed, or angry, the immune cells take on that emotion as well. These cells have intelligence! The same is true for other cells. To quote Dr. Deepak Chopra, "Every cell in the body has a mind. Every cell creates messenger chemicals. These chemicals are secreted in response to feelings, emotions, beliefs, and intentions. Whenever we have a feeling, it's happening throughout the body – at the same instant in time."

Dr. Theresa Dale, author of Transform Your Emotional DNA, a naturopath and creator of the Neuro-physical Reprogramming (NPR) protocol, states, "When we resist an emotion and/or feeling, the resistance itself creates an electromagnetic charge of energy which stores on a cellular level in the organ or gland that correlates to the particular emotions. Over time, as the pattern of resistance continues, this charged energetic pattern creates even more and more of a burden on the particular organ or gland where it is stored."

After becoming licensed by Dr. Dale through basic and advanced training in her Wellness Course, I use NPR in my private practice of transpersonal psychology. Efficiently, emotions, beliefs, and identities stored in the organ or gland from childhood are released permanently on a cellular level. This is done through employing the principle of the five-element theory of acupuncture, kinesiology (muscle testing), and high potency, organ-specific, homeopathic remedies. And thanks to NPR, counseling doesn't have to be a long, arduous ordeal of weekly visits to the "shrink" that eventually shrink your wallet.

As the twenty-first century unfolds and we feel the rapid pace in our lives and society, why shouldn't the counseling process also be accelerated? When each one of us commits to the expression of our potential, releasing forever self-pity and the victim identity, our life experience becomes a most amazing and miraculous adventure. Our family reflects our inner harmony and peace; our community is united through support and kindness, and our nation is a people honoring our Oneness. We recognize our Mother Earth as the giver of life, and the universe as the source of intelligence, as a living cell is to the body; each of them represent the microcosm and the macrocosm!

The body is a remarkable lie detector. It simply provides the information that takes us to the next step of exploring the issue and its base cause, or the core issue. It works—and it's fast. In less than one hour, an individual can retrieve knowledge that could free him/her from a lifetime of imprisonment. One case history after another verifies the research that the cell retains the energy of the resisted feeling. These feelings don't go away, even if we do everything in our power to ignore or deny them. The bottom line is that a resisted emotion persists and affects our health.

In-Sight

"Every time we express ourselves, we lose a little more emotional clutter," says Dr. Jacob Lieberman, author of *Take Off Your Glasses And See*. Since I've been involved with my own vision challenges, I've learned of many professionals working in the field who have inspired me. Dr. Lieberman correlates resisted feelings and traumatic events with vision problems. "Every person I have worked with has been able to uncover some kind of major emotional stress in the one-to-two-year period before their vision first deteriorated... It's much harder to see clearly when we aren't expressing our feelings clearly." His book has been personally helpful, as well as a validation about the importance of feeling fully what we feel when we feel it.

If we embrace the project of cleaning out the garage of "stuff" that no longer serves or supports us, it may take an hour or it may take years, but it will eventually be clean. It may not even be as overwhelming as we suspected. The task doesn't have to be repeated because we can be more aware of each piece we place on the shelf, in order to prevent the accumulation. The same holds true with the "stuff" that keeps us stuck and sabotages our dreams. Once we honor our feelings—our hurts, angers, fears, inadequacies, guilt, etc.—we can keep current with them without adding them to our "stuff." This requires our honesty and total responsibility in each moment. No matter how much we plaster on that ol' smile and boast about our PMA (or Positive Mental Attitude), that unresolved "stuff" seems to somehow creep into our lives. We have to do the work, or clean out the garage, then create the life we prefer in each moment of now. As a result, who knows what your unique contribution would be to make the planet a more peaceful place?

It's an awesome time to be living on the planet. It's a time of unlimited possibility and only our free will prevents us from experiencing the power linked with this state. A study was once done with senior citizens and people in their nineties and over. What would they have done differently? Take a guess. They'd have made more decisions and taken more risks. Are you living your life in safety, as the turtle does in his shell, or are you daring to stick your neck out and take risks? What are you waiting for?

An Attitude of Gratitude

Certainly, Anne Frank experienced her share of despondency over the circumstances of her young life. Anne Frank was a German-Jewish teenager, forced to live in a few rooms with her family and others, for twenty-five months during World War II in Germany. She frequently opened a hatch in the roof of a small room to appreciatively view the sky and smell the air. Although she knew their days were numbered in their self-imposed hideaway, she consoled her friend, Peter, as they gazed outward, by saying, "Aren't the clouds beautiful? Look at the sky." Were there moments of gratitude in her state of despondency, or were there moments of despondency in her state of gratitude?

During her suppression she wrote a diary, which helped to "shake off all [her] cares." It has been translated into sixty-seven languages and is one of the most widely read books in the world. Her memoirs indicate her strength in holding positive thoughts in the midst of such horrendous suffering and injustice. For example:

February 3, 1944 – "I've reached the point where I hardly care whether I live or die. The world will keep on turning without me, and I can't do anything to change events anyway. I'll just let matters take their course and concentrate on studying and hope that everything will be alright in the end."

July 15, 1944 – "It's a wonder I haven't abandoned all my ideals, they seem so absurd and impractical. Yet I cling to them because I still believe, in spite of everything, that people are truly good at heart."

July 15, 1944 – "I feel the suffering of millions. And yet, when I look up at the sky, I somehow feel that everything will change for the better, that this cruelty too shall end, that peace and tranquility will return once more."

She, along with her family, was taken to a concentration camp to live her remaining young years. In March of 1945, nine months after her arrest, she died of typhus at the age of fifteen years.

Horse Wisdom

I couldn't help to include a few lines from the movie, Seabiscuit, with regard to feeling despondent. Seabiscuit, a thoroughbred race house, and the underdog's champion, was a symbol of perseverance against all odds during challenging times in the early 1900's. After a severe injury, it was suggested he be put out to pasture. In his defense, his manager retorted, "You don't throw a whole life away just because you get banged up a little." "They've made him so crazy he forgot what he was born to do – just be a horse."

Where is the Seabiscuit in you? Where is the determination to surpass all odds and excel and inspire lives? What needs to be uncovered to allow it to shine through in its magnificence?

Feel despondent, but then let it go. Life is waiting for you to shine and share. Be like Seabiscuit and strive towards the finish line. After all, it's your race, and yours only.

Reflection Time:

1. Stop. Do a reality check when you are feelings depressed. Why am I feeling despondent? Make a list of thoughts you have about it.
2. When is the last time you felt despondent?
3. Do you recognize a pattern between those past events and current?
4. Did you move through it? If so, how? If not, why not?
5. What do you need to do to move the energy?
6. Do you recognize when your friends are despondent? What do they do to move the energy? Does it work?
7. Do you talk about your low feelings with others? Parents? Friends?
8. Do you seek professional help?
9. To what degree to you rely on medications as a cure?
10. Do you take responsibility for your feelings?

> *"You have the power to change the script."*
> **Earl Gould**

D is for feeling... Determined

Definition: positive, inflexible, rigorous, resolute, decided, stubborn
Opposite: easy-going, indifferent, careless, indecisive, faltering, wavering

Determined is to "keep on keeping on." Someone who is determined has a strong sense of purpose and intention. When you set your mind on something, you are determined. "I can do it, and I will do it!" How many times I've said that to myself! There's no distraction—only the goal is seen. One can be determined to do just about anything—to earn X amount of money by his fortieth birthday, to overcome a disease, to live to her fullest potential, or whatever the person sets his/her mind and heart to do!

I was determined to practice karate. When I was studying it, my Sensei (teacher) gave us a fabulous Japanese word to use that means determined, or "keep on going." The word is "gombate." Say it aloud. Gombate! What a strong word.

Our children were young, so I had to arrange for a babysitter, as I made my bi-weekly pilgrimages to East Los Angeles to study with one of the best. Neither of my teachers spoke English fluently, but I still managed to absorb the instruction. I was the only woman in a class of four to eight men (it varied), but I still had to participate in wiping up the perspiration from the wood floor after our class. Much to my surprise I was asked to partake in a demonstration to be televised at an athletic club. Yes, I accepted, never imagining in my wildest dreams that my teacher would ask me to break a board, live, on television! He just told me to "focus" in the area of strength just below my navel. The hand is only the end result. The power comes from directing and focusing on the life energy, "chi." It was a remarkable experience. I did it. My determination brought me one test away from a brown belt (white, green, brown, black). However, the challenges of life were not conducive to furthering my karate history, so I chalked it up to a grand chapter in my life and THE best form of exercise I've ever pursued. It taught me much more than physical strength; it taught me to be grounded and centered.

To Fish or Not to Fish

My friend, Alan Stanz, told me a cute story that epitomizes determination. "On my day off I thought it would be nice to go fishing. But then I heard a voice say, 'I need to practice my sax.' As morning wore on and it was getting hotter, I put on the air-conditioning and got my horn out to play. 'I would really like to go fishing,' another voice said. Ahhh, but there are a lot of bugs and mosquitoes out. I've got my music sorted out on the table, and I should just start to practice. The other voice came back and said, 'I'd really like to go fishing today.'

"I took Dizzy for a walk and told Katie, 'Don't worry if you get home from work and I'm not there – I've gone fishing.' I got my gear together, loaded the rig and drove to what I thought was a good spot to catch my limit. Up the river, I saw a fellow fisherman who had just caught two nice rainbow. I picked up my stuff and went to the bend in the river where he told me he had such good luck. It was in a spot, deep with willows and hard to get to. I threw in my line a few times, got a good hit, and the magic started to happen. I was so excited, I pulled a fish in, determined I didn't need a net to keep him. This beauty was no sooner on the bank when it got away. I couldn't believe my eyes. I turned around and managed to slip on a rock, landed on my butt, shoulder and wrist. I got drenched. My wallet, along with everything else in my pockets, was full of water. Once I got stable, I said, 'This is not going to be a good day.' I can still hear those fishermen laugh. After a few moments, another voice entered and said, 'No, I'm going to catch fish and I'm going to catch my limit.' I took my soggy body up the river and proceeded to catch six rainbow trout! Those beauties, now trapped in my freezer, far surpassed the sprained right wrist I now have to deal with." Alan was determined to get those fish!

Speaking of fish, even Nemo, the main character in the movie, *Finding Nemo*, is determined. Nemo wanted to be brave and swim into territory where he was not allowed. "I can do it, Dad. I can do it," he continually told his father.

Determination is about being centered; it has to do with pursuing goals positively. I think of Napoleon Hill's book, *Think and Grow Rich*, and the story about the gold miner who quit mining gold. He had just had it! That's it! Time out! No more! He sold his claim and off he went. A few days later someone came into the office, bought that site, dug only 300 feet, and guess what—struck gold!

Self-discipline is a key ingredient for determination. We must learn to discipline our mind if we are going to take charge of our lives and make each twenty-four hours something we will look back on with fulfillment.

Determination, perseverance, and tenacity all reward character. If the gold miner had known this and disciplined his mind, and practiced patience, he'd be rich! If you get stuck sometime—and you don't feel like being determined—call a friend who believes in you and your project and your passion. Express it! Feel it! You'll move through it! But keep going! Get back to your motive.

In the early nineties, a young woman by the name of J. K. Rowling was living in England on seventy pounds a week in state benefits. This author of the famed Harry Potter series wrote the first book in an Edinburgh café. Today, she is richer than the Queen according to the Sunday *Time's* "Rich List" and was named the wealthiest female author on the planet. According to the *Observer* out of the U.K., Rowling's fortune has quadrupled in the past two years. Was J. K. Rowling a determined person with high intention? Or did she just do what was the next thing to do? I would venture to say her astrological chart would indicate a serious opportunity for energies to be creative and outrageously abundant!

What gets us in trouble are our underlying beliefs—the ones of which we are not conscious. Sometimes our sub-conscious programming has a different agenda. You might say that one can even be determined to fail and not know it. Yes! To fail. Attached with this is an unconscious desire is to make someone wrong–there is unresolved anger at someone and guess who gets to be right? "See, I was right. I'm not smart enough to do well." "I don't deserve to prosper, to be happy, or to have a meaningful relationship." Or, it could work the other way. "You were right—I'm not making anything of my life. I believed all those things you said about me and now I'm failing. Aren't you happy?" These types of messages can really sabotage our life. We've acquired these beliefs from the time we were kids. Beliefs are the foundation of our life. Are the beliefs you have working for you or sabotaging you?

My long-time and endeared friend, Carol Merrill Burgess, is a great example of someone who is determined to make conscious choices and have a good attitude. I am so blessed to have a support team of phenomenal female friends that hold intention for the highest good. Carol was the model for the popular television game show, Let's Make a Deal from 1963-1977. She and I have one of these special relationships, like wine and cheese, it gets better with age. This is Carol's story:

"When my dear friend Alexandra asked me to reflect on the attitudes, beliefs, and choices that influenced me the most during my fourteen years on *Let's Make A Deal*, the first thing that popped up for me in the attitude department was gratitude. I realized that I was always grateful for having been chosen to do a 'dream' job. And the more I think about it now, it seems that this attitude set the stage for many good things to follow...like always wanting to do my best, not being demanding, and having wonderful relationships with those associated with the show. I also suspect it helped keep me from getting too 'puffed up' in a world where your name is on your dressing room door (with a star on it no less) and people are waiting on you hand and foot. At that point, I suspect gratitude came to my rescue more than once and, as one might expect, continues to this day to be a saving grace. I found that no matter how disappointing life can be at times, there is always something for which to be grateful."

"And this leads to my beliefs. I doubt that I ever would have been able to do any of the things I did, during my career as a model (like fashion photography, TV commercials, and game shows) had I not believed that I could do them. And yet I can't say that I started out as an especially self-confident young person either. When I think back on this, there was one incident that stands out as being pivotal in this area. In a way, I guess I could say my career was really launched at this time. I was only sixteen years old and had just lost in a beauty pageant when one of the organizers of the contest approached me and said, 'You know you really shouldn't give up on this...I suggest you try out again next year.' When I reflect on this now I realize that this person's belief in me enabled me to believe in me too. It's amazing what one sentence at the right moment can do. Anyway, I DID try out the next year and as it turned out I was victorious...I won the title of queen and one of my prizes was a modeling course, which needless to say came in handy more than once during my career. I realize that this is only one small example of the power of beliefs. And once again I find that my beliefs are just as important today as ever."

"As far as choices are concerned, I think for the most part I chose to do things that FELT right to me – I followed my intuition so to speak. Unfortunately, I can't say that by doing that I always made the 'right' decisions, but certainly I learned from them all. I guess I'm still following my intuition today. Maybe with more soul-searching as I do so, but still trusting that this is the way to go. If I'm undecided about whether to do one thing or another, I ask myself, 'Which one will make me feel the best after having done it?' That seems to be more helpful than anything else is. At this point in my life I am grateful for having discovered the activities that I can't wait to get out of bed to do each day. When I spend most of my days doing things that are interesting to me, fulfilling and helpful to others, I find that it's much easier to have a positive attitude with healthy beliefs and to make more choices with positive outcomes."

Right on Carol! Carol Merrill Burgess is one of my dearest friends and I can vouch for the fact that she walks her talk. She is determined to have a good attitude and live a good life. For many years, every morning, we walked a mountain trail and discussed everything from the improper design of toilets to the inappropriateness of allowing the elderly to drive without having more testing of their abilities and skills. Although we live across the planet from each other today, we both feel determined to continue our rich and rewarding friendship.

Mind Over Illness

Another friend, Earl Gould, displayed determination and became his own hero when his application for life insurance was declined due to test results which indicated he had prostate cancer. He became totally focused and believed he could beat this thing called cancer; he was determined! He took responsibility for what he calls "a wake-up call." Earl believes medical doctors fix the symptom but do not address the underlying abnormalities that allow the disease to manifest. Therefore, he set out on his own to do the work. He researched via the Internet and books, and became overwhelmed and exhausted with the thousands of different approaches to healing cancer. "There are no silver bullets to beating cancer. I really have no concrete proof and data as to what specific combination and factors helped me heal."

Cancer appears to negatively impact the immune system so that the body cannot heal itself in an effective way. So the key is to attempt to improve the effectiveness of the immune system so that the body can do its own natural healing. The approach that Earl used to strengthen his immune system was alternative and all-encompassing. Vitamin and herb supplements; changes in diet and lifestyle; unconventional treatments such as detoxification; bio-magnetic healings; energy work; psychic surgery; ozone and hydrothermal treatments; psychoneuroimmunology (mind, body and spirit connection); meditation; evaluating one's attitude and desire to live; and the removal of emotional and sub-conscious blockages – he tried them all!

"To beat cancer you need to be a fighter and take total responsibility for your life. You have control and are not a victim; you are not the doctor's responsibility. Cancer is a mind game. Your immune system is weakened, but what your mind can conceive, your body can build. You need to remove unbalanced energies and blockages that exist in the physical, emotion, and etheric bodies. This is best achieved in my opinion during meditation and work on the inner-plane where you can affirm, establish, and clarify your strong desire to heal. Your immune system becomes effective and healing takes place."

Earl attempts to incorporate the following into his life: self-love and will to love, forgiveness towards others as a means of self-love, personal responsibility for the growth of one's soul, compassion for self and others, inner peace and trust in the divine plan, help towards others to heal themselves, and faith, hope, love, and laughter as powerful stimulants to the immune system. Earl says you have the power to change the script. He also says he would not expect anyone to do everything he did. I call it feeling determined. Congratulations, Earl. You are a hero of mine.

It's obvious Earl had a high intention both unconsciously and consciously to restore his body to health. With intention in any positive life purpose and with determination, every dream can come true.

To stimulate determination, activate your will power in doing some things in life that you thought you could not do. Challenge yourself to do simple tasks first, and as your confidence grows, you will eventually achieve more difficult goals. Needless to say, make certain that these tasks are valuable choices. Good habits are necessary ingredients to feeling determined. Habits start with the way we think repetitively, and with how we train our minds. We can be determined to finish a project by a certain date, and if we don't reach that goal, our habits will determine how we respond to that situation. A negative attitude would look like getting down on ourselves. A more positive approach would be to acknowledge that we missed the mark and proceed to set a new date. The choice we make will determine our happiness. Once again, it's all up to us!

Reflection Time:

1. What do you feel strongly passion about to stay determined to pursue?

2. Identify ten negative habits that stand in your way of feeling determined.

3. Identify ten positive habits that support you in feeling determined.

4. Look at both lists and select the ones that support your highest good.

5. Delete the others from the list and your life.

6. Was there someone in your childhood who exemplified determination?

7. If your part in a play was to portray the determined, strong-willing character, would you be successful at the part?

8. Would it come naturally or would you be "acting?"

9. What does it take to feel determined to complete at project?

10. Where do these ingredients come from?

"Our life is only about the quality of our relationship to our self – no matter how we tend to define it as our relationship to another or others."
Stewart Emery

E is for feeling... Embarrassed

Definition: ashamed, humiliated, compromised, self-conscious
Opposite: proud, boastful, confident

To feel embarrassed is to feel uncomfortably self-conscious. Embarrassment can occur on many levels. Besides humiliation, we feel embarrassed when we're the last to be chosen for a team sport. Maybe we've said something inappropriate to someone without knowing that he or she will be offended. What about walking out of the dry cleaners, without the dry cleaning we just paid for?

While hiking one day with our Aussie Shepherd, Max, I didn't look in all directions as I responded to the call of nature. After gracefully squatting, I looked up to see the shining faces of two others out enjoying the beauty of the mountains. Our eyes met briefly and yes, it was rather embarrassing. But they were cool and turned their attention quickly away from me. I don't think their conversation skipped a beat. They were no doubt embarrassed too. The moment was a blink in the big picture, and yes, I survived it. In fact, I laughed about it once I pulled up my britches and continued my excursion. After all, I wasn't doing anything all that unique!

I recall a time when I was seven years old and invited to ride on the Greek float, a part of the big parade down Broadway, in my hometown of Lorain, Ohio. My golden curly locks were clean and shiny, and I was dressed in an evzon uniform, the traditional pleated white skirt worn by the Greek soldiers. I was so proud of my heritage and to be part of the float. About half way through the parade I just couldn't "hold it" any longer and wet my pants, soiling the lovely white tights worn under my "skirt." Oh dear, was I humiliated. The physical discomfort was not as bad as the shameful and embarrassed feelings I experienced.

Embarrassment as a Child

Other types of embarrassment are more serious. Many, many clients have shared tearful stories from when they were in school and the devastation they felt in anticipating their turn to read when reading circle time came. They were afraid they'd make a mistake, be laughed at, stared at, or whatever. One male client told me how his body would shake and perspire; his heart would beat faster just knowing his turn was coming. His mind was so active with sabotaging thoughts that there was no way he could have performed from his natural self. Unfortunately there was nobody there to say, "Take some deep breaths. You'll do just fine. Just concentrate on each word and focus on being here now. How are you feeling now? What are your thoughts? What's happening in your body? What images are in your mind? What color is your fear?"

Some teachers embarrass students. A teacher who calls attention to a student who is stumbling over his words is not compassionate. Words are powerful. Negative and destructive, they can be toxic to a young child who is eager to learn and please. A teacher makes a lasting impression, an enormous impression on a child's life, one way or another. Beliefs to instill in children are as follows:

- "Your self worth is not dependent on your answer."
- "You are not bad if your answer if incorrect."
- "You are not good if your answer is correct."

It is just what is. Learn from it and move on. Feel the embarrassment and all aspects of that concept and then let it go.

Hide and Seek

Embarrassment relates to self-confidence. If you have self-worth, nothing can damage you– nothing said or done to you. At some time or another, we will all feel embarrassed about something. We're human, and we really all do share the same feelings. Feelings are universal. However, some people let embarrassment "swallow" them, turning a small mistake into a reason to punish oneself with guilt. Again, we have the choice.

Some people go through life being embarrassed just because they're human. It has to do with wanting to hide from the world and from oneself. I've had many clients who feel embarrassed about their life. One woman came into my office and before she sat down, proceeded to tell me how she can't spell or write well and how truly dumb she believes she is. Her self-image was so low it didn't even register on my self-devised "self-esteem" barometer. On a scale from one to ten, one being the lowest, she was a negative! She didn't realize this however, until we used kinesiology (muscle testing).

She, along with too many others, doesn't have the courage to venture into the world. They're too embarrassed or too afraid they might make a mistake. They might do something wrong. So what! Who cares what people might say? Let the world know you're here! Reach out! Go for It! So, you want to try mountain biking? Do it! Yes, it's somewhat embarrassing to be a beginner, to have to get off the bike and walk the tricky parts. So? You'll feel a sense of accomplishment later for simply attempting something you've always wanted to do. And your life will be richer for it.

Maybe you've said something you're sorry for and you feel embarrassed by it. Well, clean it up! Say, "I'm embarrassed to say this but I need to communicate. I want to apologize for what I said yesterday. It wasn't supportive, and I hope you'll forgive me." Big deal! It's over! How painful was that? And believe me, it really is over IF you communicate fully. We're not here on Earth to be invisible—although many would prefer that. We're here to live life fully. When we're happy, our cells are happy, and our body hums. We project that happiness out into the world to everyone, to everything. "Life is a creation...," says Neale Donald Walsh, author of *Conversations with God*, so get busy and create more happiness and the life you want.

Feeling embarrassed is an obstacle to feeling joy and being playful in life. When we're too afraid we'll be judged or evaluated, we hold back and become rigid in our bodies as well as presentation. We lack courage to put forth who we are; before you know it our life is in the last chapters. We are still too embarrassed to express our birthright which is joy. (See "J is for feeling... Joyful" chapter!)

Feeling embarrassed to play is definitely self-imposed. And once again, it comes from fear that we'll be reprimanded and chastised. The problem is not yours, but belongs to the one who is doing the judging. This comes from his or her own embarrassment about being with someone whose behavior is playful and outrageous. It's their problem and their issue. Don't take it personally.

The personality can feel embarrassment. The mind can twist the desire to play and express joy and turn it into chaos. Take charge of your life. Take charge of your mind. You are not your most embarrassing moment. Reject those thoughts, relinquish embarrassment, and play anyhow.

Reflection Time:

1. Have you discovered the playful child within?

2. If not, why not? (Be honest now)

3. If so, what does she or he like to do to play?

4. What do you consider play?

5. When was the last time you played?

6. What do you feel embarrassed about? Your breasts being too small? Your weight? Taking the bar exam three times and failing it? Being set back a grade?

7. How many teachers stand out in your educational experience?

8. What about those teachers made them unique?

9. Ask your parents if they would be willing to share an embarrassing moment with you. Your teacher, a friend, a sibling...

10. What were your thoughts/feelings? What were your beliefs about the situation? What choices did you make about the experience? Does it still influence you?

"When you're going through hell – keep going."
Unknown

E is for feeling... Empty

Definition: spent, despondent, useless, void of life, unfulfilled, dead inside

Opposite: vital, enthusiastic, empowered, joyful, grateful

I had a client who felt empty. She said she felt dead inside—void of energy. I had great compassion for her, as she told me all the beliefs she had taken on about herself as a child. Her negative beliefs were endless. She believed she had no worth, no respect, no value. She believed she would never amount to anything—she believed it all. She tried to fill that empty hole but discovered it was bottomless.

What kind of person would believe they are useless? A person who had been told they couldn't do anything right; someone who was abandoned; a person whose relationship was torn out from under her/him; someone who suffered a major loss; someone in despair, or someone who feels sorry for herself might have this belief. To feel empty to this extent is rooted in low self-esteem. Feeling empty signifies the absence of happiness—feeling nothing, numb, unworthy of being, and out of touch. The belief systems of those who feel empty are inundated with lack, and they are separated from knowing the truth about who they really are.

Some try to satisfy the empty holes with drugs, alcohol, sex, gambling, or thrills; they just can't get full enough. Their neediness becomes manipulative as they drain their friends and relationships. Here's an interesting fact: According to the National Mental Health Association in 2001, twelve million American women suffer from clinical depression. They say it occurs more often in women then in men. However, Dr. William Pollack says "65% go misdiagnosed." Men mask their depression, or emptiness through anger and irritability, acting out in abusive behavior, while feeling too inept to express their sadness and hopelessness. Dr. Pollack also said that men's depression shows up in the high male suicide rate.

The Truth about Suicide

In America, suicide took the lives of 29,350 people in 2000. An estimated 600,000 to 750,000 people attempt suicide each year.

According to the National Institute for Mental Health, statistics indicate suicide is the third-leading cause of death among young people, ages fifteen to twenty-four and the eleventh-leading cause of death in the U.S. Males are more likely to die of suicide than females, although females are more apt to attempt suicide.

These statistics reflect an unconquered emptiness. Feeling empty is emotional bankruptcy where an individual can see no hope, are in despair, and have nobody to turn to. Often, if they do, they're too embarrassed and guilty to reach out once again. They believe they have run out of options.

Feeling empty feels like death. This death takes place while we are still breathing, and has to do with losing our joy. The actual fears involved, though still present, are subconscious in those who are feeling empty. Like any other feeling, the feeling of emptiness should be honored; feel it, explore it, experience it, release it, and replace it.

Being committed to truth and knowing our true self may seem to be idealistic, but it isn't. It just takes work.

Recharge and Re-see

Work can make great demands on us, with its long hours, intense decision-making, creative problem-solving and potentially stress-producing dilemmas. It is not uncommon or unreasonable to feel empty and depleted. For many, having more than one job is necessary to earn a living. This adds even more stress, separation, and struggle to this adventure called life. Just as a car battery occasionally needs recharging, we too need to be recharged in order to function in a balanced state with a sense of well-being.

Is this a feeling you can relate to? Is there anyone you know who has felt dead inside? At times I have felt void of joy; it is my most painful state. When I lose my joy, I feel sadness, and I lack motivation and enthusiasm. I observe the desire to desperately want my joy back, and yet I know this feeling of emptiness too, shall pass.. I feel a lack of attachment to whatever is occurring in my day, whether it's exciting news or less than exciting. Sometimes the journey is a long one. While there is probably a pill I could take, I choose to feel my emptiness and am open to the insights that come to me while meditating as well as when driving my car. So I process, I feel. I observe and I trust. I prefer to listen and receive guidance for the next step which can come from anywhere, e.g. from comments being overheard from a neighboring booth while out for dinner, witnessing a particular behavior at a shopping mall, a book, piece of art, or the purchase of a DVD player. Our guidance can come from life, if we are receptive.

One client was so needy of love she deprived herself of expressing feelings to her partner for fear he would judge, blame, or worse yet, leave her. Her fear was so great, she believed, "I'll do anything to keep my mate." She took the anger out on herself. Then her body started talking. Aches and pains from a pinched nerve in the neck led to lack of mobility in her arms. The body never lies. It is a marvelous mirror of our trauma, even self-imposed. If we can learn to listen to those aches and pains, they will serve as the mirror for what needs transformation in our life.

Another example of receiving messages from the world around me happened when my husband and I were at the river on a picture-perfect Sunday afternoon. There was a blue sky, puffy white clouds, refreshing summer breezes, and our dog Max played "fetch the stick." We were engaged in a rather intense discussion about an issue that was bothering me, when a man walked by and said to us in a friendly manner, "It doesn't get much better than this." Gene and I instantly looked at each other, refreshed by this stranger's comment. It seemed that the Universe was telling us to lighten up!

We are constantly in the act of drawing to ourselves the perfect people, situations, and experiences that will guide us to the next step. A gentleman out enjoying beauty entered our day as a reminder to add to my grateful journal! His comment brought a chuckle to us as we were aware that, although our communication was necessary, we were being reminded to see the bigger picture. Life really doesn't care if we feel empty or fulfilled. As my dad used to say, "Time marches on," regardless of how you are feeling.

As we realize that we can control our thoughts, which then affect our feelings, we inch our way to mastery and enlightenment by seeing the perfection of every situation. Trials and suffering may lead to feelings of emptiness and unhappiness, but we need to remember that they have come to awaken and remind us that we are more than our senses. Our free will is our passport to freedom and fullness. This takes self-discipline.

Once again I come back to feelings and beliefs. We can't change behavior until we change beliefs. We can't change our beliefs until we examine our attitudes. When we question our beliefs to determine if they are love or fear-based, we then start making wise choices. Get it? It's a three-ring circus. We must create new beliefs about ourselves, our worth, our purpose, and our value. As we do this, we change our thinking, which leads to speaking a different vocabulary and making more conscious choices that support our value and well-being. The end result is a reality that is filled with joy, fulfillment, harmony, and balance. It must start with you, and you must do the work. Put on your detective hat and start to truly explore your belief system, your core definitions and your perceptions of life.

Fulfilled Family

A determined client took this exact course of action. Her story follows:

"This entry is for your book, so your readers can know how much you have helped me change my life. I have had a lifetime of psychotherapy, starting at age three, and most of it didn't seem to help. In fact, some of it was detrimental. I even had psychoanalysis four times per week. Nothing seemed to help me move forward to leave the past behind. Instead, I constantly discussed my past and was continuously upset by it. My life felt empty and alone."

"When I was referred to you and you explained your system (NPR), it sounded unbelievable, but I was willing to try anything. We have had five sessions over a period of not even four months, and in that time, I know you have helped me make very significant and positive changes."

"After our first session I called my mother from the top of Baldy (ski mountain) and asked for her help in buying a home. She had never wanted to discuss it before, but did agree to help me right away. In fact, she flew up from Los Angeles and went house hunting with me, and I am now ready to move into my new home. I know the work we did together helped to shift my belief system and the very cells of my body, which allowed this to happen."

"When I went home for the holidays I got along with my sister better then I had in years. And recently I had the best visit I have ever had with my father. Alexandra, thank you so much. I am grateful I was able to find my way to you and was able to receive your help, which so far has brought me many blessings."

Certificate of Magnificence

My dear friend and soul brother, Alan Hack, created a wonderful diploma of magnificence. He sent it to me one day. Part of it says, "This is to certify that **Alexandra** has always been, is now, and will always be, a magnificent human being." How about reading that back and putting your name in the place of mine? My diploma of magnificence is framed and hangs on my wall near my diplomas from graduate schools. I gave one to our daughter, Danielle, when she earned her master's degree—a reminder of what she's heard for years.

You can honor your child and her/his magnificence at any time with your own certificate. Give your child these words today to support the foundation of her/his life with this gesture of love and truth. It's fun to give it to friends too. Because it's so unexpected, they'll be "blown away." As you reach out to express yourself through this simple activity you'll be amazed at the repercussions. You just might feel more connected, rather than empty. Try it. Unless you prefer to be one of those people who check the obituary column each day to see if they're still alive. Make changes in your life today. Don't wait until your family gathers around your bedside to support you in making your transition. You can do it, and you are worth it! Take action. *Begin by learning to connect with a force that is magnificent, then see yourself as part of it.* Start to identify yourself with this force—that of joy, wisdom, truth, and beauty.

"Try to realize you are a divine traveler. You are here for only a little while, then depart for a dissimilar and fascinating world. Do not limit your thought to one brief life and one small Earth. Remember the vastness of the Spirit that dwells within you." Thought-provoking words by Paramahansa Yogananda.

"The disillusionment of emptiness comes from failing to align one's life with the principles from which power emanates," says Dr. David R. Hawkins, from his book, *Power vs. Force: An Anatomy of Consciousness*. He correlates the lives of great musicians, composers, and conductors of our times and how they continue to live such productive lives into their eighties and nineties. "Their lives have been dedicated to the creation and embodiment of beauty...."

You are whole, total, and complete, and often appearances can fool you. I'm here to remind you, if you should ever forget, as Yogananda has in the previous quote, that you are a divine traveler.

Reflection Time:

1. Recall a time when you felt empty. What was lacking in your life when you felt that way?

2. What were your beliefs and attitudes about that issue?

3. What did your world look like?

4. Did you take responsibility for the situation?

5. To which of the characteristics on the victim/responsibility bookmark did you relate?

6. If you were to receive a certificate of magnificence, would you proudly read the words, knowing they are true, or would you feel embarrassed, undeserving or too empty to hold them?

7. Examine the repetitiveness of the pattern with regard to the current fear.

8. How are you benefiting from this belief, i.e. is it an attention-seeking device, or are you wanting sympathy, etc.?

9. Do some holistic introspection:
   Physically: nutrition, exercise, environmental influences
   Mentally: your belief system, your thoughts.
   Emotionally: your feelings
   Spiritually: your intuition, your connection to nature, your spiritual community

10. Connect with something in nature and let it speak to you about this feeling of emptiness. What is it telling you? Listen, really listen.

"If I am content with what I have, I can live simply and enjoy both prosperity and free time.

If my goals are clear, I can achieve them without fuss.

If I am at peace with myself, I will not spend my life force in conflict.

If I have learned to let go, I do not need to fear dying."

Tao Te Ching adaptation

E is for feeling... Enlightened

Definition: informed, illuminated, educated
Opposite: ignorant, illiterate, empty-headed

"Enlightenment – don't know what it is," sings male vocalist, Van Morrison in the lead song of his popular CD by the same name. I listened intently to the words, and as his pleasant voice faded, I found myself also pondering the question: What is enlightenment?

In 1784, Immanuel Kant said, "Enlightenment is man's emergence from his self-imposed immaturity. Immaturity is the inability to use one's understanding without guidance from another." His motto for enlightenment is to "have courage to lose our own understanding."

Allen Cohen, poet, teacher, writer, historian, says the Sanskrit word "moksha" which means "a state of liberation from all bondage, from all suffering; a state of infinite joy, bliss and fulfillment," is the ultimate goal of life. Sounds good to me.

Let's shed some light on the subject. "Light," the root of the word "enlightenment," replaces the dark; it illuminates and brings vision, clarity, and brightness. Traditionally the dark has been equated to ignorance whereas light stands for reason and truth.

Enlightened turns the light on, inside. It means to know you are the light. No matter what happens, you know you're the light. To me, to be enlightened means to be present in the moment. My awareness speaks the truth of "what is so." What is so in each moment? Embrace each moment for whatever it is. Remember in each moment who you are.

To "enlighten," according to the Webster's big book, means "to provide with spiritual wisdom." And under "S" in the same dictionary, we have "spirit" defined as "the vital principle or animating force traditionally believed to be within living beings." So, in this sense, enlightenment pertains to discovering a part of ourselves.

The Buddhist definition of "enlightenment" is "a final blessed state marked by the absence of desire or suffering." We are all in process, moving toward enlightenment. We can think of our lifetime as schooling, and the state of enlightenment is our graduation. Some of us are in kindergarten and some of us are completing our Ph.D.'s. Everyone is exactly where he or she has evolved to be, which is the perfect place.

But... How?

With a better understanding of the word, now we are on to explore the process of attaining this state of enlightenment. How do we become enlightened? Abraham Maslow, author of *Farthest Reaches of Human Nature*, American-born psychologist, believed that every human is born with spiritual needs and longings—the yearning for values such as truth, beauty, justice, simplicity, and wholeness. He felt we actually crave experiences in our life where we can feel most alive and fulfilled, for in them lies the sense of what the world can truly be like for us.

The Eastern philosophies have brought forth great wisdom on enlightenment. We in the West are slowly learning. Whether East or West, many would go to any length to achieve enlightenment, this state of "nirvana," or total bliss. A few even go to India and meditate in a cave for the longest time, experimenting and wanting a state of enlightenment so desperately in their lives.

Everyone has her or his own unique path. Each step of the journey is perfect in every way, no matter the appearance. The more connected we are, the more we walk in truth. The more separate and disconnected, to more we walk in fear.

It takes the power of intention and the power of commitment to be enlightened. There's a story about a young man who went to the wise master seeking enlightenment. The master led him to a lake without saying a word and pointed to a small rowboat. The young man rowed the two of them to the middle of the lake. "Put your face in the water for as long as you can," the master instructed. The young man hesitated, but knowing that wise masters can be strange, went ahead and did as he was told. When he felt he could hold his breath no longer, he began to raise his head, but a firm hand gripped his head and held it down below the surface of the water. The young man panicked, trying with all his might to lift his face, twisting his entire body, while unable to move his head. When he was about to pass out, the young man exhaled explosively into the water, and his head was yanked up at that very moment. The young man gasped and panted in an attempt to recover, staring at the wise master in bewilderment. The master responded, "Enlightenment will be yours when you want it as badly as you want to breathe." Intention is important! Without the will to grow to a higher state, we won't.

According to enlightened thinkers, life is whole, connected, and limitless. There is no separation between the world and the Self. One of life's big lessons here in Earth School is to truly understand that we are One with all of life. This truth may look like a huge responsibility to own; it may even be scary. Just go with your own experience. Be willing to explore the possibility that we are part of a greater whole. For starters, maybe we could just free ourselves of prejudice, conflict, anger, and violence. This is not easy.

In the Disney Movie, *The Lion King*, Mufasa said these words to his son, Simba: "Look. Look in the water and see your reflection. See who you are." Do you remember that? To feel enlightened is to know who you are, and that you have stuff that happens, and that the stuff is not you. It's just stuff.

The first step towards enlightenment, or discovering the truth within, is to be open and aware. This is part of the inner preparation to receive the wisdom you seek. Fine-tune all the senses (now don't forget intuition) and be alert to your inner and outer world. Pay attention to your life on a deeper level. Look for the meaning behind circumstances, rather than sailing through them "clueless," as my daughter would say. Listen to the words that come out of your mouth, and what words you receive back from others. What is the nature of these words? The tone? The quality?

Next, dare to step out and stand up for your values, for what you believe in, and for who you are. It takes courage to put yourself out there. It's risky, as others may pass judgment and criticize your thoughts and position. As part of the marriage ceremony I perform, I urge the couple "to embrace the unexpected and dance on the razor's edge." Notice who places the "stops" in your life. Who imposes the limits and the boundaries? And what are you going to do about it?

Another important point is to realize that it's the journey that matters, not necessarily the destination. In fact, enlightenment may not be a destination at all, but a "coming to" the present moment. (How's that for a paradox?) Once we've been awakened, we must trust the process and resist the impatience that may torment us. The spiritual path is not one of competition, but one of listening to the beat of our own drum. Slowly we develop, and the truth unfolds. Slowly we assert more and more of ourselves—our true selves. The rewards cannot be measured in any way. In fact, they are often beyond words.

Happy Birthday

Having a birthday can be an enlightening experience, if you perceive it as so. "Hi. If you called to wish me a Happy Birthday, I sure appreciate your thoughtfulness. Thank you so much. I'm out celebrating the special day of my birth and will enjoy hearing your greeting upon my return." This was the outgoing message on my answering machine for January 14th.

There is a purpose to birth! And I believe it is to remember who we truly are. We are here to fulfill this mission! All beautiful beings, through their uniqueness, contribute to the whole, and as we "follow our bliss" as much-admired anthropologist Joseph Campbell said, we actually affect the collective consciousness.

One day out of each year, we each have the opportunity to celebrate the moment of our birth. What do you do on your birthday to honor this special day? My birthday serves as a benchmark along the trail in my quest for Self-realization. It is an opportunity to examine and take a close look at my intention. As I do, I experience a major shift in my perspective. I've finally found what I've been searching for, and I didn't have far to look. It didn't appear in a package decorated with bows. It couldn't be bought in a store or purchased through a travel agent. I've given myself the best gift of all for my birthday—freedom. In lieu of control and struggle, I chose to allow life to teach me as it unfolds, and I trust the process.

What fun birthdays can be! I indulge in the display of colorful cards from dear friends and family, expressing sweet and loving words that penetrate my heart. One of my favorite cards from our son, Jeff, had a Dalmatian dog with colored spots on the front. He wrote inside, "I love that you have colored spots—most moms just have black ones." Christopher, our second son, sent me a card by my all time favorite card designer, Suzy's Zoo. I just love the characters and feel good from head to toe when I just look at them. (No hard feelings, Hallmark.) Marushka is my stuffed grizzly bear that was given to me by our daughter in celebration of my fortieth birthday. Marushka is propped up in my office wearing a T-shirt that says, "Where there is no love, put love, and you will find love." She may be one of the most hugged, stuffed grizzlies around.

A Treasured Gift

Happy Birthday to my beautiful...

My mother, my friend
warm and soft inside my soul
I feel your closeness within.

Thanking you with every day
for being who you are,
never for a moment forgetting your
strength, love, and support.

A gift from God we were brought together
To learn and to teach,
Back-n-forth the teeter swings
Never but a moments reach.

Soaring in the winds and dancing
on the clouds,
We will always be together
Smiling and crying for our love is endless...

I Love You...
Danielle
January 14, 1995

I believe a birthday is a beautiful landmark, a time to take stock of your life. So with eyes barely open, I honor the occasion by offering my gratitude to the Great Spirit for all my blessings, and there are so many! I'm most grateful that I am someone who is committed to conscious evolution. Yes, there will be more personal and spiritual growth. Will it ever end? I doubt it. Each year as I explore the meaning of the day, I become even more enthusiastic about my life and all I did to achieve the attitude I embrace today. I once saw a bumper sticker that read, "What are we doing here?" About thirty years ago, as I was in the midst of suffering yet another one of life's dramas, I couldn't help but wonder what I was doing here. "Won't this ever stop?" I recall thinking in frustration.

100

"There must be more to life than this."

Day after day, as I continued to listen to my intuition and experiment with the process, I came to the realization that yes, there is more to life, much more. But, it took my willingness to investigate, to read, to question, to participate, to follow, to lead, to introspect, to merge and immerse myself in almost everything to understand. It took getting off a position of being right and thinking I had the answers. It took giving up being a victim. (Sorry folks, but it has to go.) It took courage and trusting myself. The veil of ignorance slowly lifted and it became obvious that life was about learning, growing, and expanding my consciousness.

The state of enlightenment is most natural—it's our birthright and already exists. All we need to do is increase our knowing.

The Enlightening Past

One client of mine took the necessary steps to enlightenment by facing her fear of not only flying, but of airports! In her own words:

"I have always been afraid of flying. During our session I remembered an experience I had when I was a child at an airport. My memory was one of seeing my dad off on a flight to Boston because he had a horrendous hand accident and was being flown for emergency surgery. We were all outside waving goodbye to my dad and the next thing I know, my brother and I are out on a ledge with no railing and my mother is freaking out. She continued this behavior in the car and all the way home. I felt as though it was all my fault that she was so upset! I carried this memory around with me my whole life and have always been afraid to fly."

"I later found out my fear of flying was associated with this experience. After my session with Dr. Alexandra, I asked my mom about the incident. It was not at all what I had remembered. Apparently, my brother climbed out on the ledge himself, and I went after him to prevent a possible fall. I was probably four and my brother two. It was devastating. I always thought it was my fault and that had instigated the whole thing to endanger my brother. I thought that because I was older, I should have known better. I was so relieved to hear the true story that I went out to protect my brother. My mother was upset leaving my father in that condition and reacted towards us by 'freaking out.' Although I have not had the occasion to fly, I have frequented the airport many times, with dramatically different responses. In the past I would get very nervous and now I have no reaction. It's just what it is – an airport. My enlightenment happened when I found out this truth from my mother. I feel freed from the perception that kept me limited and in fear many years of my life. Amazing. Thank you Dr. Alexandra for the work that brought me to this place."

The path to awakening comes when we discover: a) lasting happiness doesn't exist in material possessions; b) security isn't found by holding onto a deteriorating relationship or job; c) peace of mind isn't necessarily achieved through weekly visits to a "shrink." Peace of mind is a process.

My friend, Peggy Warren, wrote a delightful book entitled Gathering Peace about an eleven-year-old girl who travels across the country with her family in a station wagon pulling a twenty-eight foot trailer. She wants to give her father peace for his birthday because this is all he says he wants—peace and quiet. I encourage you read it and discover how she learns about peace. Can it be given to someone as a gift? Or is it something that one can only experience for oneself, through introspection, education, and change?

The ancient sacred books all profess that the jewel is indeed within us, and once we have a glimpse of this and we begin to believe it, life takes on a new glow. Every day, every moment as we take in the breath of life, our cells respond to our new awareness. The passion pulses through our whole being as we open to a new way of living. It's scary to live on the edge, committed to speaking the truth in each moment. It's uncomfortable watching the ego dissolve. It's unsettling to know there is no turning back AND, it's the most exhilarating and energizing way to live life—for me, anyway.

In the last few lines in his song, Van Morrison sings, "You can change it, rearrange it. You're making your own reality / It's up to you." I invite you to go ahead and rearrange it—allow the beacon of light into your life to replace darkness or false beliefs and discover the vital force within.

Reflection time:

1. What's your definition of enlightenment? Sit down and "rap" with your kids about it. Or with your mom and dad about it.

2. Experiment by bringing "light" into your chores by using a chant, such as "chop wood, carry water." It may help lift spirits and keep you in the present moment.

3. How will you celebrate your birthday?

4. Did you ever give yourself a party?

5. What does peace of mind mean to you?

6. Do you experience it frequently? Rarely? Never? Consistently?

7. Do you believe you can rearrange it and that you're making your own reality?

8. Are you uninterested, slightly, or intensely interested in becoming enlightened?

9. Do you embrace, or resist the unexpected?

10. Is it comfortable for you to be in the now?

"....moving with the tide, not resisting, letting things be as they are, watching how things develop and unfold with a certain calm but interested detachment, not trying to envision or force a certain result but just watching and participating when appropriate as the 'isness' of life unfolds."

Treya Killam Wilber, *Grace and Grit*

F is for feeling... Fascinated

Definition: intrigued, curious, awestruck, amazed
Opposite: bored, disinterested, indifferent, dull

I invite you to do a little experiment. Take a moment now and reflect on some event that has troubled you in your life. Got it? Okay. Feel the feelings you have about the circumstances. Feel how these emotions weigh you down. Really get into it. Now, with all the skill you have to create your own reality, observe the same scene, but this time, view it as absolutely fascinating and mesmerizing! See it from the larger perspective that this may have occurred for some grander purpose. How does it feel now? That's quite a different feeling, isn't it? When some event fascinates us, it takes on a whole different aura. If only we could always see these situations from a perspective of fascination, our curiosity would cause a shift inside of us. We can do this with anything. Explore and experiment with this. Simply look at events from another perspective and see what happens.

All that is needed is an attitude shift. Perception makes whatever picture the mind desires to see. It's all up to you.

The above quote is from Treya Killam Wilber, a woman who died of cancer. Her husband wrote a book, *Grace and Grit*, which is a compelling story of how Treya and her husband and psychologist, Ken Wilber, endured a five-year journey encompassing her illness, treatment, and death. Treya's writing demonstrates a certain fascination with her process and is extraordinary.

Changing Positions

Hate your job? Dissatisfied with where you live? Dislike the quality of the relationship with your child? The routine in your life? What perception are your holding about each of your personal complaints?

I recall back in 1978 when I told my family I was going to India. They did not see it as fascinating. At that time, nobody but I could see this trip as an opportunity. My husband managed to find a small article in the paper about some virus affecting the brain that was being transmitted in India. Others' opinions of India were associated with death, poverty, beggary, and lack.

Consider the many professional individuals who have left lucrative jobs and careers to live in a mountain community and work in a bookstore. Do you know anybody who has done something similar? Did you find it fascinating or stupid? I once met a judge who had no regrets for leaving the bench to work a menial job in a resort town.

Many people have changed careers or professions. One man I knew left his law practice and went back to school to pursue psychology. Another woman left the stressful work of a graphic artist to become a massage therapist. Change is imminent. Even the moon changes fifteen degrees every night. Nothing remains stagnant.

When we have change we have choice. Our options are absorbing and intriguing. It's utterly fascinating to realize the choice we have in our lives. We can judge people and their choices, therefore alienating them from our friendship circle; we can envy them for their actions that took courage and willingness to risk; we could be angry with them for causing us to examine our lives, or we can support them, which will create a deeper relational connection. Choice—do we choose fascination or judgment?

We can create pain or pleasure in our reality, which all starts with our thoughts. Our minds are powerful. Thought is energy. Energy follows thought. Ernest Holmes says, "You do not change the law of gravitation, you merely change your position in it." He says the laws of the Universe work according to your belief. "The law is always a mirror reflecting our mental attitudes. The law will reflect either the belief that there is scarcity in the world, or that all the good in the world is yours to have.

Take this fact, for example. Dr. Deepak Chopra says, "Matter is frozen light." In other words, subatomic particles are energy waves of varying frequencies that interact to create the illusion of matter. It is said that the body is a number of rising and falling waves of vibrating currents of energy. Get it? The illusion of matter. The body looks and feels solid, right? The chair that you sit upon looks solid enough, right? Now take another look—see that it is actually energy. Fascinating, huh?

When we understand that a Creative Intelligence allows the planets to stay in their own orbits, water to freeze at thirty-two degrees F, leaves to drop when chlorophyll is no longer present, and that we are part of that brilliant design, we can truly manifest our dreams and goals. It starts with our thoughts. You can have thoughts about a frustrating situation turn inside out to be those of sheer fascination.

Embracing the Elders

The photograph of the crystal is associated with this chapter of "fascinated" for obvious reasons. It weighs 15,000 pounds, is from Brazil, and has been named by the owner, "Embracing the Elders." I was told, "It is the grandmother and grandfather of all crystals. Its shape, age, and feeling, portray great wisdom of many years. When you hug it, it hugs you. A three year old climbed under it and saw it even more fascinating from that vantage point. It is peace-filled." I felt utterly fascinated just being in the same room with this work of nature. The universe has wondrous gifts to humble us, if we are open to it.

Rev. John Moreland, Minister of Light on the Mountains Spiritual Center in Sun Valley, Idaho, says, "We live in a universe that is a balance of love and law. The love aspect encompasses our consciously setting intentions and being inspired to live a life focused on vision. The way that these intentions and ideas come into being in the physical is through universal laws. These are laws and not rules; they operate whether we recognize them or not. They function impersonally, working equally for all of us."

"One of the most predominant laws that affect us is that of giving and receiving. Our natural state is to go through our lives spontaneously giving and spontaneously receiving throughout each day. Unfortunately, we as humans can feel blocked in either of the polarities of this universal truth."

"Sometimes we have difficulty giving out of a fear that our resources are forever limited. At other times, we may have trouble receiving as we harbor beliefs of unworthiness. If we are experiencing a sense of stagnation or lack of flow in any area of our lives, we must challenge ourselves in taking an inner inventory of our beliefs in these areas."

"Ultimately, the law states that we receive according to the degree that we are willing to give. If we withhold from others, we will find that we do not receive to the degree we desire. We should each look at our willingness to give, not just of our financial abundance, but most importantly of ourselves in service to others. As we do so, our life experience naturally comes into balance as we embody a healthy balance of giving and receiving in our lives."

Forgiving and Living

The transformation that forgiveness brings can be fascinating. In the core of forgiveness is the notion of seeing the situation from a higher perspective. International Forgiveness Week is the second week in February, bringing a message that could release you into freedom. It's certainly worth putting the date on your calendar then including in a daily "to-do" list. Monday: Let go of the pain I harbor about_____. Tuesday: Free myself from the anchor of resentment. You get the idea. The rewards in exchange for self-righteousness are inner peace, happiness, a quiet mind, a sense of worth, integrity, and knowing our unique purpose.

The ego can get a little shaky when we start thinking about forgiveness. It will attempt to convince us that our uneasy feelings aren't real and that it's not necessary to forgive—after all, "It's really their obligation to clear the air." The voice of the ego might blare, "Apologizing is a sign of weakness." It doesn't forgive or forget, instead, it holds on. A person of inner strength is the one who is willing to clean the slate. The healthy personality knows the damage inflicted by holding onto grudges, jealousy, resentment, and bitterness. But the ego voice can emphatically overshadow the inner voice, which says, "Take a risk. Clean up your life. Express what's in your heart. Be free of the past." These are some of the reasons why it's so difficult for people to say, "I'm sorry about _____. I hope you'll accept my apology." This is an example of the importance of training the mind. Which voice do you listen to? Who's really in charge of the choices you make?

When our oldest son, Jeffrey Peter, was born, we employed a seventy-five-year-old, German baby-nurse, Dorothy Robinson, who taught me more than just how to care for a newborn. "Don't hold on to anything that's negative," Robby said. "Throw it out, just like your dirty water." The pillars of her attitude were patience, tolerance, and understanding— wise words from someone who had never taken a psychology class.

I heard about a woman say on the completion of a home improvement project, "There, Mom, I did it better than you." Her mother had passed away ten years prior to this, but obviously the daughter was still carrying the pain of an unhealed relationship with her. Until we have our relationships in tact with our parents, we will continue to allow the wounds and deep-seated angers to prevent us from realizing our full potential. Words alone won't do it; we've got to mean it, and to mean it, we've got to deal with it, understand it, feel it, and the entire pattern that manifested in that situation. Then we can release it.

Once purged from our cells, we can honestly forgive those who have hurt us or not lived up to our expectations. We can even choose to share the process with that person. We free ourselves and can begin to perceive the fascination of the situation, beyond the ego's hurt.

Most importantly we must forgive ourselves for what we did or didn't do in the past. This is an equally significant course of action that can't be dropped out. The results will be powerful.

A sincere desire must be there however, then take charge of that ego voice and proceed with the required action. Write in a journal the names of those you need to forgive. Most likely, when you close your eyes, a name or image will come to you that you had long forgotten. Just write it down. You may even feel guided to write a letter to a certain person, expressing your feelings. Great! Feel it and get it out. Purge yourself of all the guilt and suffering and commence tapping into your own strength. Look at your list again and go to the next name. Now, how about creating a list of those who may need to forgive you?

Dr. Jonas Salk, developer of the polio vaccine, says the end-result of being loving and forgiving would be "to release the power in the nucleus of each individual – a power much greater in its positive effects than atomic power is in its negative." That's some statement!

Continue the process by starting each day affirming, "There is a new patience within me, a new understanding, and a greater ability to love." Stay current by being aware of life and feelings, expressing what is necessary in the moment, and continuing to work on yourself.

Remember that blame, resentment, and bitterness are all words that keep us stuck in the past. When you say, "Let's bury the hatchet," mean it and do it. Responsibility is about the present in respect to the future. It's about looking forward not backward. It's about mastery.

The Big Screen

While in Washington D.C., I visited the Einstein planetarium in the Air and Science Museum. The Infinity Express presentation revealed that everything in the Universe is related to everything else. There were amazing facts about our galaxy and our nearest galaxy, Andromeda—that in three billion years the two will collide and form a new one. What Force holds them in their own energy field? What Infinite Intelligence? We are such a small speck in the vast scheme of Life, I thought, as I looked up from a reclining seat into a dome which held a replica of the universe. "What happens to us and our problems are so out of proportion," I said to myself.

I was so inspired by the movie *The Mirror Has Two Faces*, starring Barbra Streisand. Oh, I had such a laugh at myself after watching it! As I sat next to my kids and viewed the credits, I said to them, "Gosh, I wish I could write, produce, direct, and act in my own movie." Danielle and Jeff looked at me at the same time. We all realized what I had just said and laughed. "Mom! You already are! Remember!" Oh, those kids are so sharp—they catch me at the best times. I'm doing exactly that—writing, directing, and acting. And so are you. Are you pleased with your creation?

We can also experience something as fascinating and then, a few years down the road, see it as a mistake. At that time, we might choose to feel anger, resentment, grief, betrayal, etc. Again, it's up to us. We're so powerful. We can also see it as a fascinating scene in the movie of our life. Remember that we ARE creating it all. Life is so much more fun when we can observe it from a place of being fascinated...and from the wisdom that we are all connected.

Reflection Time:
1. What is the central theme running through your script?
2. Who are your supporting actors?
3. What kind of part do you give them?
4. What about the villain and the hero? Who plays these parts?
5. Discover a situation in your life that has been getting the best of you. Maybe a relationship, physical malady, classes at school. Experiment with the two-sides-of-the-coin idea. See it as it is now, and then choose to see it as fascinating.
6. How does your body feel when you perceive something as fascinating?
7. How about bored, uninteresting? Which do you prefer?
8. As an experiment, look out the window and gaze at an object outdoors. Now, without moving your head, just your eyes, bring your attention to something indoors—maybe on the windowsill. Now switch your gaze from the same object outdoors to the same one indoors. Going back and forth. Who is doing this? You are in charge. Where do you choose to place your focus? See how easy it is? Just choose.
9. Focus on a living creature that you might be afraid of—like spiders, snakes, jellyfish, sharks, for example. Connect to the internet and learn a few fascinating characteristics about that form of life. Does anything change for you, knowing what you learned?
10. Visit a planetarium and allow yourself to be fascinated by the exhibits and presentations. That evening gaze at the sky and be fascinated.

"Everything can be taken from a man, but one thing, the last of the human freedoms – to choose one's attitude in any given set of circumstances, to choose one's own way."

Victor Frankl, *Man's Search for Meaning*

F is for feeling... Free

Definition: unencumbered, independent, liberated
Opposite: confined, captive, bonded, trapped

Wouldn't it be thrilling to discover a new key on your key ring? Imagine that this key opens the secrets to personal freedom. What does that mean to you? What would change in your life with this new key? Pay attention to the first thing that comes to mind.

"It couldn't be that easy." Many lives are ruled by beliefs like: "Life isn't supposed to be easy –in fact, it's a struggle." "Wisdom comes with maturity and age. Then I'll be free." "My personal freedom will come when (fill in the name) changes."

Our personal freedom can manifest through our attitudes, beliefs, and choices. Such freedom takes some introspection, honesty, and the desire and willingness to change what doesn't work.

Free-wheelin'?

A thirty-two year old female client came into my office feeling depressed, sad, and considering medication. I asked her when she started feeling this way. She said when she sold her VW Eurovan. "What does it represent to you?" I asked her. "It represents the ability to take off at a moment's notice and to feel comfortable, contained, and independent. It means freedom," she responded. By using NPR (Neuro-physical Reprogramming), we determined there was resentment in her body about money and abundance. The beliefs surrounding that discovery were the following:

- I feel resentful for having to do the practical and responsible thing.
- I'll lose freedom if I'm responsible.
- The only way to have money is if you're responsible.
- I'm only deserving of money if I work hard and do the responsible thing.

110

- If I'm carefree, I'll lose money.
- Freedom equals financial security.
- Life is scary.
- Being responsible and part of the real world is scary.
- Being responsible is a "should." It's practical, but not freeing.
- Being responsible is void of adventure and flexibility and is confining.

When I asked her what kind of person would believe this, she immediately blurted out, "My father. He worked so hard all his life to be responsible and raise a family. In the process, he lost his freedom and sense of adventure, denying his feelings with alcohol." Further exploration led to the surfacing of beliefs such as "I can't feel joyful and responsible at the same time." Her identity was strongly attached with her vehicle and everything that it represented. Now that it was no longer a part of her life, she became depressed with the very thought of being responsible and establishing roots in a community. She was resentful that she couldn't feel joyful and responsible at the same time. While testing her body through kinesiology and making the statement, "I am my van," her arm remained very strong, indicating that she indeed believed, on a cellular level, that she was her van! After the process of feeling and releasing, she imagined a field with the warmth of the sun beating down on trees and water. She shifted her identification with ego-consciousness to one of soul-consciousness. She experienced timelessness and freedom in this visualization as well as a connection to her true self, one that is expansive, vast, and freed from limitation. What an incredible case history! How many of us carry around the beliefs of our parents at an unconscious level? How many of us are scared of life, of being responsible, because of what we absorbed in the early years of life? The very thought of being confined was devastating to her! Being confined meant being rooted, having a job, and sacrificing freedom—all self-imposed, all choice.

If you want to know your degree of freedom, check out how much you can do without. This might be a good clue. Attachment and freedom fit under the same umbrella.

We have the freedom of choice in every instant. However, once we act, there are always consequences of our action. We all have the same twenty-four hours; we are free to think and reason, free to feel or deny, free to act, free to take responsibility, free to sabotage, free to serve and make a difference in the world. Free will—what a gift we've been given! When we make choices based on wisdom rather than from reaction or habit, we improve our lives.

Feel It and Free It

In the case of a thirteen-year-old client who had been labeled with ADD (attention deficit disorder), his personal freedom came when he let go of a self-sabotaging belief. His parents brought him to me for counseling because he was having problems at school. Through the Neuro-physical Reprogramming, we retrieved information from the body by using kinesiology. It indicated that he carried beliefs of poor self-esteem. "Could this come from a long time ago?" he openly inquired. "Yes, indeed, it could and does," I replied.

He proceeded to share with me about the crib death of his baby brother. The fullness of the emotion that surrounded this trauma had never been felt, so the repressed and resisted feelings were stuck in his body. When the father brought him in for the next session, he was puzzled why his son was so eager for the appointment. During that session, more progress was made, because he experienced the pain rather than talking about it. He was willing to reach deep into the subconscious to reveal the old stuck feelings that had prevented him from being the joyful, loving, bright young man that he is. Now, for him, new life is rewarding and free.

A yoga instructor defined pain as "An intelligent response from the body when something is wrong." Simple and precise. However, we tend to ignore, stuff, deny, bury, medicate and/or drug our pain. Who is in charge? Where is the power? Why are we so afraid of our feelings? Feelings can set us free. They can shift the paradigm of how we perceive everything in life—everything from God to death. To free ourselves from the duality of life, pleasure/pain, joy/sadness, and health/sickness, is of utmost importance. There we "allow," instead of "resist."

Although freedom and discipline may seem like opposites on the surface, in actuality, to be truly free, one must maintain self-discipline. The greater the self-control, the greater is our freedom. This has to do with letting go of old habits and replacing them with new, healthy ones. Encumbrances of old emotional pain might be habits that have taken over our well-being. Knowing how to shape or eliminate habits can be frustrating! Maybe habits have made us feel less free, and we have had difficulty in overcoming them. It is interesting that our free will, if not used for the best interest of all, can actually imprison us. I had a client who went from drinking more than seven cups of coffee per day to not quite two in just less than three days. That was shaking a habit! That client broke out of the mold.

Are you emotionally free? Or do you get sucked into the melodrama of your life? Work toward freedom from your addictions, from the relationships that are not working, from dependency on parents. A habit will create deep grooves through repetition. Some habits are obvious, like addictions to chocolate, while others may be less obvious, like manipulating others. We are greatly influenced by our habits. As we place the emphasis on healing, which means "whole," we recapture the wisdom of the truth of who we are. This becomes our ticket to freedom.

Control of the mind is an important part of self-discipline. To what degree can we tame the wild horses of our minds and rein them in to be still? Achievement lies in the mind more so than in outer accomplishments. Control of our mind is governed by wisdom. Life can be ruled by moods, impulses, and habits, and certainly by one's environment. To know and choose what thoughts to think, words to speak, behaviors to demonstrate—this is self-control; this is freedom, and this is power. The more we look within for our wisdom, the more we experience freedom. The more we look outside for the answers, the more we perpetuate false appearances. Seek the truth in silence, in simplicity, in nature.

To be free is to act from a deep inner wisdom, rather than by habits and desires, fueled strictly by the ego. We do have free will, but remember once we act, we are responsible for that action. Consequences WILL follow. We have the freedom to choose what to do with our every twenty-four hours a day. We have the freedom to choose our thoughts, our words, and our behavior, and it's important to realize that in nature there is the Law of Cause and Effect. When we act with wisdom, rather than out of habit, we feel satisfied with our consequences. It takes intention, introspection, and action to examine this subject. It takes being true to ourselves.

Back to School

I felt tremendous freedom in my life when I disciplined myself to return to college after fifteen years. I recall it like it was yesterday, attending the open house at Antioch University in Los Angeles (a brand new satellite campus). There were maybe ten people present. At the end of the most informative and exciting evening, an alumnus sitting in the back of the room stood up and shared, "When you graduate from this college, you get much more than a diploma to hang on your wall. You get yourself." If that young man should happen to be reading this book, I want to say, "Thank you. Your words were truth." Antioch is a non-traditional education and was absolutely perfect for me. Apparently, it was also for a cousin of mine through marriage, as she learned about this unique program through a casual conversation we had one day.

Pat Train Gage took a deep journey into her roots while studying for her master's degree at Antioch University in Los Angeles. This was a time in her life when she realized she had choices. After her divorce, she knew she had a choice to be bitter and grumpy or to move on. She created a "goal board" which included teaching theatre in college and being in a long-term and loving relationship with a man who was financially solvent. She was tired of bar hopping and dating losers she supported. Pat met and dated Sandy Gage, our cousin, for five years, and he supported her freedom to pursue her bachelor's and master's degree in theatre. "My gift to you is to send you to college." And that he did.

Pat's old girlfriends, who also divorced, have chosen otherwise. "They're still sitting in the same bars, feeling sorry for themselves in their loneliness, and I have a college degree teaching what I love, married to the love of my life. I felt free when I opened to my own truth, not to others' chatter, which stifles personal freedom. Listen to your intuition and heart. Be true to yourself."

Hell and Back

Pat's adaptation of a one-act play, entitled *I Never Saw Another Butterfly*, was part of her graduate studies and also related to feeling free. This is the dramatic story, told through the eyes of the children, of life that flourished behind the facade of Terezin, the Nazi's "Model Ghetto." This emotionally moving play was presented to the public on the stage of Santa Monica City College in California.

While waiting outside the theatre to buy a ticket, I struck up a conversation with a couple. Their openness and receptivity invited me to engage with them on a heart level, for they were survivors of the Holocaust. Gerhard and Ursula Maschkowski gave me their card and said, "Contact us. We'll tell you anything you want to know." When I emailed them, asking if I could ask them a few questions, their response was, "Of course, we would be delighted to talk to you about attitude; that is partly why we are alive." The following is their story:

At the young ages of thirteen, they were both in forced labor camps, (prior to the concentration camp) and developed friendships there. "One helps the other. We all shared food. One slice of bread was cut into three pieces. Everything was shared. Today there is such waste. People don't realize what they have. There must be discipline given to the children. They throw food away – it's a sin." To this day, they don't waste food, even bread crumbs. Gerhard said, "When I hear about the children today out of line, two to three days of Auschwitz would wake them up."

Because Ursula's mother was half-Jewish, they thought there wouldn't be a problem. "One day they came to the apartment and told us to get

114

ready to leave in a few hours. And off we went to the ghetto, Terezin, in Czechoslovakia. My father was sent to Auschwitz. He was fifty-five when he was gassed. I feel more pain about his dying now that I am old (78). All those naked people in the gas chamber. People lying on top of each other. Absolutely horrible. Unbelievable that people can think of such horrible things. That people could be so mean and vicious just because of religion? We all have ten fingers on our hands."

Gerhard told me how they were liberated by the Russians (which Americans don't want to hear!). Then they were placed in a displaced persons camp where he met his future bride. In 1947, they came to America on a cargo ship and were married on May 27 at four P.M. in New York. "We went to the river and sat on a bench. And that was our honeymoon." Twelve dollars a week was the rent for one room on 95th Street. They had no education, no trade, no language, no clothing, no relatives, no money, and no normal life experiences. "We came out of hell together."

Both became very hard workers. Gerhard became a bus boy and Ursula a waitress. One day she spilled a spinach and potato dish all over her customer, who came back the next day and said, "I think I'll have a sandwich today." Their message is one you've read throughout this book. "You have to be optimistic; always try to better yourself, and have a good attitude."

They visit Germany yearly and are asked to speak in the high schools and churches. "This generation is very different. The young people want to know the details of what happened. They punish those who speak of anti-Semitism."

The conversation came to a close as Gerhard told me that they didn't believe in God. "If one exists, how could He have let this happen? I was at the ramp in Auschwitz when I saw the children going one way and the parent another. What did God say then? I weighed seventy pounds when we were liberated. Nineteen years old! It makes no sense—where was God? I didn't ask to be chosen for this."

His words were strong, but nevertheless, they portrayed a life of pain from the past as well as the gratitude of the present. They were both so delightful on the phone as they shared their experiences, often giggling like young lovers. "We went to the same hell and built our lives together, raising three children." As I heard these stories first hand, it again jolts me back to what suffering truly means.

While in Boston, I visited the Holocaust Memorial. On glass walls were numbers, one after another, numbers that at one time were names. Here is a quote from one of the glass pillars at the memorial.

"Nothing belongs to us anymore. They have taken away our clothes, our shoes, even our hair. If we speak, they will not listen to us. And if they listen, they will not understand. They have even taken away our names. My # is 174517. I will carry the tattoo on my left arm until I die."

Another quote from the memorial reads: "Ilse, a childhood friend of mine once found a raspberry in the camp and carried it in her pocket all day to present to me that night on a leaf. Imagine a world where your entire possession is one raspberry and you give it to your friend." Can you even imagine a world like this? She still had the freedom to share her one gift, a raspberry. What an amazing true story!

This portion about the atrocities of the Holocaust has one additional entry. A woman by the name of Eva Schloss, author of *Eva's Story*, stepsister to Anne Frank, came to our community and spoke to the audience after watching a play about her life. This play has been performed in many cities throughout the country for over five years. The play, *And Then They Came For Me, by James Still*, is one that depicts Eva's life, going into hiding in Amsterdam and meeting Anne Frank. Eva was sent to the concentration camp on her fifteenth birthday. As life has it, years later, her mother and Anne Frank's father married. She said Otto Frank was a changed person once this daughter's diary had been found, feeling he then had something to live for.

Feeling free is nothing to take for granted. In our outer world of course, it is a way of life for most of us. But the inner world is one where freedom is elusive. Healing the wounds of the past is what will set us free. It is obvious the Holocaust survivors' wounds are deep, yet so many seem to forgive and feel free, knowing that life should not be taken for granted.

Free To Be

On the lighter side, when our children were growing up, they listened to Marlo Thomas singing, "Free to Be You and Me." This delightful album included a variety of songs. One song described "...a land where you and me are free to be you and me." Rosy Greer, football hero, sang "...it's all right to cry. Crying takes the sad out of you." Another is entitled, "Parents Are People." There was even one about "William's Doll." The message was about being free to be who you are. When we learn as parents that it's okay to be who we are, we are modeling an important message to our children.

By modeling self-acceptance and self-control, our children learn. Children truly want to be disciplined; it means they are loved. This might be the opposite of what we think. Children want limits, want us to be consistent, want us to be clear, centered, and balanced. They want us to be real—to feel, communicate, to love unconditionally, and be accepting and non-judgmental. Through discipline, we experience feeling free, which is another word for liberation. We have liberated ourselves from oppression, from our own inner persecution, from our own bondage and imprisonment. A client once told me, "I set myself free and you reminded me where the key was."

Reflection Time:

1. To what degree are you free?
2. Have you taken on the identity of a parent?
3. Create your own "goal board" that could set you free. What do you want?
4. To what degree do habits hold power over you?
5. Now invite your partner, good friend, playmate, or someone trusted to walk you through this guided visualization. Soothing music would be a lovely background. (When you are complete with your experience, you can then guide your partner through it and compare notes when done.)

Imagine yourself right in the basket of a hot air balloon. Feel yourself in the basket – just be there. Look out, scan your surroundings, and take a breath. Now notice that there are weights keeping the basket on the ground, and let's say that these weights represent issues that are holding you back in your life. Look to see what they would be. Now, with your will, your choice, and the depth of your trust in the Universe and life, free the weights one by one from the balloon. Notice if there's any resistance to letting go of the weights. Just allow it all to be. If you've released the weights, then feel the balloon start to lift. Can you feel the freedom? If you haven't released all of the weights, you'll feel the pull holding you back from being free. Notice the expanded perception you have of everything as the basket rises, your view is much greater than when the basket was tethered. Feel the wind, the motion, and the freedom. Enjoy. Now gently bring the basket back to Earth, and know that you can experience this feeling at any time, at your choice, by breathing and staying centered, and activating your imagination.

117

"The only devil is the one that's running around in your mind."
Norman Cousins

F is for feeling... Frustrated

Definition: thwarted, nullified, angry, irritated, resistant, anxious

Opposite: facilitated, stimulated, easy-going

Why don't things go the way I want them to? Why is it taking so long to accomplish this? Why don't people just get it? Why doesn't he change? Why does she constantly make me wrong? Why is life the way it is? Oh! Such effort!

Unachieved goals can create huge feelings of frustration. Some days seem to be full of frustrating activities, like the world is out to get us. When we feel frustration, we are puzzled. What's going wrong? We've been doing all the "right" things, have the "right" attitude, and think the "right" thoughts. We may want to scream! Why doesn't our desire match our reality?

Does this sound familiar?

Frustration is a form of hidden anger, or anger that has been turned inward. It shows up in many ways: over-sleeping, clenched jaws, chronic depression, irritability, annoyance, loss of interest or caring, sarcasm, or critical verbiage. A young client of mine said the kids at school "bug" her and she's frustrated because of it, and knowing how to deal with it was beyond her scope. She shared with me, and the drama became more intensified. She blamed, envied, judged, defended, scattered, and pitied herself. These are all characteristics of the victim. The victim is a role we have all played and know too well.

If I Were President...

I will be bold and say that many of us get frustrated with politics and our leaders. Wendy Jacquet is doing what she can to affect change in governmental attitudes. Her contribution to the feeling of frustration is as follows: "As the Democratic leader in the Idaho House of Representatives, the most Republican legislature in the United States, I sometimes feel very powerless. Sometimes I feel frustrated and upset, and at times, even despondent. Sometimes I just want to lash out. When

Republicans say cruel things about my caucus members and scheme about increasing their numbers, I wonder why they are so greedy? Why do they have to have 100%?"

"But then one of my constituents will call with a serious problem and I find that I am able to fix it because when it comes to fairness, the bureaucracy works for everyone, not just Republicans. I realize that I need to make sure these negative and destructive feelings don't overcome me because I know that I am effective by working with others in a non-partisan fashion. One of my mentors told me that to achieve change, one must work through the political system. So I keep involved, I organize at the grassroots level, I have reasonable solutions and I achieve success. You will too."

"I know that too often people get discouraged and frustrated like I sometimes do. They give up because they believe that trying to accomplish something is hopeless. My counsel to people who feel like they have been beaten up by the system is: don't let it get you down. Pick yourself up, look for a different tactic or strategy, and find others to join your voice. Find people who will listen to you. Build coalitions. Continue your fight. It's important for your own self-worth, for your community, and for our country."

Thank you, Wendy, for your commitment to move through your frustration; continue to pursue your vision in making government a respectable and effective body.

Acting Out

If we're frustrated, we can be hurtful. We may speak unkindly, harshly, or without consideration. We can feel depleted with an inability to cope. "I just can't deal with this any longer" becomes our normal response. We can lash out, and in the process turn that anger inward: "I'm so stupid" or "I hate the way I draw."

We often tend to react out of victim type of frustrations rather than taking a breath and looking at an alternative behavior. What are we really feeling? To get the opposite of victim energy, visualize someone who is accountable—someone who takes total responsibility for his or her thoughts, words, and behavior. Now look closely at the fear in your life situations. Fear is the real culprit behind all our suffering. We feel fearful that we won't measure up. We feel fearful of our own capacities and self-esteem. This is why it is important to help a child understand, early on, that their task-oriented behavior has nothing to do with the nature of the child. Many beliefs started at an early age, such as "If I can't do this, there must be something wrong with me," or "No matter how hard I try, I'll never do this right." We are not our performances or accomplishments. Our true nature needs no validation of its worth, but once the identification with the ego is established, it is ongoing.

Every so often, young ones throw a tantrum. They haven't learned the art of self-discipline and understanding. But then again, many adults haven't either. Our role modeling lacks flow and ease, and children observe adult frustration and like everything else, they emulate it. Young ones then avoid anything that resembles the similar frustrating situation or activity. Based on original or core experiences and beliefs, the energy starts to build. Children require wise adults nearby to guide them. Adults need to have the communication skills to assist the child in proper expression of his or her feelings. Otherwise, the frustration turns into anger, which is a secondary feeling in this regard. If unchecked, a real problem could accelerate if anger turns into rage—an expression which is NOT natural. Anger needs to be honored and expressed. Rage is another degree—it's out-of-control anger and is lethal. Many people on the planet believe anger is bad and wrong, so they cover it with a smile and niceties. That's the mask again.

Handling Frustration

In the marvelous book, Anger, Thich Nhat Hanh states, "In our consciousness, there are blocks of pain, anger, and frustration called internal formations. They are also called knots because they tie us up and obstruct our freedom." These knots can become tighter if unchecked. The Sanskrit word for internal formation is "samyojana," which means "to crystallize." The knots can cause tremendous suffering, which is expressed through frustration. We need tools to help us undo them and the first step is mindfulness. The second is learning to embrace your pain—your shadow–your darkness.

When frustration mounts and low self-worth peaks, out of desperation, many people turn to drugs, alcohol, food, gambling, shopping, etc., anything to relieve their suffering. There are many addictive and temporary forms of relief. Self-destructive thinking follows this pattern and the energy spirals downward. Systematically, this energy flows in a closed loop and may feed on itself.

To the parents of a teenager: When you feel frustrated, just realize the benefit of having that child. With that gratitude, now you can handle any crisis. Make a few signs for yourself: "Teenager for sale – take over payments," or "Get even – live long enough to be a problem to your kid." In other words, this too shall pass. Deal with your child's frustration because it is real. Be an example of humor. Be there for your daughter as you bond more deeply through the exploration of your frustration. Be the parent who offers the emotional stability that may have not been present during your childhood years. Fathers: feel your feelings; move past feeling uncomfortable into unfamiliar territory. Mothers: Be willing to recognize and learn with your son, and identify the core feelings underneath the frustration.

There will be numerous times when you, as a parent, will say, "I've had it." You will feel like a doormat and will want to give up, but you have to keep on keeping on, trying new approaches and continuing to follow your intuition. Always be willing to search within for answers, and examine your intentions. They are looking for attention. To be accepted and loved is the bottom line. Children will often act out negatively just to get it.

Gary Zukav says, "Your intentions create the reality that you experience." Gary writes brilliantly about intention in *The Seat of the Soul.* We first need to know how intention is created. "A thought is energy, or Light, that has been shaped by consciousness. No form exists without consciousness. There is Light, and there is the shaping of Light by consciousness. This is creation." This Light that flows through us is universal energy, or the Life Force, which the Chinese call "chi."

This is the basis of making change in our lives. As a kid, I recall making cutout cookies. Mom would roll out the dough to a perfect thickness, and then I'd make the imprint into the dough with the cookie cutter I selected. If I used the reindeer cookie cutter, I got a reindeer imprint in the dough. If I used the star cookie cutter, I'd get a star. Amazing. This analogy is simplistic, but relates to what we do with the universal energy, that could be called "dough." Do we choose a "cookie cutter" that is shaped as anger, frustration, or maybe hopelessness? Well that's the kind of "cookie" we will get. Got the picture? How are you imprinting the cookie dough?

What is your intention for your life, the day, the moment? We can have a positive intention, however, it can be thwarted with frustration, jealousy, and resentment. In other words, we want to strive to be free of those unwanted influences, because this is how we achieve peace of mind and lasting happiness, a universally sought-after desire.

If we are willing to give up our "poor me" energy, and truly take responsibility for our reality, then our intentions can shift our reality. The frustration dissipates as there is nothing to resist. We just might feel more vibrant and alive, if we let go, so that we can move along to manifest our dreams and passions.

When we're not communicating truth, we can get immersed in the pain. When we do tell the truth, insights may occur. "Aha!" can shift us. Just tell the truth. The most important thing is to pay attention to the frustration. It represents a struggle in our lives somewhere. Take a look at it. Frustrated feelings are a red flag and an opportunity to grow.

I witnessed a wise two-year-old thank her Mother for buying her *The Feelings Storybook*, which I wrote 1n 1988. The book is designed to give a child the words to express feelings once they've been recognized. She learned there was no need to act out. Mom concluded that the 'terrible twos' don't have to be terrible. Little people are valuable teachers when they have the vocabulary to share what they're feeling.

There is an old adage—what we resist, will persist, and what we allow, disappears. Resistance is something like putting another log on the fire. With such fuel, the situation seems to grow more intense and more frustrating. Whether it's the behavior of another person or a circumstance in our lives, resistance will cause the tornado to blow harder.

A law of duality exists in the physical dimension. We don't know high unless we know low: large/small; chaos/order: separation/union...got it? What would be the opposite of resistance? How about embrace or better yet, desire? "Yuck, I don't want to desire my pain, I don't want to feel like my father, who I have never wanted to feel like. I don't want to desire or love the disharmony in my life, nor the repetitive dysfunctional relationship pattern." We might also think, "Why would I want to desire any of that?" Whatever we can't or won't feel, will run us! Who is in control of our lives? Where is the power? We've turned it over to that person, place, or thing. We've given our power away when we hold grudges towards another. Look how much time is spent making that person bad and wrong for their action. If they were forgiven for their "crime," they wouldn't even come up in your consciousness. Sorry to break the news, but in order to change an outer situation, we must first change our inner world. The work needs to be done within. Otherwise we have the old blame game going. What's our payoff from being a victim? We want our reality to respond to our desires. Hence, the frustration. An alternative to this point of view would be acquiring an awareness, or respect for the timing in the universe, when it doesn't seem to be aligning with our desires. Timing teaches us to let go, surrender, and trust...although climbing Mt. Everest might appear easier!

Do what is required, be involved, but then be unattached to the results. For a dramatic absence of frustration in your lives, simply release your will on people or situations. Observe how life unfolds. Solutions might just emerge that you never dreamed possible.

Keep in mind, we too are part of nature. We too are in process. Notice our lessons from nature. Trust the wisdom that the full moon will be full again every twenty-nine days, and that the birds will always fly south for the winter. Trust is an issue for many folk, and this pertains directly to control. Trusting oneself is the prerequisite for trusting others. Often we feel like we have to do everything ourselves. Another choice is to delegate and trust everything will flow.

There are other days that are magical, where everything goes our way. We're not only in the flow, we are the flow. Oh, how we long to keep up this easy mode.

I once had a fabulous dream. It was a strong voice speaking—like the strength and certainty that came from the voice of the wizard in *The Wizard of Oz*, when the curtain was pulled away and he was revealed. This voice in my dream declared, shouted, and bellowed out the words, "THE LAWS OF THE UNIVERSE ARE WORKING JUST PERFECTLY!" I woke up and started to laugh. What a dream! What a message from my unconscious! Thank you, thank you, and thank you!

When things are frustrating and life isn't cooperating, take some time out and examine your intentions. Take stock of how you feel physically, mentally, emotionally and spiritually. Watch frustration dissolve when you take my advice and feel it fully, express it healthily, and maintain the perspective that everything is happening for your highest good and the highest good of all. Believe the plan and witness its miracle.

Reflection Time:
1. Reflect on a time when you felt frustrated.
2. Does frustration feel a little like anger?
3. What were you upset about?
4. What was underneath the frustration?
5. Explore and dissect it. Gain some insight from it.
6. What needs to be said?
7. What laws of the Universe have you forgotten?
8. Can you identify your feelings beneath the frustration?
9. Can you name them, then express them?
10. Do you allow yourself to be vulnerable in front of others by expressing your frustrated feelings?

"If the only prayer you ever say in your entire life is thank you, it will be enough."

Meister Eckhart

G is for feeling... Grateful

Definition: thankful, appreciative, humbled, blessed
Opposite: insensitive, indifferent, unmindful, rude

There is so much to be grateful for! Feeling grateful opens us up to the bigger picture. It is easy to take things for granted in this world of modern conveniences. After all, we used to have to hunt and scavenge for food, go to the rivers and streams for water, and walk or ride horses to get a short distance in a long amount of time. The more perspective we have, the more gratitude we carry, and the better we feel in the present moment.

How thankful I am for each day! I get to share, to give, to feel, to be. Thanksgiving Day is experienced more than once a year on my calendar—it's everyday for me. What about you?

Gratitude was the matchmaker that allowed author Sarah Ban Breathnach to fall passionately in love with life. She says that, "Gratitude's most profound lessons are revealed through glimmers of joy." In her wonderful book, *Simple Abundance*, she claims that, "You will never find a lover who will adore, desire, caress, embrace, and delight you more than real life." We all need to recount the blessings in our lives.

I also have the *Journal of Gratitude* inspired by Breathnach's book where I was instructed to write a gratitude list. I found my entries to be so simple.

I'm grateful for:
- cozy at-home clothes
- belly aches after laughing so hard
- the movements my body makes during yoga
- being able to drive a car
- self-sticking postage stamps
- my contact lenses, organic foods, a hot shower
- community that I call home
- being able to hear the snow geese as they migrate

Oh, so much more! In short, I am grateful for the experience, the adventure and journey called life, and to feel it, all of it. I am grateful for my past, and for all the people who have played their role so perfectly in the movie I continue to produce. I am appreciative of all I have learned and remembered about my true nature—all the beautiful souls I have connected with, some like-minded and some not so like-minded. They have all played their parts well.

I had a surge of appreciation as I had the opportunity to spend an evening with four dear friends I have known for more than twenty years. As I reflected on the evening of laughter and chattering, it was a good feeling—a feeling of thankfulness for my friends. True friendship endures distance, misunderstandings, and differences of opinion. True friendship enriches our lives. My mother used to say, "If you can count your good friends on one hand, you are fortunate." Would you agree with her?

Being grateful can create a paradigm shift within us, opening up a whole new way to experience life. When we feel grateful for the support we feel from our friends and family, both human and animal, our body responds and our spirits soar.

A 2002 newsletter from the American Institute of Stress revealed survey results from research conducted on the value of strong social support. Support, it said, is a "Stress Buster." Just having a friend nearby when speaking publicly, or during some other stress-related event, can reduce the rise in heart rate and blood pressure. When dogs and cats are petted lovingly, blood pressure is lowered. When comatose patients are stroked in a kind and compassionate manner, their blood pressure is eased as well.

Through our attitude, we determine the quality of our life every moment. Through our will power, we possess the power of choice to shift the way we perceive circumstances. At times, we can slip into self-pity and find endless reasons to complain about the unfair way life is treating us. If this occurs, here's a suggestion: Try singing the bothersome complaint. Get into it. Stand in front of a mirror. Then observe any changes in your disposition. After this experiment, take a sheet of paper and create a "grateful list."

Thanks Giving, Giving Thanks

Are trees on your thankful list? Trees are known as the lungs of the planet. While walking through the woods in the gentle rain, I couldn't help but feel thankful for the magnificent towering firs and pines, and also for the little seedlings growing in their shadow. I was thankful for their purpose and how they serve us. Consider the spiritual equation between humans and trees, our out-breath is their in-breath and vice-versa. If they didn't create oxygen, we couldn't breathe.

There is a belief that the universe will fill whatever size receptacle you are holding. How large or small is the container you offer up to the universe? Do you appreciate what you're being given? Being grateful actually attracts more of what you appreciate in your life. Fascinating how it works. Appreciation and gratitude come from the heart not the head. Open your heart and let the love pour through, let the light shine in, let your soul express. You have a huge capacity to appreciate, to love, to feel. Tap into the expansive and vast nature of who you are, open that to life and be ready for the flood. It's already there. Give thanks even before you receive your food; then, just enjoy it.

Holidays make deep impressions in a child's brain. The memories of my childhood Thanksgiving were gathering around a dinner table abundant with turkey, sweet potatoes, cranberry sauce, and pumpkin pie. What were yours? Our emotional experiences have become part of our cellular structure, regardless of whether they were pleasant or dysfunctional.

If we lived our lives with an attitude that every single experience makes us who we are today, we will feel grateful. That may not be so easy to do if our childhood memories were painful. We may even feel or harbor bitterness about them. Holding onto angry and negative grudges is also an attitude of choice. As we process those hurtful moments, and move on in life, we can choose today to be grateful. What is the quality of your life today? If you've created joy and inner peace, you have much to be thankful for. If you haven't, you have some work to do. It's up to you.

As children grow into adulthood, gratitude is one of the vital emotions so important for children to understand. Being in touch with a positive feeling, like gratitude, enriches our lives. The late Norman Cousins, author of Anatomy of an Illness, stated, "...long before my own serious illness, I became convinced that creativity, the will to live, hope, faith, and love have biochemical significance and contribute strongly to healing and to well-being. The positive emotions are life-giving experiences."

The Ripple Effect of Words

The impact we have as adults is immense! I happened to see Lisa Beamer on Good Morning America speak to the nation about the loss of her husband, Todd Beamer, who was on the plane headed toward Washington, D.C. on September 11, 2001. I took notes on her talk because I was so impressed with her attitude. She recalled a teacher who gave her an invaluable lesson in gratitude. The teacher had unexpectedly lost her husband, and about a week after his death, she gave her students some words that stuck with Lisa for a lifetime. The following is how Lisa paraphrased what that teacher had taught her:

"Each of us is put here on Earth to learn, share, love, appreciate and give of ourselves. None of us knows when this fantastic experience will end. Perhaps this is the powers way of telling us that we must make the most out of every single day," the teacher said. "Please look for the little things, and cherish them...the things we often take for granted. We must make it important to notice them, for at anytime, it can all be taken away."

At what point do we realize that our words and attitudes make a difference? Lisa's teacher's attitude gave her the strength to cope with a trauma and tremendous loss in her life. Her words are now affecting a nation! The ripple effect works! Attitude is contagious.

This Abundant Universe

When we fail to be grateful for the little things, or don't cherish those relationships that mean so much, we falsely think the universe isn't giving us all we deserve and want. The only lack in the universe comes from our own attitudes, beliefs, and negative programming. This is also known as "tunnel vision," and it is a limited and restricted view of life. This thinking determines the quality of our life. By recognizing an abundant universe, and realizing that we are indeed part of nature, we can build a base for abundant thinking in every aspect of life. Abundant thinking depends on enacting a new way of thinking. Just as we change from one CD to another, we have the power to do so with our thoughts. It's our choice. The first step is awareness, followed by understanding, and then willingness.

If we choose to acknowledge that our thoughts are our responsibility, it becomes clear that prosperity is an inside job and not dependent on circumstances of the outer world. "Easier said than done," one might say. How do you feel when you make the statement, "I am open and thankful for all the wonderful and bountiful gifts the Universe has to offer me"? Do you believe it? Are you open to receive? Are your arms outstretched? Are you thankful for your life right now, just the way it is? Or are you resisting it?

Many years ago, a dear friend gave me a book entitled *Abundance Is Your Right* by Arnold Patton. It dramatically impacted my perception of abundance. One of the many staggering messages from the book is: "The average galaxy contains one hundred billion stars, while known space holds at least one hundred million galaxies." *Known* space.

When discussing abundance, the word "trust" cannot be ignored. I heard a poignant story about a young man from abroad, who had been traveling extensively in the United States who picked up odd jobs from time to time to support his love of adventure. After he had lunch with someone he'd just met in the restaurant, he picked up the check for both meals. His astonished guest questioned, "I don't understand why you want to treat me to lunch. You just told me that even though you love your lifestyle, you rarely have much money." The wayfarer said, "Yes, that's true, but I have enough money right now for both of us, and I've had a delightful time sharing with you, and I feel grateful for our meeting. So, I'd like to buy you lunch." This man's gratitude sparked generosity and a giving attitude. Thanks-giving. Makes sense, doesn't it?

My friends, Gail and Kenny, chose to embark on an adventure in their lives, referring to themselves as the turtle clan, as they meandered, in their own time, from art show to art show. They visited some of the most beautiful parts of the United States, in their thirty-four foot, refurbished RV, asking so little of life and living in a state of grace. "Simple is good," they both agreed after one year on the road.

I asked Gail to submit a few thoughts on the subject of gratitude and this is what she sent to me:

"Gratitude is a quiet prayer that walks with me into the woods to spy on animals, up the road to the mailbox, and back into my memory to the historical moment when I first became grateful. In my life, I've been banged up by various addictive abuses and several car accidents. My last serious car accident coincided with the birth of this new Millennium. My mind was adjusted because the proximity of death was in my face. 'What is life all about?' I asked myself. Certainly, living is not related to this kind of destruction."

"While I was in the altered state of consciousness needed for healing such trauma, I asked endless questions about my life and got clear answers from somewhere. I know now that I only need to move gently with love and gratitude toward the light, for a special grace watches over my life. A man who is my husband, today, showed up at my bedside and asked if I would participate in a spiritual experiment. If I would just open myself to receive, he could have his first opportunity to give unconditionally. We've kept this going for three years, just giving and receiving at every opportunity."

"Only good comes our way because I reach out for his hand and thank the Great Mystery for our love and abundance. It shows I am paying attention. Feeling truly grateful seems to propel the abundance and love, so a power circle has been created."

128

How many of us are so trusting that our needs will be met? How many are appreciative of the goodness that already exists? The more connected we feel to life, the more we can let go of worry and fear. By this, I don't mean we just sit back and say, "God will provide." Of course, we must play our part. Don't be like the woman who prayed each night to win the lottery, and one night, after her repeated request, she heard a voice say, "My dear, you've got to first buy a ticket."

Yes, we've got to take the action, but first we must be mentally ready to receive and claim the abundance and prosperity that is rightfully ours. Then we have to FEEL it in our body. What would it feel like to experience abundance? What would it feel like to be prosperous?

The True Meaning of Prosperity

Prosperity means more than money alone—it means having peace of mind. A comment from a lottery winner that got my attention was, "Money didn't change me. It changed people around me, people that I thought cared a little bit about me. But they only cared about the money." Winning the lottery did not bring him peace of mind. Prosperity means joy and love and harmony in life. It means good health. It means warm and true friends. It includes so much more then just money, which is literally only vegetable dye, tree bark and pictures of presidents who have come and gone on the planet.

So many people hold two and three jobs to meet their monthly obligations and provide for their children. They rarely have much leftover, if anything, for self-improvement. Through example, their children are learning the belief that life is a struggle. Most likely, when their children grow into adulthood, their reality will resemble that of their childhood—unless they make different choices with every thought and every exposure to truth. But who is there to stop these generational patterns of struggle and scarcity and teach new ways to a child? It could be YOU!

Rich Dad, Poor Dad, authored by Robert T. Kiyosaki, is a good reference about money beliefs. First he says you have to determine your general financial goals, then second, become financially literate so you learn to think like "the rich." www.richdad.com

Many fail to teach their children about spending wisely. Teach them early. Once again, this mantra fits. The best teacher is setting the example. What role model are you providing your child with regard to financial education? Are you preoccupied with money? Do you spend it faster than you make it? Are you frugal? Your children will learn from you, so what are you teaching? Teach them to identify financial goals and how to create a budget. Appropriately include them in the family financial matters. Help them to obtain educational materials that support this process. Teach them about the law of circulation, giving and receiving. Be open to discuss options and hear their point of view.

The Five Principles of Money

I often wonder why public education doesn't teach the four principles of money I learned in a class taken several years ago: earning, spending, investing, and saving. One important principle was left out, and it is the one I love the best, giving or tithing—one of my favorite things to do.

This information would have served me better had I known it as a young adult starting my life in the big world, rather than in the autumn of my life.

I know parents who taught their children the value of giving something to a worthy cause chosen by the child. They learned about tithing and charity at a very early age. As adults, those same children display success in all ways and continue to donate. How sad that so few have learned these valuable lessons!

There are several books on the concept of abundance. Here are my favorites:

Think and Grow Rich, by Napoleon Hill (a classic)

Creating Abundance, by Deepak Chopra

Open Your Mind to Prosperity, by Catherine Ponder

One Minute Millionaire by Mark Victor Hansen and Robert G. Allen

Rich Dad, Poor Dad, by Robert Kiyosaki

Now what? Has reading this chapter caused you to think about all the great things in your life with gratitude? Congratulations! You've taken your first steps towards a new perception and a new life. But don't stop here. The door has been opened to new ideas. Life will respond to them with opportunities and possibilities beyond your wildest dreams. Persistence will lead to your goal. Don't give up. Claim your birthright. The rewards will be astonishing in all areas: self-confidence, faith, strength of will, discipline, love, joy, peace of mind, and lasting happiness. It takes work, but believing you have, right within you, what it takes, just as the acorn has the potential to grow into a mighty oak tree, makes the journey an incredible and rewarding challenge.

Reflection Time:

1. Start your list now. In your journal, write five things you are grateful for every day for thirty days.

2. Make a list of people you appreciate and why, then tell them. (Your child, your parent, your mate, employer, employee, neighbor, baby sitter, dentist, friend, colleague are all potentials to receive your appreciation.)

3. What values, attributes, and characteristics do you appreciate about yourself.

4. Write and examine a list of beliefs you have adopted from childhood about abundance. Did your parents argue over money? What were their beliefs that most likely transferred onto you? Are any of the following in your belief system somewhere.

    • Spiritual people shouldn't be wealthy.

    • I don't deserve to be financially abundant.

    • My father never made it big, so I probably won't.

5. Do you value your friendships, and if so, do they know it?

6. What does is mean to you to have a special friend?

7. What does it take to be one?

8. If you absolutely knew you couldn't fail, what would you do to earn a living?

9. Design or buy a sweet thank you card/note and send five out every week. It need not be in return of something, but a "just because" thank you.

10. In quiet time think of the most unlikely people you know who could have possibly enhanced your life. Stretch your thinking, then determine the lesson you learned from knowing them—through their positive or negative behavior. Then if you feel moved to, send them a thank you

"Discovery"
by Gail Burkett

Something wonderful about finding ourselves.
We know what to look for after that!
We can choose to return to our old ways, but suddenly
Old habits may surprise us with uneasiness.
Cellularly altered habits are just that, transformed.
Imagine releasing the victim intelligence, for a few moments,
Look inside and find instead full responsibility in there.
Alone and fully in charge of our being and powerful.
Momentarily, our experience is pure and simple –
Trusting, open-minded, balanced and aware.
These are qualities we desire surely, there's more:
As responsible begins we are forgiving, unconditionally loving,
We feel communicative, in control and healthy,
Finally, for once, we are complete with ourselves, we are whole.
In truth, this is our real and authentic self, ours to choose.
Unless we like the burden, perhaps we have no heart desire,
To be responsible and give up the weight of the victim mind.
This is no small choice, because old habits are comfortable.
Actually, defenses, judgments, grudges, and envy are heavy;
As victims, we may choose gossipy and conditional love,
We may want to be scattered, disparaged, and limited in our thinking.
When we are victims, our life spiral turns downward into nothingness.
Or not.
The choice to be responsible for our lives simply means
Releasing the burdens of victim mentality, finally and completely.
The spiral of life was meant to wind upward toward enlightenment,
To grow into the lightness of our being, we choose and choose again.

"I am repulsed when I go out to dinner and read on the menu, 'All you can eat for $10.00.' I know that more than half the food will be thrown away…While 40,000 children daily die of starvation."

Helen Caldicott, M.D., *If You Love This Planet: A Plan to Heal the Earth*

G is for feeling…Greedy

Definition: selfish, gluttonous, miserly

Opposite: generous, open, giving, charitable, philanthropic

"Greedy" and "Scrooge" are almost synonymous. What images does Scrooge conjure up? I think of an ornery, elderly man counting his money in a dark room with no one else around. His attitude is one of bitterness and coldness. The only thing that keeps him company is his coins. I love the line in *A Christmas Carol* where Marley Jacob says, "This is the chain I fashioned in early life, link by link." Chains are synonymous with beliefs, building upon each other from childhood to tie us to a past that doesn't serve us.

The belief associated with greed is "the more one has, the happier one will be." How can I acquire more? The list is endless. More toys! More computer upgrades! More boats! Cars, clothes, houses! You name it. More is definitely better.

Greed is based on lack and scarcity, rather than abundance. We can choose to be a greedy, selfish, fear-based person, or we can choose to be a giving, open, loving person. Our body knows the difference with each choice we make. In my practice I've found that "not enough" is traced back to childhood, like many other issues. A greedy person learned to be that way. They were deprived, mostly of LOVE.

Examples of greed show up regularly in the news. The late Barbara Hutton, a screen star in the fifties, inherited a forty-two-million-dollar fortune at age six, but died with 3500 dollars in her bank accounts. Supposedly, since her childhood she gave away diamonds and furs in exchange for love she so desperately wanted. Her life was a sad commentary on what might have been.

In spite of the wealth he acquired, J. Paul Getty, recognized in the seventies as the richest man in the world, died an unhappy man.

Dennis Kozlowski, a Tyco executive whose scandalous behavior made headlines internationally when his 100 million dollar salary from Tyco couldn't cover a two-million-dollar birthday party for his wife, so the stockholders helped pay for it. It must have been some bash.

I recall seeing a photograph in a newspaper about a person who was being buried with his Cadillac. I guess he had a belief that you CAN take it with you.

How about the salaries that we pay our basketball stars in comparison to our teachers? A top athlete gets paid twenty-two million dollars over seven years for tossing a ball in a hoop, while a teacher with a master's degree gets paid 24,000 dollars a year! No offense to you sports enthusiasts. I'm talking about priorities and perspectives. Why will sponsors pay three times the amount for a spot on Monday Night Football than they will for a Peter Jennings special? Better yet, did you know that a thirty-second spot for the Super Bowl is two million dollars?

Television says they give the viewers what they want, and they go to the right sources to pay for it. How can we create a solution where we all win? It is not uncommon for a first or second year professional athlete to earn well over a million dollars per year for tossing a ball in a hoop, while some will earn three to six million a year. In contrast, a teacher with a doctorate degree, after 22 years of teaching, 190 days per year, 7.5 hours per day, is paid, $57,495!

Mouths to Feed

When enough of us are all focused on this one intention, magic will happen. If every nation were to commit to make it a single underlying principle to have everyone in their country fed, starvation would be a thing of the past. As it is, millions of people go hungry every night.

I recall one night while visiting my granddaughter, Alissa, hearing her say to her mom, "I'm hungry." She hadn't eaten much of her dinner, but as bedtime was not far off she started expressing her hunger. I couldn't help but think how many little ones on the planet say that every night, but in vain. They go to bed hungry and they spend their days hungry.

Other statistics from the International Facts on Hunger and Poverty: (www.bread.org)

- Six million children under the age of five die every year because of hunger.
- Of the 6.2 billion people in today's world, 1.2 billion live on less that one dollar per day.
- More than 840 million people in the world are malnourished–799 million of them are from the developing world. More than 153 million of them are under the age of five.

Where ARE our priorities? It's not that we don't have the means, we just don't seem to place this condition as a top, top priority. I believe greed plays a part in this choice.

Whenever we feel greedy, we have a strong urge to acquire more of anything–money, fame, friends, or toys. When we take in more food than our body wants or needs, this is greed. Did you know when the stomach is full it will hold a little less than seven cups of liquid? I was amazed when I read that fact. Gosh! How our stomachs must suffer on Thanksgiving! On this magnificent day of harvest and thanksgiving, we eat like it's our last meal. Oh, that feeling of discomfort afterwards often feels regrettable.

Possessions

December is known as that time of year when it seems that the hours and days aren't long enough to pursue the "perfect" gift. It is the time of year that stress overshadows the powerful energy that can bring insight, peace, and true joy, and when plastic money and the privilege to use it at 18% interest takes precedence over balance, common sense, and will power. And when it's all over, what do we have? Often, it's more stuff to clean, insure, repair when break down occurs, replace or duplicate when what we had was already fine. Whew!

These thoughts about possessions took me back to a previous memory of my experience with the infamous Malibu fires in Southern California, where I can still smell the smoke and envision scenes of hillsides with burnt vegetation. We were told to evacuate the premises. We carefully and selectively retrieved meaningful items from our threatened home. Fire shows no mercy for precious old pictures taken at the turn of the century or treasured mementos made by the little hands of a four-year-old. The local paper had photographed a couple comforting each other as they stood in front of the remains of a home that had been burned to the ground in the fire–a home they'd lived in for over thirty years. "It's all gone. All we have is each other," they said. "We're grateful to be alive," echoed throughout this beachside community we called home for nearly twenty years.

So I ponder, what's the message? Why do we acquire the myriad of things we do? These things just create an attachment and a "can't live without" attitude. Do we possess things or do they possess us? It seems as though we give or acquire things to satisfy a desire to impress someone or to prove something to ourselves.

Greed and ignorance are synonymous. Greed is toxic and builds on itself. Fear, lack, and scarcity, are all aspects of unfamiliarity with our true self. It is safe to say that greed and ignorance are a cause of war. The ignorance starts within by wanting to defend our righteous beliefs. Because of it, many suffer and lives are pointlessly lost. We fall into these false notions, yet there is so much abundance! To gaze at a starlit night sky is to experience the phenomenal abundance of the Universe. Check it out for yourself. We are all part of the mystery.

As part of the mystery, Michelangelo's David demonstrated that we are all originals just as the stars in the sky. He chipped away at what didn't belong. His *David* was already in the stone. We cannot be mass-produced, like a microwave or stereo player. We cannot be cloned, try as the scientists may. If we chisel away at the false identities, we can get to the David within us too.

Generous Hearts

Although we are the same, we are each different, and through our differences, we have gifts to contribute. How can a gift be a gift if it's not shared? The gift is You. Your soul doesn't know greed, although your personality or ego might. Where do you choose to put your attention?

Being generous is an attitude, a way of being that is natural, trusting, knowing, and fun. My friend, Marsha, says, "It always comes back. The more I give, the more I receive. And I just don't mean monetarily."

When selecting a special gift, we can use our intuition, creativity, imagination, and talent. The initial momentum can come from the desire to be totally generous and giving. The opposite of hoarding brings you a freedom that can't be bought. Your heart opens, and you become more focused on others rather than on yourself.

I'll give you an example. I had fun making and giving a gift to Jeff, my son. He planned a family camping trip to Canyonlands National Park in Utah. We hiked into "The Narrows," saw breathtaking desert wild flowers, and ate scrumptious outdoor meals (even in a downpour)! I captured it all on film. With those color photos, I created laminated place mats. Viola! This inexpensive gift exuded love, and Jeff felt it. "Now these are the kind of gifts that mean a lot," he said to me. The kid knows how to say the right thing, doesn't he?

So many rewards await us when we think of others first and practice random acts of kindness, feeling generous. Our imagination goes to work for us and teaches us to share ourselves. Creativity is about exploring new territories within, tapping into the desire to share, to make a difference, to touch lives.

In "Parade," a supplement to the Spokesman Review in Spokane,

Washington, I read an article about Aaron Fierstein, the C.E.O. of the Maldin Mills Textile and manufacturing plant, who demonstrated amazing compassion and philanthropy when he nearly lost his entire plant by fire. His 3,000 employees felt certain that they would be out of work. Instead of laying off his employees, this beautiful man announced he would keep all of them on his payroll for a month, while his ninety-year-old family business was being rebuilt. After a month, he paid them for a second month, and then a third. By that time, the plant was prepared to have them back at work again! This man is truly a hero! His action instilled a loyalty and devotion that any company C.E.O. would dream of having from his/her employees.

When I read the list of the opposite definitions of greedy, I affectionately think of my departed in-laws, Dorothy and Max Abrams, who were two of the most generous and philanthropic individuals I knew. They both lived long and full lives that reflected their attitudes and beliefs. City of Hope, Biomedical Treatment and Educational Institute in Los Angeles, California, was one of the many benefactors of their time, energy, and support. The walls of their home were filled with plaques, awards, and certificates of gratitude for the money they helped raise for many charitable organizations. Max and Dorothy were true role models for their children and grandchildren; their unselfish behavior has left an indelible imprint in many lives. Their example of generosity was so powerful, it touched us all. Our daughter, Danielle, paid tribute to her grandma with the following poem which was read at her memorial service:

To a Cherished Gem in My Life...How I Love Your Sparkle

Grandmas are special; they love you unconditionally. They feed you when you're hungry and ask you, "Aren't you cold?" They play solitaire and rummy, and are proud to watch you swim in the pool.

Grandmas are there to help guide the way. They are world travelers who take you to Palm Springs, Coronado, and Israel. They share their cookie stash late at night, and feed you matzo brie on Sundays. They watch you hunt for hidden matzo and usually tag the Chanukah gifts incorrectly (you never know what you'll get)!

Grandmas are role models of goodness, generosity, and strength. They are motivation for Bas Mitzvahs and to never lose site of your roots and who you are.

Grandmas make you giggle by their classic one-liners and odd little ways. They help to brighten up your day by a simple gesture and a loving embrace.

Grandmas don't miss your birthdays, and shove cake in your face when you're two. They are gifts of first bikes, first cars, first torah readings and talks of first loves.

Grandmas have recorded memories on tape with Kleenex close by. They love their family first and would do anything to see them happy. They love phone calls, tuna salad, regular visits, and cheese blintzes. They always have bagels on hand, and they love to keep their house HOT.

Grandmas are an outlet for love. They are endless givers to charities, and sell watches & purses.

Grandmas are remembered for their truth, trust and respect.

Grandmas proudly share their seventy-one years of marriage with family and friends close by. They are great dancers, cross word puzzle experts, and rarely can sit in one place at a social function—boy do they love to have a good time.

Grandmas watch Jeopardy, Wheel of Fortune, and Murder She Wrote.

Grandmas are little red-headed dolls who love going to the beauty shop; having polished nails & reject "schlumpy" dress.

Tears surface so easily as I reflect on times of our unforgettable years to-gether. I will miss you immensely and you will always be a most trea-sured gem in my heart. Blessings, light, and love. In honor of you today and always,

Danielle

Children want the gift of our laughter, our joy, and our acceptance. They want to feel respected, honored, and unconditionally loved just as they are. Adults really do want the same thing. Let's remind each other to keep things in perspective and be aware of where we choose to place our focus; let's let each other know of our unconditional love.

Won't You Be My Neighbor?

"Mister Rogers," who passed over in 2003, was a highly acclaimed television personality on PBS for twenty-five years. One year, he presented a keynote address at the National Association for the Education of Young Children conference I attended. He was a special treat. While growing up our children visited his "neighborhood" on a daily basis. We all benefited from his sincerity and creative messages intended to enrich relationships between adults and children. His feel-good songs of self-discovery were imprinted on many children.

During his keynote address, Mister Rogers invited us to observe one minute of silence to think of someone who has supported us to live our life well. "The silence is a gift," he said. His soft-spoken message touched every heart present. "Do what you love in front of your children. This is far more valuable than a box with a beautiful bow." If you love to work with clay, let the children watch you and they'll feel your love coming through. Cook, sing, garden, build–show them what you love to do. This inspires others. Unfortunately, when parents say goodbye to a child, too many are going off to a job they dislike. This too, leaves an imprint in the heart of that little one. "Whatever is mentionable, can be more manageable. Crying, feeling sad–that's part of being human. It's important to be honest with children." *Mr. Rogers Talks with Parents* is one to read. "It's not the honors, titles, or power that is of ultimate importance. It's what resides inside. Loving yourself is number one." Thank you for being my neighbor, Mr. Rogers, for the many years of helping raise our children!

So what about Scrooge? The good news is that he transformed his attitude. After all, there's a little bit of Scrooge in each one of us. Investigate it–be honest, and like Scrooge, we too, can change.

Reflection Time:
1. Remember a time you felt greedy? Generous?
2. Describe both circumstances. Which felt more natural?
3. How would a good friend characterize you? As someone who is greedy and miserly, or as someone who is generous and giving?
4. What will they say at your memorial service about your spirit of giving?
5. Write a few sentences. Be specific.
6. Be honest...If there are two pieces of cake left and you're in the kitchen alone, do you take the larger piece for yourself?
7. What would be the beliefs that comprise your "chain" that prevents you from being generous?
8. Are you greedy with your time? If so, why?
9. What are your opinions with regard to salary differences between an athlete and a teacher?
10. Were you raised with a greedy or generous mind set?

"People are only mean when they're threatened. And when they're threatened, you start only looking out for yourself."
Mitch Albom, *Tuesdays With Morrie*

G is for feeling... Guarded

Definition: cautious, defended, vulnerable, protective
Opposite: trusting, open, discerning

Bodyguards, guard dogs, and the National Guard. Human beings have a need to feel safe. When we feel attacked, we "put up our guard." Feeling guarded has its place. It is healthy to set boundaries; however, if taken to the extreme, feeling guarded can close us off from others.

Feeling guarded is a means of protecting oneself. One might create an energetic wall that says, "Nobody is allowed in here!" Some folks may project a guarded persona with an air of aloofness, arrogance, or righteousness. That aloof attitude says, "This is not an invitation to get close and get to know who I am." Their guardedness is very apparent. If we're sensitive to energy and somewhat aware, we can often feel when someone is feeling guarded. We can feel their wall and their protection.

I helped one client overcome her guardedness by having her visualize this "wall" that she had put up. During the visualization portion of the session, I asked her to talk to the wall, feel the color, shape, and density of it. I asked her what images of the past were associated with it. This was all going on inside of her as I was guiding her through the experience. Soon she spoke the words, "It's gone." She proved the theory that when a block can be FULLY experienced, it disappears. This is not uncommon. Many clients have had a similar experience. Sometimes I'll hear, "It's lighter," before it's completely gone. I simply give them space to process and soon it dissipates.

When I'm with someone who feels guarded, I often feel their coldness and definite distance. What I intuit is, "Don't even try to get to my heart." This can be their shield to hide hurt, vulnerability, and pain. A deeper thought might be, "If anybody ever caught a glimpse of that hurt, I'd dissolve." Some might fear allowing another person into their heart. They fear, "Anyone else might reject me, laugh at me, hurt me." The pain of the past won't go away. It will show up somewhere and sabotage your dreams no matter how hard a person attempts to hide it.

The Ways in Which We Guard Ourselves

We acquire an investment to guard our image. We will do whatever it takes to be liked or to be loved. If your image is associated with the type of car you drive, and the car is totaled, what happens to you? You are not your BMW.

There are other ways of "protecting" oneself. One of the manifestations of guardedness is our weight issue. Some people unconsciously add weight to their bodies in order to create a cushion of safety. Others use drugs and alcohol to bury the feelings of pain. One-third of Americans are obese. One-third! A few of the beliefs that clients have had with weight are:

- "If I'm trim, I'll be pretty and attractive. I'm fearful that men will take advantage of me, so I'll stay overweight and remain afraid to attract men."
- "I won't let anybody hurt me again. Weight protects me from being vulnerable."
- "I'll eat to avoid feeling the pain of being alone, feeling unloved and undeserving."

No matter how one chooses to "guard" oneself, when that person is determined to stay guarded, they must build their wall higher and thicker. This guardedness is always about the "L" word–Love. Deep-rooted beliefs spin: "I'm not good enough to be loved," "I'm unlovable," "Maybe no one will ever love me." These are all fears, and fear is the illusion that prevents us from living life. Fear comes and goes; it's a natural process. It is when we deny its presence that it becomes blocked and stuck in the body. We become afraid of its presence, knowing that it is there even if we don't acknowledge it. We do anything we can to cover it up to ourselves and others, even if it means shutting everyone else out.

Through my work, I meet people who really do want to tear the wall down. I help them discover how their guardedness prevents them from fully experiencing or expressing love. The first necessary ingredient is their awareness that a wall is there, and then they only need willingness to investigate its source and content. Finally, they need to discover a true desire to take action and make the necessary changes, with confidence, trust, and authentic power.

The Stress Factor

Stress is such an enormous issue in our society that it often overshadows the confidence we need to overcome and move forward.

The past becomes more stressful and turns into disease, especially when we don't feel our emotions. As a Fellow to The American Institute of Stress, I read the newsletters with amazement. Look at Post Traumatic Stress Disorder (PTSD), for example. Since the Vietnam War, the term PTSD has been used to cover a broad range of situations. Victims of rape, trauma victims, and even long-term caregivers may suffer from PTSD.

Some of the symptoms PTSD patients experience are, emotional numbing, fantasies of retaliation, feelings of alienation, difficulty in concentrating, sleep disturbances, memory loss, over-protectiveness, and a chronic or recurrent fear of losing people in their lives. So people feel guarded and protective of those emotions they've never really addressed or felt. As a result, these emotions dwell in the cells like a volcano ready to erupt.

Learn to tell the truth about your fears and experience them so they can be replaced with love. We live with either love or fear; we each get to choose. We may say, "I can't get over my fear of flying," indicating a victim energy. While, "I won't get rid of my fear of flying," represents choice and free will. What a difference a little word makes! It is indeed a choice to overcome fear. What ignorance when people say, "That's just the way I am." You learned the computer or a foreign language, right? Did you learn how to tape favorite programs on your VCR player? Come on now! We can all learn about feelings. We can learn to string the words together to better express ourselves, and we can do it without making others wrong.

We can do anything we set our minds to. We need the desire to improve our life, to manifest our dreams, to be healthy and happy, and to claim our birthright. We need a burning desire to move past appearances and bombard through the layers to get to the essence. It's never too late to learn to feel and communicate. After all, clear and honest communication means being understood and heard, specifically when we speak from our heart and listen, rather than apply our defense. There's an art to communication, and that art needs practice. Anything else comes from our ego. Whenever we need to be right, we protect our tender core with a hard exterior, which results in pain and unhappiness.

For a visual on how to break through the walls you may have created, think of the branches of the spruce trees in the spring. The trees naturally produce a protective coating on the branches. Sort of like a little cozy. This coating is very gentle, but refuses to fall off until the new growth pushes through it. Only when the new growth is strong enough to be exposed to the elements, does the protection naturally fall away. This way the new growth isn't harmed.

If you are ready to break through your own self-made protective "guard," give yourself love, time, and patience. It will simply fall away when you are ready to show your new springtime-like self to the world. And only then will you be strong enough to endure the winds and rains and even sunny sides of life. Only then can you experience all life has to offer.

Reflection Time:

1. Evaluate your eating habits. Be aware of what goes in your mouthand when you are eating food for your psyche rather than your body.

2. Notice when the numbers on the scale started changing. What event preceded it? Go back in your memory, as far as your early, early childhood. Be determined to find the answers that will help you shed that protection of emotional food.

3. What are you protecting?

4. What are your fears around this protection?

5. Take an account of the games you play in order to keep up the wall.

6. What would your life look like without the protection?

7. Do you know people who appear distant, icy, or self-protecting? Do you feel close to them? Do they allow you into their life?

8. How do those folks compare to those you know who are open and trusting?

9. Do you believe you can change and actually remove the guard?

10. Do a process with the wall, the guard, the protective aspect in your life. Talk to it. Feel it. What color is it? What body sensations does it possess? What shape is it? What images of the past are associated with it? Experience it, and then visualize soft, warm, radiant light completely dissipating it. Congratulations on being the master of your life!

"Praise and blame, gain and loss, pleasure and sorry come and go like the wind. To be happy, rest like a great tree In the midst of them all."
Jack Kornfield, *Buddha's Little Instruction Book*

H is for feeling... Happy

Definition: enthusiastic, jubilant, elated, cheerful, content, jovial

Opposite: gloomy, depressed, disheartened, dejected, miserable

What makes a person happy? One may feel happy when beginning a new love relationship, or when winning an award for their endeavors, or on one's first day of vacation in several months. Happiness means different things to different people. One person might be happiest while shopping for new clothes, while another might be happiest when skiing down a black diamond slope. But one thing is for certain–happiness is what we all strive for and hope to have an abundance of in our lives.

While listening to a radio call-in show while driving the Los Angeles freeway, a man called in and stated as part of his commentary that he was a member of MENSA, and that it had never guaranteed him any happiness. MENSA was founded in England in 1946 by Roland Berrille, a barrister, and Dr. Lance Ware, a scientist and lawyer. They had the idea of forming a society for bright people of which the only qualification for membership was a high intelligence quotient– an IQ in the top 2% of the population. So from this gentleman's point of view, even being extraordinarily brilliant didn't bring him happiness.

What else do we generally give credit to that will bring us happiness? Money and power are good starters. The right weight, perfect body, wrinkle-less facial skin, toys, toys, and more toys, the ideal partner, place to live, car, house, wardrobe, jewelry, hi-tech equipment, athletic ability, talents, etc.?

No matter how brilliant your mind, you may not be a happy person. No matter how many facelifts you undergo, or how many contracts you sign with a personal trainer, your body will change, and then what? Do you have an emotional collapse, go after the next best thing to regain your youth, or accept the fact that the source of happiness is within? It's a process.

Gifts of Happiness

A few factors that contribute to happiness are, loving yourself, loving others, laughing more, playing, letting yourself daydream, living one day at a time, being present, and giving to others. When you do something charitable or something you feel good about, your opinion of yourself, your happiness, and your joy will begin to increase.

When each child was born, Gene bought me a charm to add to my charm bracelet. With Jeff, I got one bootie; Now, I'm a Mama. Christopher's charm had two booties—a second blessing. When Danielle was born, her charm had the face of a little girl with two blue stones for the eyes that read, "One Reason for Happiness." Our three children are indeed three reasons for happiness. There is a special love with each one.

Happiness is a choice. In fact, that's the name of a book by Barry Kaufman: *Happiness is a Choice*. Kaufman says, "If happiness means that we become easier, more comfortable with ourselves, more accepting, respectful, excited, and appreciative of what we do and with whom we interface – would we not then become a gift to all those we meet? Would we not become a continually incredible gift to ourselves as well?"

Barry and his wife Suzi, share their inspiring story in this book about the benefits of choosing happiness, even though their reality said it was crazy to be happy under those circumstances. Their story started in the seventies when their son Raun was diagnosed as severely and incurably autistic. Yet Barry and Suzi refused to fall prey to "unfavorable" circumstances. Due to this amazing couple's attitude and choices, he was transformed from a mute, functionally retarded, under-thirty IQ youngster, to a highly verbal, extroverted, social, happy teenager with a near-genius IQ!

In 1983, they formed the Option Institute, a worldwide teaching center, to help thousands of troubled people from all over the world shed beliefs and behaviors about what it takes to be happy. Their twelve books have sold over three million copies in sixty-five countries and have been printed in twenty-two languages. This is a success story you want to know about. Happiness IS a choice.

What does it mean to be happy? Have you ever had an incident occur when your days are so mellow things are aligned and everything falls into place? You feel jazzed; you're livin' the good life. Then, you get a phone call. Your father just went into the hospital, your child just passed out on the playground, or your dog got hit by a car. What happens to your body? To your happiness? To your attitude?

We can choose to be distraught about any of the above mentioned scenarios and allow our feelings to influence our blood pressure, heart rate, or nervous system. Or, we can be still, take several deep breaths, reach within to our sacred reservoir and allow it to give us the support and strength we need to take the next step. Being centered and present always works.

So again, our thoughts produce our levels of happiness. The fact is 98% of the atoms in our bodies are replaced throughout each year. When we actually choose our thoughts, knowing they are replacing those atoms, we realize the extent of our power.

Outer and Inner

Unfortunately, most of us believe that if our outer world matches our desire, we're happy. If it doesn't, then we're not. Our happiness may become totally dependent on outer circumstances. That kind of happiness comes from something material, like a new car, a promotion with more salary, new roller blades with titanium frames, a diamond tennis bracelet, etc. Turning points can make us happy, like meeting a new friend who feels like a kindred spirit, going on vacation, finishing college, or feeling pleased with a remodeled kitchen. Happiness in our outer world comes and goes. It wears off, sometimes sooner than later. Fleeting happiness is based on something new or a desire fulfilled, a dream come true, or an accomplishment achieved.

Have you ever seen side-by-side pictures of each team after a big basketball tournament, or the playing field after the Rose Bowl? The contrast is uncanny. The winners glow from head to toe; they hug and maul each other, and shout how great they feel. Then, we see the losers, their heads dragging lower than the helmets held in their hands. These types of events are a marvelous venue to observe this phenomena of duality—ecstasy and depression in full bloom.

Do you know people who are incessantly buying "toys" to satisfy their longing: ATV's, clothes, electronic gadgets? The quest continues through food, gambling, sex, drugs, alcohol, and other addictions, with the thirst for self-love, worthiness and approval. We become unhappy when other people don't meet our expectations, always looking for happiness outside of ourselves. Like the song says, "Looking for love in all the wrong places." When life doesn't look like the ideal scene, we feel ripped-off and victimized by the belief that life isn't fair. As we let go of the attachment to our pictures of what we think life should be, we can surrender and accept that life is what it is. However, our mind will give us a good argument because, remember, its agenda is to keep us attached to the ego and discontent. As we move into our hearts and open into forgiveness, generosity, and compassion, we find peace.

The article, "Castaway," written by Gary Mundell and Rick Fostaod in the magazine, *Cruising World*, September 1987, is about a lone sailor who endured fifty days on a Pacific atoll (a little island or reef). On day thirty, he said, "I realized the difference between my wants and my needs and resolved to simplify my life considerably, after this whole thing was over. I didn't need all the toys to be happy. I was happy just to be alive. I realized that the difference between an adventure and an ordeal is attitude–that 90% of survival is between the ears...I lived moment by moment. I stopped passing judgment."

Princess Di had so much of everything that most people think would make them happy. She had beauty, fame, and influence. She had money, clothes, and international recognition. However, she apparently struggled with her self-worth and battled bulimia in her earlier life. Without a foundation of unconditional love and total acceptance, Diana had low self-esteem. Commoners like us, might think her possessions would bring happiness, but she suffered depression and despair. Her young life ended so tragically.

We (princesses included) are all seeking happiness, peace of mind, and serenity. We want to be fun to be around, just as we want to be around fun people. Our worries, fear, and resentment prevent us from our own happiness. The past and the future keep us stuck, and judgment sabotages contentment.

There's another kind of happiness that lasts and dwells in our inner world–contentment–inner peace. This is the happiness we all seek whether we know it or not. There is an art to living, which requires the creation of a space within where nothing can penetrate. This space is a wellspring of peace and joy; no matter what the situation, this chamber can not be penetrated.

Each of us has the power to hurt ourselves or bring joy. Nobody can make us happy, if we choose otherwise. And visa versa. Only we make our life what it is. Regardless of our circumstances, we can decide to be happy. Don't wait for life to fit an internal picture. The laws of the universe work perfectly. Accept what is and we will be happy. Resist what is, and we will be unhappy. From whom do you need permission to be happy?

The Hugging Saint
There is a saint by the name of Ammachi who is called the Hugging

Saint. People stand in a line to receive "darshan," which means "being in the audience of a holy person or diety." She has hugged over ten million people all over the world. I have been with Amma, as she is affectionately known, on two different occasions, and being hugged by her is feeling absolute, unconditional love. Her energy is electric, as she radiates an inner happiness that you can feel. It's something we all want. However, her happiness is much deeper—it's Pure Bliss.

Amma, is a Self-realized soul who has lifted the lives of many troubled people who are searching for truth. Part of her message is as follows: "If they were to just open up their hearts, they would experience the real miracle...and that miracles are happening at every moment... My child, never lose courage, never lose your trust in God or in Life, always be optimistic no matter what situation you may find yourself in... Pessimism is a form of darkness...a form of ignorance...like a curse...Only by being optimistic, will you experience that Light. By being pessimistic, you move towards greater despair and darkness."

When we can offer service and courage to those in despair, we offer a new strength to them that can relieve their struggle and ignorance. I feel we all have some duty and purpose here, and as we put our attention on that, the tribulations and trials of the personality diminish. When you choose to offer your life in service, you forget the little self and live your days as a servant to Life! "Just be kind" is a mantra I try to live by.

Try doing something for someone else rather than being self-centered. Think of someone else other than yourself. Read to someone whose vision has been impaired, take your sensitive pet to a senior home for pet therapy, or volunteer at your local school. Become a mentor for a young person starting a new business. Years on the planet really don't matter when it comes to service.

If you want to improve your life and live it from a higher state of awareness, affirm to yourself each day to seek happiness within, rather than from outer events and things. This is your choice. As we take responsibility to create happiness in our life, it ripples and becomes a gift to the world. This is the way we make a difference. This is the way we live in a peaceful world. Change yourself a little, change the world a lot.

Reflection Time:

1. How do your beliefs influence your happiness, and how do they determine the choices you make?

2. Which ones support you? Which ones sabotage you?

3. What makes you truly happy?

4. Write your beliefs down on paper and examine them.

5. What affirmation have you associated with your child's birth? What about your own?

6. Describe your attitude in general. Are you an optimist or a pessimist?

7. What selfless acts have you committed in the past year? Month? Week?

8. Happy was one of the seven dwarfs in Snow White. Can you name the other six? Which one do you resemble most?

9. If you woke up in the morning and had to choose between being the happiest or the wealthiest person on the planet, which would you choose?

10. What do your parents want for you? Happiness? Success? Financial freedom? Health? _____?

"I saw an Eagle in the sky today
Flying free upon the wind.
In my dreams I touched its wings.
Caught the wind and flew with him.

Oh what glory it was for me.
Flying free up in the sky
For dreams become reality
If in our souls they never die.

So seize the moment which is now
For your Eagle lives within
Hold the vision of your truth
Dream your Eagle and fly with Him."
Dennis Weaver

H is for feeling... Hopeful

Definition: optimistic, great expectations, confident, trustful
Opposite: despairing, hopeless, pessimistic, doubtful

Hopeful has to do with optimism. Even when things go awry, we have the choice to keep our heads high, and trust that all is as it should be, and the best possible outcome will occur. When we feel hopeful, our reality might show one thing, but we persevere with a good attitude nonetheless. This is the gist of hopeful–maintaining a positive attitude despite our circumstances.

Dr. Martin Seligman offers research on the subject of being optimistic and hopeful in his book entitled *Learned Optimism*. Thousands of questionnaires were given to depressed people in all kinds of situations. The research consistently revealed that when people are depressed, they're also pessimistic. Consistently. The clue Seligman suggests for severe depression is pre-existing pessimism. In a prison experiment, it was determined that pessimism is the fertile soil in which depression grows, particularly when the environment is hostile.

Dr. Seligman followed a group of 400 third through sixth-graders, and continues to follow them today. He found that those children who started out as optimists stayed non-depressed, or if they got depressed, they recovered quite rapidly. When major events occurred in their lives, like parents separating and/or divorcing, the pessimists went under most readily. The same is true in young adults. His most recent book, *Authentic Happiness*, is certain to impact your life.

Dr. Daniel Mark, a heart specialist at Duke University said, "Optimism is a good thing. When people give up and feel they're not going to make it, it's usually a self-fulfilling prophecy."

I went to a lecture by Dr. Bernie Siegal, physician, author, well-known inspirational lecturer, and one of the most hopeful individuals I've come across. "Change your life if you can," he says. "But if you can't – change your attitude. Choose happiness – choose to be hopeful."

Choosing to See

We see life through a set of individual filters. No two people see the same thing in the same way. Did you know that a dragonfly has 30,000 optic lenses? Can you imagine its perception of the world? Awesome! We each see situations uniquely. One person could look at a collection of plants in someone's home and think, "I'm glad I don't have plants in my home; it's another thing to care for. I don't want to be responsible for anything else." A different person might look at those plants and say, "Plants bring such life to a room. I feel such joy when I take care of mine. As I water them, I tell them how beautiful they all are, and I believe they can feel my words."

The *Talmud*, Judaism's holiest collection of books says, "We see things not how they are, but how we are." No two of us have the same set of experiences, so even if we agree, we still won't see things exactly the same way.

After his journey into space, I recall astronaut Edgar Mitchell telling the press, "This trip into space provided me with a dramatic opportunity to see the Earth and the cosmos from a totally new perspective, which caused me to question nearly everything I had believed in the past." Good for you Edgar Mitchell, for being willing to use that stupendous and rare experience to look inward.

We also hear things the way we choose to hear them. For example, my sister was visiting me at a condo we rented. As I explained the directions, I told her to turn left "at" the tennis courts. She heard me say "past" the tennis courts. She wandered around for half an hour looking for our condo. What a difference one word can make, leaving out a letter in an email address, or a wrong digit in a phone number. Be clear, don't assume, and ask questions.

I Have a Question

To teach by asking instead of telling is the basis for the Socratic Method. You may have noticed there are many questions in this book. It is intentional, as an instrumental tool for accessing inner wisdom. In his use of critical reasoning, by his unwavering commitment to truth and by his vivid example of his own life, Socrates set the standard for all subsequent Western philosophies. The fifth-century Athenian philosopher devoted himself to "free-wheeling discussions."

"Pose a question, think of a hypothetical situation, devise a line of questions and ask, 'What would you do if ___?' As facilitator, take a non-judgmental attitude."

His concept stands strong today and is practiced at The Socrates Café in Seattle, founded in the spring of 2001 by Wendy Smith. The website reads, "Welcome to the online home of Seattle Socrates Café. We meet at El Diablo Coffee Company at 1811 Queen Anne Ave. N. each Wednesday evening from 7:30 to 9:30 P.M. We are a group of people who are interested in discussing the big (and not so big) questions that affect our everyday lives, and anyone is welcome to join us - in person or online."

What is a Socrates Café? "It is a group investigation where we all help each other become better critical thinkers, re-examine our assumptions, and study the chosen question by probing it from different angles and perspectives. It is a systematic inquiry using the Socratic Method as its guiding principle (no prior experience necessary). All kinds of questions are welcome, especially those that are directly relevant to participants' actual lives and current preoccupations."

"Socrates Cafe is a facilitated discussion in which civility and respectful listening are essential. However, we are not aiming for consensus (although we occasionally surprise ourselves and arrive there), but rather for the airing, sharing, and deep consideration of diverse points of view." How's that for a hopeful template on how to communicate?

The Sunny Side

Some people just always look on the sunny side of life. They feel trusting of life and believe that things will work out for the best. When I travel to a conference, I am hopeful it will be successful in all ways. When you study for a big math test, are you hopeful your efforts will bring you a good grade?

I invite you to send away for a free little booklet with the highlights of a woman's life by the name of Peace Pilgrim. This woman was optimistic and hopeful and radiated joy. She relinquished all negative feelings. She said, "If you live in the present moment, which is really the only moment you have to live, you will be less apt to worry." In addition, "There is a criterion by which you can judge if what you are thinking and the things you are doing are right for you. And that is, have they brought you inner peace?" Did you get hope from those words? Are they bringing you contentment inside or turmoil? The booklet is called, "Steps Toward Inner Peace: Harmonious Principles for Human Living," compiled by Friends of Peace Pilgrim. All materials are free of charge and they ask only that you pay postage if possible. The organization also offers videos of live interviews of Peace Pilgrim. Send for your free materials today.

What is the alternative to this "Pollyanna" attitude? Poor health, dysfunctional relationships, unfulfilled goals, struggle and effort, negativity that impacts everyone in your space, then eventually ripples out to the world.

Disappointment and degrees of anger accompanied by sadness, empathy, and compassion is the roller coaster of global politics. Examples are: when I read about the plight of the salmon and the ignorance that surrounds their survival because of political antics, when both houses of Congress approved spending thirty-four million dollars for the UN Fund for Population Activities, but President Bush vetoed it, or when our country pulled out of the Kyoto World Environmental Conference in Japan.

One can hold an attitude that things are happening exactly this way for a reason. It may not be apparent when looking at the appearances, but I have to go beyond that and look deeper, to all I've learned in the past thirty years of embracing Truth, through personal and spiritual growth. Believing that things happen for a reason positively affects our physical, mental, emotional, spiritual health, and the overall quality of your lives. The troublesome politics may just be the Universe's way of getting enough people to take action to make a global change! I know many people who avoided politics who are now taking a stance and using their voices. The thought of like-minded people using their power to make a positive difference makes me extremely hopeful!

One such person is Erin Grunwell. She is an English teacher who put together a book entitled *The Freedom Writers Diary*. It is a compilation of essays written by her students journalizing their personal and painful youth. I feel blessed to have met and heard this young woman speak at a character education conference. She took 150 teens from hopelessness and despair to unlimited possibilities. One of her students became the brunt of a bad joke, which almost brought him to tears. When she got hold of the racial caricature that had been drawn in his likeness, she "went ballistic." She yelled, "This is the type of propaganda that the Nazis used during the Holocaust." A student questioned her, "What's the Holocaust?" When she asked the class how many had heard of the Holocaust, nobody raised their hands, but when she asked how many had been shot at, nearly every hand went up. Erin immediately decided to make tolerance the core of her curriculum by introducing new books, guest speakers, and field trips to bring history to life.

Erin said all of her training did not prepare her to be in the trenches. In other words, nothing could have prepared her to experience firsthand what it would be like to be with teens who lived with such despair and lack of hope in their lives.

When asked what made "Ms. G" so memorable to the teens, their reply was, "Past teachers didn't care about us. She asked, she listened, rather than sending us to the principal's office. She cared and it made the difference." At the time of this writing, her story is being made into a motion picture. It was challenging to determine if I was going to place Erin's story under "hopeful" or "inspiring," because she fits in both!

Of course, there is a risk in being hopeful–the risk of being let down and disappointed. One can lose faith and the negative beliefs will surface:

- "Things never turn out for me anyhow, but they do for others."
- "What's the point of being hopeful? I always get let down."
- "I did my best and it didn't help."
- "I'll always be a loser. I just don't have what it takes."

This is the point where you slip into the victim identity. "Poor me" becomes the underlying, unrecognized energy.

One male client embraced his victim identity then dissolved it to nothingness. He writes: "My work with Alexandra has been transformational. The realization that I had allowed the circumstances of my life to turn me into a person who expected to be victimized was cathartic. Releasing this victim identity through her work has had profound effects in how I relate to the world and has greatly improved my life. I'm forever grateful. Thank you, Alexandra."

Becoming aware of the victim mask we wear is a revelation. When people get it, they get it, and it transforms the way they relate to the world. I'm so proud of my clients. They are all so willing to move on, and use the energy that was expended holding on to the past for making their lives and the world more peaceful.

Take responsibility; own the results; honor your feelings, and choose. Do you really want to give these false beliefs such power? Hope is real.

It can motivate us to heights we can't even envision. Again, we have the choice! And trust me, the sunny side is much more fun.

Reflection Time:

1. Think of a time when you felt hopeful and the results were contrary to your desire. What did you do with your feelings? Did you honor them? Discuss them? Deny them? Gloss over them?

2. Think of a time when you felt hopeless. How long did it last? Did you share your feelings? Did you find yourself saying, "I'll never be that stupid again"?

3. What has been the highest, most fulfilling time in your life? Did you notice this feeling dissipating? When? Why?

4. What has been the lowest and most depressing time in your life?

5. Feel what a hopeful attitude feels like – right now. Really feel it!

6. Now feel a hopeless attitude. What is your experience of both?

7. Are your friends hopeful?

8. Do you believe people who are hopeful tend to be unrealistic?

9. What issues would you discuss if you could participate at the Socrates Café?

10. What is the source of your hope? From where does a hopeless feeling originate?

"The greatest terror a child can have is that he is not loved, and rejection is the hell he fears. I think everyone in the world to a large or small extent has felt rejection. And with rejection comes anger, and with anger some kind of crime in revenge for the rejection, and with that crime guilt – and there is the story of mankind."
John Steinbeck, *East of Eden*

H is for feeling... Hurt

Definition: wounded, damaged, rejected, impaired, tormented

Opposite: well, healed, undamaged, relieved, aided

To feel hurt is to feel humiliated, unloved, vulnerable, and weak. Maybe someone has said something that was unkind and those words really devastated us. Maybe we've felt small and insignificant around someone or a group and our feelings really hurt. Feeling hurt is an emotional wound, a mental anguish, a discomfort, and it causes pain, sometimes for a long time.

Often, there is sadness with hurt. When we are hurt, we have to decide if we will ever trust anyone again or if we'll ever love again. In the future we may be reluctant to open ourselves up to others and allow our feelings to be shared. Maybe someone hurt us so badly we made a decision to never again open ourselves up in a relationship. Out of that decision, life is lived for grieving of that deep wound which feels like it won't ever heal. How often have we heard that?

Ways We Are Hurt

So many clients have told me how hurt they were that their parents didn't go see them perform at a recital or sporting event. It may be an hour or so out of your day, folks, but attend the events in which your child is involved. It's time well spent.

In elementary school, I had such a crush on the most popular basketball player in school, who was a gorgeous hunk. He finally asked me out on a date... and then stood me up! Was I hurt? You bet I was.

Sometimes we feel hurt if a good friend says, "That outfit is not so becoming." We ask them to be honest, but do we really want them to be?

A client of mine was laughed at by her mother and grandmother. As a little girl anxious to start school, she thought she could begin kindergarten the very day she turned five years old; she didn't realize she had to wait until September! Her mother may have thought it was cute, but laughing at her without explanation contributed to this woman's self-esteem issue.

What about the three-year-old child trying to sleep but hears screaming and violence behind a closed bedroom door? A majority of my clients carry the energy of the hurt child with them. Hurt, like any other feeling, doesn't go away; it stays embedded in the body, which gets buried then covered over with a wide range of feelings. So we have to pay attention to our children's feelings, as well as our own.

"Parents can do much to help their children to master elements of emotional intelligence, not only by what they say or do directly, but also how they handle their own feelings," says Carol Hooven in *USA Weekend*, September 8-10, 1995. She says, "There are three most common inept parenting styles: ignoring feelings altogether, being too easy-going, and being contemptuous, i.e. showing no respect for children's feelings. The first one, ignoring feelings, is treating emotional upsets as trivial. The second one is leaving children to their own devices in handling emotional storms, or trying bribes to get them to stop being sad or angry. What works best is to act as an emotional coach. Take the child's feelings seriously. Try to find out what is upsetting him. The results of this action are raising children who got along better with their parents, who got upset less often, were more popular in school, and less rude. Brain circuits continue to be shaped by experiences throughout life...It's never too late for us to learn or be changed."

One Teen's Response to Hurt

"I had no other choice. Oh God. I had to. I couldn't do anything else." In May 1998, these were the words of fifteen-year-old Kip Kinkel after being arrested. First he murdered his parents, then the following day he drove to Thurston High School and opened up fire in the cafeteria; he killed two fellow students and wounded twenty-five others.

How would we describe a person like Kip, who believed he had no choice? Helpless? Hopeless? Alone? Scared? Confused? Sad? Desperate? Despondent? And maybe hurt? All of these words fit this young man who is currently serving a term of 111 years in prison, without parole.

In Kip's journal he wrote, "There is one kid above all others that I want to kill...The one reason I don't – hope that tomorrow will be better. As soon as my hope is gone, people die." Obviously, Kip was hopeless that spring day as he chose a course of action that determined his bleak future.

The question many asked as our nation experienced the confusion and anguish from such deep wounds was, why? What went wrong? We tend to look at issues surrounding the situation such as Kip's interest in guns, his association with a rough group of kids, his lack of ability to share feelings with his father out of the fear that he would get angry, therefore, being unable to bond with him. In seeking relief for a child and family, a quick fix solution might be the prescription of a drug, but shouldn't we be looking deeper? Wouldn't it be a good idea to delve into the precursor for desperate choices? We could probe the events of early childhood, investigating the years of nursery schooling and even the time of gestation. What did the child absorb through his/her environment? Why did he/she make the choices that were made? And, how did those choices influence the child's values, morality, and character as he/she grew into maturity and adulthood? What roles do the parents play in this process?

Del McElroy, from the Child Advocacy Center in Cullman, Alabama, told me of the challenges in working with adolescent boys. "They are able to relate how they physically feel, when asked. But when it comes to how they mentally feel, it's a little more difficult. When asked how they feel emotionally, they have no idea." Perhaps if Kip had the tools to recognize and express his feelings, this tragedy could have been avoided. What do you think?

Although I have no information about Kip's gestation period, I can't help but question it, as well as those critical early years. We now know that the unborn child is aware; the baby in the womb can see, hear, experience, taste, learn, AND feel. The fetus is reactive to the environment. This is the foundation on which all-learning, memory, health, and well-being are based. Joseph Chilton Pearce, author of *Magical Child*, says that,"....studies show that the emotional state of the mother influences the shape, structure, and functioning of the developing brain in her uterine infant...the environment profoundly changes the genetic structuring within us...it is the biggest influence of all our DNA."

What beliefs were absorbed during the first thirty-three months of Kip's life? Why was he tearful when discussing his relationship with his father during therapy? "He sees me as a bad kid with bad habits," he said. He told his therapist that his father expected the worst from him. And, why was Kip's father absent from any of the three months of counseling?

158

Baby Love

In a powerfully written and well-researched book, *Ghosts from the Nursery*, the authors, Robin Karr-Morse and Meredith S. Wiley, write, "From the time of late gestation to birth, we begin to develop a template of expectations about ourselves and other people, anticipating responsiveness or indifference, success or failure. This is when the foundation of who we become and how we relate to others and to the world around us is built." Recent brain research now validates this compelling message. Scientists have discovered that babies have approximately 100 billion neurons! (To put this in some sort of perspective, astronomers have found fifty billion galaxies in their telescopes. Do you think there is a parallel?) If the baby's neurons were joined end to end, they would stretch 600 miles! If that isn't astounding enough, babies in the womb actually have 200 billion neurons, but 100 billion are dropped off when the fetus is forming! Another interesting fact: The heart and the ear are the first to form—our feeling center and listening center!

Through my own psychological research over the years, I can substantiate that without exception, every client's issues originated from early childhood, and sometimes from in the uterus. They source from early experience and become the filter through which that child perceives life. They become the child's belief system. What messages did young Kip inherit that contributed to the molding of the pathways of neurons in his brain that led him on a self-destructive course?

His choices led him to the cell bed he sleeps in every night. Others with painful childhood experiences have made other choices. Another example is Anthony Godby Johnson, who was continuously subjected to physical and sexual abuse by his parents. In addition, they withheld food, a bed for him to sleep in, a coat to wear, and a toothbrush. From his book, *A Rock and a Hard Place*, Tony writes, "By the time I was five, I realized that I was alone in this world and that it was up to me to see to my own survival...I would do whatever it took... At the top of my list of wonderful things I wanted to have happen was, 'get hugs and kisses like everyone else.'"

We really are all the same; the need to be loved and to love is the thread that runs through the pearls of humanity. Tony had an exceptional experience with education and made the choice to persevere. He was awakened to the possibility of his own potential and a life he could create for himself. "...My own creativity had a great deal to do with the way I handled pain and vulnerability." He claimed teachers provided him with the hope in knowing he had the luxury of claiming his mind as his own.

I viewed another inspiring and similar example on *The Oprah Show*.

Dave Pelzer, the author of *A Child Called "It"*, an autobiography, tells the story of his abuse, starvation, and mental cruelty. He told Oprah that he ended up forgiving his mother. Oprah said, "How could you?" He responded with, "How could I not?" He says, "You have to get rid of the garbage and you have to know what you want in your life and celebrate everyday things." He says he wouldn't change one thing about his life, because if he did it would take away from his gratitude and his humility of turning his difficult past into something worthwhile. This man enlisted in the U.S. Air Force at eighteen and was hand-picked to mid-air refuel the highly-secretive SR-71 Blackbird and the F-117 Stealth Fighter, which played a major role in Operations Just Cause and Desert Shield. One of his many awards is The Outstanding Young Person of the World in 1994. Dave speaks for corporate groups, human services, and youth-at-risk. What an inspiration! He is too busy to feel hurt and bitterness. He is living in the present and making lemonade from lemons!

I was in San Diego when I extended my stay one more day so I could see and hear Dave Pelzer speak to a packed house in a Borders bookstore. Am I pleased I did! The following are a few inspiring messages I scribbled down:

- Purge what's bothering you.
- People abuse themselves.
- Become self-accountable.
- If you want a college degree, do what it takes to get it. You have to want it more than anything to do what you have to do. That's what he did.
- We all fall down; we learn when we get up.
- When you're having problems, look to see who is the common denominator.
- Resolve your issues; get the help you need to purge them out of your system.
- When we go to the bathroom, we don't put our "crap" in a bag and keep it for forty years. It goes in the toilet. FORGIVE. It frees you to live your life.
- Hate is the most destructive force on Earth. When you hate, you have no life.
- You have a choice every day.
- Have fun NOW. Make time to live a great life.
- For someone to hurt you, they have to have been hurt.
- "I wouldn't change one single second of my life."

His latest book, *Help Yourself*, has been nominated for the Pulitzer Prize. He is one inspirational and motivational soul.

If one child has been abused, it is one too many. A wonderful young man came to see me for an appointment because of mental fatigue, difficulty in concentration, and physical symptoms occurring in his muscles and joints. Sugar cravings were at a high. His very early childhood was spent sleeping in a bedroom in a cold and damp basement, where bugs crawled on the floor, while his siblings slept upstairs. Seeing shadows on the walls of the stairs prevented him from climbing them in the middle of the night for comfort. He was torn between the shadows and the bugs and dampness of this "dungeon" type bedroom, far from the ideal setting for a three-year-old. The central belief that came from this childhood was "love hurts." You can understand why. That hurt, along with anger, confusion, despair, etc., showed up in his physical pain.

I have another true story about a woman whose dinner time as a child was spent in silence, with no opportunity to share, laugh, or express. Is it any surprise to learn that one of her core, foundational beliefs, was "I have nothing of value to say"? Dinner is a social time and can be an opportunity for interaction and stimulation.

Another young woman was seeking help with a betrayal that happened in her adult life. She'd lost her trust in people after she'd suffered lies. Her hurt and devastation were deep and shook her foundation. As we explored her early years, she related the many times she would hear the yelling and fighting of her parents at night. When morning came, nothing was ever said. The children would never ask questions, share thoughts, feelings, or express concern. The parents would never discuss their problems nor admit what had transpired. Everyone in the house lived a lie. My client felt betrayed by her parents and family. A child is not supposed to grow up so intimately exposed to violence and mental abuse. The pain of those early years manifested in mistrust. Feelings DON'T go away.

What does it take to impress on new parents that having a child is easy, but raising that child is a huge responsibility? The hurt and wounded child lives in the adult. Hurt, pain, and most fears can be prevented in childhood. Role models affect us positively or negatively. It's truly astounding what capacity we have in our mind. How can one person forgive a parent because of a dysfunctional upbringing, yet another will hold on to the hurt, resentment, and bitterness throughout life? What makes the difference?

Necessary Forgiveness

The energy from the child, the adolescent, and the adult exist individually within us. We must remember that energy is a power, a force that exists in many forms. Everything is energy. Everything vibrates and has frequency. Some vibration is dense and slow, other is fine and high. Energy changes form. Rain changes to snow given a precise condition; milk changes to butter after intense churning. It's one of the Laws of Nature; we don't think about when it's happening. Hurt feelings are also energy that we can experience and transform.

When someone has hurt us deeply, we feel wounded and may want to hurt back, hold a grudge, or ignore that person. Some of us attack. "I'll never forgive so and so."

We are the masters of the moments and the feelings of our lives. Through feeling, telling the truth, and practicing forgiveness, I believe all wounds can heal. As Paramahansa Yogananda, founder of Self-Realization Fellowship, and author of the spiritual classic, *Autobiography of a Yogi* said, "You are the master of the moments of your life." If you are not, you are being small, contained, and merely existing. Take charge and be the master of your moments by being true to yourself, by being real and expressing your uniqueness through service in whatever way you are drawn to.

Daya Mata, President of Self-Realization Fellowship, says in the Winter 2003, SRF magazine, "When your feelings are hurt, that means you are thinking of yourself. Try not to let self enter into things so much. Always give others the benefit of the doubt. Say to yourself, 'Possibly they don't understand.' Sometimes it is simply thoughtlessness on the part of others that causes them to say and do things that hurt us, not that they are intentionally being mean. That effort on your part to understand them will help to eliminate your hurt feelings."

In Truth, You Can't Hurt Another

Many people avoid expressing their truth because they're afraid it will hurt someone's feelings. A client came in with the following beliefs about this very idea.

- If I hurt or offend another, they will be upset with me.
- Love will be withdrawn if I offend someone.
- It's better to accommodate others in order not to cause waves.
- Pleasing people guarantees me of love.

What we discovered was that the more she tried to accommodate her parents, the harder it was to accomplish. She kept at it because she wanted and needed their approval. Her needs became lower and lower on the ladder, until she reached the place where her feelings were completely disregarded. As we tracked these patterns, the first and primary one came at the time she was thirteen months old. Her parents brought a new baby home from the hospital. She was sitting on a couch in the living room when friends and family came to visit and adore the new addition. Filled with shame, the belief, "I hadn't been a good enough baby, so they got another one," became imbedded in her cells. "But I'll keep on trying," so that is what she's done all her fifty-one years. When she realized that she had been doing this her entire life, she made the commitment to replace the old belief with "I am enough."

It takes courage to be willing to give up what has been familiar. Who will I be? How will I be in the world? It takes recognizing yourself as the magnificent being that you are. It takes telling the truth. It requires knowing each of us is responsible for our own life. We have free will and we can choose whether or not to be hurt, to resent, to be incensed or to be kind. It's up to us. Eleanor Roosevelt said, "No one can make you feel inferior but yourself." Nobody can really hurt you unless you allow him or her to hurt you, or in other words, unless you give your power to them.

The fear of rejection can cover up communicating hurt feelings. In lieu of introspection about the hurt, it gets denied, buried and becomes stuck and then turned into resentment. What effort we go through to keep up the front and live a dysfunctional life, when we could be hugging each other!

Healing the Wounds

Speaking of hugging, Amma, the "Hugging Saint" of India, was asked at a weekend retreat I participated in, "How do you avoid running away when confronted with a difficult situation?" She responded with, "External situations don't have the power to hurt you. It is only when the mind interprets those situations that the pain bubbles up from within. The aim is to not let the mind interpret or comment on external situations. This is possible only when you learn the art of witnessing."

From now on, if someone says something that hurts your feelings, respond to it positively. One of the agreements, from the book *The Four Agreements* by don Miguel Ruiz is: "Don't take things personally." As soon as you take on what the other has said to you, you're stuck, and you've given your power away. People just do what they do; it's not because of you. Ruiz says, "You have wounds that I've touched by hurting you." What he means by this is that, when we allow our self to be hurt, there is a part of us that has not healed, and this "wound" is what is actually creating the pain. Someone just happened to come by and say something that touched that wound and opened it up to be vulnerable.

We often have the need to defend our position and we do so by retaliating. An option might be, "I feel hurt by what you said," or go deeper by taking a closer look at the feelings you're experiencing. Ask yourself if you really want to choose to feel that way. A new perspective on that same feeling can make the difference. You have a choice here. Which do you choose to do? This new conditioning will improve your relationships throughout your life.

When Albert Schweitzer was asked what it takes to be in the world, his response was, "The skin of a rhino and the wings of an angel." Do you think you could establish that balance of being thick-skinned yet still taking yourself lightly? If so, "hurt" may have lost its place in your life from this point onward!

Reflection Time:

1. When is a time you felt hurt?
2. What did you do with that feeling? How long did you feel it?
3. Are you still hurt from it? How can you free yourself from it? What are you willing to do to free yourself?
4. Is it easy or difficult for you to forgive?
5. Imagine what it would be like to never feel hurt again. What are some words to describe that feeling?
6. What do you think it takes to be in the world?
7. Make a list of other words that are synonymous to hurt.
8. Do you take things personally? What are the results if you've answered yes?
9. How often do you "assume?"
10. Do you believe you always do your best?

"The sea does not reward those who are too anxious, too greedy, or too impatient. To dig for treasures shows not only impatience and greed but lack of faith. 'Patience, patience, patience,' is what the sea teaches. Patience and faith. One should lie empty, open, choiceless as a beach – waiting for a gift from the sea."
Anne Morrow Lindbergh, *Gifts From the Sea*

I is for feeling... Impatient

Definition: restless, uneasy, intolerant, nervous, in a hurry
Opposite: forbearing, tolerant, patient, understanding

We have all experienced impatience, whether it's with a slow waiter, or being put on hold on the telephone, or with a crying child. From the time we are born, we are impatient babies wailing for our needs to be met. It seems that patience is actually a thing to be learned, and a virtue we must practice if we are to maintain a sense of happiness in our lives.

Impatience can lead to undesirable behaviors if we do not have a rein on it. We can become impetuous and abrupt, whether it's with a cashier in the market who is just learning her job, a traffic jam when there is a plane to catch, or simply with the manner in which another processes information. In our impatience, we can be rude and demonstrate immature and inappropriate behavior, all because things aren't going exactly the way we want them to go.

"God, please give me patience and give it to me now!" How is a virtue like patience acquired in a society where our hurried and harried syndrome prevails? The wondrous computer is constantly being re-designed for faster responses. Even mealtime appears accelerated because instructions on the box state, "Just add water." We inherit messages of "faster is better" in every area of life. We want the outcome, and we want it now. And when we don't get it, look out! Our patience, tolerance, and understanding disappear.

What a challenge to remain calm and centered while living in a "hurry up" world that implies there's no time to be patient. After all, "time is money" is a prevalent belief in a capitalist society. And where money is involved, anxiety and frustration well up and can take over our being. Instead, we create a full-blown case of impatience, directed at others as well as ourselves.

The Time is Now

Once I attended a retreat in Estes Park with Neale Donald Walsh, author of the *Conversation with God series*. He gave everyone watches for presents. But instead of numbers on the watch, it has the word, NOW, twelve times around the face! What a great reminder! Sure, be on time for your appointments, but always stay in the NOW. When we don't, stress creeps in.

Stress is a derivative of impatience. Just because things aren't going by our timetable, this stress expands in the body and we become more irritable, intolerant, and downright angry. When we allow those outside influences to get the best of us, we are defeated. We slip into a role of victim and wallow in self-pity, all because things aren't going our way. Maybe the line is too long, the kids are whiny, the boss is moody, or the lawn mower doesn't cut properly. When we have clear expectations, our nerves become jangled, our heart beats faster, our stomach churns, and we're out of control. The "shortage-of-time" belief dominates our thoughts and creates a sense of futility.

I met a man one day who shared with me how impatience created peril. He became irritated and anxious as he waited for a red light to change; he had no tolerance for the traffic. He had felt stressed, and that behavior led him to a heart attack right there. After one year of recuperating, he examined his life and adopted a new life style–one of gratitude and patience.

Impatience is a characteristic of the ego, while patience comes from a much higher part of us. If you think about it, impatience is a lack of trust in the plan of the Divine. Everything really is in perfect order, whether it looks that way to us or not! Everything happens at the right time. Maybe that familiar traffic light is taking way too long on red, but perhaps you missed having an accident by that extra few seconds. Or maybe you forgot something at home in your rush out the door to go to work–and when you returned for it, discovered you left the stove on. There is timing to everything. To feel impatient is to be intolerant of the natural timing of the universe and therefore disrespectful of it.

When I slip into impatience, I have momentarily forgotten the Divine Timing of the Universe. Oh no, I cannot manifest the full moon when I want. There is perfection to the order and I am part of the Universe, therefore I allow my life to unfold just perfectly. Being angry and resistant is simply unproductive.

Perfect Timing

Remember we have free will! Our highest gift is our free will. A better mode of being is to declare our desire, be thankful for it as though it had already happened, and then detach from the results. The last segment just may be the tricky part. When we truly release expectations, we participate with patience. When we are impatient, we are not living in the present moment. Stay centered, feel life, let go, move with the flow, allow what is to be exactly as it is, and observe how it all unfolds.

Patience is synonymous with love. When we express a patient attitude towards life and ourselves, we are in touch with our true essence, our bliss, our joy, and our love.

I have such respect for Olympians and their long-term goals. They may train practically their whole life, and when that moment comes, depending on their event, their competition is over in a flash. A 100-meter race will be all over in ten seconds. Olympians can stumble over a hurdle and fall or pull a muscle in a race. A slalom skier can miss a gate. A springboard diver may not execute the dive properly. A gymnast might slip on the balance beam. Many ice skaters start at such an early age, they scramble to stay upright. Yet, their gift to the world came through their dream pursued with patience.

Take the following story from Nikos Kazantzakis,' *Zorba the Greek*: "I discovered a cocoon in the bark of a tree just as the butterfly was making a hole in its case and preparing to come out. I waited awhile, but it was too long appearing, and I was impatient. I bent over it and I breathed on it to warm it. I warmed it as quickly as I could and the miracle began to happen before my eyes faster than life! The case opened, the butterfly started slowly crawling out, and I shall never forget my horror when I saw how the wings were folded back and crumpled. I tried to help it with my breath. It needed to be hatched, and patiently. The unfolding of the wings should be a gradual process in the sun. Now it was too late. My breath had forced the butterfly to appear all crumpled before its time. It struggled desperately. And a few seconds later, died in the palm of my hand."

Teachers of Patience

India's unwritten law for the truth seeker is patience. It requires patience to understand truth, along with a relentless determination and trust.

Don't we feel inspired by people who are unruffled by circumstances? Such individuals have a sense of being in charge; they radiate an aura of confidence and kindness. Their energy is relaxed, and we feel in the presence of gentleness and grace. Wouldn't you like to be this kind of person? You can be. This type of person did not purchase or borrow patience. That may be the bad news. But the good news is that patience, with many positive benefits, can be acquired and it's never too late to learn how. Make today the day you inspire yourself to look closely at this area of your life.

Patience, tolerance, and understanding are three words that have been ingrained in my heart and mind thanks to Robby, the nurse that gave us such support when our first-born, Jeffrey Peter, came into our lives in November of 1964. We grew to be dear friends. She came to visit and offered help with our other two children as well. For twenty years our friendship grew while she demonstrated patience. She shared her cozy cabin in the foothills of the Sequoias, which we frequently visited. "Nature is such a great teacher of patience," she often said. Nature evolves in a timing that we can't force.

Robbie's own little house on the prairie had no phone, no television, and no newspaper. It exuded simplicity. Clearly, it was the source for many treasured experiences for my family. We had each other and we had nature to enjoy. In fact, these trips became the foundation of a ritual that continued in our family for nineteen years while we were raising our children. Each December holiday season we would spend five or six days at different ski resorts, just enjoying being together as a family. We seemed to be more patient with each other and were able to accept whatever life presented us. Of course, we had our share of squabbles and time outs but I believe life slowed down for us individually, and in that process, we all became more patient.

My husband used to have a rather large and prolific garden. With great tenderness and care, he loved planting those miniscule seeds in their little homes. He'd gently water the invisible seedlings (but not too much) knowing they were in the ground sprouting. He would protect them from wind and weather, while pulling out even the smallest weeds, to provide the seedlings with a better chance to survive. Depending on the time of the year, it might take two to three weeks before he'd see a glimmer of a sprout above the soil. This was the first sign that the seed was alive. "As soon as they started to stick their shoots up above the ground, I had to watch out for the hungry birds. I know they need to eat too, but please not my seedlings," Gene would say.

He used a net for berries and straw or mulch for the vegetable seeds; both allowed warmth and moisture. "You can assist nature but ultimately you must rely on Her for the process. This requires patience. Timing must be right. The ground must be warm enough and soil conditions and temperature must be perfect. I'm eager to see the fruits of my labor but I can't push it. I watch it every day, but those seeds will sprout if and when they do." Gene continued, "It's like magic. Nature provides. You plant one seed and watch it grow into something beautiful. It can provide food or seeds for many years. Working in my garden is my meditation. I feel so connected to everything. Like a seed in the right environment, a child will thrive with love, nurturing, and protection."

If you truly want to learn patience, go to your animal shelter and get yourself a dog. Our dog Max is such a teacher. I say to him, "Max, do you want to go for a walk?" He takes a big stretch, wags his tail, and he's ready. Then, invariably, the phone might ring or a thought may occur to me to make an appointment. I may need a quick potty break myself, and then some water and maybe even a little nibble. And all the time, he sits, waiting patiently and unconditionally loving me. I love it when I'm on the computer and he knocks my hand off the keyboard with his snout, giving me a strong message that it's time to go play. Usually, it's past time for me to take a break. Dog lovers will know exactly what I mean. What phenomenal teachers our four-legged friends are to us!

The next time you feel burdened by impatience, try the following exercise: Feel what it feels like in your body to be impatient. Feel all the body sensations, then experience any beliefs that surface related to the impatience. Feel it, and experience it fully and deeply. Your permission to feel moves these emotions through you so they may release. The alternative is resistance, which traps the emotions in the body cells, keeps it in storage, and provides a foundation for the next associated repressed emotion. Place your intention on the awareness to create a flow rather than a trap. Notice the differences in your body as it begins to shift.

Now see yourself developing a more loving nature toward everything and everyone. The emotional charge has been taken off the feeling; you are again centered and better equipped to approach the situation from a more accurate point of view. With this simple new awareness, you'll start seeing the essence in the person or situation with whom you were so impatient, and you'll relate to them with new eyes.

So, have fun with this aspect of your growth. Remember to be kind and gentle and everything will work out. Trust that your inner butterfly or your inner sprouts are coming into being at just the right pace. So resist not and add some levity instead. Realize that what is so can be greeted with "so what!" Play a game for a day and say "so what" to the challenges that may be potential button pushers. When you say "so what" you may send your little cells spinning at such a high vibration rate that cheerfully, you will make a habit out of this practice.

Reflection Time:

1. Is there something you desperately want to happen? Are you feeling impatient, annoyed, and irritated about it?

2. If so, what are other options? How else could you "hold" this situation? Which way of learning will serve you better?

3. Ask yourself if this is a situation you can, or cannot, do something about. If you can, be assertive and patient rather than aggressive and impatient. In other words, just observe yourself and speak your truth in a respectful manner. You have the right to inquire and gain a sense of clarity about situations. Your approach can be in a manner that is expressed in a positive, rather than forceful way.

4. How would you describe your level of tolerance?

5. What pushes your buttons?

6. What/who are the teachers of patience in your life? In what way are you a teacher of tolerance?

7. How do you care for the garden of your life?

8. Has your family created a ritual that is meaningful to you?

9. Observe an aspect of nature by sitting under a tree and being present—feel what's happening around you.

10. Participate in the ancient Japanese art of flower arranging or the tea ceremony and notice your degree of patience.

"If you could really accept that you weren't ok, you could stop proving you were ok. If you could stop proving that you were ok, you could get that it was ok not to be ok. If you could get that it was ok not to be ok, you could get that you were ok the way you are. You're ok, get it?"

Werner Erhard

I is for feeling... Inadequate

Definition: defective, unworthy, flawed, marred, tainted
Opposite: confident, healthy, self-worth, plenty, enough

Feeling inadequate has to do with "coming up short." Inadequate can never be good enough, smart enough, tall enough, talented enough, on time enough, etc. Inadequate is about "doing" rather than "being." One's worth is based on what they can or cannot do, rather than who they are.

I've had many clients who were raised to believe that they're not good enough, or they'll never amount to anything. If you have ever felt this way, you have a lot of company! They could still hear the words of a parent saying, "Who do you think you are that you can do _____?" The beliefs start at a very early age, even before their second birthday. Here is a partial list of 'inadequate' beliefs:

- I am valuable only when others are dependent on me.
- It's always my fault.
- I'd better be perfect in order to earn love.
- I have nothing to give.
- If they need me, I can believe they love me.
- I'll never be able to keep up.
- I don't trust myself or feel capable to be responsible for my life.
- Other's needs are more important than mine are.

The "Perfect" Myth

We're raised in a society that puts strong emphasis on image. We get messages through the media all the time on this concept of "perfection." With so much emphasis on how our bodies look, no wonder we feel inadequate when we don't fit in those old blue jeans! But did you know

171

there are three billion women who don't look like supermodels and only about fifty who do? Most women wear a size twelve through fourteen. Did you know that one out of four college-aged women has an eating disorder? A 1995 psychological study found that three minutes spent looking at a fashion magazine caused 70% of women to feel depressed, guilty, and shameful. If we're not a perfect size six or don't have washboard abdominals, we're just not quite enough. This overflows to our possessions. We'll never have enough. By a certain time in life, we're expected to have acquired some status. We have to have more to feed these inadequate feelings.

All these feelings of inadequacy create a spiral of energy that goes downward. I had a client who had believed she was defective. She believed something was wrong with her, that she didn't have the right material to function in the world. As a result, she drew that type of person to her. She projected this belief to the world, and consequently, she was never able to make friends that were loyal, caring, and lasting.

Violence—a Self-fulfilling Prophecy

Children who grow to adulthood with the belief that they're inadequate can turn to acts of violence as a form of self-expression. Out of their repressed anger, resentment can burst forth as attacks. Unrecognized sadness and pain can turn to domestic violence, which is also linked to juvenile crime, alcoholism, and drug abuse. In addition to self-abuse, 75% of the men who abuse their wives also abuse their children. Bureau of Justice Statistics reveal that being abused and neglected as a child increases the likelihood of juvenile arrest by 59%, of adult arrest by 28%, and for a violent crime by 30%. Each year in our culture 3.5 million children who experience violence in the home go on to perpetuate violence outside the home. It's epidemic. When does this subject become a priority in our society? To what proportion must it climb? Look into the childhood of the offenders and you will find the core issue, I guarantee it.

As I read more about Andrea Kennedy, I came to learn it was and no doubt still is, a "core belief" that put her in prison today. The destructive belief that her children would be better off without her played itself out that horrendous day when she drowned her children in the bathtub. She was so low, so desperate, so depressed, that she truly believed this! Her story is a dreadful one and an example of how sabotaging and damaging our beliefs can be, unless we explore and evaluate them.

Parents, are you aware of the impact your words have on your child's life? If a child received two negative messages a day, from the time she is one-year-old to five, she will have heard 3,650 negative messages by the time she starts school! What baggage she has in her backpack! Every time you say, "You're stupid," or "You can't do anything right," you must know that those are the words that can set the stage for a dark future. "You're such a loser." Those words wound, often permanently. They can destroy a child's self-esteem. Your child's actions will reflect the belief created by those words like a self-fulfilling prophecy. Negative messages destroy children's dreams and fantasies. Rather than giving them discouraging words, honor their ideas and support their goals. Give them positive messages that will lead to confidence and a healthy self-esteem. Children need supporting words like:

- "I'm so proud of you."
- "You are such a light in my life."
- "I love your uniqueness."
- "You have choices."

My Beliefs or Yours?

When I was eighteen, I recall wanting to go to New York City to make a career in the theatre. After my experience of being in our high school performance of *Oklahoma*, I wanted to catch the next bus to New York City and pursue this dream. Along with the song and dance, I loved the excitement. I was quickly discouraged when my parents told me I had to know somebody to get ahead in that line of work. I believed it, so instead, I moved to Cleveland to work in a hospital. Borrrrrring (for me anyway). Years afterwards, I laugh at how my parents knew that I wouldn't make it unless I KNEW somebody. It was THEIR belief. My folks were simple, hard-working parents that provided me with a terrific childhood growing up on the shores of Lake Erie. They had no experience in show business. What did they know about it? Nothing. Yet, they did their best and responded to my desires from their limited knowledge. They truly did their best. But, see how influential parents can be? I believed them. I don't have regrets that I didn't follow through with my theatrical dream, nor have I made them wrong for their input. I know things work out perfectly, and if I were meant to take that journey, I would have. If my passion were strong enough, I would have gone, regardless. Their words had an impact on me.

If you're a parent or teacher, can you step back and listen to what words come out of your mouth while speaking to a child? Listen to yourself. How does it sound? Would you like to hear those words yourself? Let's say you spoke more than a few negative statements to your child, and you realized it a day or so later. It's NEVER too late to clean it up. Be real and say the words that so many find difficult to say–"I'm sorry." Your child will respect you for it, and you will be elevated as a role model.

Keep in mind that any mean behavior, such as physical, mental, or verbal abuse between parents will leave an indelible mark. So stop it. Get help now. If you can't raise a child responsibly, find them a parent who can and will. It is too easy to conceive a child, but it certainly takes skills to raise a child. So get the proper training, and be the parent you want to be. It takes education and practice, just like learning the computer, the piano, driving a car, playing a sport. Respect the job of being a parent. It's the most important job there is.

A client of mine described her experience of NPR, after attending the transpersonal counseling class I teach at Boise State University. Her words follow.

"In transpersonal class, I identified a deep emotional issue; I felt my mother never wanted me. Dr. Delis-Abrams tested me with kinesiology to confirm my feelings of unwantedness. She confirmed that my deep emotional issue stemmed from my conception, by having me hold my arm out to one side and pressing on my arm. My arm did not fall when she pressed on it, but remained firm, indicating that yes, I was holding onto the belief. Somewhere in my body, I felt unwanted. She guided me: 'Really hate the pain, the hurt, the unwantedness; now really love the hurt, the pain, the unwantedness.' As she spoke, I cried, and every ounce of my body became consumed by the feelings I had been carrying around since I was a child. The experience was very powerful. I loved and hated the emotions of hurt and pain until I felt them no more. At the end of the session, to the sound of her voice and cue, I opened my eyes. I felt a tremendous release of tension. I felt better. For the next few days, I noticed that my entire life was different."

We are now being exposed to research on the infant brain and how it absorbs. The myth that babies do not really feel or care is exactly that, a myth. From The Mind of Your Newborn Baby, author Dr. David Chamberlain writes, "I have been repeatedly confronted with the hidden wounds left by hostile words, outbursts of emotion, or worrisome questions raised at birth. These psychological 'birthmarks' can and should be avoided. Creative therapies are needed to deal with these birth-created problems." He continues, "What we find in birth memories is consistent with what is found in modern research: the newborn brain, nervous system, and physical senses are active and coordinated; a normal range of human emotions is felt and expressed while the infant mind is alert, perceptive, exploring, and busy incorporating each new experience.

From *The Wise Child*, Sonia Choquette says, "We come into this world hard-wired with a sixth sense, but children will refer to their parents to have them verify it or dismiss it. Kids are completely clear, and they learn to shut down only if they are subtly conditioned." Remarkable words to ponder on.

Maria Montessori knew this back in the forties. In her book, *The Absorbent Mind*, she states, "By the age of three, the child has already laid down the foundation of his personality as a human being." Also, "Education is not acquired by listening to words, but in virtue of experiences in which the child acts on his environment." Montessori believed that motivation came from within by a natural curiosity and love for knowledge where the impetus for learning went far beyond the classroom. When periods of disruptive behavior occur, it is because the child is trying to tell us that some great need of his is not being met. The reaction is often violent because he is literally fighting for his life.

I say, give him the vocabulary of feelings, so he can express himself. It will satisfy his frustration and dissolve his anxiety. Have you ever visited a foreign country and felt frustrated because you could not express your needs and were unable to speak the language? Well, that's how a child feels. Learn a new feeling word every day. It can be a fun and valuable game.

As you learn to recognize your feelings, through your awareness, and the art of communication, you will start to replace negative statements...

- "I'm not smart enough to manifest my dreams and live a happy life."
- "Others always seem to get the lucky break – never me."
- "I'm not good enough to deserve a beautiful relationship"
- "I don't deserve to have abundance in any area of my life."
- "I'm so stupid."

...*with positive and supportive ones such as:*

- "I can do anything if I set my mind to it.
- "Each twenty-four hours, I exercise my free will, choose my thoughts, words, and action. What power!"
- "Life is a grand adventure that I get to create."
- "I have communication skills that work!"

Keep in mind that feeling inadequate is only based on appearance. There's the power of the ego again, taking charge and bringing forth ideas that aren't true. They're all ideas, perceptions, and beliefs—what we have heard, or how we've been raised. We each have our own inadequacies, and that's what makes us human.

Just the Way You Are

An email I received is a good story of accepting our flaws:

An elderly peasant in China had two pots each hung at the ends of a pole which he carried across his neck. One of the pots had a crack in it while the other was perfect. At the end of the long walk from the stream to the house, the cracked pot arrived half-full, while the intact pot delivered its full volume of water. For two years this went on daily.

Of course, the perfect pot was proud of achieving its full potential, but the poor cracked pot was ashamed of its imperfection, and miserable that it was able to accomplish only half of what it had been made to do. After two years of abject failure, it spoke to the water-bearer one day by the stream. "I am ashamed of myself, because this crack in my side causes me to leak all the way back to your house."

The bearer said to the pot, "Did you notice that there are flowers on your side of the path, but not on the other pot's side? That's because I have always known about your flaw, so I planted flower seeds beside your side of the path, and every day while we walk back, you water them. For two years I have been able to pick those beautiful flowers to decorate the table. Without you just the way you are, there would not be this beauty to grace the house."

Brief Loss of Mother Tongue

Fear often prevents us from being just the way we are. It has a powerful effect on our psyche, as well as our mother tongue, as evidenced by the following comments from a Swiss client.

"Your assisted healing practice has been very beneficial and life changing for me. In just one visit, I experienced magical results in regaining my expression (voice) that I briefly lost, due to fear. I felt very inadequate to be stumbling in my own mother tongue. You cured me from this short but most debilitating experience. The very next day, I could not stop talking in my own Swiss language. I felt like fresh energy released back into my body, while a flash of newly-found expressions permeated my being. Only with your securely guided support, did this healing in my life happen. Thank you, Alexandra, for being in my life. Your enthusiasm towards life is infectious, very attractive and very powerful."

We are all very powerful and we are all human and sometimes forget our magnificence. Every human being has flaws and inadequacies. Look past them and focus on the good in everyone. Notice how interesting and unique we all are. Without flaws, what a boring place it would be! Your beliefs and perceptions mean everything.

Reflection Time:

1. Do you know anybody who feels inadequate in his or her life?
2. What could you do to offer support to that person to see a new reality or to see her/him self in a whole new way?
3. How would you measure your self-esteem on a scale of one to ten (low to high)?
4. Do you remember hearing negative childhood messages that need to be transformed? From whom? How frequently?
5. When are the times you feel inadequate? Or maybe it's the foundation your life has been built on. If so, when did it start?
6. What would it take for you to shift your perception from inadequate to confident, or powerless to empowered?
7. For fun, punctuate the following sentence: Woman without her man is nothing.
8. Make a list of your self-perceived inadequacies.
9. Now make another of areas where you feel adequate. Which list was easier?
10. If you have an animal does he/she view you as inadequate?

"Imagination is the beginning of creation. You imagine what you desire; you will what you imagine; and at last you create what you will."
George Bernard Shaw

I is for feeling... Inspired

Definition: motivated, illuminated, enliven, incentive
Opposite: bored, ambivalent, ho-hum, nonchalant

To feel inspired is to be psyched and recharged, to burst with new vigor and enthusiasm. When I am inspired, I feel in the flow and ready to charge ahead, through any obstacles that may arise. It's a bit comical, but sometimes when I speak in front of an audience about motivation and potential, I actually find myself being inspired by the words coming through me! I've learned these are "heart-words," when my mind meets my heart through my voice; I am inspired, so that I can best inspire others!

Inspiration feels like a gift from the Universe. In fact, "to inspire" literally means "to breathe into." Imagine inspiration as the Divine breathing into you, giving you the energy to create. I know that nothing can stop me when I'm in the flow and feel inspired to pursue my vision.

When I think of inspiration, I think of our second-born son, Christopher. In his mid-twenties, he had no clue of what he wanted to do, study, or pursue for a career. Christopher was feeling stuck in his life. One day he took a private plane ride to Baja, California. When he came back he said, "I want to take flying lessons." Well, he took those lessons, thanks to his loving and generous grandparents, and became a certified flight instructor. He went on to work with a charter company. He is currently a captain and flies a jet plane, called the Challenger, to all the romantic and not-so-romantic locations on planet Earth. That's how to use inspiration to one's advantage.

One time, Christopher had come into town for a family wedding. After a morning walk on the beach, we stopped at a local beachside restaurant for breakfast. While we waited for our table, my attention was drawn to the seagulls, foraging for food. One adult male bird in particular triggered the memorable message of the book, *Jonathan Livingston Seagull*, by Richard Bach. This bird stood in the cool morning fog, preening himself. I began to fantasize him as Jonathan, eager to share what he had just accomplished in flight. In the book, Jonathan is a seagull. He says, after

178

mastering flight, "How much more there is now to living! There's a reason to life. We can lift ourselves out of ignorance, we can find ourselves as creatures of excellence and intelligence and skill. We can be free! We can learn to fly!" However, his enthusiasm was quickly squelched as he was called to Center by the Council and accused of being irresponsible in soaring like an eagle. Instead of being honored, he was shamed and banned from the flock. "Who is more responsible than a gull who finds and follows a meaning, a higher purpose for life?" Jonathan retorted.

In the midst of inwardly cheering him on, the hostess jarred my fantasy by calling our name for the breakfast reservation. As we brushed the sand from our shoes to go in and indulge ourselves, I thanked the gull for this early morning insight. He reminded me of the Jonathan that lives in each of us and is capable of breaking free of limited thinking. This inspiring story is a classic available to all generations. I get excited about the thought of reading it to Alissa, Corianna, and other future grandchildren one day. Thank you, Richard Bach.

By the way, did you know all airplanes have attitudes? Indicators, that is. Christopher explained this concept to me. There are three for safety in the Challenger, the jet he flies. Each back up for the others—that's how important they are. The Attitude Indicator shows the aircraft's position in relation to the Earth's horizon. What a perfect metaphor on how attitude affects our path in life! What if people had an attitude indicator? Guess what? We do! It's our feelings!

Where to Find Inspiration

Sources of inspiration are everywhere! After all, everything is a product of the Creator. Inspiration strikes the core of my being. Sometimes it's like a "kick in the butt," while other times, it creeps up on me, moving me to tears. People, movies, places, smells, sounds, animals, art, even words can inspire me.

Nature in particular gives me those feelings of inspiration. Did you realize that hummingbirds weigh three and 4/10ths grams, their heart rate is 1260 beats per minute, and their wing beat is eighty per second? They have to consume more than twice their body weight of nectar per day to keep up with their metabolic rate. On a 'larger' note, I gaze in awe at the Sawtooth Mountain Range, especially when the first rays of sunshine appear on those jagged peaks. And when that moon radiates its brilliance on the snow-covered mountains, what a majestic experience!

The evolution of the salmon is amazingly inspiring. Our son Jeff, who was employed by the Idaho Fish & Game for ten years with salmon restoration, educated me about the salmon. For starters, the embryo does not eat. It lives on energy stored in the egg's droplets of orange oil. Each salmon embryo survives the winter months then develops into a miniature fish. From each egg, the embryos have everything they need to begin development with the spring thaw.

Music is also a particular source of inspiration to me. The late John Denver is one artist whose life and music continues to move me. His words from a National Public Television special are inspiring. "I want to be remembered as somebody who stood up for what I believed in and worked for. I sang it and wrote about it." In 1994, when John was dropped by RCA, he was devastated. He had lost his father, and his marriage had recently ended. His career plummeted. On October 12, 1997, John's plane crashed into the ocean. This is the sixth year since his passing. In this television special his family members were interviewed and spoke of his painful struggle. As I see it, he held strong to his identity as a celebrity, and when his career and life began going a different direction, he spiraled downward.

John touched so many lives, including our son Christopher. After our family saw him in concert in 1984, the next day Christopher, a teenager at the time, went to the beach and wrote the following poem:

"A Breath of Peace"
There would be no sadness and the fighting would have to cease.
We could see true happiness with a little breath of peace.
We can see this peace in nature, we can see this peace in love,
So why can't we believe it was intended from above?
The world is full of hate, full of fear and full of change,
With a little breath of peace, total happiness is in range.
It is an easy concept to grasp inside the mind,
So why are there problems in achieving the ties that bind?
Everything we need is right inside our souls.
But without this breath of peace, we will return into our holes.
Christopher Scott Abrams, May 20, 1984

The words in John's music are so meaningful and provide deep lessons. "As the river runs freely, the mountain doth rise. Let me touch with my fingers and see with my eyes. In the hearts of the children, a pure love still grows. Like the bright star in heaven that lights our way home. Like the flower that shatters the stone." The music that he felt so deeply, which conveyed his inner turmoil, and his extraordinary joys and profound love of nature is left as an everlasting gift to music lovers.

What about the "classics," Mozart, Brahms, Wagner, Hayden, and Beethoven to name a few? As a child, Beethoven's father, a musician and heavy drinker, would sometimes wake little Beethoven in the middle of the night to practice piano, cold, tired, with tears streaming down his cheeks. As Beethoven got older, his hearing began to leave him. He sawed off the legs to his piano, so he could feel the vibration of the music through the floor. Beethoven was prone to extreme mood swings, sometimes to the point of violence and weeping. He was miserable, mostly lonely, and stubborn. Even in the face of royalty, he refused to play at times. Some referred to him as mad. "I'm bad at everything except music," he was known to have said. Here's this amazing, brilliant, creative being who struggled so intensely in his life! Yet there was a part of him that produced these beautiful compositions! The message Beethoven's life offers is: there's a deeper part of each of us that can express and create beauty and magic and brilliance despite the circumstances.

Shanti Rahim was a mere nine years of age when she created Imagine Peace coloring books to sell for donations to the Afghan refugees. She has helped children in the world who need help. Shanti's grandmother had visited Pakistan and told her about the starving and homeless children begging in the streets. The stories moved Shanti to draw peace-theme pictures. The books are being sold for five dollars each and Nokia has agreed to match 50% of the total funds raised. (See Peace Pilgrim reference)

Christopher Reeve is the epitome of inspiration. His identity as "Superman" is remembered by some, but the contribution he has made to the physically challenged, will be remembered by many for years to come. Christopher became paralyzed in a horseback riding accident, and works continuously to bring awareness around the globe about spinal cord injuries. He lectures to raise funds for research.

I heard the story about Dana, his wife, who had made plans for a handicap ramp to be built in front of their home. He questioned why, saying it looked like a handicapped person lived there. She replied, "A handicapped person does live here." After a time of resistance and denial, it is apparent he chose to adopt a different attitude. "Out of something tragic, I can forge a new beginning." He suggests we set goals we don't think we can achieve. "We've conquered outer space, now we need to conquer inner space." What wise words! One night I saw him and his wife on 48 Hours. Dana said in the mornings after his accident, she would cry and cry, acknowledging her feelings and releasing them to go forward. What a difference this family is making to the planet!

Aloha Inspiration

I met a native Hawaiian who learned the ancient art of Lomilomi from his grandmother beginning at six years old. Lomilomi, a way of life, is an ancient Hawaiian massage form practiced for centuries. The technique reaches to the soul level to enhance healing on a physical, mental, emotional, and spiritual level. The concept of ho'oponopono, making things right through forgiveness, is part of Lomilomi. Forgiveness is the ultimate goal of ho'oponopono.

When my session with him was finished, my body was like a rubber band, loose like a baby's. He told me that knots in the body represent anger and jealousy. They form walls around the heart and it has to work harder. When those knots are dissolved you become the baby you were born as—the real you. He greets the day with gratitude in the words, "Another day in the park."

This beautiful being plays in life and is one of the most jolly and loving souls on the planet. He is kind, gentle, pure, and so inspiring; what an remarkable gift to the world.

Survival and Contributions

Here's a spectacular story of survival that I heard on almost every news station. A climber from Grand Junction, Colorado, Aaron Ralston, age twenty-seven, was pinned by a 1000-pound boulder on May 2, 2003. Choosing not to give up, he amputated his own arm with a pocketknife to free himself! He then walked out of the Canyonlands National Park after six days of being there. Wow!

We look for inspiration as well as security in our outer world. Victor Frankl said, "Once we realize that all sense of security is an illusion, then we can give up the fruitless effort of trying to pin down safe props or people. Instead, we can look inside for our security and develop ways to foster that strength." The late Victor Frankl, noted existential psychiatrist and author of *Man's Search for Meaning*, developed an approach to psychotherapy, with a core theory that man's primary motivational force is his search for meaning. "There is nothing in the world, I venture to say, that would so effectively help one to survive even the worse conditions, as the knowledge that there is meaning in one's life." This is a man who transformed years of suffering in Nazi concentration caps into insights for his life-long study of man's quest for meaning. His life was definitely an inspiration and his philosophies continue to bring enlightenment to many.

Mahatma Gandhi's attitude of non-violence began with the consideration of, "If I do this, what will be the result?" His life taught cause and effect—the laws of the universe. We are not merely puppets of destiny; we have free will and the power of choice.

Sir John Templeton is a philanthropist and humanitarian who inspired many. I learned about him and his foundation at a Character Education Partnership conference. In a video of his life, presented to the group, he said, "If I hadn't sought new paths, I would have been unable to attain so many goals." Templeton gives away over forty million dollars a year to education and charity. He began a career on Wall Street in 1937, and created the world's largest and most successful international investment funds. At ninety years young, he says, "I've got things to do. An attitude of gratitude creates blessings. Help yourself by helping others. You have the most powerful weapons on Earth – love and prayer."

Only Love Prevails – Pass It On

Despite all the examples in the world that can spark inspiration, we can also lose that inspiration, can't we? When we don't see our progress as anticipated, momentum can fade and spirits can sink. Inspiration can also dissipate when we step out of the flow and fail to stay in touch with our inner self. We can lose our focus and concentration and become deterred from our goal.

When this happens, we have to rekindle our inspiration. If that outer trigger isn't there, we can look inward for it. Yes, we each can be the source of our own inspiration. In fact, because the Source is within us, it is truly where inspiration comes from anyway. Others may look at a moonlit mountain range and think nothing of it, being absorbed in their own worlds and thoughts. In order to be inspired, we must let ourselves be inspired. It takes a sort of surrender to that which is greater than us.

It helps to surround ourselves with friends who support our dreams. I received an inspiring email that said, "Only Love Prevails – pass it on." This simple message remains on the side of my computer screen to this day. After sending it to several friends, I received a reply, "Let's remind each other of this, when we forget."

My family inspires me. At this printing we four girls have an accumulation of 170 years of marriage going for us. With twelve years difference between the eldest and youngest girl, our parents raised us quite differently, as you can imagine. They did their best, and they did well. We all feel blessed with productive and happy (most of the time anyhow) children and grandkids. We speak the truth and respect each other. For the most part, everyone gets along quite well. When we do have differences, we confront them with as much honesty and integrity as we can muster, and things get resolved. That's inspiring.

My sister Alekie, in particular, had cancer. She feels the support she received from family, friends, and the medical team pulled her through her ordeal. Some of that support included: phone calls of inquiry, rides to scheduled appointments, lovingly prepared meals from neighbors' kitchens, flowers, humorous cards, etc. They each contributed to her restored health and her exceptional attitude, which continues to this day to inspire us all.

Alekie now visits cancer patients in and out of hospitals. Her degree in medical social work is not the only education she brings to these visits; she brings true-life experience. With her delightful sense of humor, she helps to lighten up the heavy hearts to those bedridden. A rewarding and challenging chapter in her book of life, Alekie is an inspiring role model for all of her family and friends. The following are her own words about her challenge:

"Every July 4th the nation celebrates with fireworks. In July 1996, I experienced personal fireworks. I received a phone call reporting that my uterine biopsy revealed cancer. Only one month prior to this unsettling news, I inadvertently discovered a small light pink vaginal stain. Pink – a color used as a special hue on an artist's canvas and my favorite color. Little did I know that it would so strongly accent my life, in this adverse way! Life is full of choices. I chose to listen to my body and sought medical attention. I needed to be in tune with my body for the message it was sending. How well do we listen to our bodies? We marvel when we hear Mozart's 'Clarinet Concerto.' We hear our Ford Explorer telling us that it's time for a tune up. Why is it then that we turn a deaf ear to our bodies when they cry out to us? Many thoughts raced through my mind when I was told the treatment would be a complete hysterectomy. Now that my three children, my generous gifts from God, were all gone from home, and this new situation had occurred in my life, what a fascinating irony! Now that my child-bearing years were over, my uterus would develop cancer. Perhaps I was being told to also seek a change and new directions for my life. Following surgery, my treatment was radiation. Then came chemotherapy. Yes, I did lose my hair, in clumps, and purchased a wig from a caring beautician who shaved the last remaining strands. I had fun with my new 'do' even wearing it backwards, at home, looking like one of The Beatles! A dear friend told me that she thought my wig looked better than my real hair. (Only a very good friend could say that and still be a friend!)"

"No, I did not 'toss my cookies,' for as I walked down the long hall for my first chemotherapy treatment, my heart held the loving words of a very close friend, 'Chemotherapy will be your best friend.' And it was, because it gave me that extra level of assurance that I would rid my body of this cancer. I experienced disbelief, fear, anger, and 'why me,' but slowly turned a new page in this mystery I was having, as I knew a healthier attitude would aid in healing my body and that one day, I would be 'me' again...and I am! With a very loving husband, my compassionate children, unending prayers and support from family and friends, along with excellent medical care, the year passed rapidly. I now have a greater respect for the fragility of life and realize how quickly one's world can be temporarily shattered. Life does get off course, sometimes, but we need to remember that 'We cannot direct the wind, but we can adjust our sails.'"

Adjusting your sails also takes courage, but with introspection, supportive people in your life, knowing your strengths, living one day at a time, and anchoring that which is real, there isn't anything you can't do. Bravo Alekie!

Reflection Time:
1. What do you really love to do?
2. Do you spend time with people who inspire you?
3. Who or what inspires you?
4. Do you ever feel inspired with yourself? If so, write a paragraph about it. If not, why not? Give your inner critic a nap.
5. Finish the sentence: When I lose my inspiration I _____.
6. What is your definition of inspiration?
7. Where do you experience that it comes from?
8. What about the members of your immediate family is inspiring?
9. How about good friends? Do they know you feel this way about them?
10. Where or how do you express your inspiration?

"We are chemists in the laboratory of the Infinite. What then shall we produce?"

Ernest Holmes, Founder, Science of Mind

J is for feeling... Jealous

Definition: envious, resentful, grudging, suspicious
Opposite: trusting, faithful, satisfied, content

To feel jealous means to want something that you don't have. We could be jealous of the model's perfect figure, of a friend's loving husband, of a stranger's dream job. Whatever sparks the feelings of jealousy, it comes from a notion of "They have it and I don't! It's not fair!"

Feeling jealous spurs the feeling of resentment. It also triggers anger and frustration. "I want what you have, but I can't have it." "I wish I had a loving relationship." "I wish I could have a new car." "Why can't I travel as much as they do?" Do you hear a little self-pity in there? Poor me! It's the ego at work. Like all feelings, jealous is energy. It's okay to feel it, but be sure to express it and move through it. In this way, we can unlock the deep-rooted beliefs that cause the feelings of discontent, so jealousy can be dissolved for good.

I know someone who could be described as having a "jealousy identity." She rarely thinks of the silver lining. In tracking this energy, it is apparent the origination stems from low self-esteem, not feeling good enough to deserve that new coat, a paid vacation, or the ideal job. This woman always seems to feel left out and perceives life through the eyes of a victim.

We can embrace victim energy when exploring the idea of "sibling rivalry." This common expression can become a battle of wills, a struggle to compete through one's life. I believe we choose our siblings, just as we did our parents, and invited them to share our adventure in this lifetime. They perform their part in your movie. Don't be concerned if this idea seems foreign to you. No doubt you have a lot of company. I invite you to pretend to believe it for a few days and notice if your perception shifts in any way. Allow memories to surface with regard to your feelings towards your siblings.

Intention to Create

A young couple I know took two-and-a-half months and traveled around the world. Another woman who lives in Hawaii rented her home out and traveled an entire year! When she told me about it, you know what? I experienced a little bit of jealousy. "Wow! She's going to travel to all of those different cultures and countries and meet so many people! I'd like to be doing that!" My friend made this trip a priority. She focused her attention, and intention, on taking this trip. As I focus my attention on what it is that I want, I achieve results too! Let's remember this wisdom; "You know your intention by what shows up in your reality."

Dr. Deepak Chopra, author and motivational speaker, has made such an important contribution to many individuals' lives and consequently to the world. I respect him tremendously. He suggests "...you can use your intention to create your destiny." Some of the mechanics of setting intentions are to sit quietly and relax your body until you feel calm inside. Think of the outcome you want. Be specific and definite. Express it to yourself. Dr. Chopra says, "Whenever a word is backed up by intention, it enters the field of awareness as a message or a request." The universe is being put on notice that you have a certain desire. Read any of his thought-provoking books, take action, and watch yourself grow. As soon as we make choices about things, something moves inside of us. We can be still, collect ourselves, and choose. Confusion is caused by "sitting on the fence." If we hang on to the "I wish I had what they have" attitude, our self-pity will limit and paralyze us.

A perpetual obsession with the feeling of jealousy can make for dysfunction in your life. When any of the negative emotions persist too long the body will react to it. Thanks to email I received this incredible Cherokee story that was told to a grandson by a grandfather. "A fight is going on inside me", he said to the boy. "It is a terrible fight between two wolves. One is evil – he is anger, envy, sorrow, regret, greed, arrogance, self-pity, guilt, resentment, inferiority, lies, false pride, superiority, and ego. The other one is good – he is joy, peace, love, hope, serenity, humility, kindness, benevolence, empathy, generosity, truth, compassion, and faith. This same fight is going on inside you and inside every other person, too." The grandson asked, "Which wolf will win?" The wise Cherokee simply replied, "The one you feed."

Which wolf are YOU feeding? Do you experience more envy, resentment, and self-pity in your life? Or do you have joy, serenity, and compassion?

It's Not Fair!

To be envious of something or someone is also to be spiteful and show malice. We're getting into some serious energy here when we realize that these feelings encompass hostility, bitterness, hatred, animosity, and malice. Not a pretty package, and one that can cause serious complications in many areas of your life, IF not addressed directly.

Take the following scenarios, for instance:

- You didn't get the promotion you felt was your due.
- Another student won the essay contest and you just knew your submission was an absolute winner.
- The neighbors are adding onto their home, and you cringe every day you see it getting closer to completion. Meanwhile, you're dodging the stuff falling out from your closets, and the kids' toys continually offer an opportunity for practicing the hurdles.
- You find out your best friend has been having an affair with your husband, or your wife.
- All your girlfriends have bigger breasts than you do.

Can you relate to any of these examples? Sure, jealousy arises, but it doesn't have to consume us. Believe me, it will consume us if we don't acknowledge it and ask, "Where does this come from?" Am I feeling inferior, inadequate, undeserving, greedy? What's behind these feelings?

The central thread in our society today appears to be anxiety, fear, insecurity, retaliation, and depression. There's no doubt we all feel anxiety in our lives from time to time, but when it overshadows our lives, we become challenged. We even have a name for it now, anxiety disorder. This affliction is an anxiety that persists to the point that it interferes with one's daily life. It is the most common mental illness in America today, affecting nineteen million people. The range is wide and includes specific phobias, panic, obsessive-compulsive behavior, post-traumatic stress, and general anxiety. Many people turn to medications to dull the pain with a false belief that a pill will relieve the problem. Others seek professional therapy. Only a small percentage of individuals choose to change their routine of thinking, diet, and exercise. Remember this wisdom; we can't change behavior until we change beliefs.

Resentment, fear, irritation, sadness, and anxiety are emotions that are associated with feeling long-term jealousy. Long-term is when it becomes obsessive and pathological and is difficult to change.

The ego knows these feelings, not the soul. We must plant the seeds of truth in our children during the formative years, and as adults, make it a priority to embrace these feelings within ourselves, viewing them as wake-up calls, awaiting transformation. When we take one hundred percent responsibility for our feelings, we not only create more aliveness and happiness in our lives, but we also leave behind a legacy for all the children of the world.

I knew a young man who had a goal of retiring by the time he was forty. By wise planning and intention, he reached his goal. Some were jealous of his independence and freedom to travel. Others recognized his lifestyle as inspiring. I wonder how he accomplished that dream. What do I have to do to achieve a goal like that? When I spoke to this man, he said the first requirement is intention; close behind is focus, determination, and a positive mind set. Do you know of anyone with these aspirations? Talk to him/her and get the scoop on the game plan.

We may know someone who has an enviable relationship. In lieu of feeling jealous, we could respect what that person has created in his/her life, honor it, and learn from it. Say to yourself, "I'm ready for a loving relationship. What do I need to learn about myself to have a deep love in my life?"

Dreams do come true. We can have anything we want in this world. The universe is abundant! Jealousy and feelings of resentment are futile and can actually stop our dreams from coming true! Is it really worth it? Wouldn't you rather put your energy into creating your own dream life rather than coveting someone else's? If someone else is doing it, achieving it, owning it, being it, living it, then you can too. They are living proof. There is enough success for everyone. Shift perception, and shift your life.

Reflection Time:

1. Are there people in your life that push your jealous buttons?

2. Is it something they have, or something they do that you would like to have or do?

3. What is the earliest memory you have of feeling jealous? What is the next one? The next? Does this look like a pattern?

4. Are you anxious about something?

5. Make a list of your worries and a list of what you want. Ask yourself if you really want that. Make a third column to determine how you are going to achieve it, by when, and through what means. Take charge of your life.

6. Were there sibling rivalries in your family? Was it discussed? Have you overcome it? If so, through what course of action?

7. Do you harbor jealousy with a particular sibling? If yes, explore it.

8. Are you genuinely happy for people who achieve their goals? If not, you have work to do.

9. If you knew you could free yourself from the anchor that jealousy creates in your life, what would you do?

10. Stand in front of a mirror and close your eyes while you feel jealous of someone who has something you want. Feel it big time for a full minute or more. Now open your eyes and look at your image.

"The path of joy involves valuing yourself and monitoring where you put your time."

Sanaya Roman, *Living With Joy*

J is for feeling... Joyful

Definition: jolly, happy, jovial, merry, elated, delighted

Opposition: melancholy, despondent, dispirited, depressed

To feel joyful in your heart is to experience feeling really good all over. Sometimes joy comes from knowing our own purpose, doing our life's work, or knowing we're in alignment. Maybe we feel joyful because our personality and soul are aligned. When we're on target, we move forward. Sometimes we feel joyful because we're creating our dreams and they're coming true! We might even feel joyful regardless of the circumstances in our life. Our joy might come through just because we are busy being in the moment, being who we really are. Joy signals when we are onto something!

Just Open Yourself

Open yourself to life and be in touch with your birthright—love, wisdom, beauty, and abundance. Maybe our body isn't the way we'd like it to be. Maybe we don't have all the money we want. Maybe we don't have the perfect relationship or the perfect life career. We can still experience a state of joy, while we make the necessary adjustments. Joy reveals the essence of who we are. When we're in touch with that wisdom and we live our life out of that knowingness, everything is affected positively. "What we think, our positive emotions like love, hope, joy, faith, purpose, determination, festivity, and will to live, all have physiological significance," said the late Norman Cousins.

I could list so many things that bring me joy! Children are one of my greatest sources of joy. Some of you may recall Art Linkletter and his conversations with kids. Don't kids just have the best 'off the wall' comments? More good email data came to me about kids. When asked what the proper age is to get married, an eight-year-old responded with, "Eighty-four, because at that age, you don't have to work anymore and you can spend all your time loving each other in your bedroom." A five-year-old boy had a different take on the question. "Once I'm done with kindergarten, I'm going to find me a wife." Children and puppies–they're the best.

I love the four seasons! I feel joyful with each one of them: the mystery of the autumn leaves falling; the beauty, stillness, and serenity of the snow in winter; the astonishing color and blooms of spring, and the fun and joy that summer celebrations bring, such as outdoor symphonies and picnics, and hiking and water rafting. My inner child loves to play and be joyful during all the seasons.

I love the magic and freshness of spring; it seems to epitomize joy with its bursting growth. One day I can look at barren earth and the next day I see the plant known as Bleeding Heart come to life! The branches form more day by day, and then, under the branches, in perfect placement, appear beautiful little pink and red heart blossoms. Each of the hearts hang so gently and precisely from the branch, growing more fully every day. It's magical! I feel joyful inside when I watch these changes.

People Spreading Joy

There are many people out there pushing the "concept" of joy and bringing it into the mainstream. Dr. Patch Adams is one of those people. In 1972, he created The Gesundheit Institute as a creative response to the lack of joy in the healthcare industry. Costs were spiraling, caregivers were discouraged, and patients felt alienated. The purpose of The Gesundheit Institute is to "bring fun, friendship, and the joy of service back into health care!" Although not yet a physical manifestation, the Institute is proposing workshops like the one called, 'The House Calls Project.' Their Autumn, 2002 newsletter refers to this project as a mainstay of the Gesundheit philosophy, which offers new ways to generate clowning and caring service across the continent, leaving the participant with tools to sustain play, teamwork, and service right where they work.

From puns to peace, we all have our ways of improving life. Jan and Randolph Price started the first world peace meditation on New Year's Eve, where at midnight Greenwich time, people worldwide gather at certain locations or stay in their own homes to meditate on global peace. The Price's spoke one year at our Sun Valley Mountain Wellness Festival. Jan shared her experience about her NDE (near death experience). The last words she heard before she came back into her body were, "The purpose of life is JOY!" Even if you don't believe in NDE's, why not adopt that belief and discover any changes that might await? Try it!

192

The Healing Power of Joy

My dissertation was entitled, "Laughter, Enthusiasm, and Joy as Healing Modalities." I had such fun with this topic. One of the peak experiences was the interview with the late Norman Cousins in his UCLA office. What an honor to be with this gentleman. Some of our interview included the following comments:

- We don't understand health and sickness.
- We fear and expect the worst, and the worst occurs.
- Pain is the body's way of telling us something we're doing is not right – we're out of balance. Check out our lifestyle.
- Our bodies have the wisdom to deal with germs.
- Stay free from panic if we hear news we're not expecting.
- We need to educate ourselves about wellness and illness.

After the interview, we hugged while saying good-bye. There was a point when I started to release my hug. He continued hugging me saying, "I wonder how long we could stay like this." His positive energy was contagious, and I drove home that day declaring I'd never again speak a negative word. The Task Force in Psychoneuroimmunology (PNI) has been able to substantially prove this entire field and to provide the scientific evidence. PNI is the understanding of the relation between the immune system and both disease-inducing and wellness-promoting behaviors. Today it is a booming, cutting-edge, interdisciplinary field including a wide variety of practices such as acupuncture, tai chi, relaxation techniques, yoga, nutritional modification, and body work. Cousins was a pioneer in the subject, as I interviewed him in the mid-eighties, when it was not yet researched and proven that these previously-listed practices had value in the promotion of wellness and management of chronic illness.

He told me he came to UCLA with an obsession to find or help develop scientific evidence behind what he wrote about in his book, Anatomy of an Illness. The program brought in actors who can summon their emotions and be put through hypothetical exercises where they react as if those situations were real. "We discovered there are specific changes in the endocrine and immune system, even though the situations are imaginary."

Learning to Play

Another visionary in the field of joy is Dr. O. Fred Donaldson. He is the author of *Playing By Heart*, a play therapist, educational consultant, and presenter who conducts workshops internationally on his ongoing research pertaining to play with children, dolphins, and wolves. I've had the honor to interview and be with this extraordinarily sensitive man in several seminars. "Play is the child's natural expression of joy and wholeness," he said. "Adults need to relearn how to play in order to understand and support children in gentler ways. Play may also help us to regain our youthful enthusiasm and sense of connectedness."

Here is more of what Fred has to teach:

"The difference between contest and play can be briefly stated as: In contest, life is to be lived as won. In original play, life is to be lived as one. The best definition of play I know of was given to me by David, a five-year-old boy. He said, "Fred, play is when we don't know that we're different from each other.'"

"Play and contest are two different operating systems of relationship. Contest is based on fear in which relationships have a context of fight, flight, freeze; they are characterized by blame, fault, and revenge. In contests, we hide from ourselves the disturbing fact that every victory is a funeral. Original play is a system of relationships based on the safety and love of creating a sense of sanctuary. Original play is a sense of belonging and kindness – kindness, not as a sense of social niceness, but a realization that all life is of only one kind. How's this?"

"It's now been thirty-four years of playing. I don't find much change in human adults around the world either geographically or historically in terms of their ability to truly play rather than contest with life."

"At the same time, I'm continually taught new lessons by the children and animals. For example, a lioness leaping on my back taught me about the connection between fierceness and gentleness. Being charged by two rhinos taught me the real feeling of peace. I learned from a teenage girl living in a squatter camp in Manila and a four-year-old boy in a township in South Africa that children, who we continue to ignore, are truly bearers of promise."

"The choice to play in a world of contest is difficult and requires courage. Most adults do continue to not know there is a real and practical choice outside of contest behavior. Adults talk about peace and conflict resolution as if they are ideas and not physical as well as emotional responses. Playing in a South African prison with young male serious offenders and with street kids in Manila and South Africa has shown me that they can even, with the profound aggression and violence they have experienced, choose, when given the opportunity, an alternative they didn't know existed."

"Resolving conflict is not enough. We must substitute something for conflict so that the feelings, emotions, and actions simply don't arise in the first place. So, 'in the first place' is original play. Psychiatrists and neuroscientists who have thought about this with me have suggested that I've played for so long that the fear-flight, fight, freeze response has been altered in my brain. That play is a deeper response system than either fear or sex. Nurturing the play response to life creates an entirely different human with a different brain. So original play is not about self-defense – it is about self-disappearance – the result is that even in the face of an attack there is no attacker, no victim."

"I am working to establish sanctuaries for children in places (Hawaii, Sweden, Cape Town, South Africa) around the world. The idea is that the best sanctuary for a child is another human being. A "sanctuaryist" is a person who can mentor for children the kindness, belonging, love, and safety of play under any and all circumstances." Intrigued? Read Fred's book. It's fascinating.

The Play Class

I used to teach a class at a junior college on the subject of play–a lost art for many. It was through a program called Elder Hostel, which offered education and fun to participants aged sixty and older. The focus of the program was to learn the benefits of play in our lives. In several cases, the students felt embarrassment over looking foolish in their form of play, and chose to hold back. Most were eager and ready to engage.

The purpose of the class is to discover the playful, magical child that exists within us all. The only requirement is a willingness to be open to new ideas, new beliefs, and discover the true source of our joy. During the first session, students were asked why this particular class was selected. The answers varied to some degree, but the central thread was, "I've become too serious as an adult and yearn to have more fun in life." I encouraged students to keep a "Joyful Journal" and visit toy stores. One student brought in a small doll wrapped in a cozy flannel blanket. "I never had a doll," she said. "Being brought up on a farm, doing chores, rather than play, filled our days. I just never learned how to play."

In the first class, I posed a question to the group: "What do you consider play, and how do you incorporate it in your life?"

Andy and Fran of California had celebrated their fiftieth anniversary the previous year. For them, worldwide travel is play. They love planning trips and writing about their fascinating experiences.

Connie "plays" by wearing fun clothes, like fruit salad earrings and bright purple blouses.

Maria is a "snowbird" residing in cold country for the summer and heading south before the white stuff starts to fall. She has teddy bears that reside in both homes and serve many purposes. She dresses them up creatively and talks to them as a means of sharing her concerns and feelings. "It works too," Maria assured the group. "I always feel better after our sessions." (I asked her to keep this quiet – I didn't want to lose my livelihood!) Maria also plays when she adventures. "There's only one prerequisite for my adventures." We all listened intently as the secret was divulged. "I must do it alone!" Whether it is taking a hike in uncharted territory or planning a major trip to an unfamiliar culture, Maria is a dedicated student of play.

Cathy, the coordinator of the program and another serious student of play, shared her watch with the group. This "out-of-the-ordinary" timepiece made us all smile and lighten up, activating the joyful feelings inside. Its brightly colored numbers light up when the hands on the watch indicate the hour. When it is two P.M., two bright lights emanate from the watch. It's a fun way to remind the bearer to "lighten up."

Betty, a woman from Washington, has taken a trip once a month for the past two years. "So what if plans don't go exactly as scheduled." she said. "When you travel, you just learn to go with the flow."

Then there was Linda from Texas (age seventy-seven, but who's counting?). Linda swims in the ocean or a pool every day–alone. This was her eighteenth Elder Hostel experience. She looked so alive in her purple jacket, fuchsia blouse, and natural snow-white hair. During the first portion of the class she fought back tears, and then finally broke down and told us that, only months ago, she'd lost her husband and was missing him. "When do you stop feeling sorry for yourself?" she said reluctantly. This courageous and lovely woman was so willing to share her heart as she is in the process of moving on to another chapter in her life. The group's response was compassionate and supportive, and before long, Linda was inquiring about my colorful juggling scarves, wanting to sign up for instruction. Juggling scarves are much like juggling balls, but because these are scarves, they stay in the air longer. Later in the week, Linda was the subject of a front-page photo in the newspaper. Doing what? Learning how to juggle, of course. What an inspiration!

The class concluded with balloons for all students as a playful "reward" for each participant as they expressed their gratitude and appreciation for feeling safe enough to share their inner child with the group.

Another class I had great fun teaching was called "Discovering the Joy Within." Remember, an acronym for JOY is, "Just Open Yourself." Some of the questions explored during my course were:

- What does "joy within" mean?
- What are the benefits in learning how to live a more joyful life?
- How is this "opening" process achievable?

"I'm not willing to allow anyone to steal my joy!" one of the participants emphatically declared. One gentleman celebrating birthday number seventy-two said, "I feel so grateful that you presented this class. I needed to have a reaffirmation of what I'd been learning over the years. I also think it's good to hear it from an outside source." One student discovered the value of true communication. "It felt good to share my honest feelings," she said. "The heaviness I'd been harboring went away." And yet another realized, "I can affect a change in my perception of situations and in doing so, let go of frustration in trying to change people."

During the last session, a student volunteered his personal growth lesson. For him, the class was about competition. "I had only learned to compete, not to play. I now realize that competition can be an excellent way to have fun, so long as participating, not winning, is the goal." We each perceive competition in our own way and there are many ways to acquire "winner" status. Others said that, they indeed had become more open. A mother of two young children became particularly aware of her intuition and was more open to its loving guidance and wisdom.

Did the class discover the joy within? I'd say yes. In fact, they all graduated with honors. They learned the value of incorporating play into life. Yes, joy and play are synonymous, along with laugher and enthusiasm. The main lesson is simple; Lighten Up.

Why do I love to teach? Because I get to play with people like those mentioned. Hopefully, it's a mutually beneficial experience, but at times I feel the motive is purely selfish. The students enhance my every breath as they continue to provide me with precious memories and priceless lessons here in Earth School.

We've all been given a most precious gift, the gift of life, and the opportunity to express our aliveness. The quality of that life is our job. How we choose to express aliveness is how we experience fulfillment in life. This is called a PMA, or Positive Mental Attitude. Only we control what we think. Only we determine the content of our thoughts. Our choices either empower us or destroy us. Just as we select a flavor of ice cream, which sweater to wear, or what to eat for breakfast, we choose our thoughts about life, self-image, our past, and our future. We choose our thoughts today. How exciting to know we are in charge!

Yet there are times when we just can't seem to muster up that good ol' PMA. Instead we may be feeling any one of the hundreds of emotions we're capable of feeling, like rejection, anger, or fear. Well, that's just fine. The moment we resist what we are feeling, the longer it will persist. Transformations come when we allow our thoughts to be exactly what they are—waves of energy that move. They come, they go, they're not good or bad, they just are. If we judge our feelings and prevent them from being expressed, they take up residency in the body and eventually block the free flow of life force, prana, hence the beginning of dis-ease.

When our negative thoughts creep in and tend to consume us, we can honor them in the moment, and then choose to keep or release them. Are they truth for us today or part of a belief system that has outrun its course? Maybe they were absorbed in early childhood as a means of protection and survival. The question now is, do they serve you? Are they supportive to your goals in life? If not, dismiss them and replace them with thoughts that are nurturing and loving. No matter what our present conditions, this is how we empower ourselves.

So where is the source of joy to be found? From within us, just as the fragrance of the musk comes from within the musk deer. We become the masters when we take responsibility for our lives. Albert Einstein said, "There are two ways to live our life – one as if everything was a miracle and the other as if nothing was a miracle. The choice is ours."

Reflection Time:

1. What brings you joy?
2. What gets you in touch with your joy?
3. To what degree do you allow yourself to play, laugh, and be spontaneous?
4. Have you discovered the playful child within? If not, why not? If so, what does she or he like to do to play?
5. When was the last time you played? What do you consider play?
6. Start a Joyful Journal and let the thoughts and feelings flow.
7. What's your favorite season and why?
8. Would you consider your friends positive influences in your life?
9. Is doing something outrageous a natural or foreign thought to you? If not, what's the limitation?
10. When is the last time you laughed at yourself for doing something silly?

"Decide to forgive, for resentment is negative. Resentment is poisonous. Resentment diminishes and devours the self. Be the first to forgive, to smile, and to take the first step, and you will see happiness bloom on the face of your human brother or sister. Be always the first..."
Robert Mueller

J is for feeling... Judgmental

Definition: discerning, discriminating, critical

Opposite: accepting, allowing, amenable

Imagine the occupation of being a judge. What comes to mind? Perhaps the judge is someone in a basic black robe with a stern expression on his or her face and a gavel in hand, ready to quiet anyone caught disturbing the judiciary process. Most likely, the judge is on a stand, above and separate from all else in the courtroom.

Sometimes judgment is necessary when discerning certain situations. A judge must see the situation from an objective point of view, which gives relevance to the height and distance from those being prosecuted. A fair judge takes note of all sides of the case and makes a decision based on the arguments and evidence presented. Intellect and intuition must come into play, as well as an ability to maintain emotional detachment.

People love to "play the judge." There is an element of superiority that accompanies this feeling. Being judgmental can be addictive. One can become so judgmental of people or events that one actually loses perspective rather than gains it! Too often, when one judges another's behavior or choices, it is a means to criticize it or label it wrong, therefore making the "judge" right and "better." This kind of judgment often comes from a state of arrogance. No one can know what is best for someone else ultimately.

Judgment can have to do with ignoring the neighbor because you heard that she was cheating on her husband. It can be as devious as gossiping about the new woman in town who showed up to last night's party wearing a tacky outfit. It can be as ruthless as ending a friendship over a single argument. And judgment can be as simple as labeling a painting or person or plant as "ugly" or "pretty." Any "opinion" is, in fact, a judgment. And while it is sometimes necessary to form a judgment, like when getting into a car with a driver who has had too much to drink, sometimes a judgment can be a way of harming another instead of protecting oneself.

The Lady and the Monks

There is a story of two monks who are traveling in heavy rain where huge puddles of water had formed. They encountered a woman in distress who wasn't able to cross over to reach her village. The elder monk picked her up and carried her over the puddle. He joined the other monk, and they continued their long journey. The other monk was clearly disturbed and preoccupied. The elder monk asked what was bothering him. The other monk responded, "I did not like that you picked up the woman and carried her like that. It is not appropriate behavior of a monk to do so." The elder monk smiled and replied, "I picked up that woman and put her down a long time ago, but it seems you're still carrying her."

Judgment is a trait that comes from that which we are not. We have a personality, but it is not our true nature. Our essence, our soul, would not and does not judge. Soulfulness honors and respects the life process. Soul only knows pure joy, love, and peace. When we are identified with our personality, we tend to judge. In fact, one man candidly shared with me that it takes him tremendous awareness and self-discipline to not judge. He believes it is a prevalent trait in many, if not all, people. Most people do not readily admit to judgment but he feels it is widespread, like a virus. What do you think? He is not proud about this part of himself. It just seems to come up, he says, like it's natural. He said he gets hurt and angry if he's been judged, yet, he is aware of himself judging others.

Learning not to judge can be a real challenge. We begin when we are truthful with ourselves. Look at the standards you have set for yourself and others. Have you set them up to win or to lose? Have you based them on what you'd like to see in your own life, or are they based on someone else's idea of what your life experience should be?

The results of judging another are actually an extension of self-judgment. Have you noticed that people who seem highly dissatisfied with their own lives are the ones most prone to gossiping and other forms of judging others? It is simply because they need to find a reason to make the lack of happiness in their own lives okay, by pointing out the so-called faults in others. Yet, if we simply realize what we do in our life is really the best we can do in any given circumstance, judgment loses its grip. When we stop judging ourselves, we stop judging others, and vice versa.

My sister Clara had a shift of perspective after visiting the space museum in Florida. She had always judged the U.S. space program and questioned its budget. However, while walking through the museum, she educated herself with the fascinating exhibits including various missiles, rockets, and the history of astronauts, to name a few. She was amazed and enlightened about this program and could now see, through her personal experience of it, the place it plays in history. In addition, she realized her pre-judgment and wondered if she had the same pattern affecting other areas of her life. Lesson learned. Replacing ignorance with wisdom is life altering.

Words and Cells

Like so many "issues," judging others or feeling constantly judged stems from childhood. Few have the words to stand up to those who judge. Many children are judged cruelly by their peers, and in turn, many children judge cruelly. Where does a child "pick up" the judgmental attitude? And how does the child who is picked on handle it? Many children are inept and have little confidence to stand up for themselves, so they take the consequences. They may be separated from a group, labeled, or ultimately left alone as a devastating result. So why say anything? Should we just take it?

We, as a species, have yet to realize the tremendous power of our thoughts and words. Words either bond us with someone or they separate us. Words can either criticize or acknowledge. Words are either healing or they're destructive. Our thoughts and words not only have an impact on others, but especially on ourselves.

Are these words, which are actually thoughts expressed through language, real? After mapping the brain and the pathways of neuropeptides through the body, neuroscientist Dr. Candace Pert, determined that the thoughts themselves invoke chemical reactions in the brain, which then flow to different parts of the body. I listened to an audio tape from a presentation she did at a wellness conference. Although abstract, or non-material, thoughts instantaneously influence our bodies on a physical level. Sometimes it's beneficial and other times it is not. Her ongoing research indicates that the body "listens in" and is influenced by our thoughts. Dr. Pert stated that "the cellular level is the most subtle level of being awakened. It gives you an increased ability to be touched by life and respond to it." So if we're even thinking negative and judgmental thoughts about ourselves, our body gets it. Our cells get it. We have a choice, to replace judgment with thoughts and words that will enhance good health and happiness.

Judgment affects your life wherever you are. One person can feel miserable being at the beach, getting all sandy and yucky, being bothered by the damp, sea air, while another loves the sound of the waves and nestles into the warmth of the sand. The same falls true in the desert, as demonstrated by the following.

Meet "Mr. Desert"

After taking a long and warm walk near the Santa Rosa Visitor Center on a very hot afternoon, I sought rest under the only shade tree nearby. I later learned this was an old Palo Verde tree, meaning green pole in Spanish. I was so pleased to meander to this place of quiet, because what I found was a large granite boulder with a plaque displaying a photo and inscription from Randall Henderson, 1888-1970.

Randall Henderson, also known as "Mr. Desert," Founder of the Protective Desert Council in 1936, was interviewed by *Desert Magazine*. His words are most pertinent to the topic of this book: *"There are two kinds of deserts. One is a grim and desolate wasteland, home of venomous reptiles and stinging insects, thorn-covered plants and trees, and unbearable heat. This is the desert seen by those strangers speeding along the highway, impatient to be out of the damnable country, seeing only the mask. The other desert is the real desert whose character is hidden except to those who come with friendliness and understanding. It offers gifts of health and sunshine, skies studded with diamonds, breezes that bear no poison, a landscape with pastel colors, such as no artist can duplicate. To those who come with friendliness, it gives friendliness, courage, strength, and character. Those seeking relaxation, find release from the world of manmade troubles. For those seeking beauty, the desert offers nature's rarest artistry."*

Once again, there are two ways to look at everything. It's all about attitude! Even a desert can be cruel or generous considering your attitude. It's always your choice!

Take time to get in touch with your inner judge. Is she or he just? Or does she make up her mind too quickly? Does he allow others to express themselves in his presence? Or does he suppress others with preconceptions? Remind yourself of the effects of judging yourself and others harshly. After all, judgment is a prison cell of its own.

Reflection Time:

1. Be honest with yourself. Do you tend to judge others?
2. If so, in what way? Skin color? Behavior? Success? Physical appearance?
3. How do you judge yourself? To what degree on a scale of 1-10?
    1-periodically
    3-frequently
    5-mostofthetime
    7-prettyhard
    10-harshly
4. Is it okay for you to feel any way you feel?
5. Is it okay to talk about your feelings? Even the angry ones?
6. How about being who you are? Or do you have to please someone to feel loved?
7. When were you judged as a child?
8. When did you feel unaccepted the way you were?
9. Experiment with judging something in nature—a dried-up river bed, wildflowers, a star-studded sky. Judge with high intensity. What are your thoughts about it?
10. What was the defining moment in your childhood when you felt criticized? Maybe by a teacher? Parent? Sibling?

"We all come into this world with a keen psychic awareness."
James Van Praugh

K is for feeling... Keen

Definition: intellectually acute, highly sensitive, vivid, piercing, intense
Opposite: dull, numb, out of sorts

If I'm feeling keen, I feel like I'm onto something. I feel good, in my element, even snazzy! Colors look brighter, food tastes richer, and smells are more intense. Life is on the HIGH setting. Or maybe I'm just tuned into the higher source...

The word "keen" has a variety of meanings. We could have a keen intellect or a keen intuition. Although the intellect and the intuition are seemingly different, they do relate. Both have to do with using the senses to gather information. The difference is that the intellect uses the brain, and the intuition uses the sixth sense, or feelings.

How sharp is your intellect? Is it as keen as it was when you were going to high school or more so? Some believe that as we age we lose our keen intellectual edge. Stand above the general case and strive to disprove those beliefs. Maintain an interest and exuberance for life and the millions of things there are to learn. Experience the whole universe to keep intellectually and physically keen. Continue to spend time with the young, embrace new ideas, challenge the ruts we may have made for ourselves, and explore new parts of the world or the town we live in. These ideas and your own will ensure a keen desire for future experiences.

The Oracle Within

On the other hand, intuition is a sixth sense, and an infallible teacher of truth. We have to learn to distinguish it from our ego's agenda. Once we hear it, we need to trust it, take risks, and act on it.

Intuition is just beginning to get a foothold in our society. For the past few hundred years, schools in the West focused on developing the intellect rather than intuition. We've been taught to think with a certain mind set, trained with a certain framework logically, linearly, realistically. To step outside of that means being labeled weird and uncooperative. Thanks to the "New Age" movement, this is shifting...slowly.

Intuition is not a New Age phenomenon however. In other cultures, intuition has been the fad for eons. For example, in India, children are taught to meditate in schools. In the Orient, many companies take meditation or Tai Chi breaks, rather than coffee breaks. And surely the American Indians paid attention to their inner voices. A medicine man would give time and deep contemplation before treating a patient. And the youth of the culture were sent on vision quests to find out where their destinies would take them. They would then return to the Elders for help interpreting what they received. Similarly, people would go to see the oracle, or prophet, at the sacred center in Greece called Delphi. Indeed, people have looked for thousands of years for guidance and answers from an intuitive source. The Greek word for "oracle" is, in fact, "divine voice."

Delphi is located on the flank of Mount Parnassos, and has been recognized as the sacred center of Greece. My visit to "tous Delphous," as it is referred to in Greek, was an enriching time for me, as I turned deeper in the oracle within my being. "Each person is a microcosm, a reflection of the entire universe in miniature, and at the center of the soul exists the oracle of the heart. When one becomes aware of this voice from the center, at that point the soul becomes cognizant of its manifest nature: a mediator between worlds, a one and a many, a point from which creation springs, a word, a world, an oracle, a song." These profound words come from David Fideler, written in the journal entitled GNOSIS, Fall 1987.

James van Praugh, a renowned medium, author, and lecturer, tells us that everyone has a psychic within them. Not me, you say? Look again. Have you ever experienced listening to your wise inner voice? That indeed is your very own oracle, guiding you along your true path. Your inner voice may reveal itself through a tight feeling of dread in your stomach, or you may actually hear a voice, or you may get a flash in your mind's eye. However your inner voice speaks to you, you can be sure that it has something of value to share with you.

This powerful story comes from a Self-Realization Fellowship magazine. Many years ago in Bhopal, India, there was an intense explosion at a chemical company. As the story goes, a sixteen-year-old girl was left in charge of a commune in this community. Everyone had left the day the eruption happened. The shocking sounds would have sent most into a state of terror and alarm, but this young girl did not panic. Instead she sat to meditate and, in the quiet of her mind, received instructions on how to save her life.

"Turn on the fan," she heard from within. "Drink water, get under the covers to protect your skin." She did exactly that but would fall asleep until a voice would come and say, "Wake up; drink more water." When finally she was rescued, the hospital staff told her she took the best precautions that saved her life; she reduced her breathing (through meditation), flushed the system (by drinking water), circulated the air (with the fan), and reduced skin exposure (being under the covers). If you choose to call this common sense, fine. How many of us would stay so calm to use our good judgment?

Intuition is known as the voice of the soul, or the sixth sense. It was my thesis topic in graduate school. "Intuition: The Infallible Teacher of Truth." I have recorded some of the material along with a thirty minute meditation onto a CD, called Inner Realms, for educational purposes, as well as to relax and center. The quality of this sense is keen, acute, and razor-sharp. The word comes from Sanskrit meaning "that which flows from itself, needing nothing else." We perceive the world with our five senses, but our sixth transcends the world and we simply know. It can't even be explained. We just know. The more we're in the state of relaxed awareness, the more we can receive intuitive messages. It comes from another source, beyond our logical and rational understanding. When we put linear thinking aside we can open to the creative part of ourselves. The answers will come in a new way to solve our dilemmas, and we see with new eyes. It is time to look within for the answers, not outside, giving our power away to the "authority." We DO know what's best for us. This is one example of how intuition and a keen awareness can affect our every day life.

There is a parable about the musk deer who smelled an intoxicating aroma in the air. He started looking for the sweet smell and became frantic in his search, as he was unsuccessful in finding it. He climbed to the tops of the cliffs and was so anxious in his pursuit, that he fell to his death on the valley floor. A hunter comes by, takes a knife and slits open his belly to remove the sought after, luscious-smelling musk oil.

Too many of us are no longer satisfied with the trinkets of the world. We're looking for that keen sense of guidance and wisdom within ourselves. The shift in the belief that it is no longer outside of us, but within, is occurring now in our reality. We're being forced to make many shifts–from fear to love, from doubt to faith, from separateness to wholeness, from resentment to forgiveness. We are preparing to be alert and feel our keen sense of Self through sharpening our awareness and acknowledging our own potential.

What is bliss if not the keenest edge of joy? What is death if not the keenest experience of loss to the living and of greatest curiosity to the dying? Keen is not the middle ground–it is not beige. It is a firm commitment to one feeling or sensation, intense pain or pleasure. In life, the most pungent, most enthusiastic, or the most desirous belong in the rank of keen.

There seem to be many opportunities in life to remember intense experiences of pain, but what of the pleasures and excitements. What of our most keen desires? Within each of us is the keen desire to experience the essence of life, the truth. And, the quickest route to that end is through Self-exploration, and a desire to use the intellect AND the intuition to discovery the Self and the world we are living in.

Do you dare to look for the joy within? Do you dare to cease the search in the outer world and claim your birthright? The yearning can be over when you proclaim your boldness and truth. Get in touch with your keen sense of awareness and your inner ability to be self-directed, and each day will be a true celebration.

Memories

Start with remembering the smell of the holiday season just by thinking about it. A memory often flashes with a keen smell–the recognition of times from the past. Those fleeting sensory memories show us the impact those experiences had in our lives. Can you think of occasions when the smells, sights, and noises were so keen you will never forget them? When you turn all of your sensory inputs to high, those memories have a lasting impact. What do you want to fill your memory cells with? When you think about it, every keen experience, whether of pain or pleasure, is a memory for tomorrow. We can create those memories through the choices we make of how we occupy our moments.

In December of 1986, after a deep meditation I asked for direction regarding my state of mind. I picked up a pen and started writing. The following healing words literally flowed through me:

"My dear one....know that the tears that momentarily come to you now, and the tears that you have shed in the past are truly representative of the beliefs being shed from you. There is now standing a beautiful soul, like the Christmas tree before any lights and ornaments have been added. It stands alone, rich with color and unique in its own special beauty. The tree appears to have been cut down, separated from its source, but it is not. The tree lives for its span, then, the form changes. Its beauty touches something in all who look and something deeper for those who look deeper. You, like the tree, are now standing in all your own beauty with no need for the tinsel. Stand simply with the knowingness that you are never alone. There is a humbleness about the

207

tree, a purity that sets it apart from the ones made from plastic or laden with artificial snow. You're never alone. Why would I ever leave you? I couldn't – We are One."

Tap into your intuition, and you too, will be amazed at what comes through.

What channel are you on?

One of the classes I attended at the Self-Realization Fellowship World-wide Convocation was on the subject of intuition. The idea of having two channels on satellite television was presented. One is the sensory channel that offers sports, romance, sitcoms, promotional gifts that you can't live without and much more. The other is the intuition channel, offering peace, truth, bliss, lasting joy and higher consciousness. We are provided with both channels and we can change the button on the remote at any time.

When you choose to change to the intuition channel, you discipline yourself to sit in silence daily and develop a calmly receptive mind and heart. To sharpen the intuition takes practice, patience and perseverance. Initially, ask the Universe, "What is it I need to know about this challenge I am facing?" Let it go, then enter the stillness; quiet the restless mind and calm the thoughts, while practicing concentrated breathing. Allow yourself to be. Then after the period of meditation, be open to receive your answers through your intuition. You may be given several different perspectives, so introspect and be highly sensitive about the information offered. Refrain from judging. Once you let go of the way you think it should be, your intuition begins to flow. This is an important point. I have a fabric scroll that hangs adjacent to a patio door in our home that reads:

"In the end what matters most is
how well did you live,
how well did you love,
how well did you let go."

Reflection Time:

1. How are you staying keen in life? How and what are you exploring?

2. Test your intuition. This takes a playful attitude! The next time your phone rings, refrain from looking at caller ID, and take a moment to "feel" who it is on the other line. Start simply. Is it someone you are close to, or a stranger? Are they male or female? Later, make specific guesses. You may surprise yourself!

3. Take up a new hobby that exercises your intellect. Do math equations, or learn how your car engine works. Your brain needs exercise too!

4. What senses do you "use" the most? Are you a tactile person, touching the clothes when you shop? Do you learn better, when lessons are written on the chalkboard, or through an auditory lecture?

5. Take the intuition quiz:

   - What prevents us from acting on our intuition?
     1. the ego
     2. the five senses
     3. a righteous belief system
     4. all of the above
   - Our intuition is part of our nature at birth. True or False?
   - Intuition comes through best during
     1. activity
     2. stillness
     3. in dialogue with another
   - When I don't have a ready answer I tend to be:
     1. patient
     2. clumsy
   - When working on a difficult problem I usually:
     1. concentrate on finding the solution
     2. play around with the possibilities
   - In most cases, change:
     1. makes me nervous
     2. is exciting to me

(There are no specific answers to this quiz. However, use your intuition, as you have them inside.)

"Practice random acts of kindness."
The Random Acts of Kindness Foundation

K is for feeling... Kindhearted

Definition: considerate, respectful, generous, good-hearted
Opposite: self-absorbed, rude, cruel, brutal

"Kindhearted" has to do with compassion. When one's heart is kind, he or she has the ability to feel empathy and take the actions necessary to help others when there is a need. Kindheartedness means to care. We have the ability to be kind and care about other humans, animals, the environment, and ourselves if we so choose. Kindness is one of the most beautiful virtues a person can express. It builds character and the sooner it is taught, through example and understanding, the better.

Character Counts is an organization whose educational framework rests on the Six Pillars of Character: trustworthiness, responsibility, respect, fairness, citizenship, and caring. As kindness is synonymous to caring, you realize why it is so important to live our individual lives being kind. We demonstrate kindness through our actions. There are many opportunities for us to show our kindheartedness. Whether it be by wiping up the soap and water on the counter in a public bathroom, leaving it neat for the next person, or taking a meal to the neighbor after he's just had surgery; these seemingly small actions mean you care. It means being considerate. It means being thoughtful.

Thoughtful, kindhearted, caring, and compassionate, all these words describe my good friend, Herman Roup, who was our neighbor for many years. Teri, Herman's wife, told me the story of how Herman had gifted a pair of glasses to one of the girls in his daughter's elementary class. The teacher had expressed her appreciation for his gesture, but explained that the little girl's sister also needed glasses and that it wouldn't be fair to give to just one. Without hesitation Herman said, "Okay, get her some too!" Total selfless service.

Kindness is a virtue that relates to character development. How do we teach kindness if we feel anger, greed, and frustration? Kindness is a reflection of how we feel about ourselves. When we have a low opinion of ourselves, and feel we don't deserve to have good things happen, kindness may not be easy to express. When we have a healthy self-esteem, we may realize we are all connected. When we do for someone else, we're also doing something for ourselves.

Without kindness, we feel separate and lonely. Taoist Master Lao Tzu said: "From the One came the two, from the two the three, and from the three came the Ten Thousand Things." When we begin to recognize the one in the many, we naturally become more kindhearted. Doesn't that make sense? We would comprehend that we are all connected. We are all part of each other. We are all part of the One.

Email Humor from the Mouths of Babes

Maybe a life partner has the quality of being kindhearted, but how do we find out? Let's ask the kids and have a few guffaws. When children were asked how you decide who you're going to marry, here is the perception by Kirsten, age ten, on the subject (thanks to internet sharing):

- "No person really decides before they grow up who they're going to marry. God decides it all, way before, and you get to find out later who you're stuck with."

Another favorite when asked about dating:

- "Dates are for having fun, and people should use them to get to know each other. Even boys have something to say if you listen long enough." Eight-year-old wisdom.

Here's an answer to the question of what you'd do on a first date that turned sour.

- Nine-year-old Craig said, "I'd run home and play dead. The next day I would call all the newspapers and make sure they wrote about me in all the dead columns."

We need to laugh more to open our hearts and not take things so seriously. I believe this helps us to be kindhearted. When our hearts laugh and sing, it helps us to overcome what looks like a heavy situation. Don't take my word for it. Try it.

As volunteer staff I was involved in a personal growth seminar in Bombay, India years ago, and was fascinated to hear participants as they stood up and shared very similar types of problems: "My children fight so much," "My employee doesn't appear to produce for me," "Everyone is always in such a hurry." It was a clear display that we are indeed connected. In the U.S., we're not that different in our dreams and ambitions. We want to be happy, to be loved, to love, to be comfortable, and to feel inner peace. We want our children to be healthy and happy. We all want to live the best life we possibly can.

I observed an autopsy of a young man in his thirties. He was traveling in a car at 130 miles per hour when he died. Every choice this man had made during his young life brought him to that stainless steel table. I also realized that "we are all the same under the skin" literally! Beneath our very thin layer of skin, we all have blood that runs through our veins, a heart that feels pain and joy, and a mind that reasons. The color of our skin truly means nothing.

At a counseling conference I learned of a program called CHOICES. It is a powerful, interactive seminar designed to help middle and high school students realize that they can take charge of their lives. Since 1985, CHOICES has helped millions of kids in the U.S. and Canada to shape their futures. Children learn what factors in their lives are under their control and which are not, and then what they can do about it. Self-discipline is the key. You can become a volunteer for this program and make a difference in children's lives. It's a fabulous concept, and it works.

On a similar note, I learned of a school in Southern California called, The School with Gentle Eyes, a.k.a., the Community Learning Center. Formed in 1983, their mission is to celebrate each child and their family's uniqueness. The school's philosophy is based on kindness and support, instead of competition. They initiated a program called "The Earthkeeper Program," which promotes an ecologically healthy planet. Also, each year, five students are chosen to demonstrate their unique gifts to win a scholarship. Each child took a turn exhibiting their particular talent—one exhibited art, another read poetry, another demonstrated skill in computer graphics, one sang, and one played the cello. Yet, after their performances, the five young people asked the board if they could divide the scholarship into five equal parts. Through this type of education, children learn not only academics, but also life skills like caring, kindness, and sensitivity.

Today the tradition continues. Instead of one scholarship, there are five. In fact their theme for 2004 is, "It's a Wonderful World, We are World Peacemakers." Laia Hansen, a teacher affiliated with the school, says, "We are focusing on peace and problem solving. One of our activities will be an interact-simulation Internet cruise. We are going to imagine that we are members of Advance Teams sent out by the United Nations to explore the diversity in our world and see if we can create solutions for the problems that arise from our differences. The students will learn some computer skills, world geography, problem solving, and have fun in the process. As you can see, this is no small task."

Kathie Housden shared with me what a rich experience it was teaching in The School with Gentle Eyes (or Community Learning Center) for nine years. She created a team of students, parents, and teachers who all worked together for the best possible education for the children who attended. "The dedication to have the spiritual value of kindness as the bottom line was inspiring to all of us who were there–to be the most we could be and bring forth the best in everyone around us. The values of the programs brought forth – Earthkeepers, Peace Studies, World Community, Community Service as well as the academic subjects taught in regular programs, have stayed with these students even in to their college years. To know this 'School Within a School' is still in existence and is about to celebrate its twentieth anniversary is a real thrill. I am incredibly grateful to have had the privilege to serve here," Kathie said. Kathie's outward glow, radiant and peaceful energy, all come from having made such a huge difference in the lives of so many young people.

The Children are Watching

Unfortunately, there are too many people who have been disrespectful to Mother Earth and polluted her streams, lakes, and oceans. Each act of disrespect for the Earth creates a wound inside of us. Regrettably, many people who hold very high positions in our legislative system make inconsiderate decisions for the planet. They could use their power to make decisions that do not just benefit individuals, but the planet as a whole. I believe many politicians have their priorities out of balance.

The actions of our world leaders have a great effect on everyone. How confusing it must be for children to grow up with a system that sends murderers to the electric chair and wages war on foreign countries! Consequently, children learn through our role modeling. They learn to either be kind and gentle or unkind, rude, and demanding. It's up to us what we do with our modeled behavior. Remember when you act–the children are watching!

To live life with an attitude of kindness is living from our essence. I understand we may not always be kind, but it is something to strive toward. We interact with many people during the day, over the telephone or in person, who may sometimes be a challenge. At times we may not encounter the sharpest, quickest, or even friendliest individuals at the bank or at the market. Be kind anyway. You'll be amazed at how often the other person's attitude will be affected by your own. You make a difference and if you want to prove it, begin a kindness campaign of your own.

I feel kind to little creatures that invade our home from time to time. They have the right to live too. I gently escort them outside on a little piece of paper or in a glass. Our world needs people to be kind. Teach children early in their young lives to respect life. They will emulate you. If you get freaky about seeing a spider and your little one is within eyeshot, they will form their personal decisions about spiders by observing you.

Kindness is Compassion

Janis Frawley-Holler wrote in "Island Lesson," Hemispheres, 2003 about the island of St. Barts. "Kindness toward one another is the highlight of living here. It's a waste of energy to yell, be pushy, and angry. It takes a lot less energy to be kind. It's just our island's attitude." Get me a ticket there!

I remember a time I was extremely impatient and intolerant with someone on the phone. After I'd hung up, my body told me it wasn't over. It was definitely incomplete. When I'm being unkind toward another person, my body knows it, and my cells respond accordingly. I couldn't go on with my work, so I called that person back and apologized for my rudeness. She appreciated it, and thanked me.

To be kind is to be compassionate. You have no idea what that person on the other end of the phone may be going through at the moment of your interaction. He could have just come from an upsetting meeting with his child's teacher, or she could have just been told that her husband wanted a divorce.

We've all had the experience of behaving unkindly. We just need to own it (take responsibility for) and take the time to set it right, then feel the benefits of that action. Open, honest communication is always the solution for anything. You'll be a happier person when you choose to be kind. Be kind when nobody is looking. When you choose kindness, rather than cruel, critical, or teasing words, you will feel good about yourself. Be the kind of person your dog thinks you are. We are all different, so instead of judging those who are unlike you, be kind to them. Why would you want to put someone down and inflict suffering in his or her life? Would you want to be that person? Evaluate from where your critique comes, correct your actions, and modify your behavior. You are the one who gets to choose. Choose kindness.

Random Acts of Kindness

I met a young woman who had a senior project in high school based on the notion of practicing random acts of kindness. She started a program with abused and abandoned children, suggesting different ways they could be kind in spite of what had happened to them. What an inspiring program!

Suggestions for random acts of kindness:

- Take someone a flower. Give someone an unexpected gift.
- Leave several quarters lying around in an active children's park.
- Pay the toll for the car behind you.
- Walk a dog from the local shelter.
- Pick up litter.
- Listen – just listen.
- Send a thank you note for no apparent reason – just because.

When my friend Gail moved to my hometown, she began to wave at everybody. She often walked her dog, Sierra, down the same road and waved at every person she passed. "Half-a-hug" is what she thought with each wave and when people started waving back, their wave made it a whole hug.

I attended a conference in Santa Clara, California, being held at The Westin Hotel. I was delighted to discover they offered Heavenly Beds®, Heavenly Showers®, Heavenly Cribs®, AND (the best part), Heavenly Dog Beds® for your pets! Max could come with me and live in style for a few days. When I went up to my room, there it was–a large three-foot square pillow covered with white satin-like fabric, no less, and two stainless steel bowls next to it. This is a dog-friendly hotel–one that gets my kudos.

I can attest to only two out of the three "Heavenly" extras The Westin offered – absolutely delicious sleeping and bathing conditions. When I checked out, I spoke to the Front Office Manager, Allen Chin, and expressed my appreciation for the "Heavenly" stay at their hotel. He told me Westin has always had innovative ideas. "We were the first to become a dog-friendly property, as well as providing our unique "Heavenly" experience. Westin is also part of Starwood Preferred Guest®, which was voted the number one hotel guest loyalty program in the world for the fourth consecutive year." Congrats to you, Westin Hotel, on your creativity, unique marketing ideas, and determination to be of service–all results of being kind-hearted to pets!

All the rest of this book could be filled with such ideas! You have your own too; just do them. They do make a difference. They can be so simple yet so rewarding! It becomes addictive –and what a fabulous way to get high!

If we awake to the sensitive part of ourselves, we can all practice kindness in our lives. Tune in and do what is appropriate. Put yourself

215

out there and take a risk. It will be well worth your effort.

Being kindhearted is essential in building relationships. Doing something nice for someone else is kindhearted. It could be the simplest of gestures, like bringing your child a cup of cocoa when she's studying for a test. Maybe something unexpected—a gift, a phone call, a hug when you meet your friend in the post office and she's on the verge of tears. Outwardly it looks like you're doing this for someone else, but inwardly you're feeling terrific about who you are. You don't even expect anything in return, because it's done out of the kindness mode inside.

Being kindhearted is being thoughtful. It's taking time from ourselves and giving it to another. But often we don't take the time to be thoughtful, because we're so busy. We're so busy being busy.

My friend Shannon calls me when I'm gone for more than a few weeks. She'll leave the kindest message on my voice mail, "Hey, I miss you. How's it goin'?" It touches my heart immensely. Small gesture, huge impact.

Many people claim to think about doing something for someone, but they don't get around to it. The thought is nice, yes, but the action is even better. That's what demonstrates the thoughtfulness and the sincere expression of kindness. It has a magical way of opening up the love in our hearts, and the love within us is meant to flow. As we act on our kindness, it opens up the love in others. Funny how that works.

Often the smallest gestures are the most touching. Some examples in my life are:

- the card from my all-time favorite card company, Suzie's Zoo, which Christopher sent me for Mother's Day;
- the matching T-shirts Danielle gave Gene and I for our anniversary with twenty on the back;
- and, the flowers Jeff sent me for Valentine's Day, stating on the card that I would always be his favorite Valentine. Music to a mother's ears.

Our time is a gift we give to others. Take the time to be thoughtful. Do something for someone else, however small or incidental you might think it is. It will make you feel so good; you will want to do it again, and again, and again.

Reflection Time:

1. What could you do to make someone, anyone, even someone you don't know, happy?

2. Do a little experiment with someone and take turns criticizing each other. How does it feel? Now be kind to each other. How does that feel? Notice the difference.

3. How do you want to live your life? Start to develop the capacity to "see the one in the many," as Lao Tzu suggested.

4. What kind of things could you do for your parents that would be exhibiting kindness?

5. What kind of attitude harms the environment? Beliefs? Choices?

6. What can you do today to help the environment and change these attitudes and beliefs?

7. Who are the thoughtful people in your life?

8. When was the last time you did something that was kindhearted?

9. If you had only one minute to create a list of kind gestures what would they be?

10. Do you think your friends truly care about you? Why? Why not?

"No place in all of my travels have I seen such loneliness as I have seen in the poverty of affluence in America."

Mother Theresa

L is for feeling... Lonely

Definition: solitary, desolate, forlorn, remote, alienated, rejected

Opposite: intimate, close, connected

We have all felt lonely at some time in our lives. Maybe we just broke up with a girlfriend, or lost a loved one, or simply feel alone in our beliefs and opinions. When someone feels lonely, he or she feels as though no one could understand what he or she is going through. Maybe they feel cut off from humankind and the Greater Source. Maybe they feel like a support system is lacking, or that no one cares. Lonely is a feeling that can overwhelm and a sense of desperation or urgency.

One time, when Max, our puppy, had just come back from visiting his brother, Sachi, he was feeling very lonely. I found him one morning lying in front of my full-length mirror looking at himself and whimpering a mournful cry. He missed the company of his brother, who looks just like him, and hoped to find something of his playmate in his own reflection. When he feels lonely, I pet him and tell him I understand.

Mother Theresa dealt with many of the poor and suffering in the world, and had something to say about lonely. A couple from Massachusetts spent time serving in one of the late Mother Theresa's orphanages in Calcutta. When they were leaving, Mother Theresa spoke to them, "I have seen the starving in the slums of Calcutta, but in your country I have seen an even greater hunger–that is the hunger to be loved. No place in all of my travels have I seen such loneliness as I have seen in the poverty of affluence in America. I have seen the rejected–these are your starving."

Mother Theresa saw loneliness as the need to be loved. It is interesting that she pinpointed Americans as feeling this way. We live in a country of such abundance! We have grocery stores with foods from around the world; we have shops with any style or color of clothing; we have cars and homes and so much more! Yet, people are not happy. There are so many of us–yet we still feel lonely. Why? So many feel isolated and climb into their holes and feel self-pity.

This amazingly compassionate woman also said, "You don't water the leaves or the fruit of a tree. You water the roots–its source." You have to water the source or the rest will dry up. So let's "water" or pay attention to the source of loneliness. How can we ever feel alone when we have the constant companion of our mind? Our mind is continually active, isn't it? It's busy judging self and others; it encourages and sabotages; it brings up painful memories, and it supports progress. Our mind is there to play with and laugh at. It's also there to be disciplined. How can we ever really be alone? But first we have to know there is more to us than our mind. There is the self (with the little "s" and the Self, with the big "S"). It seems to me that the innermost core of all loneliness is a yearning to know and merge with our lost Self. Often, before we do that, we get to know our mind quite well. It is sometimes referred to as "monkey chatter."

We could reach out to our friends. If you don't have any, make them. Reach out to your community through service. Reach out to the universe for your spirit guides many would refer to as angels. You say you don't believe in angels? Fine with me–your choice.

Continue then to listen and honor the monkey mind, or the sabotaging beliefs that keep you lonely. What would happen to your life if you broke all those ties to the past, your skepticism and cynicism, and truly celebrated your relationships? To actually come to your relationships with a magic wand and say they are perfect just the way they are, because you said so.

While visiting Hawaii, Gene and I sat at a picnic table to have a vanilla latte and a muffin. A young man who was also having something to eat was at the same table. Sensing his loneliness, I started talking to him and we continued for over an hour. One lovely aspect of vacations is that there is no time, no appointments, no hurry. Anyhow, Francis M. Primeaux, Jr., is also known as Eagle Feather Walks in the Dawn. He told us he is a chief in the Lakota Sioux Nation, located in Rosebud, South Dakota. After our intimate visit and bonding, he invited us to the yearly Sun Dance, which is an incredible spiritual event, lasting nine days, at the end of summer, including a four-day vision quest.

I can hardly put into words what this experience meant to Gene and me. We spoke of the atrocities of his people imposed by "the white man" and asked him if he was bitter as a result. He said, "My mind is better than that." He told us of his love for Mother Earth. "Mother Earth is the true Mother. Without her there would be no life." He served our country in the U.S. Army for nine years and was in Hawaii working when we met him. Our moments together were very special. His humbleness and pride came through naturally, and it connected us to him on a soul level. We parted hearing the words in his native language, "Mitahu Oyasin," which means "we are all related." I send blessings and gratitude to you Eagle Feather Who Walks in the Dawn for touching our lives. The universe has precise ways of uniting us to recognize and achieve our wholeness.

To give up making others wrong, means giving up being right. Are you big enough to do this? *A Course in Miracles* asks, "Do you prefer that you be right or happy?" Maybe your answer is to be "right." Fine and dandy. That's cool. The universe doesn't really care. Just know reality WILL reflect that choice.

Alone or Lonely?

In order to conquer loneliness, we must change our attitude, and see the feeling of loneliness as a gift coming our way. Let's start off with the question, "Do you enjoy your own company, or do you always have to have someone around you?" Is going away for a weekend by yourself a fascinating or scary idea? How about just a day outing, even for an hour or two, as Julia Cameron suggests in *The Artist's Way*?

I remember being in an airport one time waiting for a flight. We can have so much fun being with our minds in airports thinking thoughts like, "Hey look at that luggage; now that I like." "That hat is so cute. I'd look good in that style, but I don't like the color." "How can she walk in those high heels?" "Why is he talking so loud on his cell phone? I'm not interested in his conversation, and I doubt that anyone else is either." My mind is such a companion! Can you relate to this?

All by Myself

I personally indulge in alone time. In 1990 I was asked to perform a wedding for the daughter of a friend of mine. It would be my first, and I felt rather unprepared. The demands at home prevented me from spending the necessary time to create a beautiful ceremony for her daughter and future son-in-law. The time was drawing near, and I felt the need to get away by myself. A retreat spot that was tranquil and quiet is what I was searching for—a place to be alone. I retrieved my "Getaways Close to Home" file and discovered a haven in the nearby mountains that appeared to fill my requirements.

After a pleasant journey, I reached my destination and drove up the long dirt road lined with huge grand firs, ponderosa pines, aspen, and birch. I was in awe of the beauty that welcomed and embraced me. It felt good to be there. Perfect, I thought, just perfect. The innkeeper and her young son warmly greeted me. They showed me the layout and amenities. There were three cabins in the meadow, which were surrounded by 160 acres of private, heavily-treed property. Beyond that was National Forest land. There would be no other guests; I would have the entire area to myself. "Be aware of what you ask for," the expression goes. "You just might get it." I asked for alone, and alone is what I got!

After a few deep breaths in the crystalline air to acknowledge my blessings, I unloaded my gear into the Thoreau-style cabin. Inside the functional, cozy, log shelter was a wood stove, bathroom, kitchenette, and separate bedroom with hurricane lamps all around. What more does one really need? Like Thoreau, I craved the simple life. He didn't even want a door mat offered to him by a friend. "Just something else to clean," he retorted.

I propped up the pillows, sat on the bed, swung out the windows, and gazed upon a "Kodak moment." Wow! It was exquisite. My senses were alive with the smell, sight, and feel of autumn blowing through the windows. In a few moments, I acclimated to the silence. Acres and acres, abundant with wildlife and natural beauty, provided me with the inspiration to accomplish my task.

The scene was breathtaking. I gazed out at a pristine wilderness and connected to the power behind its stillness. I felt the solitude throughout my whole being as my mind started to calm and my awareness became even more astute. Periodically, fearful thoughts attempted to invade my peaceful state like, "What if something happens to me; there's nobody in ear shot." And, "It's lonely out here with nobody to talk to or even see." Fortunately, I successfully took charge of those negative thoughts and ushered them along their way.

Yes, I was alone, but I didn't feel lonely. It felt absolutely wonderful. In fact, I noticed the initial confidence in the project being restored as I started to settle in. My energy level seemed to surge. I felt emerging creativity and excitement about co-creating with Great Spirit. I was hardly alone.

Certainly, as night follows day, the format and words of the ceremony began to flow. Frequent outings in the woods didn't throw me off my purpose; they became part of the process. I trusted that the time spent appreciating nature would be beneficial to the whole. The sun and wind, and the moments spent swinging in the hammock listening to the sounds of the mountains, all contributed to a magical experience.

I felt gratitude for my thirty hours in this remote hideaway; I completed my mission, and felt renewed in all ways. When I shared it with others, I was somewhat taken back when the responses had a similar chime,

"Weren't you scared being out there all alone?" I responded with, "There are many who feel alone while in a crowded city, or lying next to someone in the same bed." No, I didn't feel scared, nor did I feel alone, but I could appreciate and respect their apprehension.

So what does aloneness really mean? I was alone physically, and yet I felt connected. It appeared to enrich and empower me. I felt united with nature and supported in my belief that I can never be alone. My thoughts can initiate fear and doubt, or love and trust. I choose the latter.

This brief interlude of aloneness reminded me how much I value spending time with myself. I like me. I like my company. I love and respect nature and prefer its sounds to that of freeway traffic. During this time, ringing phones and appointments ceased to exist. Demands and stress were nonexistent, because I knew and trusted the ceremony would turn out perfectly. My entire body slowed down and seemed to gently say, "Thank you." Although I didn't realize it at the time, this was a blessed gift I gave myself. I vowed I wouldn't need an excuse next time.

Now when are you going to set up a magical experience with yourself?

P.S. The bride was beautiful, and the groom, ever so handsome. Cabo San Lucas in Baja, Mexico was the scene for the exchange of vows. I performed the marriage ceremony on the shores of a magnificent white beach with the waves of the Pacific Ocean crashing in the background. It was like something out of a movie, and quite a romantic first page in the book of their united life.

Reflection Time:

1. When you are alone, do you feel lonely? What deep-rooted beliefs are causing this feeling? How could you overcome it?

2. How do you reach out to others? To your community?

3. Who is your support network? Do you let them know how much you appreciate them?

4. When was the last time you went out and did something that you like to do all by yourself?

5. Would you be willing to schedule some alone time for yourself within the next week?

6. Is this a scary thought? Could you view it as fascinating?

7. Is there a day, or particular time of the day, during the week that you feel lonely? Friday nights, Sundays, the first thing in the morning? Why these particular times?

8. Do you acknowledge your lonely feelings?

9. Make a list of the people who love you. Do you experience their love?

10. Does intimacy intimidate you?

NAMASTE: *I honor the place in you in which the entire universe dwells. I honor the place in you, which is of love, of truth, of light, and of peace. When you are in that place in you and I am in that place in me, we are One.*

L is for feeling... Loving

Definition: affectionate, devoted, caring, fond

Opposite: heartless, cruel, unkind, mean, hateful, fearful

"Love sweet love." "Only love prevails." "All you need is love." Valentine's Day, hearts, and chocolate candy. When one feels loving, most likely his/her heart is wide open, ready to give and receive from the core of his or her being. Whether "loving" by hugging a child, writing a check to a favorite charity or by kissing your partner affectionately, one thing is for sure–the world would be a desolate place without love. After all "Love makes the world go 'round."

This feeling word has been the source for numerous books, countless seminars and classes, thousands of popular songs, and innumerable poems. One such class was taught at the University of Southern California by the late Leo Buscaglia, a professor, lecturer, and author of many popular books. His audiences fell in love with him through his wit, his hugs, and genuineness.

Following are some of his quotes about love.

- "A total immersion in life offers the best classroom for learning to love."
- "The loving person is one who cares about her/himself."
- "Seeing the continual wonder and joy is being alive."
- "A loving relationship is the unconditional acceptance of another person."
- "To live in love is life's greatest challenge."

From his book entitled *Love*, he states, "Vulnerability is always at the heart of love." I would agree with him. When we open our hearts, we're open to hurt, disappointment, rejection, and pain. We're also open to peace, joy, contentment, and beauty.

Love is Free

The subject of peace and love need not be confined to Christmas and Valentine's Day. Regardless of all effort by the human mind to capture these terms, love and peace have no boundaries. When do we realize that love grows when it is expressed? There is no limit to where it goes or to whom or what it touches. Love is free! What dams up the harmonic current of love are human limitations such as jealousy and possessiveness. Love is expansive, not restrictive. Ultimately, love is all there is.

Unconditional love means exactly that, unconditional, no matter what. Mine was challenged a bit I recall, when I was a new California resident and felt a desire for a furry companion. I saw an ad in the paper for poodle puppies and decided to take the big leap and share my life with a furry friend. I was employed at a hospital in LA, so after work I went out to the valley to pick up my new puppy. Keep in mind I wore a white uniform when I worked. The puppy and I bonded immediately, in my experience anyhow. He was so frightened sitting in the back seat of the car, periodically expressing through his squeals and cries, I pulled off one of the famous California freeways and reached around, took him out of his little box, and put him on my lap, knowing that I could give him the comfort and nurturing he was looking for. He must have felt loved and very much at home, because after a few moments, I felt a warm sensation in my lap. I looked into the sweet puppy's eyes and all I could experience was unconditional love for this dear, sweet animal who was no longer with her mother and with me, a stranger. It was a bit odd to drive the distance home in this condition. That I will leave to your imagination.

Expressing Love

There are countless ways to express love, and they need not be the stereotypical mushy, gushy ways either. Sure, a mother shows her love by cooing to her baby, and a boyfriend shows his love by sending a poem to his sweetheart. But feeling loving is so much broader than the typical notion of love! In fact, because we are all unique individuals, we can only show love in our own way. Realize this about yourself. An artist may show his love for trees by sketching them. A teacher may show his love for travel by teaching a foreign language. A writer may show her love for nature by writing an article on camping.

When we identify with our essence of love, our reality looks so different. Once we've anchored ourselves in our purpose and our passion, life becomes more joyful. A tetherball is attached to a cord, then attached to the pole. It gets whacked back and forth from clockwise to counter clockwise, but the ball always comes back to the center pole. It doesn't go anywhere. When we identify ourselves with our truth, with love, with our spirit, no matter what happens in our lives, we'll be anchored to our loving energy. As a tetherball, even when we're knocked this way or that, we are constantly coming back to center. There's no place to go looking for love—it's right here.

My research over the past thirty years has proven this is all we want—to be loved, accepted, and to be who we are. Besides acceptance, I feel love is synonymous with enthusiasm, compassion, trust, and bliss. A wider view of love includes gratitude, honesty, responsibility, and heart-centered communication.

In 1975, I participated in a day-long course called, "Celebrating Your Relationships," offered by "est," a human potential growth program. One of the thousand-plus participants stood up and asked questions pertaining to his relationship with his father and lady friend and some others. He spoke about how they don't relate to him and wouldn't play nor share intimately with him. "I come to them with love and acceptance and they won't play. There is no relationship." Werner Erhard, the founder of est, was conducting the seminar that day. He said, "They have the capacity for love but their expression of it is bound up. Their inability to love is their highest expression of love. It's a bound-up absolute love for you. If you can accept that, and if you come to the relationship being joyful and celebrate the relationship exactly as it is, it will provide the heat to melt whatever is there, and miracles will happen." The auditorium roared with acknowledgement of those words.

Dr. Gerald G. Jampolski, founder of the Center of Attitudinal Healing in California, says, "Teach love, for that is what you are." He wrote a book in 1979 called *Love is Letting Go of Fear*. It is about re-training our minds. He wrote, "Fear always distorts our perception and confuses us as to what is going on. Love is the total absence of fear. Love, then, is really everything that is of value, and fear can offer us nothing because it is nothing."

Our communications with others must be based in honesty, and we must join together for the good of all. Many are afraid to love because they've been so wounded in the past. Yet refusing to love any further is only cutting one off from oneself.

When we hold grudges, harbor hate, and seek revenge, we teach another message with a different vibration. That vibration comes through beliefs that don't serve us. Dr. Jampolsky goes on to say, "The world we see that seems so insane is the result of a belief system that is not working. To perceive the world differently, we must be willing to change our belief system, let the past slip away, expand our sense of now, and dissolve the fear in our minds." This leads us to union and away from separation.

When I'm feeling loving, I'm connected with my soul. I see myself as a wave of the ocean of Creative Infinite Intelligence that is Love. Ignorance of this truth can be replaced at any moment when I choose to acknowledge the wisdom that I am love. It is my source. The more I feel it and give it away, the more it manifests in my life through abundance, joy, opportunity, and laughter. All I need to do is be it – feel it – live it. Where there is no love, put love, and you will feel love.

Live in Love

If love is acceptance, and you actually accepted people for who they are, how would your life be different? Why would we want to change someone so badly when we realize the result is resentment? Resentment is one of the bricks in a wall that prevents love from being expressed.

How would it be different if you could have your relationships be exactly the way you'd want them to be? What would it look like? How would it impact your life? Imagine if you could live your life this way for one day? What would it mean to a person you might never see again? We never know what the next moment brings. A phone call or a knock at the door could drastically change our lives. A client shared with me the time someone from the U.S. Government knocked on her family's door to give them the news that her brother had died in combat. What shocking news to hear, in the middle of having a typical morning breakfast.

So, if you actually knew this about another's destiny (as well as your own), how would you live your life? I invite you to experiment and try it for one day. Live your life like you knew you'd never see that person again. What would be different? Maybe you could stretch it two days, then three, then maybe every day you could actually live your life in love, allowing people to be exactly the way they are and the way they are not.

Too many people on the planet FEEL unloved. Yes, parents love their kids, but why is it kids don't FEEL loved? We're all looking to be unconditionally loved. There is a difference. This is love with only love strings attached. "No matter what, my love is always there for you." Through quality time together, we show love. Through awareness of feelings and the skill to express them, we feel love. Then, we speak it sincerely, and be it, under all circumstances. Choose love.

The experience of love that heals and transforms the quality of our lives is an attitude of the hearts. When we walk into a dark room and turn on the light, nothing is altered, yet everything has changed. Every person is a radiating center of energy.

Love is the River of Life

Love is the energy which leads us down the river of life. In nature's infinite wisdom, love and life flow with a constant and ever changing motion. Love is a cascade. Love is a calm eddy. On this tributary of love and life, we join at a confluence which brings two bodies of love together as one. In these two bodies which are one, love becomes stronger and deeper, changing and constant, tumultuous and serene. Love will flow together and ride as one, down the river of life. **Shannon Orr**

Reflection Time:

1. What areas of your life are in conflict?
2. How would you describe the relationship with your father, mother, siblings.
3. What about your relationship to money?
4. What is your definition of love?
5. Are you aware of the times in your life when your heart is blocked from expressing love?
6. Do you have the skills to shift moments like this?
7. Write a love letter to someone you know that you want to communicate with, including yourself. Simply begin with the hot feelings you have for that person. Write word after word and just let them flow. Speak of your resentment, irritation, feelings of betrayal. Get in touch with your feelings and share them on paper. Just write. Get the energy that's inside of you on a piece of paper. Share your frustrations, disappointments, and your anger. When you feel complete, do a simple ritual with fire in a safe location. Let the energy now on the paper be consumed by fire. Feel complete. Now write a letter to the same person, sharing your needs and open your heart to allow the love to flow through you. The purpose of this letter is to move the energy within you, not necessarily to send it to that person. This is a cathartic process, and it will help.

How to Write A Love Letter

Writing has a powerful effect on our emotional state. The following exercise is designed to help you fully express feelings that may have lain dormant for a long time, or may be too intense and jumbled for you to process effectively. You'll find it helpful in expressing what you feel, especially if you're having difficulty

letting go, forgiving, grieving for or being appropriately angry at someone.

THIS LETTER IS NOT DESIGNED TO BE MAILED TO ANYONE. After you write it, you may decide to write another appropriately adjusted letter for the other person to read. The point of this is to let your feelings out, uncensored and unedited.

Begin by expressing your anger, resentment and blame and allow yourself to move through the other levels until you get down to the love. You may find your feelings begin pouring out as you write. If so, just go with what you feel. If you get stuck or confused, the following suggested lead-in phrases may help you.

A.   Anger and Blame

      I hate it when...

      I get so irritated when you...

      I resent that you...

      I am so annoyed at your...

B.   Hurt and Sadness

      I feel disappointed that you...

      I am hurt because...

      I feel unhappy and neglected after you...

      I feel sadness every time you...

C.   Fear and Insecurity

      I feel frightened when you...

      I am scared to hear you...

      I feel insecure when...

      I feel rejected when I see you...

D. Guilt and Responsibility

       I'm sorry that...

       I'll never...

       I don't deserve to have...

       I didn't mean to...

E. Love, Forgiveness, Understanding and Desire

       I love you when...

       I appreciate your...

       I forgive you for...

       I feel loving because of...

Now, put the letter away for a couple of days, then re-read it and decide if you want to share part of it with the other person. If you are writing to someone who has passed on, you may want to burn the letter to symbolically 'send' it.

Used with author permission. Adapted from It Ends with You: Grow Up and Out of Dysfunction (New Page Books, 2003) ISBN 1-56414-548-4 by Tina B. Tessina.

"Laughter and humor integrate the physiological, the psychological, and the social events and processes that shape each person as do few other phenomena."

Raymond A. Moody, Jr. M.D., *Laugh After Laugh:*
The Healing Power of Humor

L is for feeling... Loyal

Definition: faithful, devoted, dependable, unfailing
Opposite: disloyal, treacherous, false

To be loyal is to be faithful, trustworthy, or dedicated. Loyalty indicates strong character and represents a person of conviction. Loyalty is one of the characteristics for the astrological sign of Capricorn, which happens to be my sun sign. I feel loyalty for my friends, my personal passion, and the values I've learned from long experience.

Being trustworthy is also an aspect of loyalty. It means you can be counted on to keep your word. Synonymous words would be determination, reliability, and truthfulness. Can you rely on people if they are fickle or often change their minds? I want a friend I can count on for support when I forget to be kind. That support might be calling me on my stuff. That's a loyal friend.

I have attracted loyal friends in my life that I feel grateful for. At one time, Carol, Bobbie, and I all lived in LA. Now I'm in Idaho, Carol's in Australia, and Bobbie's in California. We still have our reunions. Another special friend, Judy, met me at the airport after not seeing each other after a long time. We were so engrossed in being together, that I almost missed my connecting flight. Distance does not interfere with loyalty amongst friends.

When we practice loyalty, we stand up for ourselves, believe in ourselves, and have unwavering faith. Your loyalty as a friend means you are willing to do whatever it takes to clear up a miscommunication. A friend of mine and I had an uncomfortable situation like this. She said many words that hurt me, and I honored her feelings, knowing that somehow this would all work out. I heard her point of view and asked if she would be willing to hear mine. It didn't happen immediately, but it did happen. Our love and loyalty for each other overturned those few painful moments. We are united and committed to purge ignorance and replace it always with wisdom.

231

Furry Friends

Lessons about loyalty come from animals too. In Native American cultures, animals represent certain "medicine." Dogs are known to have the medicine of loyalty. The notion of the loyal dog turns up over and over again in Hollywood, from *Old Yeller* to Lassie to *Turner and Hooch* to *The Truth about Cats and Dogs*. Man's best friend has won hearts over and over again.

Writers and filmmakers have written and produced innumerable books and films about our four-legged friends because they know what pulls on our hearts. We can learn lessons through animals that can solidify our purpose and passion. If you haven't seen the movie *My Dog Skip*, do so! It was a tearjerker for me. One of the best lines at the end is, "He's buried under the Elm tree. No, he's buried in my heart."

Speaking of dogs, I have a few "Dogs' Letters to God" (email wisdom) that I'd like to share and which are worth a chuckle:

- "Dear God, How come people love to smell flowers, but seldom smell one another? Where are their priorities?"
- "Dear God, When we get to heaven can we sit on your couch? Or is it the same old story?"
- "Dear God, Can you undo what that doctor did?"

Loyalty has long been a pet characteristic and hard to match. Animals can open our hearts after being closed for years; they can bring an incredible amount of comfort to a suffering soul, as well as one in physical pain. This is loyalty, compassion, and sensitivity beyond words. It's no wonder why many people prefer them to adults!

Max has been so loyal to me while writing this book. In the last few months of intensity and dedication to complete it, he stayed near my side, curled up, looking like a black and white fur ball. And then he'd hear, "Good-bye" from AOL, as I'd sign off for the night (which could be anywhere from midnight to 2:30 A.M.). He'd take a good stretch then follow me down the hall to my bedroom to snuggle on his lamb's wool-covered bed. His sweet soul gives love unconditionally and his loyalty is beyond measure. What joy he has brought to my life!

Committed

One can have a profound loyalty to other things, including a cause. I was intensely involved with the clean air movement while living in Los Angeles in the sixties. We called our group, "Write for Your Life," because we believed if people were educated, they would then write to their elected officials so they could properly represent the people. Once we'd been heard from, obviously, our action would make a difference. However, it didn't exactly work that way. That's when I started to question who exactly these elected officials do represent.

I protested with other mothers and our children in front of Standard Oil in downtown L.A. because of lead in our gasoline. I developed a vehement loyalty to a cause—the environment. What started as protesting air pollution, merged into oil, then land pollution, then food, chemicals, sprays, dyes, treatment of animals for food, and sweeteners. Basically, we were advocates for the quality of life. It is still a cause I feel strongly about.

Go Bruins!

While I was out protesting, my husband Gene was home watching his Bruins on television. He is loyal to his alma mater, UCLA. Many times his loyalty is tested, but he remains loyal to the team, even when they don't perform exactly the way he prefers. Go Bruins Go! But they don't always go!

One year his team was in the Rose Bowl game. Moments before the kickoff, I said to my husband, "I'm going to watch your Bruins play ball," which in itself was a display of loyalty. Although shocked by my spontaneous gesture, he was totally thrilled to have my company as he anticipated my cheerleading support. So there we were on New Year's Day, nestled in our usual positions on the sofa, Gene in his blue and gold alumni hat and me with a large bowl of popcorn, discussing offensive and defensive star players. However, being true to my nature, I couldn't help but draw analogies to the game and life and loyalty.

Both teams were bursting with enthusiasm as the game began. Before long, the action was inundated with turnovers, fumbles, and interceptions, which caused emotional havoc in our home. Groaning of varied intensity permeated the room every time the Bruins had a mishap.

The analogy: The team is psyched up with a plan in mind and intention is high. They have the ball. Effort is in full swing; they're going for it, headed for the touchdown line. In a moment, it all changes. Someone drops the ball. A player with a different-colored jersey catches the ball. A pass is too short, too long, too high, or too wide. Bummer! It doesn't happen according to the plan. The paradox of life is quite evident, as the other team cheers outrageously.

The nature of competition creates a fierce test for loyalty. You might feel loyal to your dear friend until she gets the part in the play you tried out for and felt you deserved. Or your loyalty to a fellow worker turns to treachery when you hear the news of his promotion and salary increase.

Have there been times in your life when you've felt loyal and committed to a plan, done all the right things, and were headed for your goal? Then something happened and turned everything around. INTERCEPTION. Your goal is disrupted. You scratch your head and wonder what happened.

Have there been times when your loyalty has been challenged?

- Your dear friend and business partner is disloyal by covering up certain important transactions. Your faith has been destroyed through this behavior, and your relationship has changed forever.
- You've given your all to a community organization that you've been loyal to for years. Another board member says something hurtful, you retreat and your loyalty to the organization is compromised. What to do?
- 'Blood is thicker than water' takes on new meaning as your relationship with your family is threatened because of a family lawsuit over an inheritance. Loyalty is replaced with bitterness, revenge, and lack of forgiveness.

You could add your own story to the list, yes? There are times when our loyalty is questioned and it makes us evaluate how loyal we truly are, which is a good thing. They say, "Test your beliefs through experience; don't just believe something." Is your loyalty one sided? Should loyalty be a two-way experience?

Friendship

Being a loyal friend makes me feel good about myself. I believe it has strengthened my character, and I am proud to be a loyal friend. There have been times when I chose to leave a friendship, as it just played itself out. We were on different paths and lost touch with each other, and that's okay. Our days are full and how many quality friendships can we maintain anyhow?

I strive to preserve my friendships through communication. If I notice the calls always going one way, it is a sign for me to question and communicate. Many people hold onto friends for the wrong reasons. Maybe it looks and sounds good to have soooooo many friends and such an active social calendar. Being loyal seems to require a certain amount of effort and intention, wouldn't you say?

A colleague expressed to me her pain because of the lack of loyalty from what she considered a long-time, close friend. "This 'friend' of mine called me, by accident, after not hearing from her for such a long time. I wondered about the nervousness in her voice, as we talked about trivial matters. The next day someone told me this 'good friend' was dating my ex-boyfriend. Why didn't she say something? I felt hurt and disappointed and betrayed. How could a dear friend do that to me? It has nothing to do with wanting him back or feeling jealous, it's about her betrayal of our friendship that I thought we both valued as special. The quality of our relationship was based on truth and integrity and this is what hurts, as apparently there was a lack of it on her part. Now that my anger has subsided, I have more clarity as how to approach the situation. I'm going to pick up the phone, discuss it with her, clear the air, and express my feelings in a mature manner. This action will put me in the driver's seat and will take me out of the victim role." THIS is an empowered woman. Good for you.

Well, back to the UCLA game. They lost. It took some time that day for Gene to recover from the 1994 Rose Bowl results, but I moved on and celebrated a brand new year, once again realizing lessons that enhance the quality of life about loyalty, friendships, and loss–even from watching a football game.

Reflection Time:

1. What or who are you loyal to in your life?

2. Are your friends loyal to you?

3. What causes in your life are strong enough to rouse your passion and loyalty?

4. If you own a pet, reflect on the times he/she demonstrated loyalty to you.

5. Do you feel loyal to your family members just because they are blood relatives?

6. Do you feel loyal to your country, even when you are opposed to decisions that are being made?

7. Has a parent been a role model demonstrating loyalty for you? If so, in what way? If not, why do you suppose that is?

8. Do you experience yourself as being loyal? If so, how? If not, why not?

9. Have you ever felt your loyalty has been betrayed? Taken advantage of? Discounted?

10. Is there one person who you KNOW will never let you down?

"We all have the ability to manifest divine magic. It's bubbling under the surface of our lives all the time."
Linda Forman, *Dreaming in Real Time*

M is for feeling... Magical

Definition: enchanting, mystical, mysterious, wondrous
Opposite: common, simple, dull, plain, conventional

The word "magical" evokes images of wizards and fairies and unicorns and Harry Potter and *The Lord of the Rings*. Magic seems to have gotten "hip" in the mainstream media. But what about feeling magical? When I feel magical, I feel like I've tapped into my inner mystique, my inner priestess, and I feel sparkly! It is the feeling of being invincible! In other words, there isn't anything I can't do. Whatever the chronological age of our body, there is a child that lives in our heart-mind with characteristics such as acceptance, purity, honesty, spontaneity, uniqueness, imagination, innocence, and resilience—all relative to magic.

Feeling that your inner magical child is alive and ready contributes to feeling masterful. I think the positive connotations of the word "masterful" are "confident, strong, centered, empowered, ingenious, amazing, and incredible... Magical." When I'm feeling masterful, I am oh-so-connected to my atma (soul).

In Sync

Once I was cross-country skiing on the bike path near our Nordic center. I watched many others skate-skiing, which is a more graceful, more aerobic form of cross-country skiing—a cross between skiing and roller-skating. I thought to myself, "I could do that. All I need are some instructions." (I found out later, one also needs a certain type of ski!) I skied around the next bend and noticed a folded pink piece of paper in the snow. Having a habit of picking up litter, I retrieved this piece to throw away later. It appeared to be so nice and clean, and I felt an urge to see what it was. Indeed, I opened it up and read the content. It said, "Techniques on How to Skate Ski"! I threw back my head, laughed, and said, "Thank you!" to the Universe.

One of my favorite card lines is Suzy's Zoo. There is no local store that carries it. After regularly shopping for cards at one particular store,

I just happened to ask if they would consider it, given the many aisles of greeting cards available to their customers. The answer? "It's been ordered and will be here in about two months." Instant gratification. "Small things," you might say. Hey, the Law doesn't measure by size.

Some of us have lost touch with the magical child within. Where did she/he go? Why have some of us settled for a life of mediocrity rather than a life of magic? Mediocrity means moderate to low in quality. Our mind-talk might lead us into a mediocre life, or we could choose a life of magic, instead. Create your destiny. Be masterful and live a life of magic!

To quote from one of my favorite books, *Illusions*, Richard Bach says, "Every person, all of the events of your life, are there because you have drawn them to you. What you choose to do with them is up to you."

Until you commit to something, you're "on the fence." W.H. Murray, a member of the Scottish expedition to Mt. Everest observed that "until one is committed there is always hesitancy."

Dream Time

My sister, Georgia, had her own magic happen when she was invited to become a member of the prestigious circumnavigator club. She says, "As a prior flight attendant for American Airlines, I was always intrigued with the magic of travel, geography, and foreign cultures. I took a journey, circling the world in one continuous trip in the same direction, which qualified me to join this international club whereby people such as General McArthur, Neil Armstrong, Lowell Thomas, and Norman Vincent Peale are some of the members. It takes a positive attitude, self-confidence, plus determination to accomplish things you may not have ever imagined or wondered possible. This adventure of mine was the high point of my travel escapades, meeting people of other cultures in their homes; it was completely magical."

Are you living your dreams? Do you even still have a dream? Dreams are often thwarted when we grow into adulthood. Dreams are what we want to do, rather than what we settled for in order to earn a living. Fantasy and dreams are healthy. As parents, do you support or squelch your child's dreams? As children, do you allow your dreams to be squelched?

A mother wanted an appointment with me for the purpose of clearing away anything that could possibly squelch her daughter's dreams. She was intent on eliminating any old beliefs that would act as an obstacle to being the best mother for her two-year-old daughter. She wrote,

"Sometimes I think back to my sessions with Alexandra, and I can't really explain what happened. What 'magic' occurred with her in those two sessions is still a phenomena. All I know is that I was ready to move past my old self and be who I was truly meant to be. The work we did together pushed me onto a new path without the old constraints holding me back. Now, I feel in my body, my heart, and my soul – more present. I'm happier with who I am and freer to be me. I'm also more open to my husband, my daughter, my family...more open to give and accept love, which is the reason I was put on the planet. Thank you, thank you, thank you." It sounds like her intention was fulfilled.

Jenny's View

About ten years ago, I interviewed children about their beliefs and attitudes. One young lady, Jenny Miller, age eleven, particularly impressed me. She had an absolutely magical attitude! It's obvious her parents raised her with a set of beliefs and values that have provided a strong foundation, as well as with life skills to live a happy and abundant adult life. They operate an outdoor program for children and adults in Colorado. The following are some of the questions and answers from the interview:

ADA: How have your parents brought you up? What values have they instilled in you?

JM: They taught me to be honest, to accept myself as I am, and not to worry about what anybody else says.

ADA: Would you say it's important to understand your feelings?

JM: Yes, because they can all build up and then explode and it's all really complicated.

ADA: What happens when it explodes and gets complicated?

JM: Then you feel insecure.

ADA: Would you say that you are in touch with your feelings?

JM: Yes, I usually talk to my friends and parents.

ADA: Do you feel like you can share anything with your parents? If so, why?

JM: They did the same with me. They trusted me.

ADA: Wow. That's really important. How did it make you feel when they shared their feelings with you?

JM: Maybe important.

ADA: What about feeling included in their life?

JM: Yes.

ADA: How would you measure your self-esteem?

JM: Eight or nine; maybe ten after basketball.

ADA: Why do you think that is, an eleven-year-old that feels so good about herself?

JM: I get good grades. Things that don't make sense I push aside they don't really bother me.

ADA: What kind of beliefs do you have about yourself and life?

JM: I believe I can do anything I want to.

ADA: How did you learn to believe that way? Where did it come from?

JM: My parents taught me this way. You have to have confidence to do anything, and without it, you can't do it.

ADA: Why do you think young people take drugs?

JM: Because they have problems, and they think it will fix them, and that is not the way to do it.

ADA: What would be the way to do it?

JM: Talk to somebody. Don't do something stupid just to get away from things because they won't help.

At the time of this printing Jennifer is now 22; enrolled in a semester abroad in the Dominican Republic; and is a junior attending Lewis & Clark College with a double major - International Affairs and Hispanic Studies. How inspiring! Like Jennifer and other magical children, when I'm feeling magical, there's nothing I can't do! I think something, visualize it, put energy there, and it happens.

Shanti Shanti

Another inspiring story about a family who demonstrates keeping magic alive comes from Linda Forman, author of *Dreaming in Real Time*. Her book is about her Sanskrit-chanting daughters who call themselves Shanti Shanti, and the magic that accompanies her life. Shanti Shanti has gained world recognition for their universally-spiritual concerts, chanting ancient Vedic recitations in Sanskrit and performing their original pop music written by their father, Bob Forman. The girls are incredibly gifted musicians, and along with their CDs and performances, are committed to this passion they feel. But what is most amazing is how the girls got involved with this rare art form.

Linda's absolutely fascinating message is as follows:

"It's important to listen to your children. It started when I was just barely pregnant with Sara, and Andrea, who was a toddler, brought

Acknowledged

Helice Bridges

Thank You for making the dream come true... A blue ribbon acknowledgement for every person in the world by the year 2004, creating dignity and respect among all people.

Aware

Challenged

Bethany Hamilton

Compassion

ADA & Ram Dass

Challenged

Creative

Kathleen Mardian

Daring

ADA Backcountry Outing

Despondent

In spite of everything,
I still believe that people are truly good at heart.

Anne Frank

Idaho Anne Frank
Human Rights Memorial

Fascinated

Embracing the Elders

Free

Boston Holocaust Memorial

Inspiration

Alekie Bennhoff

Christopher, my son The Pilot
& the Attitude Indicator

Joyful

Allissa ready for gymnastics

Bleeding Heart

Kindhearted

Lonely

Max & Sachi

Gene & ADA

Loyal

Gene, the Bruin Fan

Magical

Nurtured

Odd

Nostalgic

Cousin Hareklea preparing traditional Greek food

ADA on the walk from the spring

Uncle George & Daddy

Daddy's home in Lala Elias, Greece

Passionate

Painting by Jeff Abrams

My Trusty Backpack

Pacific Coast Highway, Malibu, CA

Peaceful

Resistant

Buddy

Supported

ADA & daugther Danielle

Supported

The Abrams Family

Tolerant

Unique

Corianna Sakura Abrams

Unique

Georgia, Alekie, Clara, ALexandra

Upset

Joanne. Mark & Steven Goldberg

Wise

Ryan & Page

Wise

PHONE:
(208) 733-4678

6 June, '03

2045 HILLCREST DRIVE
TWIN FALLS, IDAHO
83301

DAVID R. MEAD

Surveyor of sunrises/sunsets, clouds and storms;
Inspector of untamed paths, ridgetops and meadows;
Sharer in the passing parade.

Venturesome

Tom, Melissa, Tate, Trevor Boley

Wondrous

Yearning

Max

Youthful

Aunt Fannie celebrating her 100 birthday

Betrayed

Ryan, age 5

Frustrated

Tyler, age 8

Grateful

Becky, age 11

Greedy

COLOR OR DRAW ON THIS PAGE
Letter N Feeling Needy

Stephanie, age 8

Need a house. I need food. I need a bed.

Happy

It's a boy!

On January 7th, 1996, my baby brother was born. When we were driving to the hospital, a snow storm came. I was afraid that we might not make it to the hospital. When we got to the hospital everyone was relieved. I was exhausted because it was midnight.

The next day I was anxious to see the baby! It was awesome to watch him being born! It was fun to watch him in the nursery. I liked the cafeteria. When my sister and I got back to the room, Jared was asleep. I was glad to have a baby brother after having two sisters.

Natalie, age 9

Overwhelmed

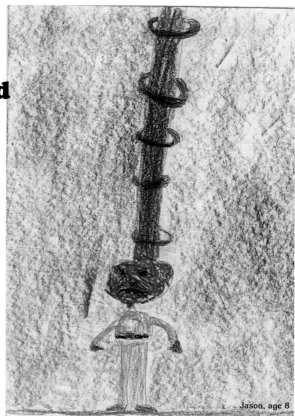

Jason, age 8

Trapped

Katie, age 7

Unloved

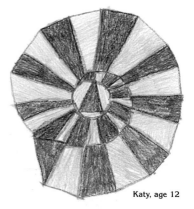

Katy, age 12

HERO

When you need a hero
Is anyubody really there
To show you that the world can be a good place?
When nobody's there,
That's when you look inside yourself.

When you need to cry
Is there a shoulder to grab
To comfort you?
When everybody's gone
That's when you lean on yourself.

You need a hero,
You need to cry
You need to love
You need yourself,
You can always count on yourself.

Katy, 7th grade, age 12

Tara, age 13

Alissa

Are you taking time to smell the roses?

me my Ayurvedic book and asked me which side of the page I read. (Ayurvedia is a 5,000-year-old perfected holistic health care system aimed at maintaining balance of life energies within us, rather than focusing on symptoms.) In this book, one side of the page is written in "devanagari," a written form of Sanskrit, and the other side is in English. She pointed to the Sanskrit page and said, "I can read this, Mommy." I was in disbelief and it took months and months to digest it. She had knowledge of a very complex language. How could children be fluent in a language that they never spoke and that was never spoken in the house? There was no way to explain it, it just appeared. Andrea wanted to chant this ancient Sanskrit language with a partner."

"I knew there wasn't a Sanskrit-chanting partner in Sparks, Nevada. And once she realized this, she'd then understand she couldn't do it either. I recall walking down the hallway and heard these two voices coming out of Andrea's bedroom. Bob and I slowly opened the door and Andrea said, "Look Mommy, Sara can do this, and she can do it even faster than me." Andrea was nine and Sara, seven. We slowly closed the door, and I felt like the wind had been knocked out of me. We didn't even speak. So now we have this with two – what to do now?"

"We became pro-active, contacted major universities, and bought textbooks. Andrea inhaled them all. 'If I read it before I go to bed, in the morning, I'll know it all.' She could not demonstrate this ability with any other subject."

Linda refers to her family unit as ordinary and says, "We all have the ability to manifest divine magic. It's bubbling under the surface of our lives, all the time."

Linda's advice on parenting is: "We are not giving our children a childhood anymore. Their little nervous systems can't take it all. It's there for a reason and they need time to nurture their own nervous system at the pace they're supposed to grow. Don't assume your children are going to do bad behavior because others are. Believe that your child is smarter and knows better than to demonstrate negativity. Expect them to live the highest. Condoning bad behavior can validate the parents' bad behavior."

"Listen to them and spend time with your kids. Talk to them and take a stand on issues. It's part of listening. Don't be afraid to set boundaries. I know of a story about a child who drank a large amount of poisonous liquid because she had so much rage toward her mother. Set boundaries – they need and want them."

"Don't be afraid they won't like you if you tell them what to do. Fulfill your child and your life will be fulfilled. Don't worry about yourself and get into 'poor me.' An incredible mechanism is to think about others and aid in their fulfillment."

Besides being an Ayurvedic practitioner, Linda travels with the family and is an authentic spokesperson for the group. Bob, the father, accompanies the girls and Micah, the younger brother, is enjoying his unique childhood.

Allow the magic to bubble up in your life but first believe it is possible and that you deserve to live a magical life. It goes with the territory here on plant Earth. Children don't question, they simply are present, encountering each moment of now with shear delight. Living your dreams is not supposed to be for only the rich and famous. Set your intentions, create your goal boards, clean up your past, and you too will be on the road to manifestation. Then just watch the sparks fly. I'd call that magic!

Reflection Time:

1. Is there something preventing you from committing yourself to a life of magic?
2. I invite you to explore what that something might be. Examine your beliefs and your dreams. Weed out the beliefs that don't work for you.
3. By writing down your dreams, evaluate which have manifested and which have not. What steps have you taken and not taken in order to achieve your goals?
4. Do you believe you deserve to have your dreams come true? Do you have passion behind your dreams?
5. Find a good friend or join a group of like-minded people who will mutually support goals and dreams.
6. Do you believe in magic? If so, what does it mean to you?
7. Do you ever intend to create something you want to find by a certain day and time? Try it. After that has been done, let it go and discover what happens.
8. Do you find Linda's daughters to possess a kind of magic? What is your reasoning behind their unique ability?
9. Are there beliefs that keep you conventional and dull?
10. Play with the idea of being magical for a day.

M is for feeling... Martyred

Definition: poor me, victim, torture, low self-esteem

Opposite: empowered, receptive

Have you ever said the following to yourself?

- "I'm doing it all."
- "Oh you don't have to show up; I can get it done by myself."
- "I have so much to do (sigh), but somehow I'll try to squeeze it in."
- "Just to make sure it turns out the way I want, I guess I'd better take charge of planning the event."
- "I'm so tired and not really feeling well, but I'll do it, because there's nobody else."
- "Feel sorry for me because my childhood was so rough."
- "I have so much pain in my life; nothing ever works out for me."
- "There's just always so much on my plate I have to juggle."

These are all thought-forms of the martyr, the one who is always doing everything, but never getting the credit, the one who feels sorry for him or herself, the one who acts out the role of the underdog. To be feeling martyred is the opposite of feeling empowered. Somewhere along the line, the martyr has given away his or her power for whatever reason.

Have you ever known people whose lives are so incredibly full of drama? Their script could be in the soap operas! They take on more and more and then feel resentful; rarely, can they acknowledge it to themselves or others.

Many martyrs don't feel worthy unless there is a task to be done. They become human doings, rather than human beings, taking on more and more, out of lack of love and respect for themselves. A martyr can actually attempt to make someone else feel inferior to detract from his or her own feelings of inadequacy.

A martyr will feel undeserving of quiet time and self-pampering and will take on more projects, responsibilities, or assignments. It may even be under the guise of helping humankind.

The Caregiver

Caregivers tend to get into this feeling. They can easily lose sight of their original mission, because they're so identified with their caregiver identity. Others often recognize it before the martyr does because friends and relations can sense the passive hostility and bitterness. The martyr's comments may become mean and vicious. Blame then becomes the next hidden agenda. The rat goes down yet another spiral of the maze.

Gail was a client who overcame her martyr identity. While doing Ph.D. work, she agreed to provide elder care for her parents. After she moved into their home, she also became a Girl Scout volunteer, creating and organizing new events for girls. If cook, laundress, shopper, student, and nurse were not enough, Gail took her parents on every out-of-town trip to their doctor. After two years, the wear and tear became unbearable. In just one amazing session, I helped Gail recognize and come to terms with her martyr behavior. Before long, her parents moved to assisted living, and Gail was swept away, in love with Kenny, her husband and best friend. There's no room in her life for martyr now, though Gail remains vigilant and so loving to her parents.

The Superhero

Another characteristic of this feeling is the one of manipulation. Depending on the situation, manipulation can be unconscious or conscious. Most likely, indirectly taught by a parent, the identity of being a "Superhero" (someone who believes they can do it all) gets them what they want.

Here's a hypothetical example: Janet takes on the responsibility of yet another project for her organization. It's more work for her and she's overextended herself once again. She asks Candy if she would assist her with a particular aspect of the project. After some consideration, Candy declines. Janet attempts to persuade her into accepting. When Candy feels intimidated and manipulated by Janet's behavior, she decides to accept because of her insecurity. When she calls Janet to advise her of her decision, Janet says, "Never mind, I'll do it myself," which engrains her martyr identity another groove deeper.

When one has low self-esteem, one becomes a target for such circumstances. However, when we take responsibility for drawing that situation or person to us and ask ourselves "why?" we don't take on the victim energy and are more likely to free ourselves from the pattern.

Manipulation shows its face in many ways. It can be as subtle as a twisting of words to our benefit, or it can also be very direct, as we pout and maybe hang up on someone, instead of continuing an uncomfortable communication. We might walk out of a room rather than confronting the issue. That's manipulation.

The Inner Critic, the Judge, and the Pleaser

We actually have many aspects of ourselves, like the Superhero previously mentioned. In their book *Voice Dialogue: A Tool for Transformation*, Dr. Hal Stone and Sidra Winkelman have revised a technique called "Voice Dialogue." Using this tool a client begins to work with his or her many sub-personalities. One of these personalities is called, "The Inner Critic." Born very early in life, this is the inner voice that has nothing good to say about us. "The Inner Judge," another heavy hitter, criticizes others. Dr. Stone uses this example, "Let's say you grew up in a family where you learned that it is important to be nice. You are rewarded with love and perhaps even praise when you are nice. You are punished by the withdrawal of affection, or actual verbal or physical punishment, when you are not nice. Being nice becomes one of your basic rules for living. Through being nice, you relate to others and learn how to avoid pain." It becomes an archetype through which you live your life. Through the identification of being nice, we become a "pleaser," then center our lives around making things nice for others–pleasing them for approval, for love, for attention. In doing so, we frequently deny our own needs and therefore are not true to ourselves.

Have you recognized yourself in any of the above examples? Do you see these traits in any of your friends or family members? Recognize the difference between making sacrifices for a cause or out of love for another, and making sacrifices for sympathy and attention. If your choices are bringing light into a situation, your intentions are high; if they bring a burden to you or others, look again.

Reflection Time:

1. Think of a time that you felt entrenched in the role of martyr. What did it feel like?

2. Did you recognize it as martyr energy?

3. What does your to-do list look like?

4. Are you a task-oriented person?

5. Do you integrate free time for yourself into your day?

6. When playing a martyr role, ask yourself what the payoff is.

7. In what way is this role working for you? How are your needs being met?

8. How could you turn it around so you're feeling empowered, and not in the role of playing the victim?

9. Now that you have an idea of how, are you ready and willing to do so?

10. Do you recognize martyr in others?

"The thought manifests as the word.
The word manifests as the deed
The deed develops into habit.
And habit hardens into character
So watch the thought and its ways with
Care and let it spring from love
Born out of concern for all beings."
Buddha

M is for feeling... Mindful

Definition: attentive, observant, watchful, thoughtful

Opposite: mindless, oblivious, dazed, bemused, absorbed

To be mindful is to be aware. Feeling mindful is feeling intent on something, whether it is cleaning your home, dissecting a crossword puzzle, or dressing yourself for the day. Being mindful is paying attention, probably in great detail, with concentration. Being mindful is being completely present in whatever you many be doing. A friend of mine used to tell her children to "be mindful" rather than "be careful" when they went out to play. I always liked that. It has a similar meaning in that it says, "Think about what you are doing before and when you are doing it."

You are what you think. Watch your thoughts. Pay attention to your inner world as well as your outer activities. This can be done in motion as well as in stillness. Experiment with watching your thoughts without attachment to them. Allow them to flow in and out like the ebb and flow of the sea. When we still our minds in relaxation, our thoughts are allowed to be fluid and move. It's simple—observe and be centered. Seek fluidity through awareness. Notice your mind and mindfulness will be yours.

In *Zen Mind, Beginner's Mind*, author Shunryu Suzuki refers to mindfulness as follows:

- Stable thinking, which means accepting things as they are without difficulty.

- Having a mind that is soft and open enough to understand things as they are.

247

- Concentrating. "Thinking which is divided is not true thinking."
- Being ready to see things with our whole mind.
- There is no effort to think when we are prepared for thinking.
- Wisdom comes out of your mindfulness – it is not something to learn.
- Being ready for observing things, and being ready for thinking. This is called "emptiness of your mind."

Detach and Unlatch

One key is attachment. Once we attach, then we employ our emotions. In activity, when we observe our thoughts we gradually develop witness consciousness. Again, we seek no attachment to our thoughts, we just let them come and go, while being aware, ready, and attentive.

As we simply watch and observe our thoughts, we accept them as they are, and remain unattached. Most likely, at first this discipline requires some effort; notice it, honor it, and respect the present moment.

Ligia Dantes, an old friend, is author of *The Unmanifest Self*. She suggests there are many ways to live our lives mindfully. She describes contemplative living as choosing to live someplace with clean air and a quality of life that aligns with us. As contemplative beings, we are mindful of what way we eat, maybe even growing our own food, and we're aware of our company. In short, we intentionally notice how we spend our day and night.

Ligia says the following about mindfulness: "Caring for others, caring for the totality of humanity – this is being mindful. A way of living in the universe – not just living in a home." It's imperative we start thinking in terms of ourselves as the microcosm within the macrocosm. We are not alone.

In *The Dancing WuLi Masters*, Gary Zukav says that wood fibers are actually patterns of cells, which, when magnified, are patterns of molecules, which when magnified, are patterns of atoms, which are patterns of subatomic particles. "In other words, matter is actually a series of patterns out of focus. The search for the ultimate stuff of the universe ends with the discovery that there isn't any." From Maui to Mt. Shasta, I participated in many of Gary's gatherings and found them fascinating. *The Seat of the Soul* really spoke to me.

According to quantum mechanics, we cannot eliminate ourselves from what we are seeing. Objectivity does not exist. We are a part of nature. As we learn to think of ourselves in terms of expansiveness, vast, formless and limitless, we start to claim our birthright. Be mindful of all of life, from the smallest particle of the atom to the infinite vastness of black holes.

Live with love and gratefulness, peace and harmony. Observe, being mindful of the way you interact with others.

Yoga and Stress

In the practice of yoga, we want to be mindful. Yoga is not competitive. It is observation, balance, concentration, calm, ease, release, and openness. One of my teachers shared with us a comment made by a 98 year old yoga student. The suggestion is that with each pose, we make an offering. I liked that. As we open our chest and body, we open and offer ourselves to the Universe. Ancient and empowering, yoga is much more than specific asanas (poses). It is the integration of body, mind, and spirit.

I know a woman who teaches yoga to children. She shared with me the ease and grace through which they do their practice. It can't help but affect their daily lives. In lieu of Ritalin, parents might offer a clean and pure diet along with yoga.

From an American Institute of Stress newsletter (Number 7, 1992), an Associated Press dispatch comments, "Stress is turning kids into pencil-chewing, teeth-gritting, bundles of nerves and represents a major contributor to increased teen drug use and suicide. Kids are pressured to have sex at twelve, get high at thirteen, and get even at fourteen." Apparently it is not unusual to see anxiety attacks in children of nine years, along with stress-related ulcers before the age of twelve.

The newsletter, which further stated, "Fierce competition, hostility, aggression, and other early signs of Type A coronary prone behavior are prevalent at the nursery school level." This particular newsletter refers to stress and children as the "new American tragedy." Parents, we need to have some recognition of our children's inner world! Children know about stress, ask them.

Mindfulness is what we want to teach our children in order to lay the groundwork for a responsible life. To achieve this WE must know and live mindfulness.

Being Mindful Could Save the Species

Are you aware of this fact: 1.2 billion pounds of pesticides are used in homes, gardens, schools, workplaces, farms and forests? Pesticides are now most often used without our knowledge. What is being sprayed on the food you're eating? Be aware. Be mindful of it. Be ready with an open mind and concentration. Northwest Coalition for Alternatives to Pesticides works to protect people and the environment by advancing healthy solutions to pest problems.

Is it mindful to contaminate our planet, our food, and our bodies with toxic elements? We seem to be apathetic and take it for granted that this is just the way it is. It seems to me we need to be more mindful, more caring, more insightful, more intuitive, and more connected. This is the first step and it always begins with each individual. If we want more peace, we have to become more peaceful. If we want more financial abundance in our life, we have to learn to give money away. If we want more understanding from others, we have to be more understanding of others. If we want to receive from Mother Earth, we have to give and care for her.

Someone once said that the mind is a beautiful thing. Indeed, it is. But it is obvious that we, as a species, take beauty for granted, considering our polluted streams and devastated forests. Are we also taking the beauty of our minds for granted? What if everyone committed to use our minds for the greatest good of ALL? Can you imagine how powerful and glorious our world could be, if we all dedicated ourselves to that? Maybe that's the bottom line of being mindful. When we focus our attention on the present, being aware and centered, our minds can only be used at their highest potential. So, think smart, think now, think good, and be mindful of your shifting reality!

Reflection Time:

1. What do you believe the mind to be?
2. Where do you think your mind is located?
3. What do you think it means to be mindful?
4. What do you believe it is up to?
5. What do you think the mind's function and purpose is?
6. Does it serve you? If so, how?
7. Do you believe it could ever sabotage you?
8. When your mind talks to you, who is it talking to?
9. Who chooses what the mind thinks?
10. Do some reading or researching on the Web regarding the mind. Educate yourself about who you may believe you are.

> *"The anthropological record shows us that psychologist Abraham Maslow was right when he hypothesized that human nature is good and instinctively seeks the divine, and that humans only become dysfunctional when they grow up in a sick culture which produces violent and damaged humans."*

Thom Hartman, *The Last Hours of Ancient Sunlight:*
Waking To Personal and Global Transformation

N is for feeling... Neglected

Definition: abandoned, uncared-for, ignored, unwanted

Opposite: attention, care, concern, consideration

When we feel left out, ignored, unimportant, or forgotten, we feel neglected. We might feel abandoned or even invisible. As a parent, we can feel neglected by a child. As a child, we can feel neglected by a parent.

Business partners can feel neglected by one another, as well as life partners. We can feel neglected as an employee or as a friend. A pet can feel neglected by the owner. Once, when I was gone, I neglected to ask someone to water a plant in my office. When I returned, I gave it that first drink of water it had yearned for to survive. Almost before my eyes, that plant came back to life. How remarkable and what a demonstration!

A story was forwarded to me by email about a young boy who felt neglected. The little boy watched as his father sighed and popped open a beer and sat on the couch to watch TV after yet another long day at work. The little boy quietly went up to his father and asked him how much he earned per hour. The father responded with a cold, "It's none of your business," and turned the volume on the TV up. The son asked again, almost pleading. Irritably, the father answered, "Twenty dollars. Now go on." The son ran off to his room, but came back with yet another question. "Dad, can I have ten dollars?" The father, now close to the point of anger said, "What for?" The little boy pulled out some one dollar bills and some quarters. "I need ten more dollars to make twenty. So if you give it to me, I will have twenty dollars. Then I'll have enough to buy an hour of your time."

I had a young client who, as a boy, was thrilled to be invited on a business trip with his father. Yet when they got there, he had to sit in hotel rooms until his father returned. At the end of each day, his father was too tired to satisfy his son's curiosity and excitement about being in a new city. This was often repeated as he grew older. It made no difference whether or not they traveled or stayed in the same town. The boy acquired the belief "Anything is more important than me." He felt neglected. He never felt like he was a priority in his father's life.

If we would just water each other more, and ourselves, think how we'd flourish and thrive. Instead, we seem to always be so busy. Meals prepared with love and attention have been replaced with fast foods. I was given a "snack" on an airplane trip and looked at the ingredients on the package. It took me almost as long to read the list as it did to reach my destination. Well, not quite, but it did contain forty-one ingredients. A far cry from 'fresh is best.' It's become my habit to examine labels. Check out the list on your popular dry cereal boxes. Can you guess the number of dyes in Skittles? How about your child's toothpaste?

Food for Love

Neglect shows up in many areas of people's lives these days. Neglect means lack of care, either of ourselves, or others. For example, a staggering number of children are obese. Lack of exercise, overindulgent lifestyles, and processed foods seem to be contributing factors. Oprah featured the subject of children's obesity on one of her television programs. It was brought out that no child is overweight alone, and that it is a family problem. She emphasized, "This issue is not about blaming the parent; it's about understanding."

To that, I would add–it's about education and searching for the core beliefs and issues to the cause of the onset. When did it start? What was happening in the life of the family at that time? A divorce? A move? A set back in school? Be the detective and don't stop until you have the answers. Then be pro-active until there is insight and a breakthrough on the subject. Don't give up. Be determined to seek until you find the answers.

"It all starts in childhood," says Gerald S. Berenson, a Tulane University physician who founded the Bogalusa Heart Study, a continuing thirty-year study of 14,000 children and young adults, making it perhaps the longest and most detailed study of children in the world. "Half these kids are going to die of heart disease eventually," Dr. Berenson says. "But we know there is a window of opportunity where parents can have an impact."

Recent data indicates that about 15% of U.S. children, aged six through nineteen, are severely overweight or obese based on their body-mass index (BMI). These figures have doubled over the past twenty years. The Mayo Clinic says, "This is the most dramatic increase of obesity in history. The issue of childhood obesity starts with prevention – empowering children to be in control of their bodies and helping parents and grandparents like you, make the right decisions with regard to nutrition and exercise." From a February 28, 2002 report, it goes on to say that, "Depression is the most common emotional effect of obesity in kids. Starting as early as three to five years, kids are often called names, have difficulty making friends, are excluded from activities, and are picked last for teams." Adults are making choices for these little ones, and it is obvious the choices are not the best ones. We must become more aware as the role models for our children. It is part of the responsibilities of being a parent. These overweight kids need love and attention. They need to FEEL loved and cared for.

What are we feeding our children? What are we allowing our children to drink? Are they taking in the amount of pure water their bodies need, or do they consume soft drinks, filled with artificial sweeteners and caffeine?

Here's an issue that might be thought of as neglectful on the part of our government. What are we doing about our latest threat to our natural foods? Genetically Modified Foods (GMOs) pose human health issues, environmental and wildlife concerns, economic implications and ethical and social concerns. We don't even KNOW the effects on the human body, the most perfectly designed system on the planet. Even though "93% of the public believes that genetically modified foods should be labeled," no labeling is mandatory in our country. (ABC news survey, June, 2001)

To better prepare a child for life in today's society, they need nutritional education. We need to examine our beliefs and change our behavior if we are going to make a difference in our children's lives. We need to do it now.

On the other hand, young women who suffer from anorexia and bulimia are the victims of emotional neglect. The one thing they can control is their intake of food. Eating disorders are striking children at young and younger ages. Forty percent of the nine and ten-year old girls are trying to lose weight, according to a study in *Pediatrics*, the Journal of the American Academy of Pediatrics. These girls are not overweight in the first place.

I had the opportunity to interview Dr. Ira Sacker during the time when I was a host on a radio program. Author of *Dying to be Thin* and a twenty-five-year veteran in this field, Dr. Sacker said, "Their behavior in action is a mechanism of control, and the control is for underlying issues that are unresolved, creating anxiety or depression." Are these teens possibly feeling neglected? Feeling unloved? Feeling low self-esteem? This is a serious condition and parents need to tell the truth about it rather than denying it. Don't close your eyes to what you know is true. Be aware, listen, and pay attention.

H2O

When a plane accident occurs, the black box is sought after. When a fire happens, we look to see what the cause is. What causes the damage to a tree, a river to flood, an area to experience drought? We look into these kinds of things with a fine-toothed comb; however, Western medicine continues to look at the symptoms and still only guesses at the cause. How often are we willing to look into our own situations with such scrutiny to find the cause? Even the investigation is of value. It signifies a desire to know the truth. I've often thought that we care for our automobiles better than we do our bodies, making certain the filter and the oil is regularly changed. One way we neglect our body is through the lack of water.

How many glasses of water do you drink a day? After reading the following, you may want to include more. Daniella Chace, MS, CN, nutritionist, teaches us how to calculate how much water your body needs. "Take your weight and divide it in half and that gives you the number of ounces of water you need per day as a baseline. Add thirty-two ounces to this number if you live in a dry climate such as high elevation. Also add an additional thirty-two ounces of water for every hour of high intensity exercise. It is also important that we take in electrolytes. Potassium, magnesium and sodium are electrical conductors necessary for nerve and heart function."

Why water? Our body needs it! We're made up of almost 80% of it, and then we lose it by urinating, sweating, and breathing. See how much each organ uses daily:

Intestines	1/2 glass daily
Lungs	2 glasses daily
Kidneys	5 1/2 glasses daily
Breathing	1 1/3 glasses daily
Skin	2 glasses daily

Water is the natural way for us to get rid of harmful toxins. Daniella Chace gives us some more startling statistics. She says that 75% of Americans are chronically dehydrated, that thirst is often mistaken for hunger, and even mild dehydration can slow down one's metabolism by

3%. One can eliminate daytime fatigue and "fuzzy" thinking by drinking water, as well as ease back and joint pain. Water is also known to reduce the risk of cancer and improve the immune system. (Write for Dani's water handout.)

If that wasn't enough, a local colleague, Casey Wood, who teaches classes in Emotional Mastery, writes that "sixteen ounces or more immediately after or during an emotional blast will help your body cope with the overload. Also, if you do not drink extra water you can feel achy muscles, headache, nausea, tingly hips, thighs, forearms, or aching elbows. That feeling is toxic overload." Ms. Wood suggests that high emotions can build up within our systems and that water can help! So, next time you argue with your partner, drink a lot or water, take a bath, and/or go sit by a creek or the ocean!

Joc Bell of Trinity Water talks about the benefits of spring water. Trinity Water comes from "Paradise, Idaho from 2.2 miles deep into the Earth. It comes up under its own pressure, as an offering. It comes up through quartz crystals, a protective chamber. We collect it without wounding it, leaving it whole, organic, and alive. There is no signature to the water. It's unmarked, without imprints – pure." He says that our tap water, on the other hand, is tainted with "jet fuels and rocket fuels, pesticides and soap detergents that get into deep well aquifers."

Is this really the way we want to treat water, which sustains life as we know it?!

Now, think about this. What is our nation's drink of choice? Take a guess. The active ingredient in this drink is phosphoric acid with a pH of 2.8. It will dissolve a nail in about four days. Many studies have been done. Try our own.

What about our beloved soft drinks? According to the website www.cspinet.org, in 2001, Americans spent over sixty-one billion dollars on soft drinks alone! That year, the industry produced fifteen billion gallons of soft drinks, twice as much as in 1974. Soft drinks are American's single biggest source of refined sugars. And what does this substance do for our bodies? For every soft drink or sugar-sweetened beverage a child drinks every day, their obesity risk appears to jump 60%.

Get this–in many states, the highway patrol carries a particular soft-drink in the truck to remove blood from the highway after a car accident. Put a T-bone steak in a bowl of the same drink, and in two days, it will be gone. Use it to clean your toilet, remove rust spots from chrome car bumpers by rubbing it with a rumpled piece of aluminum foil dipped in this drink of choice. Any time you're having car battery problems, just pour it on and watch the corrosion from the battery terminals transform

What must it be doing to your muscles and bones?

As a point of interest, Coca-Cola spent almost 300 million dollars in 2000, on media advertising, and the entire soft-drink industry spent over 700 million dollars. Between 1986 and 1997, the four major companies spent 6.8 billion dollars on advertising. Soft-drinks are a huge business.

My friend, Lisa Marie Goold, has a solution to these sugar-sweetened drinks. It's a tea called Rooibus, which is African for "red bush." Classified as a food, Rooibus is in the legume (bean) family. It is one hundred percent pure and is grown only in South Africa, used to establish electrolytes in the body. Rooibus contains the antioxidants of green teas, is naturally caffeine-free, has no oxalic acid, nor traces of tannic acid. Would you rather consume a medicinal tea—or something that removes battery acid?

As founder of The Sunn Institute, distributor of Rooibus, Lisa formed a group called, PASS, Parents Alternatives to Sugared Solutions. She shares the following with parents and others who care about the health of children.

"Being a parent is both a tremendous opportunity and serious responsibility. Our children are a most precious gift and they deserve the very best of our energies, time, knowledge, and experience. As parents we realize that there is nothing that surpasses the joy and satisfaction of giving the very finest to our children in the formative years of their lives."

"The scientific and medical world overflows with evidence-based studies, as well as supporting and time-tested anecdotal confirmation, highlighting the negative effects of highly sugared solutions on our young. Commercial availability and targeted advertising for these products is everywhere we look. Sodas, fruit drinks, food bars that are no better than candy bars, powdered concentrates, even sport drinks are all filled with calorie-adding, hydration-sapping, nutrition-depleting sweeteners. When we read the listing of ingredients on much of what our families drink and eat, all too often the bad sugars, (such as high fructose corn syrup) in some form, are the major component."

"It is time to step out, be counted, and say loudly and most clearly that enough is enough! We do care about what our children drink and eat. Concerned parents must stand up to corporate America and put their children's health first." Thank you Lisa.

Are you neglecting your body's need for water and good nutritional food? If our children are eating their happiness away, what are we feeding ourselves? What is your diet like? How many nights this week did you have pizza? Take out food? What is your food history? Do you eat psychological food?

Be There

Not only do our bodies need healthy foods and to "be watered," but our spirits, or souls, do as well. When they are quite little, young children need to be assured of their security. Feeling abandoned does not establish a foundation for a life of protection, safety and immunity. The absence of a parent can be physically or emotionally traumatic. In some cases, a parent may be home consistently; however, distance and separation may still exist. If a child is not allowed to talk during mealtime, or if he or she is sent to their room without knowing why, a child will feel neglected. They may grow up feeling ignored and with non-existent skills of listening and respect.

Most parents do not intentionally neglect their children. We are human and have the tendency to get caught up in our accelerated lifestyle. We can unconsciously neglect those we love and care about. If appropriate, we can apologize to our children. It's never too late. Relationship repairs just require being aware. Some evolved pre-school teachers say, "Use your words." Use feeling words and express yourself to the person directly involved. This will move the energy. Share with the person directly involved, not to your friend about your husband, not to your husband about your employer, not at the water fountain about your boss.

Being willing to acquire impeccable communication skills is one way of caring for yourself and giving attention to your well-being. You are worth it. Don't wait for others to do it either. Learn to treat yourself with dignity and respect and you will never feel neglected. If those times come, just "use your words" and share your feelings with the appropriate person.

Care for your body by taking the time to eat healthy meals during the day, to make certain you sleep on an excellent mattress, to breath clean air and drink pure water. These are just a few ways of taking care of your self. When you do, you become an example for your child, and others. It may require changing habits that have become familiar, but who you are is much bigger than your habits. Caring for yourself shows you have self-respect and self-worth. Be good to you. You deserve it. (See "N is for feeling... Nurtured")

Reflection Time:

1. Is someone you know feeling neglected?

2. What suggestion could you offer that person?

3. Did you feel neglected, abandoned, left out during childhood? As an adult?

4. Start today and look at the labels on what you are eating. Notice how different you feel when you pay attention.

5. Are you drinking enough water? Are you sure it's pure?

6. What are you neglecting in your life? How might you be n glecting yourself?

7. How many soft drinks do you consume in a week? What about your children?

8. Do you sometimes feel the only area of your life you can control is how you eat?

9. Do you have quality one-on-one time with your father?

10. How many meals during the week does your family eat together?

N is for feeling... Nostalgic

Definition: sentimental, yearning, longing
Opposite: cold, regretful, removed

To feel nostalgic is to feel reminiscent of the past–to pull up old memories from our mind's memory bank. Maybe there is a longing to have things be the way they were. Or we may want to go back and rewrite the script. We may question, "What would I have done differently?" On the other hand, we may want it to stay just as it was.

To be reflective is healthy when we can apply it to improving ourselves today. However, we can also get burdened with regret and remorse, which are elements of feeling nostalgic. "If I had only done ____, my life would have been happier today." Or, "Why didn't I try harder at my marriage?" The remorse tugs away at your heart. "Did I really give that job my best?" Guilt is a prison embroiled with toxic energy that can create dis-ease. It can prevent us from being happy enough to create meaningful relationships.

The Good Ol' Days

How many times have you heard or said the phrase, "Those were the good ol' days?" I remember going on drives with my dad when my sister and I took turns steering the car. No seatbelts. No air bags. And we rode our bikes all over town without helmets. We didn't have video games or ninety-nine channels on cable. No DVDs. No personal computers with Internet chat-rooms. No personal cell phones. We talked to our friends during and after school about boys. (Well, not everything has changed!)

Although I don't remember the first day of school, there was definitely no preschool. My mother had to tolerate us until first grade. I knew that when my father said "No," he meant it. I knew my life would turn out even if I didn't get what I wanted at the moment. And at the end of a long summer day, I went with my mom to the A & W drive-in root beer stand, and ordered frothy cold, really good root beer, served in an authentic frosted glass mug. We rolled down our window and the young server propped the tray on the side of our car door. They just don't make root beer like that anymore!

My mother was always home with us, a rare thing these days. She made us potato pancakes for lunch after a long walk home from school, no matter the weather. She was such a homemaker. Gardening, baking, sewing; she did it all. I recall her sewing a matching wool-pleated skirt and jacket outfit for my sister and I, like we were twins. Her bread was always homemade, as were the poppy seed rolls. "Kapama" was a specialty – a Greek rice dish that we all loved. (Those were the meat-eating days. (That was a long time back!) When I'm working in the yard, I FEEL like her. It is a good feeling. Thank you, Mom, for teaching me so much about living a simple life, the connection to the earth and to my soul.

Milk Train

When I was eight years old, my father sent me on a milk train, (which was a train that stopped at almost every town, probably every ten minutes) from Lorain, Ohio, my hometown, to Athens, Ohio, where my sister Clara and new brother-in-law John had just set up their first home. What accompanied me on this trip was a roll of linoleum twice the height of me! My father was in the furniture business and because my sister and her new husband were students, they needed all the help they could get in fixing up their tiny trailer. Just imagine–what you would have to do today to transport a roll of linoleum?

What ever happened to the simplicity of trains? I wouldn't be too excited about getting on a milk train again, but what about Amtrak? It's faster these days traveling at 150 miles an hour. And look at these statistics: Where airplanes pollute 17.45 ounces per passenger per mile, Amtrak only pollutes three ounces, and in 2003, airplanes consumed 15.9 billions of dollars in government subsidies, while Amtrak only took 1.04 billion. Feeling nostalgic could also save big bucks and the environment to boot! ("Trains, Planes, and Pains" by Blaire Tindall, Sierra Club Magazine, Nov/Dec 2003)

I found myself feeling nostalgic as I started omitting names from my Palm Pilot. What a kick! Every unsuccessful business venture and the contact person, my son's ex-girlfriends, acquaintances I haven't spoken with in about twenty years, highly recommended health references, and more, triggered my nostalgia as both pleasant, sad, regretful, resentful memories associated with each deletion arose. I noticed every time I saw on the screen, "Are you sure you want to delete this record?" I had the opportunity to also delete the negative emotions that were associated with that entry. Our mind is a phenomenal computer and we can delete as easily as I did with my Palm Pilot. That's the power of choice. That's the power of free-will. That is innately part of our hardware.

Nostalgic thoughts may also include thoughts about love and joy. They might often be accompanied by a big grin on our face. Some memories are priceless. Such nostalgic thoughts for me include raising our kids in Malibu, California, living on the edge of a continent, with spontaneous mid-week dinners at the beach, and going on trips to Alaska and Hawaii. All these thoughts warm my heart. We would load the van with the Christmas decorations and head for our sacred hide-away cabin in the Sequoias. We all recall that family ritual with fondness. Another ritual we had was every Sunday night, after baths and getting on jammies for bed, we watched Marlin Perkins on *Wild Kingdom*, then Lassie, and sometimes Disney. It was simple–but not as simple as how my father was raised.

Getting Back to My Roots

I yearned to visit and explore my roots in my father's homeland, so in 1985, I made a pilgrimage to Greece. That trip filled me up with a lifetime of nostalgic feelings.

Thousands visit Olympia, located in the southern portion of Greece at the edge of the Mediterranean each year, because it is the birthplace of the Olympic Games. Up a winding mountain road, just eighteen kilometers from Olympia, sits the small village called Lala. Although tourists rarely frequent this countryside, heavily dotted with olive trees, it is of great importance to me. Lala is the birthplace of my father, Peter Delis.

As a child, I often heard the stories about life in Lala, its simple folk, and its simple lifestyle, which centered on basic needs. Survival was a challenge from morning until night. Regardless of age, everyone had to share in the endless chores required to survive.

As a young lad, my father's job was fetching the family's water supply–not an easy task. Daily, he would load the donkey with sturdy barrels and walk down a rocky and rutted path to a central spring where cold, pure, crystal-clear water was abundant. Mother Earth generously provided for the people of this humble barrio. Although the water was used sparingly, three trips were always required. Morning, noon, and evening, every day, back and forth, my father went to the spring to fulfill his obligation. After all, they were a family of eight with chickens, goats, and sheep who also needed their share. I imagine he must have dreamed how glorious it would be one day to see water flowing directly from a tap inside the house.

Paying jobs were non-existent in Lala, which added to the difficulty of their mountain existence. At age sixteen in 1906, Daddy took his second trip out of the village and boarded a boat for a strange and new country called America. His sheer act of courage and vision for an improved life must have overshadowed the fact that he was unable to speak English. Although an older brother had preceded him and a younger one was to follow, I can imagine how frightening it must have been for him to leave behind the only life he'd ever known.

He arrived at Ellis Island with nothing. In 1916, after ten years of hard work in a variety of jobs, washing dishes at New York's posh hotel, the Waldorf-Astoria, a tanning factory and working on the railroad, he and his brothers organized a family furniture business. They settled in Lorain, Ohio, and Delis Bros. Furniture Store was established. All of the deliveries were made by horse and buggy. Coupled with sincerity and integrity, their reputation of selling only quality merchandise soon spread throughout the area. Eventually, with their hard work and determination to succeed, they had a highly respected and prosperous business.

Although outwardly their dream manifested, individually the brothers held another dream deep within their hearts. Jointly, they made a commitment to sponsor the enormous and costly project of bringing water directly into the homes of the Lala villagers. Little by little, hard-earned dollars were sent from America and eventually, their dream became a reality.

As an adult I grew curious about Lala, the infamous spring, and the climate that assisted in growing "cherries as big as golf balls," according to my father. The appropriate time had come for me to meander the land of my roots and the birthplace of democracy. My husband held down the fort, but that was fairly easy with only our child, Danielle, home at that time.

I'd often envisioned traveling for an extended adventure in Greece and learning the language of the Greek people — the language of my heart. I followed my inner guidance wherever it guided me, day by day, moment to moment. I would surrender and trust my heart. It never let me down. In fact, that experience transformed my life forever.

As springtime emerged, my journey led to Lala. The countryside was spectacular, baby lambs and freshly planted gardens stood out as signs of new life everywhere. The days in Lala held even greater meaning for me because I was able to stay with my cousins who lived in the house where Daddy was born. Though showing signs of age, the hundred-year-old dwelling stood sturdy. A large photograph of my grandparents dominated the dining area; it had hung untouched for more than ninety years.

The outdoor bathroom was remarkable, just as I had imagined. This functional little room adjacent to the house held a tank on the wall for bath water. Every other day the water for my shower was heated in the kitchen and poured into the tank. In the middle of the night, I often stumbled down the creaky and tenuous stairs to use the facilities, but I always stopped to feel the peace that permeated the area.

Delectable meals were prepared in a crude outdoor oven, which was heated with wood. If the required temperature was 400 degrees, Hareklea, added a few more sticks. But, to achieve 250 degrees, several would be removed. She was a master! In amazement, I watched, as she knew intuitively just how hot she needed it, to prepare the meals

One day, my cousin Stavros, Hareklea's husband, told me the central water pump had broken. We would have to go directly to the spring for our water until repairs were made. How ironic, I thought. I had fed the animals, took the sheep out to pasture, even milked the goats, and now I would go for water, just as Daddy had done as a child.

We drove down the rocky road in the ol' pick-up. I was told it hadn't changed much over the years. The fragrance of the Scotch Broom perfumed the air. I felt the excitement build within along that bumpy road, and I gazed upward in awe at the azure sky and rejoiced in that one event.

Then I heard it! The rushing and powerful sound of water! As we approached I could see nature's gift bursting forth from the Earth. It spilled over and created the stream, which followed gravity downhill. The force of water carved a path into the hillside and provided life to everything.

I intently explored the area and infused myself with images of Daddy's past. As I neared the old pump house, which emitted cool, damp energy, my body started to shiver. I peered through a gate of heavy wire to behold, hanging on an inner wall, a marble plaque. After years of weathering, the inscription was barely legible. What I could decipher was a message honoring the Georgakopoulos brothers for the contribution they had made to their place of birth, Lala Elias. (My dad had to change his name to Delis when he came to Ellis Island because Georgakopoulos was too long.)

I felt incredibly proud of my father and all he had endured. I could almost hear him saying, "Learn to be satisfied," a prevailing theme from childhood. Waves of anxiety surged through me as I reflected on anguished times I'd given him. It was so hard to understand all of this as a kid, but because of all I'd been exposed to during this visit, his words had new meaning. Given how he was raised, I knew that he did the very best he could do. My tears flowed as freely as the water from the spring, and my heart was full of compassion and love.

I helped my cousins fill large containers and load them in the pick-up. Just as we prepared to leave the spring, I noticed an old man with his donkey, laden on both sides with wood and water, starting his ascent up the hill. What a dear and useful animal these donkeys are, with their marvelous big ears, and whose unforgettable calls echo through the hillsides of Greece! "May I walk your donkey back to the village?" I asked the stranger in my broken Greek. His look told me he thought I was "trelee" (crazy). With a twinkle in his eyes he gave me the rope to his furry, loyal friend. This was the icing on the cake; I was thrilled to lead his "guythudee" (donkey) over the rough terrain back to the village. Literally, I walked in my father's footsteps, overwhelmed with emotion.

With the opportunity to study the language, learn more of the culture, and attempt to relate to my father's primitive lifestyle, I gained a deeper and more meaningful understanding of him and of myself. I strongly urge everyone to explore his or her own roots; the past may certainly be the light that replaces the dark. As a reminder of Daddy's roots and a lesson in humility, a small wooden donkey statue adorns my kitchen windowsill. "Made in Greece" is stamped on the bottom.

I hope you enjoyed my trip down "Nostalgia Lane," and I hope it encourages you to take your own journey. It's good to reflect and introspect. It gives us depth and soul and supports us in making choices today that will be fond and heartwarming memories tomorrow.

Reflection Time:

1. What do you focus on when you reminisce?

2. When you feel nostalgic, do you experience the pain or the pleasure? Do you allow the pain to take you on a depressing downhill journey? Or do you honor and learn from it and move on?

3. What will you create? Remember that our choices today become our nostalgia tomorrow.

4. How about writing your own story of a nostalgic trip?

5. Is there a journey in your mind you've wanted to make a reality? If so, what is preventing it from happening?

6. What is most painful about your childhood? Do you resist those memories? If yes,

   try honoring and learning from them as a gift for your growth.

7. Do you ever take the time to allow another to be nostalgic?

8. If there is a home in your area for the elderly, consider visiting and just talking to the folks you meet.

9. Do you know about your parents roots?

10. Are your mementos in a safe place? What would you save, if your home was in danger?

"If our children are to approve of themselves, they must see that we approve of ourselves."

Maya Angelou

N is for feeling... Nurtured

Definition: nourished, cared for, deservingly loved
Opposite: neglected, ignored, undeserving

To feel nurtured is to feel loved, cared for, and appreciated. There is a satisfaction that comes with feeling nurtured. One feels fulfilled in some way.

The first step in feeling nurtured is to have the wisdom to know you deserve to be nurtured. Often, we wait for others to nurture us and then feel sorry for ourselves when they don't. We might get stuck when our expectations aren't being met. Sure, it's nice to have someone offer a backrub or to make us our favorite meal, but ultimately we each must self-nurture.

Go Ahead – Be Pampered

When do you feel deserving of being pampered, and given attention? Maybe some people will allow it on their birthday, but what about the other 364 days? After a long, particularly tedious workday, can you take yourself out to dinner with a friend? If you believe you need an excuse to nurture yourself, chances are you may not feel worthy of this special treatment.

Many years ago, I started a ritual of having my lady friends over for a luncheon to celebrate my birth. This is a pattern that continues to this day. In fact, on my last birthday, I invited twenty-four sweet souls over to help mark the day. We had such fun. Before we ate our catered, (cook on my birthday? No way!), but simple lunch, we formed a circle and one by one, I acknowledged each woman for who she is and the contribution she has made to my life. That is a warm fuzzy kind of feeling for everyone!

I often nurture myself with a visit to Chapter One, our local bookstore, and browse the shelves until something speaks to me. At the same time, I visit the organic juice bar and have Ananda make me a special liquid salad. I do love my books. Even when alone, I don't feel lonely, especially when I'm into a good book.

A massage from Shannon is another way I care for myself. Sometimes, a foot massage is simply delicious. Travel is another love of mine; I go right down to Southern California to visit Alissa and Corianna, our granddaughters. Nothing can divert my attention when I am with them. I completely nurture myself by playing, singing, eating, bathing, napping, reading, puzzling, photographing, baking, cleaning, cuddling, crying, learning, exploring, laughing, creating, and adventuring. You name it.

Other ways to nurture ourselves that don't involve spending a lot money might be: spending time with people we want to be with; doing things that give us joy; walking, fishing, or going out in nature; simply celebrating life! Sailing, garden work (or is it play?), nurturing flowers or vegetables, and having long phone conversations with old, distant friends we seldom see, are all favorites of mine.

Mentoring can be very self-nurturing. My friend, Joyce, spends time with a woman who lives at a shelter for abused women. On her weekly visits, sometimes they have lunch while other times they just walk. The woman benefits from knowing someone cares, and Joyce feels fulfilled because she's offered a small part of herself to someone else. Mentoring this woman may be small to Joyce, but it's so big for the woman who receives nurturing.

It is wondrous to me that we have the ability to make a difference in a person's life when we become a mentor. I believe all children are at-risk, not just the ones labeled as such. *Newsweek* senior editor, John Alter, says "No one succeeds in America without some kind of mentor-parent, teacher, coach, older friend to offer guidance along the way." ("Mentoring Makes a Difference", *Newsweek*, November 2, 1998) One study done by Public/Private Ventures indicates that children who are mentored are less than half as likely to abuse drugs or alcohol. Corporate volunteerism can influence a young person tremendously. All mentoring efforts result in a win-win situation. Perhaps, more businesses could be encouraged to commit company time to make a difference in children's lives.

Taking a Time Out

If we don't self-nurture, we can become depressed, dis-eased, feel lonely, or feel sorry for ourselves. If we live in our own little selfish world, we risk becoming so self-absorbed that ignorance overshadows the truth. Lack of self-nurturing can show up physically in the body, as it did with me, in my much-valued right wrist!

There was a time when I was working long hours on the computer. During the night, I would notice numbness in my fingers. This went on for several months, as I sought different types of care. After many visits to my chiropractor, it was recommended that I have it tested for carpal tunnel. As the numbness was not getting better, I chose to follow the suggestion. I had a nerve conduction study and electromyography to test my condition. After extensive testing, I was told I had severe carpal tunnel syndrome and needed surgery immediately. Time to investigate deeper. The blocked energy was not getting through my wrist. I learned that the energy to my hand comes from a nerve leading from my spine! It was interesting information that led me to explore alternatives.

This all happened during the winter when we migrate, like the birds, to the desert. The timing was perfect. Instead of surgery, I chose to eliminate wheat, sugar, and dairy from my diet, along with treating myself to rest and relaxation for about three weeks.

Once I got settled into my routine, I started to examine all aspects of this condition: mental, emotional, spiritual, as well as physical. I explored the beliefs associated with this body sensation to divulge a deeper meaning. I reflected on it being my right hand, which is the outgoing energy (the left hand is receiving). My business was now a "teen-ager" and symbolically I determined the belief that it (my business) wanted attention after years of putting so much energy outward to make it successful. It was demanding attention and it was showing up in the numbness of my right hand. (This may be another time for some of you readers to stretch your thinking.)

It was a significant insight. As I continued to learn through my intuitive wisdom, I sought chiropractic care and alkalized my body by drinking two to three quarts of a green drink daily. The body started to respond favorably. I learned from reading that an acidic body can create dis-ease. The *pH Miracle* by Robert O. Young, Ph.D. and Shelley Redford Young will provide you with more than you wanted to know on the benefits of alkalizing the body. Making corrections in my lifestyle has brought restored health to my hand.

Good Night

A cute story about nurturing and caring for yourself comes from the back of a "Sleepytime" box from Celestial Seasoning herbal teas. David Jacoby offers his quotes on napping. He states that "the tall ones" would suggest to us when we were young, "I think someone's tired." Off we'd go for a nap, feeling refreshed and cheerful afterwards. "When we woke, the world somehow made sense again." As tall ones, living in a complicated world, with no one to tell us to slow down, once again, we need to take responsibility and slow ourselves down. This action is caring for our selves, rather than living like a mole whose nature is to burrow in the underground. (See "M is for feeling...Martyred," and "N is for feeling...Neglected")

Reflection Time:

1. When was the last time you took a nap?
2. Do you feel like you deserve to be nurtured?
3. If yes, do you nurture yourself or wait for others?
4. In what ways do you feel nurtured?
5. What rituals are regular caring rituals for you?
6. Who are the people, places, things, and activities you choose that are associated with good feelings?
7. Do you allow others to nurture you?
8. Is it more important for you to take care of others, rather than yourself?
9. What would have to happen in order for you to place yourself at the top of your priority list?
10. When was the last time you had a green drink, or a liquid salad?

"If a man does not keep pace with his companions, perhaps it is because he hears a different drummer. Let him step to the music which he hears, however measured or far away."

Henry David Thoreau

O is for feeling... Odd

Definition: unusual, peculiar, different, curious, eccentric
Opposite: normal, structured, average

We've all heard the expression "odd-ball." The term usually refers to someone who is "marching to the beat of a different drummer," and is considered peculiar or just plain weird. But is being odd really so bad?

My clients may think I'm odd when they read the sign in my office that says, "Please solve your problems before you come in to see me so it will be easier for me to help you." I guess that could be a little odd. It always provokes a chuckle.

The one who steps out of the main stream and chooses another path may be laughed at, ridiculed, shamed, belittled, humiliated, feared, bullied, judged, criticized, badgered, labeled – odd. During your last airline flight, did you happen to think, one hundred years ago, on June 8, 2003, of those two odd Wright brothers who made their first successful flight? It lasted only seconds, but nonetheless it was successful. The passion they shared for flight was beyond ridicule and judgment. It was an idea whose time had come, and these two brothers were the open receptacles of the manifestation of the vision. These boys are heroes in my opinion, but I wonder what people thought of them then?

If it weren't for those who depart from the everyday, life would seriously lack in diversity, and it is likely few changes would ever occur. Initially change can feel odd. New beliefs and new patterns may take a while to get used to–like a new pair of sneakers. For example, try crossing your hands or feet in the opposite way you normally cross them. Try it now. Does it feel "odd?"

Why does our culture think it's odd or weird to turn to an acupuncturist for healing, when Chinese medicine has been around for about five thousand years? More people are looking for change in their health care and acupuncture is an option.

Without change, there can be no growth, either individually or collectively. Albert Einstein said that insanity was doing the same thing over and over again and expecting different results. By the way, what did folks think of Albert Einstein and his ways and appearance? Unusual? Odd? Yes, and Albert Einstein had a profound perspective on life, especially his belief in the grandeur of the universe. He revolutionized our understanding of modern physics, yet his manner, humility, compassion, and humor are as memorable as his scientific achievements.

Where would we be if we'd not been blessed with those who possess unusual gifts and a willingness to share them despite the fact they might be considered odd? Consider someone you have known who is odd. What is it that made him or her so different? Did you feel comfortable with that individual? Was the experience of spending time around her or him a challenge? Why?

We often commit to that which is certain and safe rather than different and risky. It takes a sense of security within to step out to that different drummer. It also takes somebody who is committed to listening to that voice and pursuing at all costs. Humiliation and labeling matters not when the heart is filled with the passion to step out of the norm and live or speak your conviction.

Most of us eventually conform to the usual and take the path of least resistance. Many of those individuals who are odd challenge us to take a closer look at ourselves, but do we? Or do we lash out with make-wrongs and petty innuendoes, unconsciously feeling threatened by their oddness? Those odd ones often express or behave in ways we may secretly envy. We may feel too uncomfortable to even entertain the thought of their unique behavior.

When we watch our children turn into teenagers, originality is often stymied. Being odd is truly frowned upon because it could mean exclusion. Different means exclusion. It is best to look the part, speak the language, and live the loss of your own uniqueness. From Anthea Paul's book, *girlosophy, a soul survivor kit*, writes, "If you want to achieve stunningly different results, you need to adopt a spectacularly different approach." Ms. Paul has compiled a work of art that is both unique and creative–a book for young women urging each to find and be true to their own drummer. One of the many requirements to become a "girlosopher" is to have an open heart and an open mind. This book is an absolute must for every home.

Dare to Be Weird

On a recent little journey with my granddaughter, Alissa, to a quiet and sacred park, she spent each minute examining her surroundings.

When she approached a flower, she pushed her entire tiny face into its fragrant bud. She delighted in the texture and smell of the flower. If you and I were to do that in front of a full audience, it might be considered odd. Whenever we were thrilled as children, we danced or jumped up and down; that would be considered odd behavior for us as adults. Teenagers seem to get away with being odd a little easier than adults do. Wearing black lipstick, for example, would look pretty strange on a fifty-year-old, but is considered an aspect of teen angst for adolescents.

When do we cease to express ourselves in those un-self-conscious ways of the child? Is the "acting out" of adolescence really a last ditch effort to hang on to a most precious connection with the miracle of a diverse universe? Why do we accept the norms of society, if it might mean a compromise for our personal gifts and ways of expression? We don't have to have the genius of Einstein or the inventiveness of the Wright brothers; we can acknowledge our own personal oddity. Each of us has a unique way. We perceive our universe, and that perception makes life a personal prison or haven. We each have a way of expressing what we know. Do we believe we won't find acceptance or love by being ourselves or by following our dreams? Could be.

There is always an element of risk in being who we truly are. But when we take that risk, follow our thoughts and imagination to the finish, and act on our deepest desires in the moment, we've found the magic formula for the life we each deserve. I read a marketing piece about a woman who is a dog communicator. It stated that in her childhood, she dreamed of becoming a fairy godmother to animals. Lydia Hiby's client list numbers over 60,000 from every state in the United States and also European countries with many beginning as skeptics. I would imagine Lydia has been viewed, more than once, as odd. Break the mold, step outside, reach your arms to the heavens, and enjoy being odd. It's great fun and rewarding too!

Some people think being deaf is odd. My friend, Venda Levy, would disagree. Here are her very insightful thoughts and attitudes about being hearing impaired.

"Being deaf in life may have some limits. Not much different than anyone else except we cannot hear. We may be frustrated trying to make a phone call. We have a TDD (special telecommunication line for hearing impaired) that you can type to communicate. When we call through Relay Service Operator to have a three-way conversation, they always tend to hang up, thinking it's telemarketing or a survey."

"My husband and I don't go out to watch a movie at the theatre because we don't want to waste money, because we don't understand

272

the whole story of the movie. Instead we buy or rent a DVD movie that has closed caption so we can read what each person is saying. We also have close caption for television too. We have light flashers around the house when the phone rings."

"The deaf myth is still alive. People still think deaf people can't do anything. However, we notice people in California, New York, and Washington, D.C. tend to accept and respect deaf people."

"We talk, read lips, as well as do sign language. We have three children and all three can hear normally. They all know sign language. At first when they were very young and discovered we were deaf, they tended to feel sad, disappointed, and a little embarrassed. We explained to them that we cannot hear but we do wear hearing aids to help us to hear sounds. For example, we can hear people talk and 'hear' music as we feel the beat and vibrations of the sounds."

"When we are around a group of people, we try to communicate, but it's hard for us to understand and we get lost and bored easily, as we feel left out. It is easier to communicate one on one. We've lost many friends for no reason. We haven't done anything to them, but it's their loss. We feel they do not accept us or show any respect for who we are. In other words we are lonely. We like to have company to share laughter and joy. Mostly, we live a normal life just like anyone else."

I asked Venda if she and husband, Jimmy, ever feel sorry for themselves because of their hearing loss. "Feeling sorry for myself? No, not at all. We have both overcome this situation."

Here are some comments with regard to their children's attitudes. "Sheena is six years old and gets frustrated that we can't hear, wishing we could, but happy that our hearing aids helps us. Elijah is nine. He doesn't care and loves us, no matter if we're deaf or not. He likes the idea of us being handicapped, so we can easily and quickly find a parking space. He gets upset when someone says bad things about us behind our back. Max is twelve years old and feels sorry for us. He gets upset and is sad at how rude some people are, and how badly they treat us. He thought we were lucky being deaf when one time the airline made a mistake and put us in first class seating."

Thank you, Venda, for sharing your heart. I know it will give all of us more insight on how physically challenged people might be challenged.

Being Weird Can Be Weird

Cartoonist Gary Larson spoke at a high school graduation class and encouraged the graduates to, "Dare to be weird." My interpretation

– dare to be yourself in the face of criticism and judgment. Dare to be odd – unusual – out of the ordinary. Maybe being weird is donating your weekly allowance or salary to a homeless shelter. Maybe it means doing a spontaneous cartwheel while walking through the park. Or maybe it means telling a stranger they are beautiful. I support that kind of weird.

Since childhood we've always been told what to do: brush your teeth; do your homework; clean your room; go to bed; get in the car, it's soccer time; eat your broccoli; be polite, etc. Are you waiting for permission to live your life? And I mean your life, not someone else's idea of your life. When will you give yourself permission?

Out-of-the-ordinary situations may feel odd, but also fascinating, if we embrace the moment and what is transpiring.

Lights Out

My nephew, Brian, and many other New Yorkers gave themselves permission to feel somewhat odd during the black out in July of 2003 in New York City. He described the experience as a "blast." He said, "Midtown traffic was shut down and no subways were operating, so I walked four miles to get home. Sidewalks were packed, so many were walking the streets. Long lines of people were waiting for free ice cream being given away before it melted. And everybody was buying pizza for dinner. I fulfilled a dream and directed traffic with our neighbor. It was awesome. People were really appreciative. It was after dark so a woman loaned me the blinking dog collar from her Great Dane, which I hung around my neck along with the flashlight I was already using. My buddy had a glowing light stick and together we worked a three-way intersection for an hour, letting emergency vehicles and buses take priority, and pretty much 'kicking butt' doing it. Drivers asked for directions, which we happily provided. Eventually, uniformed NYPD showed up and observed that we were doing a fine job, so they just let us continue running the intersection until they had three guys to take it over. Once they came, up went the flares, we exchanged handshakes and gave ground. People were sitting out on stoops with candles and wine. Restaurants were jam-packed. An impromptu sing-along broke out on a popular side street. There were lots and lots of people out gathering, eating, drinking, without any signs of discontent. Someone said they heard the power would come on in a few hours and got the reply, 'I don't want it to come on!' It was truly an incredible night. And it was indeed odd, to see a city usually made up of light, sound, and traffic, cease in a backdrop of darkness and a momentum all its own."

Being odd is being unique; it's being yourself, following your own inner drummer with strength and determination. The compass remains at true North even while you may walk in different directions. True North could equate to trusting yourself to follow your bliss. There will be many manipulating you to follow their path, preaching that you have been "satanized" and strayed away, but these are the times when True North is constant.

The message from one of my favorite books of all time, a children's story entitled *How Joe the Bear and Sam the Mouse Got Together,* by Beatrice Schenk de Regniers, is one to remember. I read it to my kids in the 1960s; it is now out of print. In the story, Joe and Sam meet on the street and would like to spend time together, however they can't figure out their similar interests. Just before they are about to sadly part ways they become aware of the fact that they both like to eat ice cream together at three o'clock. So Joe and Sam can each live their unique lives, but still get together at three o'clock to eat ice cream. What a great message to teach our children. We are all different! And there are ways we can come together if we choose to.

It takes courage and conviction to step to the music of a different drummer. Build your truth on what you know to be real and step to the music of your own drummer. Allow yourself the luxury of being a bit odd today and love yourself for it! You are a unique and fantastic creation who contributes to the whole of the universe. Let the universe hear your voice and witness your special dance!

Reflection Time:

1. Before you go to sleep tonight, make a list of the things you wish you had done, the things you wish you had said, the dress you wish you had purchased.

2. Imagine a life less ordinary, more crisp, and more exciting. Imagine the life you would have if you stepped over the line of normalcy and into the world of odd for a moment.

3. In the morning, intend to do just one thing you've wanted to do for ages. Some ideas might be:

   a. Tell someone you love him or her that you've been meaning to tell, but were afraid of how it might be viewed.

   b. Push your face into a flower and feel the texture and truly smell the fragrance—even if there are seventy-five people standing next to you.

   c. Tell the grocery clerk you appreciate her/him for being there to help you.

   d. Live a little and wear red with pink, or purple with yellow. What could it hurt?

   e. Dye your hair the color that you love, but are afraid everyone else will see as a bit too strange. I once saw a young man at the mall with the most beautiful blue hair and told him so. He was flattered and acknowledged that he loved it too.

4. Jot down in a journal something you'd like to see improved in your world. There might be an invention inside of you!

5. Question the order you've created in your life. Are they all rules by which you want to continue living?

6. How many odd friends do you have? In what way do you view them as odd?

7. If your parents were odd, was it embarrassing for you?

8. If your children are odd, is it embarrassing for you?

9. Are people odd or is behavior odd?

10. Create the most odd scenario of life you can think of. Brainstorm with a friend. Write a screenplay. You might want to submit it for consideration.

"A mind that is stretched by a new experience can never go back to its old dimensions."

Oliver Wendell Holmes

O is for feeling... Open-minded

Definition: tolerant, broad-minded, liberal, unbiased
Opposite: narrow-minded, bigoted, judgmental, set

To be open-minded is to be receptive to new ideas. When one feels open-minded, one might be in a situation where they must be open-minded! Most likely, this person is faced with something they have never thought about before, and it causes them to take a second look, perhaps seeing it from a new perspective. On the other hand, some folks are naturally open-minded, constantly seeking new stimuli philosophically, ethically, emotionally, and intellectually. I would be so bold to say that if you are reading this book, you are probably experiencing open-mindedness in some form!

Outside of the Box

I needed to have my desk moved from one room to another. It was a rather heavy desk and my husband and I couldn't figure out how we were going to get it through two doors and a hallway. It just didn't measure up that it was going to fit. So I decided to wait for Brandon, who helps us with projects around the house and is one of the most sincerely kind humans on the planet. Brandon walked into the room as I walked out to answer a ringing telephone. When I came back into the room, the desk was almost in its final destination! "Oh, my goodness! It fit! Brandon, you're brilliant. You put it on its side!" This was a perfect demonstration of open-mindedness. Brandon thought outside the box and succeeded with ease.

Being open-minded might sound like this: "How interesting. Tell me your thoughts." The response may be quite fascinating IF you choose to be open. You may still own your old opinion after you've heard and explored the other point of view, but you allowed yourself to be open to new possibilities, and to consider another way of seeing something.

Check out the following list:

Blocked Attitudes	Open-Minded Attitudes
That's a dumb idea.	That's an interesting idea...let's explore it.
They'll never want to do that.	Let's run that idea by the group.
I don't have the time.	My day is full; can I get to it tomorrow?
It will never work.	It just might work.
Get down to Earth.	I admire your vision.
That's not my problem.	I have a few minutes to hear what's going on, then I can refer you to the right person.
Get real.	That's fascinating.
You can't teach an old dog new tricks.	I'm willing to give it a try.
That's not practical.	It's fun to think out of the box.
Why did you think of that?	I respect how your mind thinks.
We managed so far without it.	I wonder where we could fit it in?
Let's think about it for awhile.	I'll be prepared to make a decision tomorrow by 5 P.M.
It won't work for us	This looks challenging, let's go for it.
It's too much effort to put into practice.	Looks like a lot of work; are you willing to commit?
We've always done it this way.	Change is so healthy.
We better not rock the boat.	Let's present this as a solution.
We should study it some more.	We have studied this enough; it's time to choose.
You're a dreamer.	I admire your unlimited thinking.
Maybe it worked elsewhere, it won't work here.	Let's connect with those for whom it worked.
You're a Pollyanna.	Your positive energy is a tremendous asset.
What a problem this is!	There are so many solutions and options.

There's still substantial controversy about the alternative or complementary approach to healing, in spite of the throngs of individuals who choose and prefer it to traditional methods. What an opportunity to see how set in our ways we just might be, how committed we are to our old belief systems, even when they don't work for us! When we're open-minded, we're willing to listen, to explore, and recognize that there may be another way, no matter how bizarre, or how far from mainstream that way might appear. We actually become aware and awakened to a new power that has been there all the time.

Know Thyself

"Know thyself," said Socrates, the Greek philosopher. These legendary words have as much meaning today as when he first said them centuries ago. We can choose outside assistance in the process of getting to know ourselves, such as going to counseling. Many still consider counseling as a sign of weakness or rather "odd." The stigma of "lying on the couch, talking to a shrink" is one that unfortunately still remains in our society. (Remember, I'm a stretch.) Here are a few other ideas that originate in closed minds to act as stoppers to counseling: "I can't really afford counseling." "People should be able to handle their own problems." "I just can't see myself talking to a stranger about these issues." "It takes too much work to change habits and beliefs. It's so-n-so's fault anyway."

Subconsciously though, the message might really be, "Am I worth it–all the time, the money, the attention, the caring?"

I had a client tell me he never dreamed he'd be making a call for counseling help. His first time visit to therapy was at age forty-two. His accumulated pain was so intense, he felt forced to reach out. There is a quote that fits this situation. "And the day came when the risk to remain tight in a bud was more painful than the risk it took to blossom," Fritz Perls, the father of Gestalt therapy, once said.

And what about those who don't ask for help? I felt sadness and concern when I read about a Seattle police officer who took his own life. I pondered the question: "What stops us from reaching out and seeking assistance with life's challenges?" Supposedly the officer was asked if he wanted time with the staff psychologist and declined the opportunity. I wondered what beliefs prevented him from being open to counseling.

Just as our physical needs are readily tended to, our mental health also deserves attention. We must be open-minded to recognize this. Everyday, negative emotions are more widely recognized to be directly associated with disease. We live in an increasing stressful society, one that is capable of placing serious demands on the body, mind, and soul. A skilled heart-centered practitioner can guide us to the root of our pain. That is where we've got to start.

I used to frequent one road that had innumerable patch-jobs to repair holes. Every time a storm came, the road buckled and the crews were out again applying another bandage. The transportation department avoided the source of the problem for two long, hard winters. Finally someone realized the patches didn't work. The road is now completely redone and is functional through the heaviest of storms.

Isn't this what we want? To function with sound mind and judgment as the storms come into our lives? If a boat isn't well anchored in the harbor and a storm comes, the rains and gusts toss it onto the rocks. Every vessel that is securely fixed withstands turbulence and turmoil. Security isn't found in the outer world. Only through a solid foundation in our inner environment will we find peace and security.

So which fear will get to you first? The fear that will eventually come when you're at the end of the rope or the fear of getting to know yourself? One day I received a fax from a friend that read, "Psychiatrists tell us that one out of every four of us is mentally ill. Check your friends. If three seem all right, you're it."

Smog Alarm

I have been hot on the human potential path since the sixties, when once again, driving down the road with a friend, I took my anger out on the Los Angeles smog. My dear friend in the passenger seat said, "It's really hard to be around you." That's when I decided to seek out a "shrink." I'll never forget Dr. Ira Carson, behind his impressive desk, on the twenty-fifth floor of a luxurious office building, which overlooked...the smog. Perfect setting for an anti-pollution rabble-rouser.

Week after week, I lashed out at the injustices of humankind; how unfair it all was; the atrocities committed by our own federal government on our Native American brothers. The list went on and on and on, until the day came when I got that the pollution was really within. The changes happened appropriately once I was ready to be open and replace my ignorance with understanding.

This counseling created a life review. My childhood had been really fun. I was born the last of four daughters and believed that I wasn't really wanted because of my gender. Four girls? I did my share of acting out because I didn't have the vocabulary to express myself. Everything worked out as it always does. Each experience brought me closer to where I am right now in my life.

It's a comfort to know there are counselors who are dedicated, trained to listen, and whose very being says, "I care about you, I believe in you, I know who you are." Counseling can awaken the seed that says: "I am worthy of a fulfilling life. I make a difference. I deserve the very best." Affirming these truths establishes a center within us of strength, goodness, and harmony. It promotes the growth of something in ourselves for which we all yearn.

Just as we're advised not to wait until it rains to repair the roof, the same is true for counseling experiences. It is important to make certain you see a quality practitioner who cares about you, is somewhat Self-realized, who will address the subject of responsibility in the first session. Ask for a clear short-term program design. There are many directions one might take: dance/art therapy, group therapy, individual session, spiritual or transpersonal counseling, family sessions, and even programs you can do alone for self-improvement. Or come and see me.

Cultural Differences

The following entry is from a young man who has worked at improving himself by being open-minded and embracing a new culture, a new country and a new perspective. I applaud him for what he has had to endure, especially since 9/11. Mohamed Milad writes in his own words about his attitude and feelings towards America.

"I was happy to come here because America is known as the most powerful country in the world. Everybody talks about the American dream in my country (Tunisia) and France. It's a great opportunity to start a job and to make things happen in your life."

"People are open-minded here; they have freedom to speak their minds. And it was a good opportunity for me to learn about the culture that we don't learn much about in our own school."

"The connection I had with the American people I first met here was exactly what I had expected – open-minded. Then I got to know Robin, my wife, and her family; everyone seemed willing to help me out as a foreigner. I felt no bias."

"My first feeling after September 11, 2001, is that it was something that didn't touch (affect) only America, but it touched all other countries. It's like Americans said, 'the twin towers themselves represented international cultures.'"

"As a Muslim, I felt totally dirty and too small in the eyes of everyone around me because of this bad publicity that the news media gave to the

281

Muslim religion. After the attack, I also felt at the same time that this powerful, untouchable country that represents freedom CAN be hurt. I thought now America has to open her eyes, the people of America have to open their eyes to other countries and what America has done or not done for other countries and how American culture has affected other countries."

"All I dreamed about – the power, freedom, and untouchableness - turned to a nightmare because what happened shows me that no country is bigger than another country and that the attack came for a reason. The attacks showed the powerful countries that what they've done to the other countries (influences) without realizing the impacts is coming back to haunt them."

"I think Americans need to open their eyes for what goes on in other parts of the world and to stop thinking that America is the best. Americans need to open their eyes to notice what's going on in other countries."

"Did Americans change for the better after September 11? No, not after what Bush did. Well, yes they did change for the better – until the second Gulf War. The time after September 11 has changed Americans on the fact that they started to ask what's going on in other countries. People started to ask what's going on with Israel and Palestine and in the Gulf area, but it didn't take long for Bush to come up with the idea to go after Saddam. That kept the American mind busy so Americans don't find out what's going on in the rest of the world. I think that every time I introduce myself as Mohammed it surprises people, and then I think they wonder what I'm still doing in America."

"Yes I think some of my friends and family are upset that I married an American girl – more friends than family – but I tell them that it's my life and everybody's different. One person can't represent a country all by herself."

"I try to send the message to people around me about my religion – that we're not about violence. I try to, through my actions, show people that Islam is not a devilish, evil religion."

Thank you, Mohammed, for your honest, sincere, and important participation in this book. I trust it will make the reader reflect and look inward, being open-minded.

When will the day come when we can each interact with other beings, open-minded and kind, with the respect that we are different, and yet we're all the same? Although no two digestive systems are the same, they all produce the same results. Set an intention each morning that you will be open to see a soul beneath each person's personality, no matter what kind of craziness and imbalance may be transpiring in their lives. Observe the patterns.

Belief Settings

While setting up a tennis ball machine to practice my backhands, I learned more about life. If I set it at random, it gives me balls at random. If I set it at fast, it gives me the ball to hit at a faster pace. High, low, slow, backhand, forehand. I could select whatever I wanted the machine to feed me. Just like our beliefs. Set them and they'll continue to give you what you've ordered up.

When we have an opinion about something, we can be closed about seeing anything that might be in opposition to that point of view. Blinders become fixed and tunnel vision feels safe. "It's my way or the highway." We become so enmeshed with our own perception that we believe we are right, so therefore others MUST be wrong. Being judgmental, rigid, and set in ones way is also the opposite of being open-minded. Being unwilling to even entertain another way of seeing a situation could also be stubbornness.

Wouldn't life be easy if everyone we encountered thought the same way we do and shared similar perspectives? If you agreed with that question, look again. It's diversity in thought that makes us grow as humans. We learn from others different ways and opinions. Let others challenge your beliefs. Maybe you'll change your mind, or maybe you'll become even stronger in your convictions, realizing the deeper truth of what you already know. It's people who think differently than we do who challenge our beliefs. Those individuals and their positions are our teachers. They are gifts to our evolution as a species. How we respond is what brings harmony – or hatred.

To be closed and stuck on a position is also being resistant to open-mindedness. The closed-minded have all the answers and can be self-righteous and arrogant. Underlying that façade, however, is fear and threat. A threat to the ego sends out messages of fear because the ego will do anything to maintain righteousness. Remember that the ego's only purpose is to survive. Hidden is a fear of being exposed to another's belief because it's just too scary to consider that another might be right. It could challenge your belief system, then who would you be? Maybe unbalanced? Maybe unaligned? Maybe someone who doesn't know all the answers? Maybe in need of a shrink?

The closed mind is one of contraction, almost shrinking inside, which is the exact opposite of our expansive, vast nature. The blocked mind is so restrictive that it can't recognize or even identify anything that it is not akin to. This is the mind of limitation, narrowness, and fear.

The humble person demonstrates a sign of greatness by saying: "That's really interesting. And this is how I see it." That mind is receptive, trusting, and allowing. It comes from kindness and respect and open-mindedness. It is not threatened by a new idea that is opposite. It is not on a position. It neither diminishes nor shrinks. Quite the contrary, an open mind is a healthy mind that considers everything knowing the source of ideas is infinite. We are merely receptors for the birth of ideas that allow for the evolutionary process. Did they laugh at Einstein? What about the Wright brothers? And Alexander Graham Bell? I wonder if IBM is still laughing at Bill Gates, as they did when his idea was presented to them? Open-mindedness is what it's going to take to move forward as a culture and as a planet. Practice it, and watch the world expand.

Reflection Time:
1. Why do you think someone would not want to hear or consider another opinion?
2. Have you ever considered counseling?
3. Analyze a point of view or opinion you have that you feel strongly about. Describe it to someone or write it down, in length.
4. How do you feel about sharing it with someone?
5. Make a list of five positions you are strongly attached to. Out of those five, which three could you not give up? And out of those three which one position could you simply not give up?
6. What is the investment you have in it? How does it serve you? Is it threatening to even think about giving it up?
7. Do you pay attention to your fondest wishes and fantasies with an open heart and mind?
8. Develop the power of imagination and visualization for achieving your goals.
9. Do you confront obstacles in your path by looking at more than one angle?
10. Do you take responsibility for creating your own life and fulfillment?

"Choose a job you love and you'll never have to work a day in your life."
Confucius

O is for feeling... Overwhelmed

Definition: stressed, pressured, floundering
Opposite: centered, calm, trusting, in balance, flow

Everything feels out of control. You have a deadline for work, your kids are getting in trouble at school, your spouse seems distant, your bathroom has a leak in it, your car needs an oil change, and your dog has fleas! You wonder, "Will it ever stop?" When someone feels overwhelmed, his or her life has snowballed into one big mess.

Even atoms get stressed, from what I understand, after hearing local physicist, Marcia Grabow, speak to our Light on the Mountains Spiritual Center about quantum physics. Research indicates that "when there is a constant perturbing of the atom it collapses and can't make a transition. When it is constantly bombarded with a laser, it's unable to make the transition, as normal." The world of atomic and subatomic particles is truly wondrous.

Stress is a worldwide epidemic. It's affecting the quality of our life, our health, our well-being. So how can we learn to practice the art of balance and harmony? The center of every tornado is calm. From time to time, we will all no doubt feel like our lives are synonymous with a tornado. To feel calm, no matter what our circumstances, is truly a remarkable state of being.

We learn to be calmly active and actively calm. In that place, we can perform at any given moment. It's like an anchor–solid, centered, connected. When we operate out of that place, we don't become the victims of anything going on.

Our circumstances don't have to change because we have a new attitude, or do they? Our attitude of being in charge promotes calmness. We know what to do inside of ourselves to make the necessary adjustments, and then we handle whatever is happening in our reality. Rather then:

- There's just too much to do.
- There's not enough time to do it.

- I can't think clearly anymore. I'm starting to make mistakes.
- My body isn't cooperating or responding anymore.
- I'm experiencing the S-word (stress) to the max.
- There's no way out! I'm feeling desperate.
- I can't make this deadline.

Take a deep breath. Relax. Step back and look to see what's happening. When did you start giving your power away? What is this stress really about? Worrying and anxiety are designed to play havoc with your body. When fear steps in, we lose it altogether. Our mental composure goes out the window along with our spiritual balance.

The Happy Waiter

While in Jackson Hole, Wyoming for the Teton Wellness Festival, one of my dinners was spent at the Mangy Moose Restaurant. I asked one of the gentlemen that scurried around purposefully about the variety of old flags on the walls. From there, a conversation struck. His name was Ari Borshell, and he was general manager of the restaurant. One thing led to another, and before I knew it, he told me of his education in criminal justice and how at one point, he considered law school. Eventually, he acquired a teaching certificate, but in his first year, was thrown into the sixth grade as a teacher, with more girl students than he knew how to deal with! After one year, he left teaching and came to the Tetons to ski. That was twelve years ago (1991). Having never worked in a restaurant and not knowing the 'how-tos' of being a server, he applied for a job at the Mangy Moose. "I liked people, and I was good being with people."

Today, Ari could be overwhelmed with running this continuously busy restaurant and supervising a staff of 163. But instead, he relies on his good attitude, which always seems to get him through. In hiring people, he almost dismisses the interview. "I can teach people how to serve but not how to get along with people." Send them my way, Ari.

The S-word

Our stressed-out lives are affecting our children directly. Children are naturally innocent, but when their worlds are out of balance and dysfunctional, they act out. In their innocence, they can say the most darling things. It takes great awareness and dedication to be a parent. It takes time–quality time–to interact and communicate effectively. As adult role models, we need to handle our "stuff" first, before we take on the awesome responsibility of parenting. I completely understand that we are all doing the best we can do at any given moment, but we need to continue our expansion, growth, personal experimentation, and be more committed to self-improvement.

When I attended a conference in Colorado for Educators of Young Children, I met several little ones who attended with their mothers. They reminded me how up-front children are and how natural it is for them "to tell it like it is." I chatted with a most delightful first grader, and after she told me her name, I asked, "How old are you, Natasha?" She replied, "I'm six. How old are you?" Her innocent response took me by surprise, but I chuckled and provided her answer. She simply said, "Oh."

At one of the breaks, a teacher told a sweet story of a grandmother who exclaimed to her four-year-old, who had just played in the mud, "My, you're pretty dirty." The little one replied, "I'm even prettier when I'm clean."

On my phone messages, I heard from a client who had previously spoken with me about her concern over her child's attitude. She phoned because she thought I would enjoy hearing his comment. After she told him about the counseling appointment she'd made for him to see me, the five-year-old retorted, "I don't want to see an attitude doctor." I got quite a chuckle out of my new specialty. His remarkable statement is actually quite accurate. Aren't children delightful? I now refer to myself as "the Attitude Doc."

Doing Machines

The late Erma Bombeck had written poignant comments pertaining to what she would do if she had the opportunity to live her life over. "I would have gone to bed when I was sick, instead of pretending the earth would go into a holding pattern if I wasn't there for the day." Such good advice for those of us who become overwhelmed with our to-do lists and turn into doing machines.

But what happens to change this innocence? Every day there are more and more cases of stress-related diseases in children. At an early age, children are not taught expressive vocabulary for their feelings. Out of frustration, they act out and create serious problems in their lives. James H. Humphrey, author of *Stress Management for Elementary Schools*, reveals reasons behind these truths:

- The expectations on children today are intense.
- Their schedules are often quite demanding.
- Excessive exposure to electronic games can produce hypertension and eye strain.
- The necessary role models have less and less time to spend in child rearing.

287

- Many parents lack skills to raise children.
- Children often feel unaccepted for who they are.
- Time for daydreaming, exploration, and play has become regarded as unproductive.
- Fear seems to be an underlying emotion. Teachers are afraid to touch; parents are   afraid for the safety of their children; children then learn to be afraid of "strangers." Fear and doubt seem to have replaced love and trust.
- The value of our sixth sense, intuition, is usually not valued, encouraged, or taught in schools or at home. Intuition leads to self-reliance and self-empowerment.
- Children with extreme sensitivity are being overlooked, in lieu of being nurtured and understood.
- Teens are getting to middle school without learning the basics of the paradigm that they are one hundred percent responsible for their lives.
- The law of cause and effect may not be explained and comprehended at home or at school.
- Children may feel an underlying pressure to please mom and dad to earn their love. Parents unfulfilled desires may be projected onto their children.

We adults need to recognize, confront, and resolve the personal issues that dramatically affect young lives. It is time for all of us, as teachers, parents, or influential adults, to release the old emotions and beliefs that are destructive, not only to ourselves but to our young people. Layers of experience with shame, guilt, and fault have been proven to be barriers to the joy and love we want and desire. If we are to enjoy good mental and physical health we must release the darkness of the past and see today as a bright light, full of potential and opportunity.

Dr. Ron Smotherman, author of *Playball: The Miracle of Children*, says, "You can learn more from a child about those things that mean the most to you in life than from any professor, psychologist, or theologian. Children teach by being, not by being full of information."

Rather than being, many children are becoming "stressed out," often raised by single parents who struggle, suffer, and feel overwhelmed. Others are exposed to highly competitive parent role models trying to strike it big in a highly competitive world. Too many children are fed fast foods which are highly processed and lack nutrients that are vital to strong healthy bodies.If 60% of all visits to a family doctor are connected to a psychological issue, maybe, just maybe, there are a lot of people on the planet who aren't coping very well. Twenty-five percent of hospital admissions are mental health related. I would say those individuals are not being treated appropriately. They no doubt have been given a pacifying medication to stabilize and off they go. The insurance information from Online.com continues by stating that 50% of all sick day absences are linked to psychological issues. Joe Robinson has written a book called *Work to Live: A Guide to Getting a Life.* Do you have a life? Although the above statistics do not outwardly use the word "overwhelmed," it is obviously contagious.

How many people do you know who are feeling overwhelmed in their life right now? How can you recognize this? ABC news reported that of twenty major industrial nations, seventeen have laws that require a month or more of vacation per year. The United States has no such law and it was reported that the average vacation days per year taken is 10.2 days.

Overcoming Overwhelmed

Overwhelmed can be embraced by introspection, acceptance, evaluation, making different choices, and trust. As we actively connect with ourselves, we clearly see the benefit of appreciating, allowing, and honoring the child's true nature, even the child within ourselves. The world of a child is magic, play, enthusiasm, laughter, trust, imagination, innocence, resilience, knowing, freedom, honesty, creativity, and joy. All of these traits and more exist within each adult. Appreciate and honor this part of yourself, and overwhelmed will lose its meaning.

Reflection Time:

1. What action can you take to be the calm in the center of chaos?
2. Detach for just a brief moment and ask yourself how much of what is happening, you can or can't control?
3. What part of your tornado is self-imposed?
4. How can you relieve the strain, the tension, the feeling that you're spent and can't do one more thing?
5. Where is your priority?
6. What can you do right now to take care of you?
7. Are you feeling overwhelmed in your life at this time? With what? With whom?
8. How much time off do you take per year? How do you spend it?
9. Do you check in with work if you are away? Do you eat lunch while working?
10. Observe your children. If you are stressed, is it affecting them? How?

"Choice – it's a beautiful thing. Be decisive. Act powerfully. Make a decision and put energy, belief, and pure intention behind it."
  Anthea Paul, *girlosophy*

P is for feeling... Passionate

Definition: zealous, eager, enthusiastic, excited, inspired
Opposite: lifeless, bored, detached, indifferent, apathetic

Passion is fire! To feel passionate is to feel that fire within roaring up. One can be passionately in love, passionate about a cause, or passionate for life in general. There is an intensity of feeling when passion is aroused.

My experience of being and feeling passionate is to feel deeply, very deeply about my personal connection to something. If I don't experience passion in some way, often I feel I am not being true to myself. I must live my dream, my life, and my passion. My body will let me know it when I'm not. Everything in my life would let me know it.

Maybe your passion is something that you really love doing, like singing or dancing. One of my passions is contributing to peoples' lives. Others' passions may be to build a car or make quilts. Passion is something that turns you on inside. Passion creates a feeling of connection, and you know it when you're doing it.

I have a friend who recently opened a restaurant. She's so happy! She looks happy. She smiles all the time. She's just delighted! She prepares wonderful food with wonderful loving vibrations and her customers benefit from her happiness and her food.

Entrepreneurs have passion. They are creative people. Once you have that creativity to follow through with a new idea, you must have a team of supportive people to make it happen. You get the disappointments, but you still keep going. My son, Jeff, is starting a community radio station in Boise, Idaho. The Boise Community Radio Project is "for those who don't need a corporate shepherd." Jeff is living authentically. He's living for what he believes in, and he's taking action.

One could say "I believe in being healthy," but if she smokes, then she's not living authentically. Identify your values, define them, prioritize them, then work to align in living them. Write your own personal mission statement. Keeping your agreements is part of living an authentic life. Be appreciative and grateful.

ABCs

There are many people I know who have a passion for reading. Their personal libraries resemble an annex of the Smithsonian (Slight exaggeration?). However, statistics from California Literacy say 74% of the children who are poor readers in the third grade remained poor readers in the ninth grade. Thirty-five percent of students with learning disabilities drop out of high school, despite the fact that many students have above average intelligence. Fifty to sixty percent of adolescents with substance abuse problems have learning disabilities. It's embarrassing and humiliating to live in a nation of abundance, opportunity, and mentorship, and know that so many people cannot read. According to the National Institute of Health, at least ten million, or approximately one child in five, is affected by reading disabilities.

Dr. Suki Stone, founder of Reading Right, is as passionate about teaching children to read as I am about empowering children in the area of emotional literacy. Suki shared the following thoughts with me about passion: "Passion is to me pursuing your first of many loves and being focused with that love. My love is teaching these kids to read. It sustains me in going forward."

"It's been ten years since I've had a salary," Suki told me. "Part of my passion is my understanding of faith and divine timing. I'm driven to making a difference in the world, and it's through my faith that I believe there is a reason for my passion. I knew I had a greater goal than just being in a classroom and that goal was to reach children in a unique way, which turned out to be my reading program. These skills could carry them through their lives and help them develop their own passion."

"I was invited to work with teen-age boys at a lock-up facility outside of San Diego. These boys had very low self-esteem and weren't able to take a drink of water without escort. At first it was kind of frightening being there because it was so regimented. But the kids helped me overcome my fears. Kids were yelled at. If one stepped out of place, they were reprimanded. As I talked to the kids I was able to get over my fears."

"One young boy, sixteen years of age, was incarcerated for drug use. After working with him he told me, 'I've learned so much from the vocabulary, thesaurus, and The Feeling's Dictionary that I want to transform my life and not come back to this place.' (He's now off of drugs and put his life back on course.)"

Another young man, at age seventeen, wrote the following after working with Suki in her brilliant program:

"Dear Dr. Delis-Abrams, *The Feelings Dictionary* is pleasurable because I can write things about how I feel. I can write when I'm bored. The meanings of the words are simple to understand. It's a good book to write my poetry, stories, and draw pictures in my journal. Thank you for creating this book."

Keep in mind these words are from a teen-age boy who was at the Campo Center for one hundred days because he had gone back on drugs after being clean for a long time. The drug addiction had "fried" his brain and he lost some of his "brain power," which was a major contributor to his reading disabilities.

Suki told me, "He never had read any books – just looked through magazines. In the program he brought books back to his bunk and was very excited about it. He just loved your 'Dictionary.' And yet another young boy also got so much benefit from The Feelings Dictionary/ Journal. He was sixteen and read at a third-grade level. He was very eager to participate in my reading program. He liked the idea of using the blank pages in the back of the dictionary to write his feelings using the words from the dictionary portion. His eyes glowed when I handed it to him. He had been told innumerable times he would never amount to anything, but after the reading program, he was aspiring to become a writer."

"The boys expressed a desire to read but felt my program wouldn't be that different. After the first hour they said, 'I really like this program. I'm learning so much. I think I may even be smarter than my girlfriend.' One kid said, 'I love waking up in the morning because I look forward to literacy class.'"

"In addition to being a boost to their self-esteem, four out of ten became literacy experts in their dorms. Once they started to read, they felt confident and started to help other people. The others also learned to read."

"My compassion was for those at the facility who would stop to talk to me about wanting to get into the program, but didn't qualify."

Dr. Suki teaches people to read in twelve sessions. And at the time of this printing, she has just closed her business after fifteen years. She said, "People have said they wanted to help and that they care about children, but it has been difficult to keep this program alive." Political reasons prevented her from significant opportunity that would have catapulted her career and been an enormous help to a huge population of illiteracy. The Attitude Doc says to Suki: "After fifteen years of being an advocate for children, I hear ya!"

Grandma Behind Bars

The late Barbara Weidner was a woman who lived her passion. She was the Founder and Director of Grandmothers for Peace. In 1982 at the age of seventy-two, she started her activism when she learned that nuclear weapons were stockpiled at a nearby Air Force Base. Before she knew it, she and others were marching for peace. She carried a sign, made by her ten-year-old granddaughter that identified her as a "Grandmother for Peace."

Barbara said, "As a grandmother, I could no longer remain silent as our world rushes on its collision course with disaster which threatens the lives and futures of all children everywhere, and the future of this beautiful planet itself." Seven women were arrested on Good Friday for civil disobedience and sentenced to serve 120 hours of community service. "We do not encourage people to break the law. Our actions should teach people and children to scrutinize laws against human life and they should be broken to prove a point." This was a woman with passion.

Designer Babies?

In his recent book, *Enough: Staying Human in an Engineered Age*, environmentalist Bill McKibben makes a passionate case that "inheritable alteration," or producing "designer babies" would rob future generations of the chance to determine their own identities. He states that, "If science can make everything perfect, there would be little incentive to be good stewards of our own bodies or of the rest of the world." He believes humans are not in need of "radical overhaul, improvement, or augmentation." He continues, "As we are now constituted, we are plenty good enough." (From *Sierra Club Magazine* Nov/Dec 2003; article by Jennifer Hattam)

In a Newsweek article, April 10, 2000, scientist Robert Sapolsky says, "It's not all in the genes. The environment you grow up in is as important as your DNA in determining the person you become... A particular gene can have a different effect depending on the environment... Genes are turned on and off by environmental factors. The human body is made up of about 100 trillion cells. Inside every cell is a nucleus that contains forty-six packets or chromosomes. Each chromosome contains a single, tightly coiled molecule called DNA. It's estimated that within the DNA there are up to 100,000 genes positioned like towns and cities along a major highway." The article says scientists have undertaken a complex task known as the Human GENOME Project "to determine the precise order of chemical units in human DNA." When completed, the data would take a person twenty-four hours a day for twenty-six years to read.

This human body is a miracle! I'm grateful for those who are passionate in their work in trusting the process of life to be the miracle it is.

Had I altered my son's DNA, I would not have the son I have today, a deeply caring, sensitive, artistic, creative soul. It started quite young. Jeffrey Peter, our oldest, loved to draw from the time he was old enough to hold a crayon and had an amazing eye for detail. He also loved the ocean and investigating the tide pools near our home. We supplied him with markers, chalk, charcoal, drawing boards, and other art supplies to support that love. Jeff followed both of his passions and graduated from Humboldt State University with a double major, one in Oceanography and the other in Art. His passion was allowed to flourish and has influenced his adult life. Today, one of Jeff's passions includes restoring the salmon to the Northwest and loving the great outdoors.

Natural Passion

One of my passions is for spirituality and from this comes my passion for nature. That's why I live where I do — Idaho, The Wilderness State. It feeds my soul. Seeing the first rays of sunlight on the top of 9,000 foot peaks takes my breath away.

There is a bumper sticker that drew my attention on the freeway one day – "Wilderness, Land of No Use." Hogwash, I say, and what disrespect! What else nourishes our physical, mental, emotional, and spiritual well-being like being in nature? That's my passionate point of view. I know of many people who don't have tremendous passion for the great outdoors and that's okay. Just don't trash it for future generations if they choose to visit and see wildlife.

Hiking, backpacking, picking up litter in the forest, or just taking a walk on a trail with our dog in the middle of the day can recharge me. What does it do for you? Wilderness can provide this benefit if we allow ourselves the time to connect and let its power penetrate our cells. The Earth places no demands on us. As Sierra Club founder, John Muir, said, "Visit the mountains and get their glad tidings...cares will fall away like the falling leaves." His wisdom goes deeper, "Thousands of tired, nerve-shaken, over-civilized people are beginning to find out that going to the mountains is going home; that wilderness is a necessity...as fountains of life."

One of the healing ingredients in wilderness is silence. Ligia Dantes says, "Silence is one of the most powerful yet least utilized energies available to human beings. More can happen in a moment of silence than in months of discussion." Wilderness may be the only place left to discover true silence.

After seeing the movie *Winged Migration*, I can say that the migration of birds is not a quiet experience. However, it is moving and heartening as you witness actual portions of different species of bird migration that have been filmed from cameras perched on hot air balloons, glider wings, and other small aircraft. It takes passion to photograph and produce a film of this nature. Bird hunters, please see this film before you pick up your rifle. The film shows virtual footage of the life of these migrating birds, which consists of flying back and forth, north and south in search of food. The snow goose flies over the same landmarks, 1500 miles from the Gulf of Mexico to the Arctic twice a year in a migratory pattern instilled by the stars and the sun. Their inner guidance is a message to us all.

The Loop

An outing in the wilderness gives us an opportunity to explore inner space. For example, my friends Ken and Suzy gladly accompanied me when I invited them to hike up to Alice Lake in the Sawtooth National Recreational Area. It was one of the spots on my checklist, so I was excited when then said, "Let's go."

So we walked in on a picture perfect day at 9:30 in the morning, got to our destination, went skinny dipping, then decided to do the loop as the day was so magnificent, and we felt it was doable. The "loop," although incredibly beautiful, turned out to be one that took us by lakes that weren't even on our maps, playing tricks on our estimated locations. Each time we started up again after rest and waterfall playtime, we'd say, "giddy-up," which always brought a roar of laughter.

We finally walked out at 8:30 in the evening by the light of a quarter moon. Although our "PMA's" stayed steady, the opportunity to explore inner space came frequently as the mind relentlessly wanted to make me wrong for making the choice of doing the loop. It was a continual struggle with the mind, those last few hours, as we had eaten all our food and were starting to run out of water. "Why didn't you bring a better map? "Why did you consent to do this loop anyhow?" "Gene (my husband) is going to be concerned about me because it's so much later than he expected me home." "Do I have enough gas to get us back, knowing that all stations will be closed by the time we get to the highway?" The mind doing its thing, thriving on worry.

Meanwhile, we got back to my car where I could read in my hiking book about "the loop hike," which indicated it was eighteen miles. I just walked eighteen miles in one day. That's about three-quarters of a marathon. Hallelujah. Thank you, body, for your support. Thank you mind, for allowing me to honor and ignore your tempting thoughts to make myself wrong for undergoing such a trip. Thank you feelings, for surfacing so I could feel you all. Thank you Spirit, for guiding me along, one step at a time. As a suggestion, if you set off on an excursion such as this one, make sure you are with fun people who like to laugh. Thank you, Ken and Suzy, for sharing my passion for adventure. When you have passion for something, you can overcome any odds because your heart is fulfilled. My love for the Sawtooths was the conveyor belt that kept me going.

Nature exudes incredible beauty and wonders beyond our comprehension. With more and more people living in big cities, our connection with the natural environment and feeling a bond to Earth and to life is critical to our well-being. Understanding the mysteries of nature helps us return to a state of 'little children,' filled with awe and delight.

Consider the spider, whose belly spews forth a thread so she can create an intricate and perfectly designed web of silk. (Had any luck with that procedure lately?) Did you know salmon find their way back to their birthplace using currents, the Earth's magnetic forces, and the stars? That's rather impressive. After traveling 900 river miles, they smell their way back to the very riffle in which they were born. What about hummingbirds that beat their little wings furiously at 170 beats per minute. Both mother and father hummingbird build a nest, two inches in diameter, to support the continuance of their species. The miracle list of nature is endless.

Consider how we treat Mother Earth for all she gives us physically, emotionally, mentally, and spiritually. Our species, Homo sapiens or human beings, rape her mountainsides, pollute her waterways, and obstruct the natural pathways for salmon to perpetuate life. In general, we impart ecological damage that is inexcusable. The atrocities perpetuated are unbelievable, yet her restorative powers keep us from destroying our species – for the time being anyway.

Imagine one hundred million trees are ground up every year to produce the 4.5 million tons of junk mail that clutter our mailboxes. We each receive about one-and-a-half trees worth of junk mail in a year. The average person spends eight months of his or her life opening junk mail. (Research facts from the newsletter of the Environmental Resource Center, Ketchum, Idaho.) The Direct Marketing Association (DMA) estimates that listing your name with their mail preference service will stop about 75% of all national mailings coming to your home for about five years. **www.dmaconsumers.org**

Up, Up and Away

One day a year is set to pay tribute to our Mother Earth, our Home. I'm proud to say, I was involved with a group of mothers who believed strongly that they made a difference. It was the first Earth Day, 1970, when a powerful group of homemakers marched purposefully throughout significant locations in the Los Angeles area, shouting "Hey, hey, let's make every day Earth Day." We had passion. Boy, did we. We juggled a placard in one hand and a child with a peanut-butter sandwich in another as we proudly displayed our ecology buttons.

I reflected on those days as I came across an audio-tape of a lecture from the Windstar Conference in Aspen, Colorado by Rusty Schweickart. He described the Earth from space as "an incredibly beautiful place." Traveling at a speed of 17,600 miles per hour, we can circle the Earth in just ninety minutes. We don't have to be an astronaut hurling our craft through space to feel Rusty's truth about the Earth's beauty. We only need to take a moment and STOP, take a breath, look around and appreciate the Earth's incredibly beauty.

Nature gives greater clarity–a new perspective. Astronaut Edgar Mitchell said: "The trip into space provided me with a dramatic opportunity to see the Earth and the cosmos from a totally new perspective. This new perception caused me to question nearly everything I had believed in the past." Shift Happens!

Chief Joseph of the Nez Perce once said, "The Earth and myself are of one mind." No teaching could be more fundamental to our young people than this message–the teaching of love and respect, for oneself, and for our magnificent Earth.

Imagine, at the time of this writing no one alive today will ever see this close encounter between Mars and the moon again that we're experiencing now. The next time Mars may come this close is in 2287. No human being has seen this site in recorded history. I was awed by that. Extraordinary.

As life becomes more complex, it is even more important to reap the gifts that our Earth has to offer, mostly the gift of healing. In return for merely opening our hearts to her wisdom, we can become subtly strengthened and profoundly renewed by her beauty and perfection.

You deserve to pursue your passion, whatever it is (as long as you don't harm anyone). Start today. Discover it, connect with it, live it.

"Hey, hey, let's make every day Earth Day."

Reflection Time:

1. What do you feel passionate about?

2. Are you doing it? Are you experiencing passion in your life? If not – why not? If you are, in what way?

3. Write down the ten things that you love doing most in your life.

4. Prioritize the list, with those you love the most descending to those you feel less passionate about. They have a mind of their own as they struggle to be on top.

5. How much time are you spending on your passions? Do you have a support?

6. Must you take risks to do the things on this list? What's holding you back from living your passion?

7. What if anything were your parents passionate about?

8. If you were to draw a picture expressing your passion, what colors would you use?

9. What benefits do you suppose you would be provided through a journey to space?

10. Have you identified the passions of your children?

P is for feeling... Peaceful

Definition: serene, restful, calm, content
Opposite: violent, disturbed, turbulent, noisy

"Peace...it does not mean to be in a place where there is no noise, trouble or hard work. It means to be in the midst of those things and still be calm in your heart." This anonymous quote was written on a card given to me by Michael, my son-in-law, for my birthday. The love coming through his personal inscription floods my heart. I am so blessed to have acquired another son.

To experience peace within requires honoring the self. Treasuring who we are includes recognizing the valleys and peaks in life. When we can observe our thoughts and behavior without judgment and criticism, we come to appreciate ourselves, by trusting and honoring our process. Through this behavior we learn to be tolerant with ourselves, which leads to being tolerant of others. We can respect the differences and allow each to have their own opinion and point of view. As we live our life in this manner, trusting and honoring the process of life, we become more at peace; when we don't, peace becomes elusive. We know it's there, but how do we access it? It can slip through our fingers like sand. We are then into the other nature of our duality.

Peace Pilgrim

As long as we have this duality on the physical plane and as long as we have a Department of Defense, then why not have a Department of Peace? A woman who called herself Peace Pilgrim posed this question as part of her peace pilgrimage from 1953- 1981. She vowed to "remain a wanderer until mankind has learned the way of peace, walking until given shelter and fasting until given food." She dedicated her life to a pilgrimage, walking more than 25,000 miles, with only one message: "This is the way of peace: Overcome evil with good, falsehood with truth, and hatred with love." She talked with people on dusty roads and city streets, in churches, colleges, to civic groups, and on TV and the radio, discussing peace within and without. Her pilgrimage covered the entire peace picture—peace among nations, groups, individuals, and the very important inner peace, because that is where peace begins.

"We need a Peace Department in our national government to do extensive research on peaceful ways of resolving conflicts," she said again and again. "We need to set up mechanisms to avoid physical violence in a world where psychological violence still exists. All nations need to give up one right to the United Nations – the right to make war." Provocative and intriguing ideals came from this woman. As a penniless pilgrim, she basically surrendered her life to the moment, with no agenda, because she knew the next moment of 'now' would present something remarkable. She lived with an appreciation of every ride, every meal, and every opportunity to share her thoughts about peace. These became her greatest gifts.

She began her pilgrimage of twenty-eight years walking for peace, January 1, New Year's Day of 1953, at the Rose Parade in Pasadena, California. A policeman tapped her on the shoulder as she walked in the parade route and said "What we need is thousands like you." After removing fear, anger, and hatred from her own life, she decided she wanted to help others replace negative and harmful feelings in their lives with love and peacefulness. She believed that world peace would come when enough people had attained inner peace.

Her message continues through the Friends of Peace Pilgrim, who disseminate her materials free of charge, including newsletters that are most informative. They only ask that you pay postage if possible.

Peace Out

An impending threat of war seems to frequently be present on our planet. Sometimes more imminent than others. Peace Pilgrim's message is more vital than ever. Keep in mind, peace does not mean the absence of war. We can still hold vengeance and greed, anger and hostility in our hearts, and live without war...and vice versa. Once again we touch on the idea that we can experience peace within, regardless of our outer conditions.

One of the most heart-warming experiences I've seen on television was watching the soldiers reunite with their families after the Gulf war. Tears of joy and gratitude were openly shed as fathers adoringly gazed upon a child they'd never seen. Husbands and wives appeared in ecstasy as they embraced tightly, and parents showed relief on their faces after weeks of anxiety. This wasn't the soaps. This was real life. The thought of losing someone we love is indeed painful and this goes hand in hand with war.

My first association with war was as a child. I knew intuitively it was the opposite of peace. Although war and peace happen in our outer world, they truly exist within us. War is felt through inner struggle, torment, unrest, darkness, depression, and turmoil. Peace is felt through joy, harmony, alignment, lightness, contentment, and love.

Thanks to Congressman Kucinich, a bill establishing non-violence as an organizing principle of American society cultivating an array of peace-building policies and procedures, may one day become legislation along with the citizen lobbying effort to create a U. S. Department of Peace.

World peace and the expression of love will be achieved when enough people attain inner peace and realize they indeed are love and joy. But how does this seemingly monumental task occur? For starters, each one of us can participate, every day at noon, by discontinuing our activity, and for a minute (or more if you choose) think peaceful and loving thoughts about life and about our planet.

John Randolph Price, is the co-founder with his wife, Jan, of "The Quartus Foundation," a spiritual research and communications organization formed in 1981, located in Boerne, Texas, near San Antonio. I was so impressed with their presentation at the Sun Valley Mountain Wellness Festival.

He has devoted more than twenty-five years to researching the philosophic mysteries of Ancient Wisdom and integrating those teachings with spiritual metaphysics in the writing of his many books. He and Jan are the originators of "World Healing Day," a global mind-link that began on December 31, 1986. Millions today, join in each New Year's Eve day, all at the same time, all over the world to meditate on peace. John personally discovered, "Consciousness actually shifts, and you move into a realm you may not have even known existed, a realm of joy, peace, bliss, ecstasy, and great clarity of mind." If even a portion of his testimony were accurate, wouldn't it be worthwhile to include this practice in our day?

The Ideal World

Every person is a radiating center of energy. We can and do make a difference in the world by thinking thoughts of peace and love. Gandhi said, "Peace between countries must rest on the solid foundation of love between individuals."

Many years have passed since the Gulf War, and I wonder about those who were seen and interviewed by the media as they were reunited after the threat of permanent separation was felt. What is the quality of their relationships today? Are they taking each other for granted or are they creating appreciation and joy in each moment of being together?

I recall being particularly touched by a father whose son was in the hospital in serious condition. "We've said 'I love you' to each other more since he's been back than we have in his whole life," he told the television-viewing audience in a teary voice. I felt his sadness over this realization and pondered just how many others in the world there must be who block their love from its natural flow and imprison it. Why do we wait till threat of loss hits our homes to share the healing energy of love?

While reflecting more on the subject, I recollected an interview on 20/20 that Barbara Walters had with General Norman Schwartzkoff. In her probing yet sensitive manner, she asked him questions about his past, his strengths and his feelings. It was inspiring to experience him in a new light. Wet-eyed, humble, and proud, he shared memories of his father, revealing a tender, gentle soul underneath that rough exterior.

Many have "fought" for peace over the years. Thich Nhat Hanh, author of many books and a Vietnamese Buddhist monk, worked tirelessly for peace in Vietnam and helped rebuild destroyed villages. Through his writings, he urges that opposing forces talk about their suffering, fears, and despairs in a public forum so all the world can hear. "We can listen without judging, without condemning, in order to understand the experience of both sides. This would prepare the ground of understanding for peace talks to occur."

Martin Luther King nominated Thich Nhat Hanh for the Nobel Peace Prize. Let's take his wisdom and apply it to our own lives–to our family, our homeowners' association, the local planning and zoning department, our Congress, our immediate community, and finally to those people we interact with on a daily basis. Is this too much to ask? Is this closer to an ideal world? If your answer is yes, what must happen to create the ideal world? So, if we accept the premise of Thich Nhat Hanh and Peace Pilgrim's model for peace, what do we need to do to put it in place?

Gandhi practiced reverence for all life, "ahimsa," which is more than non-violence. This action requires self-discipline. Are you ready to practice this? Are our children ready to?

Paul Coleman, also known as Earthwalker, is walking and planting trees for peace and global environmental protection. His pilgrimage from England to China began on November 2, 2000. Paul is currently in Africa having walked 15,000 kilometers to date. He has planted 25,000 trees in 350 tree planting ceremonies and events in fourteen countries. You can find journal updates at www.earthwalker.com, and keep track of Mr. Coleman as he spreads his own unique message of peace across the world.

When a certain number of us achieve the awareness that we do make a difference, and live our life that way, more and more will join in; together we will create a strong field of energy picked up by almost everyone to spread peace across the Earth. It's a matter of choice. YOU could be the one to cause the shift.

So in other words, the first action of this concept shifts the energy of fear, anger, and hatred to energy focused on love, peace, and joy. Any negative belief prevents us from knowing who we truly are, or even knowing we possess a soul. If we could only realize we are not our position, our body, or our personality. We are here to remember who we are, claim our true identity, be of service to our fellow travelers and make the planet better for having been here.

How can we begin this process? First of all, we must be introspective and turn the searchlight inward.

Create a Sacred Space

What supports this process is meditation, which is not really all that mystical. It's simply taking the time to be still and be open to receive. Dennis Weaver says, "Meditation gives you a sense of caring, a sense of humility, a sense of gratefulness, because in meditation you experience that which satisfies you like nothing else in this world can." In this place of tranquility, you will eventually experience a calmness that is like the reflection of the full moon on a still body of water. In that space we can hear the voice of our intuition, the infallible teacher of truth. There is no restlessness, no searching, no striving.

Create a sacred space in your home for meditation. The purpose is consistency. For instance, when you sit in the same chair day after day, positive vibrations build up in layers. This supports your practice.

- Begin your practice with soothing sounds/music. After a few minutes, turn the volume slowly lower until it is off.
- Start to observe your breath – as you inhale think "calm" and on the exhale "down." It becomes a mantra.
- Notice passing thoughts and acknowledge, "that is my mind," then come back to your breath.

Spend at least twenty minutes twice a day in meditation. This is your most important appointment of the day. Meditation is cumulative.

Don't expect to become "enlightened" in the first twenty-minute session. Meditation comes of its own accord when the body and mind are totally relaxed, and all expectations are removed. We do the practice just for the sake of doing it. We become self-disciplined when time is set aside to sit, and we still our body and our mind. The challenge of quieting the mind may be a life-long endeavor. A truly quiet mind is well worth our time.

Meditation is no longer perceived as a "woo-woo" weird activity. Dr. Herbert Benson founded the Mind/Body Medical institute and argues that "Meditators counteracted the stress-induced fight-or-flight response and achieved a calmer, happier state. In his book, *The Relaxation Response*, he states, "All I've done is put a biological explanation on techniques that people have been using for thousands of years."

The August 4, 2003 issue of Time magazine sports actress Heather Graham on the cover, and featured meditation in the health section. She says, "At the end of the day all that star stuff doesn't mean anything. Transcendental meditation reminds you that it is how you feel inside that is important. If you have that, you have everything."

Joel Stein's article, "Just Say Om," in the same issue of Time, states that ten million American adults practice meditation every day. The latest science says people who meditate will probably outlive others who don't by quite a few years. It not only boosts the immune system, it may be rewiring their brains to reduce stress. It's recommended by physicians to control the pain of chronic diseases, like heart conditions, AIDS, cancer, and infertility. It helps restore balance in psychiatric disturbances such as depression, hyperactivity, and ADD (attention deficit disorder). Contentment, inner peace, and a calmer, happier state are some of the benefits. Great article! Thanks Joel.

Love and peace have no boundaries, regardless of all effort by the human mind to capture them. Do we realize that love grows when it is expressed? There is no limit to where it goes or whom or what it touches. Love is free! What dams up the harmonic current of love are human limitations such as jealousy and possessiveness. Love is expansive, not restrictive. Ultimately, love is all there is. All we need to do is light our own candle of peace, shedding light and love so others may light theirs from ours.

Reflection Time:

1. Do you consider quiet time of value? If so, are you allowing a portion of each day to be spent in meditation?

2. Do you find value in creating a sacred space in your home? Have you done so? (I.e.: a portion of a bedroom, a quiet hallway–any place where you can create a small altar comprised of objects that touch your heart.) Use candles, essential oils or incense, music, wool or silk cloth to enhance your space.

3. Have you done something to make someone else's life a little easier?

4. Observe your thoughts and notice to what degree you give your power to the mind.

5. See the best in others through positive perception.

6. What areas of your life are in conflict? Relationship? Finances? Health? Purpose? Career?

7. What can you do about this? Take one at a time and analyze it; ask a friend to support you in exploration and resolution. Check your attitudes, beliefs, and choices in each category.

8. Try this visualization observation: After several minutes of breathing and observing any thoughts, allowing them to flow in and outward, gently recall a time in your life when you felt peaceful. Feel it – the colors, sounds, body sensations – feel the peace and the accompanying feelings – joy, serenity, connectedness. Allow that image to ripple throughout your body. The more intently you feel and connect with this experience, the more you will feel the caressing warmth of peace and love. Now expand that peace even further beyond your body, beyond the room, your community, your country, your global home, your universe. "I am infinite. I am peace."

9. Did you experience war or peace in your childhood? Have you honored it?

10. What is your experience with war?

"I can't do this. I can't do this. I can't fight this...and in feeling my hopelessness I was suddenly suspended in time. No, I thought, I cannot fight this. My panic is not working for me....and I succumbed to whatever was meant to be."
  Mariel Hemingway, *Finding My Balance*

P is for feeling... Powerless

Definition: ineffective, weak, helpless
Opposite: powerful, strong, confident

When we feel powerless, we have given our power away and have become victimized. That's it! That's the bottom line. There is nothing else to say on this word. But as long as I have an almost blank screen in front of me, I might as well keep going.

I'm Not Worthy!

Let's say you're in an employee review. Your heart is beating so loud, you're certain it can be heard throughout the room. Two superiors are sitting across from you. They read a list of observations that were made of your performance. Their ratings were much lower than you expected. After all, using the same criteria, you rated yourself much higher. Wow! What a shock! You are given the verdict as if you were on trial. There is no recourse or opportunity to defend your point of view. Armor goes up and you become defensive. You feel weak, helpless, misunderstood, inferior, deflated, embarrassed, treated unfairly and...powerless. You hear only negatives. There is nothing positive about anything that you've done. Your ego has turned to mush, and your mind plays havoc with the words you're hearing. "But I thought I'd been doing a fairly good job. How could they have observed otherwise? What can I do now? "I'm finished," your mind retaliates.

The interview is over and you are feeling dejected and unmotivated to perform at a higher level. Your self-esteem is low, and your body is tense and stressed. You have no control over your mind; rampant thoughts take over your shaky sense of well-being. All social affairs you had planned with family members are cancelled because your feeling of inferiority predominates. You make up excuses for not attending, which reflects your level of personal integrity. You have nothing to offer the family, or even Harry, the pet hamster. You're crying out for validation, "Yes, you are a good person. Yes, you have accomplished great things. Yes, you are of value." However, these messages don't immediately come and all you hear is the inner mantra, "I am not worthy."

The question is, what will you do with these feelings and thoughts that have completely taken over your life? Let's explore the choices of two hypothetical scenarios.

Betsy tried to heal her wounds with a call to her boyfriend. She proceeded to blast everyone she could think of that works with her. She was in attack mode and even her boyfriend, who was willing to listen, became affected by her negative energy. She vented, yes, but in a way that was harmful to everyone. In lieu of sharing her feelings and observing her thoughts, she came across like a bulldozer, dumped on her beau, then hung up on him when he lovingly attempted to probe her position. She developed a migraine, followed the next day by a fender bender accident, and all of that was topped off with a notice that her apartment will be converted into condominiums and she must move. "What next?" she complained.

Meanwhile, we have Gary who experiences an almost identical scenario with his job review interview. As the less-than-favorable comments were being read to him, he noticed his mind ready to grab on to self-pity and make others wrong. At that moment of observation, he brought his attention back to the moment. He noticed his breathing, the tone of the voice doing the reading, the temperature in the room, the chair he sat on, the lighting, the sensations of his body. He became the witness of every moment because he fully used his senses. There was no need to interpret what was said, he was just aware with no judgment, allowed everything to be, just as Eckhart Tolle, author of *The Power of Now* suggests in his book.

Tolle writes, "The present moment is as it is. Observe how the mind labels it and how this labeling process...creates pain and unhappiness. By watching the mechanics of the mind, you step out of its resistance patterns, and you can then allow the present moment to be. This will give you a taste of the state of inner freedom from external conditions, the state of true inner peace...Accept the present moment as if you had chosen it. Work with it, not against it – make it your friend and ally, not your enemy...This will miraculously transform your whole life."

It's a challenge to stay in the present moment when there is an enormous incompletion in your life. Not knowing can make us feel powerless and out of control.

Missing Pieces

The following submission is from a woman who is gaining her strength back after feeling powerless, knowing there is nothing else she can do to locate her missing brother.

"Jay is the kind of brother who would drop any plans to be with me if I needed him. His sense of humor has given our family over the years the laughter we needed to get along well in life. All Jay's life, he would demonstrate mischievous behavior that caused him to be somewhat embarrassed. At those times Jay managed to produce a huge smile that seemed to neutralize all those who were near."

On September 17th, 2001, Jay disappeared. "I received a call from Jenny, who had not seen or heard from Jay in two days. The Sheriff's Department found the vehicle Jay was driving parked at an unoccupied house in a nearby neighborhood. Then, we heard about a 10-foot fall Jay had taken, landing on pavement. Pam, a friend who was with him, said he was unconscious for a couple of minutes. Jay did not want to go to the hospital. They went to Pam's home nearby to rest. Jay left in the vehicle later that afternoon, not to be seen again. From this information we concluded that in a state of confusion from the head trauma, he had parked at the wrong house and wandered off into the woods where he died of a brain hemorrhage."

"Search and Rescue were on the site within hours. Our family and friends joined in a three day search."

"I was overwhelmed as I searched for my brother's dead body; wanting to find him, but afraid of seeing him. When the search finally ended, I headed for my bed."

"I felt grief for Jay, I felt grief for my family and I felt grief for Jay's 7 year old son, A.J. A.J. lost his father, his best friend, his roommate and his ski buddy. Jay had moved to the town where I lived, three years earlier with his son. My two children are the same age as A.J. We became two single parents, working together as a family to raise our three children. We were really three single parents with three kids because Eric, my former husband, was there with us as a single parent too."

"Soon after the disappearance, a friend's psychic told me I would find Jay's body in the river south of the search area. With waders and my friend, down the river we searched. I wanted to find Jay, though my fear in seeing his body overwhelmed me. I cried a lot during these searches. We traveled four miles down river. No Jay. Back to my bed I went, in a state of mental, physical and emotional exhaustion. Other friend's psychic's readings took me into the hills and canyons outside

309

the original search area with scent dogs. In my mind, it was horrific. The visuals that came to me as I searched and in my sleep grew more gruesome with time."

"Soon the snow came. Snow covered any possible scent a dog might find. The snow covered the ground and any clues that might still be there. Searching was over for the winter. I felt powerless. I lived in a state of gloom. I cried often, I missed my brother. I missed his calls to ask what he should wear on a date. I missed discussing what we were doing with the kids for the weekend. I missed him listening to my problems. I missed his huge grin that he wore often."

"I thought about Jay dead and I thought about him alive. I thought of every possible scenario. I thought about someone knocking at my door at any minute with news of Jay's body being found. I thought about arriving home and seeing Jay on my couch. He would be wearing a guilty, "I made a big mistake," face with that huge grin sneaking through."

"I did not like leaving my home. It was safe. When I went out, people would ask if there was any word of my brother. This happened at the grocery store, on the bike path, at the post office, at parties, on the ski hill, at concerts, at my office and everywhere I turned there was the question about Jay, whether I was in the mood to go there or not. This question still comes up when I leave the safety of my home."

"When spring came we had a lead. We were told that, unbeknownst to us, Jay had been in some trouble. We were told that Jay died suddenly (brain hemorrhage) in front of the bad guys, who put his body in a mine out one of the canyons. In my desperation to find Jay, I believed this. Off I went again, with a friend into the many mines..."

"The next tragedy in my life was when Jenny, A.J.'s mother took A.J. to live with her in another state. I felt my family was lost and broken."

"Depression set heavily into my heart. I thought it was grief, but after a long while, too long, I was diagnosed with depression. I did not want to live anymore. The hopelessness and the grief felt too great. I could not imagine feeling better ever in my life. For the first time in my life I understood why people commit suicide. I would never take my own life, though I prayed often to be taken by an accident or a disease."

"That summer a body was found in a reservoir outside of Boise. The investigators knew it was male, but nothing else, until further research on the body. This threw me, and my family, into a panic. I dropped my plans for the morning and chose to go for a long walk, breathe deeply, and get some fresh air. I felt more empowered when I returned and better equipped to deal with the day. A picture of the belt that was around the torso of the body, appeared on the front page of the Boise State Newspaper. Our family agreed that it was not the kind of thing Jay would ever wear. It was not Jay, thank God."

"I do not know if Jay is dead or alive. It is much easier to focus my thoughts on the latter. My fantasy is that Jay needed a break from non-stop single parenting and the many pressures he was under with opening a new business and dealing with some difficult issues at the time. I like to believe that he took off for a couple days, which turned into a whole town search. Because of his embarrassment he was unable to return home."

"I like to think Jay is out there. That someday I will see that huge mischievous grin again. Though this is my hope, I still search for Jay's body whenever I am in the woods, any woods."

The family tries to go on with life and be in the moment, yet this unknown in their lives plays a powerful role and is overshadowing any thought of staying present. Feeling powerless is real and must be processed and worked with. How? By feeling in each moment of now.

I have recommended Eckhart Tolle's book, *The Power of Now* to this woman in hopes that it will be of some comfort. Could his advice be too simple to be effective?

I invite you to experiment and discover the answers for yourself. Reading this life-transforming book flooded my memory bank of the days in the seventies when I participated in "est," the human potential growth seminar that offered an entertaining and profound way to explore our true nature. Werner Erhard, who I have mentioned sporadically throughout this book, was a pioneer who introduced the powerful idea that we are not our mind, which was a stimulus response mechanism but something much more powerful. One of his many great one-liners is, "Be more interested than interesting." After the sixty-hour course, participants were invited to sign up for supportive ten-week classes, entitled, "What's So" and "Be Here Now." To you, Werner, wherever you are today, having your own challenges, I say thank you for pushing so many people's buttons and providing a most remarkable experience to hundreds of thousands of individuals.

Re-training the Mind
So dear reader, whenever you feel worry, anxiety, unease, tension, or stress, your attention is no doubt in the future or past. When you feel resentment, guilt, remorse, bitterness, despair, sadness, or a lack of

forgiveness, you are in the past or future. The present moment, the true and real present moment, holds only love and joy. With a focus on either the past or the future, you have given your power away. There is only power in the present moment, being centered, aware, allowing what is so to be exactly as it is. There is only power in taking responsibility for your life. Feeling powerless is taking on the identity of being a victim, which embraces conflict and DRAMA–the energy that ego delights in.

What better time to take charge of the ego than in early childhood? But how to do it? Brother Anandamoy puts it nicely in the Self-Realization booklet in the Summer 2003 issue: "Modern schooling leaves out the most essential aspects needed to cope with life. It omits training the mind – how to transmute negative, destructive thoughts into constructive positive ones. It leaves out mastery over emotion and feelings – meaning not suppression, but redirecting destructive emotions into positive channels and transmuting them into higher, spiritual feelings. It leaves out control over the life energy, by which one can resist harmful temptations and desires. It's incredible how many vital skills are neglected."

So, the earlier one is taught to train the mind, the more one is in charge of the mind. When you understand that the purpose of the ego is to survive, and it feels threatened when you are in the present, being in your truth, you will realize the ego energy is not who you really are. Learn about how the ego operates–how it must defend in order to be right. It's just doing its job. It will be a truly fascinating research project, I guarantee you.

My dear friend, Bobbi, wrote the following:

"It was August 1977. I believed then it was the worst year of my life. My whole world was in disarray and nothing like I thought it was supposed to be. When did the fairytale end — or, more to the point, did it ever really begin? This I pondered while looking out of the airplane window into the vastness of space and the illusion of time. I was on my way to Greece, running from a nightmare into what I hoped and prayed was a new and bright beginning. With my two young children in tow, I could only hope I was doing the right thing."

"Living in Greece was not easy. Being a tourist had been so different. Now the reality of being a single mom, starting anew in a foreign land, seemed to be a daunting task indeed, not at all like I thought it would or should be! Without my Greek relatives, I'm not sure I would have made it through that long, bitter cold winter in one piece - such was my distress and anger over a failed marriage and unfaithful partner. I wanted so much for my children – exposure to different landscapes and ancient cultures – but behind the veil of sweetness and courage, I was an empty shell, navigating without a compass and insecure with every labored decision I made. I was on my own, and I was really scared."

"I felt powerless. The sadness of my looming divorce was overwhelming and seemingly uncontrollable to me. I felt doomed to a life of grief and permanent pain. It was at this point that I wrote my sweet friend, Alexandra, sharing my revelations of inadequacy and bewilderment at the 'unfair hand' I had be dealt. Why me? My moaning and despair got a quick response from Alexandra. 'Bobbi, you have a choice here,' she said in her written response to me. 'You can view this as an opportunity to grow, or you can choose to wallow in your grief. It's up to you. Which will it be?' I was absolutely stunned at the thought she had presented me. It had never occurred to me that I had a choice in this vast emotional dilemma. The thought that I did not have to grieve the rest of my life was like an epiphany – a wondrous surprise in my world of turmoil and unpredictability.

"Yes, this could be my chance to really grow, to turn my life and sadness around into something worthwhile. It was an exciting challenge and realization that I might actually experience happiness again, just by changing my attitude and belief system. Reading her letter and groping with its meaning was a turning point in my life, and the beginning of a new path that has become my life's journey."

"Thanks to Alexandra's wise counsel, my sojourn in Greece was the beginning of my empowerment. I returned to America with a new and positive attitude that continues to evolve. With the help of many dear and supportive friends, my journey is one of openness and acceptance to life's challenges and grace. I know that I can influence the circumstances of my life with the choices or non-choices I make. I know that I choose my reality by my response to every condition in my life. And that is power. And it all started a long time ago in a foreign land when I thought my life was doomed and there was no way out. But I learned, through loving encouragement, there always is. It's just a matter of choice."

Your choice: Claim your power and be in the moment as the truth of who you are, or give your power away to the past or future – the mind. Either place will bring you obvious results. Notice them and be aware.

Reflection Time:

1. Reflect on the last time you were upset, troubled, or emotional about a situation in your life. Dissect it. How connected did you feel to your power? Who did you blame? Who did you have compassion for? How did it feel? Did you confront it? Did you move through it consciously or did it subside and diminish?

2. Notice if you developed any physical symptoms afterwards, i.e.: upset stomach, blurred vision, headache, a skin rash, or overall soreness.

3. Practice being in the now; take a walk with a child and just be with her or him. Surrender to that child for twenty minutes.

4. Can you recall the first time in your childhood you felt powerless, or were told something that led you to believe you could not affect the situation?

5. Make a list of your traits that deem you powerless. Look at them one at a time. Do you REALLY believe this about yourself? Do you want to?

6. If not, make another list of your traits that deem you powerful. Now choose. I invite you to observe the results of the windshield wiper experiment. Get in your car and turn on the wipers. Choose to look at them going back and forth. Now choose to look at the road or the hood of your car or the window. Notice how readily you were able to shift your attention from one to the other.
   You're so clever. You can choose to focus on anything you choose – that's how powerful you are.

7. Do you have beliefs about power and gender? For example: "Men are more powerful than women."

8. Are you afraid of your power?

9. Do you recognize a difference between persona and authentic power?

10. Was there a person in your childhood that you considered as powerful that scared you?

"I noticed, growing up with bullies all around me, that I had turned into a bully myself. I had learned to believe that I needed to be aggressive if I was going to survive in this world."

Terrance Webster-Doyle, *Why Is Everyone Always Picking On Me:*
A Guide to Handling Bullies

Q is for feeling... Quarrelsome

Definition: argumentative, combative, belligerent, complaining
Opposite: easy-going, agreeable, good-natured, non-resistant

To feel quarrelsome most likely means that there is some sort of feud, fight, or argument happening. One cannot quarrel with oneself! There is most likely another party involved.

When you are feeling quarrelsome, you may experience a rage inside of you that is sitting like a volcano. Your child may say, "Mommy, the phone's ringing," when you are busy doing something else. The child keeps telling you that the phone is ringing, so you snap at her, "Just answer it!" This quarrelsome, argumentative, and explosive nature is sourced in anger and deep pain that hasn't been acknowledged.

The Flunkie

I had a client who displayed such inner turmoil. Her out-of-control emotion, which made her so quick to argue and attack and explode, was sourced in the experience of flunking the third grade, which was the one report card her mother kept. The volcano inside of her started building each time the teacher would indicate she was having trouble in certain areas. Her mother would sign the "bad" report cards, send it back to the teacher, never attempting to help her child or get a tutor. The identity of being a "flunkie" had anchored itself in the cellular structure.

Today, in her fifties, she came to me, associating herself with being a hardened person constantly corrected all of her life–stupid, dumb, uneducated, uninteresting—a "flunkie." In sum, people are argumentative because they have those volcanic embers inside of them that are linked to the past. Something simple can act as a bellow to awaken those embers and cause the explosion.

Fools Argue

Have you ever known anyone who always appears ready for combat? At the drop of a hat, he/she can engage in an argument with fervor and conviction. Conflict appears to be a claimable birthright. Paramahansa Yogananda said, "Wise men discuss, fools argue." Which are you?

If someone is quarrelsome, they may be looking for anything to react to, like the pickpocket who meets the saint but sees only his pockets. I attended an evening featuring Thomas Crum, author of *The Magic of Conflict* and Akido master. I offered to participate with him on stage in a demonstration of using energy to work with conflict. His words to the audience are as important today as they were then: "Choose to be centered. Centering occurs when the mind, body, and spirit become fully integrated in dynamic balance and connectedness with the world around us. This is a heightened awareness and sensitivity, a feeling that everything is perfect the way it is."

When we're feeling quarrelsome, we're suffering. It's as if our anger is on simmer, but then we react, and the gas is turned up to a boil. We must watch our "anger pots," and take care this doesn't happen. Once again, we have a choice to act out, assert our righteousness, make others wrong, raise our voice, speak hurtful words, be ornery, and get even... .OR we can embrace our anger as a part of us that needs taking care of. Recognize it with awareness, mindfulness, feeling, and introspection.

Let's do a mini-analysis of how our combative Mr. X or Ms. Y grew up. This is a person who needs to be aggressive in order to be heard. If I have to scream in order to be heard, there is a fear in me that I have never been heard and what I have to say is not important and no one will listen. These thoughts don't just happen. They have been acquired and learned from childhood. Many clients have related personal stories of how their words, feelings, and presence were denied. They inhaled the beliefs that said, "What I say doesn't matter," and "My presence isn't important." They unconsciously formed the foundation of how to relate to people.

When President Bush decided not to send the thirty-four million dollars approved by both houses of Congress for the UN Fund for Population Activities which provided contraception, family planning and safe births, and worked against the spread of HIV and against female genital mutilation of the poorest countries of the world, did Jane Roberts and Lois Abraham lash out with quarrelsome behavior? No, they choose instead to start a symbolic protest by asking thirty-four million women (and men too) to send one dollar each to the United Nations which would prevent two million unwanted pregnancies, 800,000 induced abortions, forty-seven maternal deaths, and 77,000 infant and child deaths. They chose a pro-active attitude, or positive affirmative action. By sending in my dollar, I believe I have made a contribution to combat ignorance and conflict.

What Do YOU Think?

Each time we ask a child her opinion, she acquires value. Her belief becomes, "What I have to say makes a difference." Her point of view is important. However, if the opinions and ideas of our Mr. X were ignored as a child, or he was laughed at or negated, he may have matured with the belief that "I've got to get my point across, no matter what."

If a child feels fatigued or is asked to do something he doesn't want to do, he will be combative and reactive. Children will look for reasons to find fault with anything. Unless dealt with by the adult appropriately, through kindness and understanding and patience, the child will start to build on that experience.

Ruthann Saphier, author of *Parenting Tips for the Strung Out Mom and Dad* and a parenting coach, has some wise words to offer on this subject:

"I have been teaching parenting classes for thirteen years. I see many parents over-controlling and over-indulging their children. Quarrels emerge in families when children are not given positive ways to have power or control in their lives. I see modern parents doing everything for their children to be efficient in the short term. However, parenting is much more than simply feeding, clothing, sheltering, and chauffeuring. It is character building. This takes time. Parents need to take the time to train their children in practical life skills like getting dressed and making their own lunches. 'But we're so rushed in the morning, and I do it so much faster.' Every time you 'do for' your child what she or he can do for her or himself you are creating a handicapped child, one who is unable to do specific tasks and one who perceives her or himself as inadequate. Every time you 'do for' your children, you take their power away."

"Spoiled, incapable children are discouraged. See misbehaving and quarrelsome children as waving a big flag that says, 'I feel discouraged!'

"Find ways your children can contribute to your family life. For example, consider making lunches the night before, teach them how and then notice their efforts and achievements. 'I see you've made a healthy lunch for yourself. Thanks for cooperating.' Giving lots of encouragement will create....confident, capable young people, and will lead to harmonious family life, and steer the dynamics away from quarrels."

Great advice from a lady who knows!

Drama Kings and Queens

When someone is being quarrelsome most likely they:

- Feel insecure (core identity)
- Have a need to be right and/or make the other wrong
- Are unable to hear another perspective
- Feel separate
- Are abrasive and alienate easily
- Show no respect or care for another opinion
- Intimidate as others back down
- Are manipulative
- React defensively and explosively to others points of view
- Do not demonstrate patience, tolerance, or understanding
- Project past experiences into the current conflict, with no recognition of it
- Feel fear at some unconscious level

What a lot of drama! The first questions to ask ourselves: are we willing to drop all that drama to make changes in our life; are we ready for a new way to relate to others as well as ourselves?

Inner discontent is the source of feeling quarrelsome. Once again, when the inner world is chaotic or feels unhappy with a situation, it will be projected into life. If any little thing occurs, it becomes the trigger for the release of all the discontent. In conflict, our body undergoes stress and does not perform optimally. We are not taught skills to embrace conflict. Our body tenses and our tissues aren't soft. There's effort and we feel a need to attack. We set up our situation in order to win and establish a point of view of being the only correct one. We operate out of a deep unconscious pattern where we seem or feel out of control. We're on a treadmill and there's no stopping us now. We are invested in this position and nothing will throw us off. People may start to avoid us as we may start to avoid those who are quarrelsome, ready to break into conflict at any moment, even when discussing anything other than the two big no-no's – religion and politics.

How do you respond to a person who is being quarrelsome?

- Recognize that this energy is a reflection of something in you.
- Realize that you have a choice. Do you become one of Pavlov's dogs, merely reacting to the "bell?" Or do you move into your

heart and feel understanding and compassion for this individual?

- Breathe. Allow the moment to be exactly as it is.
- You might say something like, "It sounds like you're feeling angry about something."
- Or, "I'm feeling really attacked by your position."
- Or ask, "Would another time be better to discuss this?" knowing that it takes time for anger to cool down.

At one of the many conferences where I had an exhibit, I met a woman who told me this story of when she was a playground attendant at an elementary school: Some children had been quarreling so she sent them "to the wall," ordering them to hold hands and not to come away until they had made up. They fussed about doing it, but the rules were set. It took about fifteen minutes, but sure enough, they made up! The little girl, now in college, happened to see Sue after ten or so years, and told her how much that event stuck with her even to that day. Like the Beatles say, "We can work it out."

Nothing to Oppose

Sometimes when we're feeling quarrelsome, we feel negative–pessimistic rather than optimistic, as if nothing is going right. Those gray clouds seem to constantly hover over us, and we forget that the sun is just in back of those clouds. We're irritable, in despair, and react in a quarrelsome manner. We are convinced nothing will ever shift. Everything we attempt to do seems to be thwarted. Our outlook becomes dark, dreary, defeated, and dismal. Some people are so familiar with this knee-jerk reaction that ends up challenging someone and making them wrong, (and you right) that they aren't even aware their negative, quarrelsome demeanor is turning people off. It is the filter through which they experience life. Yet others are aware, and still continue the sabotaging behavior. It has become a habit. Very much like an addiction, while others slip into it from time to time. Which category are you in?

The next time you're ready to tear into someone – STOP – don't do it. You have that ability. I guarantee this is possible. Remember the time you were planning a surprise party for someone and you started to say something that would give it away, then caught yourself and didn't say it? You know exactly what I mean. We are capable of monitoring what comes out of our mouth. We simply need to be more aware – more conscious – more present.

Before you blurt out something that can be damaging or destructive, look inward and ask where you're out of balance. Why are you feeling upset and irritable? What would be the consequences of your lashing? What isn't working in your life? What is the source of your stress? Just STOP. Be present and look inward. I guarantee you will have more friends and like yourself a whole lot better.

And the next time someone is ready to tear into you – STOP – just observe that behavior and notice it and don't feed it. How? By not reacting to it. Respond with responsibility and simply acknowledge it. A response could be, "Interesting," or "Hummm, I never saw it that way before," or "That is a fascinating point of view. Thanks for sharing it with me."

When there is nothing to oppose, miracles happen.

Reflection Time:

1. What do you really want – drama or happiness?

2. How invested are you in your position? In the identity that you know doesn't serve you?

3. When were your feelings first denied?

4. Do you have "knee-jerk" reactions, or do you respond?

5. Would you rather be happy or right?

6. Is quarrelsome a way of describing yourself?

7. What in your early life was painful and when did you start denying that pain by covering it up with the need to be right, argumentative, and combative?

8. Dialogue with the controller in you and discover what she or he has to say.

9. Is there a particular person who you spar with? If yes, who, and why?

10. Experiment with your response when another starts quarreling with you. Resist not and simply allow. Then congratulate yourself for expanding to be bigger than that situation.

"Dear God,
What is it like when you die? Nobody will tell me. I just want to know, I
don't want to do it."
Your friend, Mike
Children's Letters to God

Q is for feeling... Queasy

Definition: uneasy, nauseous, indisposed, sick
Opposite: hardy, well, strong, stable

I would say there are two different kinds of queasy. One kind of queasy is when we feel physically ill. Maybe something we ate or saw didn't sit right with us, so we feel a little nauseous and upset. When the stomach is all upside down, that's a physical kind of queasy.

The other kind is an emotional queasy. We might feel uneasy, anxious, edgy, restless, troubled, uptight, or worried. This emotional queasiness might surface when we know we need to confront someone and the feeling persists with our avoidance. Our queasiness can actually take us into a deeper physical discomfort. Few are comfortable with confrontation, although there is profound value in communicating our feelings. Perhaps the confrontation was put off long enough to slip, conveniently, into your subconscious state. Every time you see that person, you know it's still there. Yuck—that queasy feeling arises again.

Listen to your feelings. What's happening? There is an insect in your house that you wish were outside. What about that meeting that you have tomorrow that you're not prepared for? Is there a sense of feeling scattered and out of balance? Maybe your child is acting in a suspicious manner? How about that loan you made to your partner and now you feel uncomfortable asking the payment plans?

Queasy, out of balance, jittery feelings in the stomach refuse to go away. We think, "What if I don't do well? What if I freeze and draw blanks on all the answers I know I know?" Our minds go ballistic. We have no control over the negative thoughts and uneasy feelings. When we slam-dunk ourselves into the future, all the wrong scenes appear on our life's screen. What to do with these queasy feelings? STOP. BREATHE. Get to the present moment. Stay present, study, and prepare for this adventure, for this experience, or for this endeavor. Get support, create enough time to learn how to study for it, and ask friends for help. Parents may offer suggestions; ask for guidance from the universe. Take responsibility, become self-empowered, and stay present. Everything works out – always – for your highest good. This is a truth, believe it or not.

Life or Death

Now, there is a subject I'd like to explore in relation to "queasy." This is the subject of dying and death. People feel "queasy" even when the word "death" is mentioned. Funerals surely stimulate these feelings within us because they directly force us to look at our own mortality.

Everybody has his own perception of death, or her own experience and beliefs about it. It's unfortunate we don't talk about it more openly, sharing our feelings, thoughts, and beliefs with our children as they grow up.

While in India I had the opportunity to witness a ritual processional for someone who had died. Their version of a funeral is quite different than ours here in the West. The mourners paraded behind the body, which was prostrated on a scant wooden board for all to see, and was covered with a multitude of orange marigolds. A variety of instruments were played as the procession concluded at the final resting spot where the body was placed on a plank supported by four posts. Dry leaves and grasses covered the plank entirely in a huge mound. Once everyone gathered, a flame, which represented purification and freedom, ignited the leaves. Within moments, the scene became a crematorium, as good-byes were chanted, sung, and spoken by the survivors. That was a most amazing experience for me.

Witnessing death can certainly bring perspective. One morning I left my home to go into town to meet a client and had just turned right onto the Highway 75 when I saw two birds fly in front of the car just ahead of me. One was hit. It instantly fell to its death. The people in the car proceeded forward. There was nothing that they could do; it was all over so quickly. I pondered if the other bird wondered what had happened to its companion. In one split second, the timing of the Universe brought this car and this bird together, and it was all over for the bird. No time for a last good-bye. My eyes welled up with tears, and I cried the remaining ten minutes to my office, feeling this experience. As I write about it, it still touches me. I think of what is really important in our day, and I even question my own activity and importance in fulfilling a self-imposed mission here in this lifetime. The idea of balance is prevalent in my consciousness as I reflect on this morning's gift to me. Balance. What an art to accomplish it! I'm grateful I have the awareness that will lead me to wise choices.

Embracing Life

The Buddhist perspective on dying and death says that when we have fully embraced death, we can then truly live. Once we are prepared to die, we will then be best prepared to live.

Most people would feel afraid if surrounded by a pack of wolves, but Dr. Fred Donaldson plays with them, as well as children and dolphins all over the world. Fred has a Ph.D. in education and is the author of an inspiring book for all ages entitled *Playing by Heart*, mentioned earlier. Fred defines play as "a universal solvent dissolving the categories, hierarchies, and fears with which we coerce the world."

I met Fred at "The Power of Laughter and Play Conference," I attended when I was in graduate school. We quickly connected, and he granted me an interview for my dissertation on "Laughter, Enthusiasm, and Joy as Healing Modalities." I am always fascinated when we connect periodically and I hear of his amazing international experiences. Fred is incredibly sensitive, compassionate and such a beautiful soul. What an honor to know him.

One of the most touching and challenging experiences Fred had was with a five-year-old boy who was dying of leukemia. The little boy really wanted to "play" with Fred. When Fred plays, he gets down on the ground and rolls around. The boy's parents were afraid that the roly-poly roughness would hasten his death. The little boy came to Fred one day and asked if he could have a meeting with his parents. They all met, and the little boy said, "I want to play with Fred, and I know that I'm going to die sooner than the three of you, but I want to live my life as though I wasn't." The foursome decided to allow the little boy to play with Fred, so Fred and the boy played and played and played. The little boy just loved every minute of it. Within a month he died. After his death, his parents and Fred had another meeting and wondered if they had done the right thing. It was determined they had made the right decision allowing him this joyful experience. Fred said it was one of the most powerful lessons he had ever had on "trusting in life." His book will take you on a fascinating journey of empowerment. If you were facing death, would you be able to embrace life like this little boy did?

The Journey

At a women's retreat I participated in, Marlo Morgan, author of *Mutant Messages Down Under*, told the group that the Aborigines have a wise greeting they offer when a baby is born, "Welcome. We love you and support you on your journey." Interestingly enough, the same message is repeated when someone dies, "We love you and support you on your journey." Death is not ignored or feared. Instead, it is seen as a continuum, rather than an end, like reading the next chapter of a fascinating book.

A long time friend of mine, Laura Larsen, a RN, provides relevant information and resources for anyone who wants to broaden her or his knowledge about the subject of death in her book, *Facing the Final Mystery: A Guidebook for Discussing End-Of-Life Issues*. It is a book to prepare for end-of-life issues now, before a crisis occurs. The purpose of this book includes the exploration of the importance of in-depth conversations about dying and death, as well as support for those who choose to feel well-versed rather than queasy about the end of life. She says that "facing the final mystery" would include such activities as having your financial documents in order as well as "quality of life" and medical documents established. Ms. Larsen talks about the durable power of attorney for health as well as exploring and communicating feelings to loved ones, creating a team, and visualizing the dream. She helps you take care of "the business of living and dying." Regular folk, health professionals, people of all faiths, and therapists–we can all benefit from this extensive guidebook. It's about getting your life in order before you die, whether it be the nitty-gritty legal stuff, or healing a relationship with an estranged sibling. Thank you, Laura, for the courage to compile this book; it's a job well done!

In the Arena

I heard a one-liner that brought a hearty laugh to my heart. "Live your life so the minister at your funeral doesn't have to lie."

My nephew by marriage, Dave Jones, offers the parts of the eulogy that his brother Jim gave at their father's funeral. It is a quote from Theodore Roosevelt.

"It is not the critic who counts; not the man who points out how the strong man stumbled or where the doer of deeds could have done better. The credit belongs to the man who is actually in the arena, whose face is marred by dust and sweat and blood; who strives valiantly, who errs and comes short again and again because there is no effort without error and shortcoming; but he who does actually strive to do the deeds; who knows the great enthusiasm, the great devotion; who spends himself in a worthy cause; who at the best knows in the end the triumph of high achievement and who at the worst, if he fails, at least failed, while daring greatly, so that his place shall never be with those cold and timid souls who know neither victory nor defeat."

Dave also says the following about his father's death: "I don't think I ever felt queasy during that period. To be sure, I felt shocked, emotional, empty, deeply saddened, worried for my Mom, abandoned, and left with an immeasurable sense of loss that I have never felt before. I guess I equate queasy with an uneasy physical discomfort or nausea. I really never felt that during the aftermath of Dad's death – rather more of a psychological wringer that left me emotionally wiped out." My memories of Dave's father can be described as someone with a remarkably positive attitude. His mother also lives her life this way. Quite a legacy to be proud of for their two sons, and of so many more.

Returning the Jewels

The following is a story from the Talmud (Judaism's holy book) called "The Jewels" that may provide a new perspective on death:

One Sabbath, while Rabbi Meir was in the House of Study, his two sons fell in a well and were drowned. Grief-stricken, his wife, Beruriah, carried them into her room and covered them. In the evening, when Rabbi Meir returned, he asked, "Where are the children? I missed them at the House of Study."

Instead of replying, Beruriah handed him a goblet of wine for the recital of the Havdalah Service. Rabbi Meir drank from the goblet and again asked, "Where are the children?"

"You will see them soon," Beruriah turned to her husband. "I would like to ask you a question. Not long ago, some precious jewels were entrusted to my care. I became so attached to them that I regarded them as my own. Now the owner has come to reclaim them. What shall I do?"

"I am surprised that you, who know the Law, should ask such a question," Rabbi Meir said. "Naturally, the jewels belong to their owner, and must be returned."

Beruriah then gently led her husband to the room and lifted the sheet from the bodies of their dead sons. "My sons! My sons!" cried Rabbi Meir.

Tearfully, Beruriah reminded him. "Did you not say that we must restore to the Owner that which He has entrusted to our care? Our sons were the jewels which God had left with us."

Together they wept and they said, "The Lord hath given, the Lord hath taken away; blessed in the name of the Lord."

A New Attitude

Geoff and Linda Bushell lost their beloved twenty-one-year-old son, "Boo," in an accident on the Salmon River. Taken from the back cover of her book, *Forever In Our Hearts*, "Linda not only details the death of her only child and the ensuing period of grieving but also the ways in which the guidance of intuitive and impassioned friends helped her to begin a spiritual quest that led her to a reconnection with Boo."

Linda was one of my first neighbors when I moved to Sun Valley. We bonded almost immediately. She has picked up her life and has reactivated a dormant creative gift–jewelry design. I have such respect for what this mother has been through and how her resilience has set her on a new chapter of her life. She brings us up to date with the following entry:

"Alexandra asked me to write something about my lifestyle today – how I am getting along in my life after the loss of my only child. It is always difficult for me to put my feelings into words. I can only say that I have had some of the happiest moments of my life and some of the saddest. What I have learned is you make your life whatever you want it to be by your beliefs and choices. I still miss my son in the physical world, yet I believe that all of our experiences, good and bad, are just experiences in our life – our physical life. I feel so fortunate to have had the gift of what I consider the most precious of all, the love between a parent and child. The fact that Boo is no longer here does not take away from the gift. I had twenty-one years of sharing my life with another spirit. Without a doubt, I would still have chosen to have this child, had I known on the conscious level, he would have been here for only twenty-one years. Absolutely. To have the experience of loving and sharing life with another spirit is the joy. The loss is only temporary. As the old saying goes, 'it is better to have loved and lost than to never have loved at all.' "

"And, how am I doing today? I am great. My life is better with the knowledge my son gave me, by leaving at such an early age. It's the knowledge of eternal life, how precious life is and how quickly time goes by. Boo taught me to be grateful for every day, being aware of the choices we make. He taught me the gift of life."

Blessings to you, Linda; your attitude is illuminating and touches my heart.

If we are feeling queasy about death, once again, we can choose a new attitude. And with a new attitude comes a new set of beliefs. There are many options, believe it or not. These are for you to consider and determine which, if any, will replace the feeling of queasy when the subject of death arises. Your choice. Feeling morbid of the very mention of the word, "death," is a clue, a red flag, to resisting the subject. Some even feel if it is discussed, it will be wished upon them. We in the West have been taught to deny death or fear it. It smells like RESISTANCE to me! One suggestion to lighten up the queasy subject of death: rent a video called *Defending Your Life*. It's such fun.

So, if we can embrace this subject, we can dissolve the fear and the resistance, face death, and truly start to live, as the Buddhists say. We can replace ignorance of the afterlife with wisdom as we pursue optional beliefs. If and when queasy comes to visit the body, feeling our way through it will bring us to the truth.

Reflection Time:

1. What do you do with your queasy feelings?
2. Do you embrace and honor them, looking deeper into the feeling?
3. How often do you ignore them? Take medications to make them go away? Deny them?
4. How often do you embrace them?
5. What thoughts were going through your mind as you read about the Indian ritual of death?
6. Do you feel queasy about the subject of death?
7. Is the subject of death an untouchable one for you? For your partner? Your child? Your parent?
8. Do you give your power away to challenging life situations?
9. How do you want to be remembered? Are you living your life this way? How long would your obituary be in the paper?
10. Are you "prepared" for the final mystery?

"How can you buy or sell the sky, the warmth of the land? The idea is strange to us. If we do not own the freshness of the air and the sparkle of the water, how can you buy them? ...Every part of this Earth is sacred to my people...This we know. All things are connected...man did not weave the web of life; he is merely a strand in it. Whatever he does to the web, he does to himself...So, if we sell our land, love it as we've loved it. Care for it as we've cared for it...And preserve it for your children..."

Words from a translation of Chief Seattle's reply to President Franklin Pierce in December of 1854 when the U.S. requested to buy two million acres of Indian land in the Northwest.

Q is for feeling...Quiet

Definition: peaceful, silent, calm, tranquil, serene

Opposite: active, noisy, loud, clamorous, boisterous

Shhhh. Be quiet. Listen. Shhhh. When one feels quiet, everything around him or her is quiet too. It's the difference between shouting and whispering. Or maybe one feels quiet because the environment is quiet.

The benefits of quiet are numerous and outstanding. Dr. Albert Schweitzer, humanitarian, physician, and philosopher, is someone I've always respected. In fact, he and I share the same birthday. My favorite quote of his is, "It's supposed to be a professional secret, but I'll tell you anyway. We doctors do nothing, we only help and encourage the doctor within."

To be aware of our own doctor within, we need to be quiet and listen. We can physically be quiet, take a walk in the woods, sit against a tree, and just listen. Being in stillness is a very wonderful experience.

We also need to learn to quiet our minds, especially in the quickening of our culture. The Jewish tradition, Shabbot, which starts on Friday at sunset and continues through sunset on Saturday, is about being quiet within. It's a peaceful day, one that's dedicated to rest. Orthodox Jews won't drive and do not even use the phone. What do they do? They share, they walk, or they read. My in-laws took us all to Israel and the day we arrived happened to be Shabbot. Even the elevator was quiet because on Shabbot, it didn't operate.

Quieting the Mind

I have a vivid memory about feeling quiet when I came home to Idaho from a conference–alone. This was a different experience for me, because my husband, Gene was not home to greet me with open arms, nor Max, our Aussie Shepherd, with wagging tail. They were both in California waiting my return in several days. I walked into a house that was incredibly quiet. Only the tick-tock of a family heirloom mantel clock broke the silence. I even heard the heater come on. Initially it was rather peculiar. Soon it felt incredibly peaceful and highly enjoyable. Then, my mind started to rise like the phoenix out of the ashes! "I better lock the door," my mind said, although we rarely lock the door in our safe community. "Did I put the garage door down?" "Is there a light in the library?" My mind even led me to think I saw Max out of the corner of my eye, and I found myself looking for him under Gene's desk, like he'd be ready to go out for a walk (which was always now)!

I soon realized what was going on. When in a quiet environment, the mind's chattering becomes more apparent. How resistant the mind can be to quietness! Breathe. Shhhh. Breathe. It's my understanding the greatest challenge is to control one's mind. I can personally attest to that after over thirty years of meditating. It may sound like I'm a slow learner, but I'm not alone in this challenge! The mind is like a herd of wild horses. It is up to us, the disciplinarian, to calm the mind and take charge of the reins. To do this takes tremendous practice and commitment. That night my practice paid off. I was in control of those thoughts.

As I prepared for a good night's sleep, the quietness became delicious. After hearing the only other voice, my computer, which said, "You've got mail," I luxuriated in my hot shower, and climbed into our awesome bed, under a snuggly down comforter to sip my favorite bedtime tea out of my Sawtooth National Recreational Area volunteer mug. Ahhhhh, life is good. The light can't go off until reading several chapters of an engrossing and inspiring book! This completes my nightly ritual. Quiet is good.

Now, Class, Let's Listen to Our Thoughts

And, as important as this is, are our children taught this in school? Unfortunately, our schools leave out this most essential aspect needed to cope with life–the training of the mind! Our children are not learning at an early age to be still and to be introduced to the "invisible intruder" called the mind. I've observed children when they are afraid and how that initial thought can catapult into a major frenzy. Thanks to my friend Katie, a preschool teacher, at least one little girl on the planet knows the power of her mind.

"Emily, a bright and cheerful four-year-old, was extremely frightful of the sound of large trucks. As the school was next to a construction site, this became a problem. She would tremble, cry, and whine, and run to me or one of the other teachers every time the trucks started up. One day, when a truck began 'growling,' I led Emily to the window and sat with her, letting her watch the trucks. She grasped my hand in fear as I explained to her, 'What is making you afraid is a thought in your mind. The trucks can't hurt you. Do you see how it is a thought that is making you scared?' Emily quieted somewhat; it seemed as if she was thinking about her thoughts! Eventually, after a few days of this, she came to me when the trucks were being loud and said proudly, 'Miss Katie, I'm not scared of the trucks anymore.'"

These are the lessons that empower a child and cultivate a healthy adult. In 1988, I was invited to speak about the subject of meditation at an elementary school. I brought my singing crystal bowl, which is a bowl made out of quartz crystal and when stroked with a wooden stick creates a song – sounds that stimulate and awaken the unknown parts of our selves. I played the bowl for the class and guided them through a meditation. The following are some of the comments I received in thank you letters from the individual children:

- "I really love your crystal bowl."
- "The meditation was neat."
- "It felt good when we meditated with you. "
- "I felt free and could fly."
- "Could you come back one day?"
- "I imagined I was the most beautiful girl in the land of flower groves."
- "The part you said about our body being a vehicle was very interesting."

Children know what's up! We have so much to learn from them, if we can only quiet our ego long enough to listen and nurture their spirits.

Nature's Gift

John Denver (one of my champions) sought out the quiet places in our country – Alaska, the Colorado River, and Yellowstone, and said this about nature. "Nature comforts me and gives me solace. It is a place I feel listened to." In the last film he produced for National Public Television, he spoke of serenity, how he feels peace in nature, while observing wildlife. He spoke out for the wilderness, saying, "That aspect of our life is disappearing." Being in nature strengthened him; it felt like home. It's ironic that the last song he wrote for this program was entitled "Coming Home." John passed on in 1997, at the age of fifty-four, feeling the freedom of flight, which he loved so much.

Quiet, tranquility, and calm is best developed as an inner experience. This may well be the only place we can find quiet. With the intense growth of civilization we have less access to the quiet of nature. Does it matter to you that the existence of the old growth trees is in danger? If it doesn't, it should. What is an even more startling fact is that out of all the forests in the entire world, Greenpeace International states that 76% of the planet's original primary forests have been destroyed or degraded! Three-fourths of the forests have been destroyed! Can you imagine what it would be like not having a place to retreat to experience quiet? Not to mention beauty, simplicity, and the other wonders of nature.

Seeking Quiet

Tranquility is synonymous with peace of mind. Now think, are there people on the planet who would beg, steal, and borrow for peace of mind? Many seekers often look in the wrong places. They yearn to satisfy their inner cravings and thirsts by acquiring the old, as well as the new, such as the antique automobile, the latest and best sound system in the steam room, the fastest and most efficient skis, racecars, bikes, you name it. Fast is better, for it is one way we are forced to stay in the moment. Only the finest of materials from far off places can satisfy the unique adornments for the home. For what? All to make us feel important and worthy. A variety of "toys" will be sought after in lieu of quiet moments as a means of avoiding our own company. Rather interesting dynamics we engage in.

The Blizzard of '04

There is a dichotomy in the quietness of falling snow. New Year's Day 2004, we were invited to a friend's home to view a live satellite presentation by Gurumayi, the head of Siddha Yoga Foundation. We chose to brave the heavy snowfall and journey up a canyon to bring in 2004 with special friends and a sacred message which was "Experience Your Own Power." It was well-worth our adventurous journey home, as it had been snowing two inches per hour New Year's Eve and into the day. That is a lot of snow. Our little caravan was going to stay together as we started our three mile escapade down the canyon, but we got stuck in a bank during the first few minutes because we couldn't see! White on white—there was no distinction of the main road and the bank. Friends came to the rescue, offering selfless service, exactly what was talked about in the presentation.

We got stuck again one-half mile from our home, but once back, I settled into the moment and felt the quiet of the snow. Once home, we noticed our outdoor table had accumulated a total of about four feet of snow!

The incredible beauty of this fresh snowfall is hard to describe. Peacefulness and quiet beyond words–a pervading stillness. Even the shadows of the sunlight that appeared on the crystalline snow were quiet, in their majesty. The fir trees bent, heavy with the flocking of snowflakes one upon another, demonstrating evidence of the power of one upon one upon one.

Quiet is good.

Reflection Time:

1. Take a walk in the woods, seek to visit quiet places, find the few wild or sacred spots left on the planet. Go someplace where it's still and allow your thoughts to calm down – allow them to be quiet. How does it feel?

2. Does your mind quiet down? If yes, after about how long? If not, why do you suppose?

3. Where do you feel "at home?"

4. Do you seek out quiet? Quiet places? Quiet moments? If you don't, why not?

5. If you don't, do you not find quiet of value quiet?

6. Do you feel comfortable with quiet?

7. Take a weekend morning and go visit a quiet, natural place. Take nothing to "entertain" yourself. Offer yourself to the trees, streams, birds, sky, and insects. Talk to them – yes, that's what I said – talk to them. Then listen; listen for the answer.

8. What lesson did you learn from Emily?

9. Do you think "Shabbot" has value?

10. If you feel moved to do so, write a short letter to your local official in response to Chief Seattle's words.

"You can't create in opposition to anything."
Werner Erhard

R is for feeling... Resistant

Definition: unyielding, defiant, antagonistic, rebellious
Opposite: accepting, allowing, desiring

To feel resistant is to not want something to be the way it is. To resist is to fight whatever it is that already exists. If you're suffering, you're resisting something.

Have you heard the expression, "To resist is to persist?" "We can allow life to flow and evolve from joy, or we can resist, create disease, and grow from experience," said Dr. Theresa Dale, naturopathic physician and author of *Transforming Your Emotional DNA*. In her remarkable book, Theresa discusses resistance and the immune system. "Vulnerability to disease manifests in the human body when an individual resists feeling an emotion, as it actually lowers the immune system. Whenever you have pain, there is a resistance to something or someone. Resistance implies pain."

So, resisting is like pushing against something. It is an inner tug-of-war. When we refuse to accept responsibility, we have resistance. Resistance can affect us by making us feel stuck. It may physically affect our colon and our elimination process. The answer to resistance is to simply allow ourselves to experience and actually embrace the layers of resisted emotions and beliefs. Then, our body will balance itself out on a cellular level.

To look at this area a little more closely, I offer a suggestion: Make a list of the things that you're resisting in your life. This alone will help stimulate some shift and heighten awareness. Then buy Dr. Dale's book and learn how to dissolve the beliefs that are sabotaging your dreams and goals.

Eckhart Tolle in *The Power of Now* says, "Not only your psychological form but also your physical form, your body, becomes hard and rigid through resistance. Tension arises in different parts of the body, and the body as a whole contracts. The free flow of life energy through the body, which is essential for its healthy functioning, is greatly restricted...unless you practice surrender in your everyday life...the resistance pattern has not been dissolved."

You Can't Resist a Mirror

We've got to love what we want to let go of. If I'm resisting my friend's indifference towards me, I've got to love that she's being indifferent. If I want to let go of being dependent, I've got to love my dependency. If my father has not been responsive to me during my childhood, behaving as if work is a priority, I've got to embrace the idea that he is unresponsive. If I get annoyed that my paychecks barely make it to the next one, I have to love that I run out of money before my next paycheck. Get the idea? It's more than acceptance. It's actually honoring that energy because it's there! You've just been resisting it. As you choose to desire what you've been resisting, your heart opens, your struggle ceases, and your pain is relieved. Whether we're comfortable or uncomfortable really makes no difference to the Universe. Everything is happening to wake us up! Each trial is an opportunity. Never blame anyone for anything that is happening to you. That is a wholesome attitude. "How am I behaving?" is the question to ask yourself. "What is my attitude about the situation?"

If somebody is irritating you, chances are good that quality or something like it is within you. Introspection helps us own that rather than resist it. The desire to change must be there. The desire to see your true nature helps you to understand this. Our experiences are all trying to tell us something, as well as the interactions in our relationships. Why be resistant to the lesson? Rather than being defensive, which is coming from your ego, use it as a catalyst for your inner search.

If your child's behavior is upsetting, frustrating, and provoking, I ask you, Mom and Dad, what are you resisting? What do you see in your child that is a reflection of you? Someone once said, "You can't preach against the darkness until you've seen it in yourself first." Talk to your child from your heart. She or he will not change as long as you're making her or him wrong. What does she feel inside? Stop, look and listen. Refrain from resisting what is. Trust the process. Look inside of yourself and be honest with yourself and your child. Take responsibility for this reality. Seek good help from a professional who will get to the core issues.

See if any of the following relate to you or someone you know:

- When we resist taking 100% responsibility for our life, we blame others and become the victim.

- When we resist feeling vulnerable, we can hide it with a mask of confidence that never allows another person to get close to us.

- When we resist letting go of control, we fear trusting life. When we resist exploring the unfulfilling patterns in relationships, we can feel lonely and separate.

- When we resist recognizing who we truly are, we live with inadequacies and unworthiness.
- When we resist our past, it acts as an anchor and prevents us from the present.
- When we resist the way people are, we criticize and judge which keeps us separate.
- When we resist acknowledging our weaknesses, we're not being honest with ourselves.
- When we resist our humanness, we portray a perfectionist identity.
- When we resist love, we live in fear.
- When we resist looking inward for the answers, we can act impulsively and not in our highest interest.
- When we resist accepting who we are, we will continue judging others.

What Buddy Taught Me

We have so much to learn from our animal friends. They teach about resistance through its opposite, which is acceptance.

I'm in awe of the unconditional love and trust that pets have for their owners. I recall an opportunity we had to dog-sit for five months for our son, Jeff's, Aussie Shepherd. Following are ten lessons I learned from one very trusting furry friend, named Buddy, who closed his eyes for the last time when he was sixteen years old.

Buddy taught me many tips about being in the moment:

First thing in the morning before he moved, he stretched; first the front legs, then the rear. After a big yawn he strolled out the front door to greet the day. *Stretching our muscles is so healthy for the body. Any yoga enthusiast can give you the beneficial details.*

In no time, Buddy felt comfortable in our home. My son, the adventurer, allowed little grass to grow under his feet over the past years, so his loyal and trusted friend made every new environment his home. Change is exciting! *Fear of change is limiting.*

This dog had incredible concentration. During a game of catch, he'd intensely focus on the rubber ball until it was in his mouth. Nothing could distract him from "sit" and "stay" while he waited to get his biscuit. *We become empowered when our attention acts like a laser beam to produce the results we desire.*

Buddy most definitely possessed the "call of the wild." When he was after the scent of an animal during our morning walk ritual, there was virtually nothing I could do to make him "heel." *There is incredible power in concentration, focus, and staying on purpose.*

One minute he would be taking a "dog nap" and in the next, be ready to play, big time. *Play is always a moment away for us too, if we recognize it. Accept the invitation when it comes, or instigate it. Play does reduce stress. Believe it.*

One morning we allowed Buddy to go out on our bedroom deck, a new environment for him. He investigated all of the area with natural curiosity. *We all have a curious inner child. Do we allow that child to express curiosity, or are we too busy being an adult?*

The excitement didn't stop. The same food, the same time, the same bowl. Yet, every night, at approximately 6:00 P.M., Buddy got so excited when I picked up his bowl and headed for that big bag of feed. He watched diligently as I put in just the right amount. His tail wagged and he could hardly wait until I put down his once-a-day feast. He got excited for dinner, for taking a walk, for getting in the car, for getting brushed, or getting a biscuit; he got excited about everything! If each dog year were equivalent to seven adult years, he would have been one hundred and twelve. *Does our society support a lifestyle of excitement in the "golden years," or does it promote "over the hill at forty?" Excitement is created in our own mind, through our attitudes, beliefs, and choices.*

After being gone only a few hours, I was always greeted like I'd been gone for days. His unconditional love and trust was beautiful. *Is our love for partner or children unconditional? Is our love for life unconditional? Do we choose trust?*

Buddy was also loyal. He preferred to be nearby, even when I moved to another room. He was also very protective; he was "on purpose" as he guarded his domain. *Do we express to our loved ones how much we care about them, while they are here, or do we carry regret and guilt after they pass on, because we didn't show our love and share our heart?*

Last, but certainly not least, the most powerful lesson came in the form of the stick game. Buddy would tug, and I'd tug back. It continued until I tired of the game. One day, I happened to just hold the end of the stick and didn't tug at it. After a few moments, much to my surprise, he released the stick. The game was over. What a lesson! The game will go on as long as we keep tugging. *Are you resisting something that is causing you to suffer? Resist what we don't want and it will persist. Allow and it will disappear.*

Experiment on your own, as I did with Buddy. Maybe you too will be awed by the results.

Buddy has been treated better than many humans treat each other. Throughout his life, he was given food and water, lots and lots of love, and the freedom to be who he is. In return, he gave so much more.

Repressed, resisted feelings do not go away! If anything, they grow more intense. So release your resistance, surrender, and breathe into what is already happening. Stop playing tug-of-war with whatever wants to play tug-of-war with you, and the game will end before it even begins!

Reflection Time:
1. If you have an animal watch him or her for a few days;
2. Note his or her behavior; watch the eating pattern, etc.
3. How much love do they give you? Is it conditional or not?
4. How much love do you give back?
5. Has Buddy inspired you to find the lessons in your life? If so, in what way?
6. What are the three most important issues you are resisting, or avoiding at this time? Make a "resistance list" and be willing to tell the truth about each item on your list.
7. How would you describe your willingness to embrace these situations?
8. How have you been dealing with them up to now? Has it worked? If not, why not?
9. Have you explored other perspectives in resolving them?
10. In what ways does resistance show up in your life?

"Don't laugh at me,
Don't call me names.
Don't get your pleasure from my pain...."
Song from Project Respect, Sung by Peter Yarrow

R is for feeling... Respectful

Definition: considerate, courteous, reverent
Opposite: uncaring, rude, impolite

Being respectful is an attitude that comes from a deep, inner belief that it's good to honor and care about people and their rights. When we show respect, we honor another's point of view or opinion. We are being respectful of another's journey, their choices, path, and their own unique process. Each person has rights. We each deserve to have our privacy respected, as well as our opinions. Problems arise when we think our rights are more important than someone else's.

When we feel respectful, we have embraced the shadow within ourselves, and we've learned to respect our own journey, our own process, and can therefore be respectful of others. Respecting others' property is equally as important. Whenever we borrow something from another person, we must make certain we return it. I will often loan a book to a friend and frequently have need of it and can't find it. I feel "F for frustrated" because I haven't written down the name of the person I loaned it to. In most cases, I get it back, sooner or later. Being respectful of others' belongings means living with integrity and honesty – two character traits related to respect.

With our deluge of cell phones, I find many people being less than respectful with regard to their public conversations. I really don't care to be exposed to hearing a business transaction or personal interactions. People seem to talk louder while on a cell phone, and I feel it is disrespectful. When I receive a call while in the market, I will walk outside and take my call there. Awareness. Choice. Many people walk the aisles chatting away. What are your thoughts about cell phones? How about when you go to a movie and someone's cell rings?

Respect Your Elders

Unfortunately, our society does not respect the elderly, as other cultures do. Many of the elderly spend the last days of their lifetimes in nursing homes. They are offered institutionalized food, loaded with carbs and cooked to death. Often, they're drugged so they don't cause problems, like ADHD children. Their main source of entertainment is television.

Why don't we respect their lives enough to seek their wisdom and their stories? Their years on the planet have surely earned them something. How about asking your grandparents what it was like when they were young, what it was like when they went out on a date, or how much money they earned at their first job? Ask them for stories of places they've seen or what each decade taught them.

This brings back memories about my visits to the Jewish Home for the Aged. I remember all the folks there, because I interviewed and recorded many of their lives on tape. They lived fascinating lives. One couple had escaped the concentration camp and they told me the details of that saga. I admired their bravery as they relayed those painful days to me. "Your children must be indeed touched by hearing these tales," I stated. "Oh, they haven't heard them – not like you have. They're too busy." Everybody is so busy. What is everybody so busy doing? Opportunities to be still and respectful slip by because people are wrapped up in their own lives, their own pain, and their own drama.

I happened to notice an ad in the classified section of an organization looking to hire someone to care for a disabled person. They were willing to pay all of six dollars and fifty cents an hour to pay for this gigantic task and responsibility. Six dollars and fifty cents per hour were the proposed wages for someone to fill a job description that required sensitivity, caring, compassionate, strength, and kindness. This is ludicrous. Where is the respect shown in this unfortunate but true example?

Respect Your Kids

The good ol' golden rule – treat others the way you would like to be treated. That is a strong message to live by as examples for our children.

Most families have rules. If I choose to break those rules and cause disruptions, I am being disrespectful to those who love and support me. In that scenario, I'm behaving in a way that is hurtful to them, but even more so, to myself. If I visit my daughter and see a letter on her desk from someone I am curious about, I demonstrate disrespect if I choose to open it and read it. Or, if I'm in earshot of a very personal phone conversation and choose to stay there and intentionally listen, I am being disrespectful.

What about our children? Do we truly respect them? Politicians talk a good game, but do their actions support their words? In my experience they don't. One cliché refers to our children as our future and how we have to invest in their quality education and safe after-school programs. Many of us understand the importance of the arts in a child's life: drama, music, theater, and art. Why don't our politicians read research that supports arts education? When the budget has to be cut, why are these often the programs that are eliminated? Why do teachers have to dip into their own pockets to invest in products that support emotional growth and character development? Respect at the most fundamental level must be continually sought. From the government to the individual child seems like a long way for respect to travel. The trickle-down movement needs help all along the way. Yet, how many schools actually teach feelings communication on a daily basis? Emotional awareness is instrumental to a child's capacity to learn and grow into a healthy, fully-realized adult.

I recall presenting a session at an early childhood conference and learning that one of the best attended workshops was one that presented ideas on how to teach math principals using only the barest of supplies. If that doesn't demonstrate an attitude of lack, I don't know what does! Our children deserve better. In fact, they deserve the best.

We MUST be respectful of our children. When we understand they are wise souls in small bodies, we will definitely be awakened. Listen to them. Use eye contact. Ask your children for solutions, for consequences to their own unacceptable behavior. Include them in that decision-making process. When we model respectfulness for our children, they become respectful themselves. Use kind language and positive tones, letting them know that you care. Refrain from interrupting them. Acknowledge a child when they are being respectful, thanking them, and praising them to build their self-esteem. Teach them to appreciate their own accomplishments as well as those of others. Children are so fresh to life. They are authentic and they feel deeply. They live in the moment and don't have the years of debris and filters that adults have which sabotage dreams and goals.

Two teachers, Janie Hamilton and Maria Loew wrote a curriculum for kindergarten through sixth grade called Character Connection. It has gained national attention and won awards. They started the Character Connection Homework Program with the simple idea of developing character traits such as respect, responsibility, compassion, and service learning. "We gave our parents homework to discuss with their children. Although a few busy parents complained at first, most participate regularly. We have noticed the climate of our classroom changed. There is more respect, more compassion for one another. Start young. The road is more or less paved once they start high school."

I received an email entitled "I've Learned," a series of one-liners about life, by children. For example, "I've learned that when Mommy and Daddy yell at each other it scares me." This was from a five-year-old. "I've learned that it always makes me feel good to see my parents holding hands." A child aged thirteen said this. Children are more in touch with their innate wisdom and sensitivity than many adults are. They are pure love. Here's one more: "I've learned that I can swim faster when I eat fish sticks because they're fish!" Age seven. Go figure.

Project Respect, founded by Peter Yarrow (of Peter, Paul and Mary), is a non-profit organization working to transform schools, camps, and organizations (focused on children and youth) into more compassionate, safe, and respectful environments. Operation Respect developed the "Don't Laugh At Me" program, utilizing music and video along with curriculum guides. As of this writing, more than 60,000 copies of this curriculum have been distributed to educators. Peter performed at the Character Education conference I attended, singing the tender song that is the basis for this program, "Don't Laugh At Me." Kathleen Kennedy-Townsend also addressed the audience and said 160,000 kids in our nation's schools don't go to school because of fear of being bullied. Respect for one another is fundamental in preparing a child for life.

Respect Your Mother

We can't talk about respect and ignore our Mother Earth—our source of sustenance. As her air and waterways become more polluted, we see disrespect. As wildlife habitat is used to feed cattle or ticky-tacky-little-house-all-in-a-row developments, we can see the results of the lack of respect we've demonstrated. The choices we have made were not with the Earth's best interest. Respecting all of life is important. Whether it's a two-legged, a four-legged, or a multi-legged friend, trees, or our winged companions, we all share this Earth together. Do we forget we have free choice, and we can choose to change our ways and change the direction we're headed?

Animals in particular seem to be suffering due to our lack of respect. Thousands of animals suffer every day due to animal testing and abominable conditions in which they live. From the national bestseller,

Anger, author Thich Nhat Hanh says, "Nowadays, chickens are raised in large scale modern farms where they cannot walk, run, or seek food in the soil. They are fed solely by humans...kept in small cages and cannot move at all. Day and night, they have to stand. They have no right to walk or run. Imagine that you have to stand day and night in just one place. You would become mad, so the chickens become mad."

If we had respect for these animals that are consumed by a mass population, they would be raised on free-range farms to lay their eggs according to nature rather than the creation of artificial days and nights with indoor lighting. He continues, "The chickens believe that twenty-four hours have passed and then they produce more eggs....There is much suffering in the chickens. They express their anger and frustration by attacking the chickens next to them. They use their beaks to peck and wound each other." Because they bleed, suffer, and die, the farmers now cut the beaks off the chickens to prevent them from attacking each other out of their frustration. Is this reverence for life? Is this showing respect for the food that feeds our bodies, our temples? If you choose to eat veal, I urge you to educate yourself on how those calves are raised for your pleasure.

There is a company called Daily Blessings Food, Inc. that specializes in superior quality meat. Diane Hollen, owner of Daily Blessings, personally told me about the trials and errors of raising cattle. "Our cows are [now] raised in a healthy environment in lush, green pastures. They drink fresh, clean water, the feed is certified organic, and they receive no antibiotics or hormones...We count our blessings that in our world of factory farming, we are able to provide a very special product." (Hence, the name of their company)

Previously, people had told her that she would have to expand, by adding more cattle, for her business to survive. She took their advice, but had to confine the cows to feeding lots, rather than letting them loose in the pasture. Within a few years, the cows started to show diseases, including cancer, foot problems, and twisted stomachs. She later found out that it was due to lack of exercise and the unnatural diet of corn. Then when the calves began to be born abnormally (the mother retained the placenta after calving due to a prolapsed uterus), Diane looked at her babies, and said, "This is not the way to go." She said, "Forget it," and opened the gates and put them back into pasture. After that, no more sickly cows. In fact, "the veterinarian has rarely been back." Diane has made it her duty to see that her cows are not only healthy, but happy. Happy and healthy go hand in hand, don't they? And respect is at the source of both.

You might need to stretch your thinking on this next bit of information about the correlation between how an animal is treated and how it affects the person who eats the meat. The American Institute of Stress Newsletter, 1999, Issue 9, states, "When a cow, pig, chicken, turkey, or any domestic farm animal is under severe stress due to fear or pain, increased levels of stress-related hormones like adrenaline and cortisone are found not only in the blood, but also in body tissues. Primitive man and kosher butchers sacrificed animals by 'blood letting,' a procedure used so that [the animals] lapsed into a painless coma before perishing. As a result, the hormone content of this meat was much lower. Modern slaughtering practices tend to cause extreme fear in animals, resulting in the production of abnormally high amounts of these hormones and other compounds. There is good evidence that these chemicals remain in the tissues, and can have significant physiological effects when consumed." Food for thought.

Here are "Ten Reasons to Buy Organic," written by Sylvia Towse for *Organic Times* Spring 1992.

1. Protect future generations. Children receive four times more exposure to cancer-causing pesticides in food.

2. Prevent soil erosion. Three billion tons of topsoil is eroded each year with conventional farming.

3. Protect water quality. Pesticides pollute our water!

4. Save energy. Modern farming uses more petroleum than any other single industry, consuming 12% of the country's total energy supply!

5. Keep chemicals off your plate. Pesticides are designed to kill! Humans are not immune to their affects. Pesticides cause cancer, birth defects, nerve damage, and genetic mutation.

6. Protect farm worker health. Farmers exposed to pesticides have six times greater risk than non-farmers of contracting cancer.

7. Help small farmers.

8. Support a true economy. Conventional farming uses our tax money.

9. Promote bio-diversity. Neither the soil nor its crops can handle the same crop year after year.

10. Taste better flavor. Definitely!

Big Bad Wolf?

Have we grown wiser? In the thirties, out of irrational fear, people shot and killed most of the wolves in the United States, and they became fugitives. Wolves have an acute sense. They are smart. They can travel fifty miles in a twenty-four hour day – day after day after day. Can you do that? If I had my way, the Little Red Riding Hood fable would be eliminated from all children's libraries and retailers' bookshelves. How unfair it is to raise our children with the notion that wolves are "big and bad."

Mark Hoff, who wrote *The Art of the Wild*, says, "The Ancient Athenians had such respect for wolves that they passed an official decree ordering any man who killed a wolf to pay for its funeral."

I couldn't help but think of all the past research and books I've read about the wolves, as well as learning about their patterns, while visiting the Wolf Education Research Center, in Winchester, Idaho. Jeremy Heft is the main wolf handler for the captive wolves of The Sawtooth Pack, which were raised in captivity by Jim Dutcher in the nineties for research. The instinct is there but the knowing isn't. Animals understand more than we can imagine. For example, Jeremy told me how he cannot go into the wolf compound if he is in any way compromised because the wolves will sense it. If he is feeling irritated or tense about anything, he must process these feelings first before he walks the perimeter, proving to be a marvelous therapist.

Selling the Earth

We can't leave the subject of respect without addressing the lack of respect shown to our Native American Indians. When the U.S. Government offered to buy two million acres of Indian land in the Northwest in 1854, Chief Seattle responded with what has been described as the most beautiful and prophetic statement ever made about the environment. It has been titled, "How Can You Buy or Sell the Earth?" The last paragraph is as follows:

"If we agree, it will be to secure the reservation you have promised. There, perhaps, we may live out our brief days as we wish. When the last red man has vanished from the Earth, and his memory is only the shadow of a cloud moving across the prairie, these shores and forests will still hold the spirits of my people. For they love this Earth as a newborn loves its mother's heartbeat."

"So, if we sell our land, love it as we've loved it. Care for it as we've cared for it. Hold in your mind the memory of the land as it is when you take it. And preserve it for your children, and love it...as God loves us all. One thing we know. Our God is the same God. This Earth is precious to Him. Even the white man cannot be exempt from the common destiny. We may be brothers after all. We shall see..."

To be respectful of life is to feel reverence. Without respect, we have chaos, everybody doing what they want to do when they want to do it. Life is sacred, and we are all connected like a web of life. We leave behind the most important part of who we are with our loved ones. Wouldn't you consider respectfulness something of value to leave behind after you've taken your last breath? Our relationships are the most important "ship" we're on. Do you treat your relationship with the Earth, yourself, your wild relatives, as well as your not-so-wild ones, with respect and reverence? Reverence grows from within like wisdom. The restoration of respect begins one person at a time.

Reflection Time:

1. Using a scale of 1 to 10, one being low and ten being high, where would you rate your self-respect?
2. How is it reflected in your world?
3. What is sacred to you?
4. What do you feel reverent about?
5. Do you respect your parents? Why or why not?
6. Do you respect your children and their opinions, regardless of age?
7. Did you learn to respect the Earth and her resources? If so, how and from whom?
8. If not, are you educated today about this topic?
9. Are you aware of the relationship between self-respect and respecting others?
10. Do you experience yourself as one with the earth? Connected to all of life?

R is for feeling... Responsible

**Definition: accountable, reliable, obligate, bound
Opposite: exempt, irresponsible**

To be responsible is to acknowledge our own self as a source or cause, to be accountable. The definition I learned was, "Responsibility starts with the willingness to experience yourself as cause in the matter." It is not fault, blame, shame, guilt, or burden; those are judgments and evaluations of good and bad, right and wrong, better and worse. Responsibility begins with a willingness to deal with each situation from the point of view that you are the source of what you are, what you do, and what you have.

For example, this story comes from an article from *Self-Realization Fellowship*, Fall 2001, "Transmute Anger, Prevent Violence," by Arun Gandhi, the grandson of Mahatma Gandhi. In it he tells of a time he had just started learning to drive. His grandfather had told him to drive him into the city, take him to a meeting, take the car in for service, and then pick him up at exactly five o'clock. After dropping his grandfather off at his meeting, Arun went to a double-feature movie. At 5:30 he realized he was late, picked up the car at the service station, and it was 6 o'clock before he got to his grandfather. He was asked why he was late. Arun stumbled forwards as he blamed it on the car not being ready, unaware that his grandfather had called the garage. "I must think about what I have done wrong to raise you, for you to lie to me. In order for me to do that, I am going to walk home." For five-and-a-half hours, Arun followed his grandfather eighteen miles while he was in constant turmoil just because of a lie. That story happened over fifty years ago and, needless to say, has made a huge imprint on Arun's life. Another time, his wise grandfather also pulled him aside after he fought with his close friend over a soccer match and spoke gently to him, "Don't get into the habit of blaming others for everything. Always first take a good look at yourself and your contribution before blaming others."

It's Not My Fault!

Responsibility includes responding with ability, good judgment, dependability, reliability, and trustworthiness. All these words are synonymous with being responsible.

Responsibility is a state of being from our choice. We either take responsibility for the situation of the life we create through our thoughts, words and actions, or we blame others and make ourselves the victim.

Responsibility is the only place where we have power because once we state "how it is" and take responsibility for it, we can change it. The ticket is to own it in the first place. The game of making others wrong eventually catches up with us. We feel drained, sick, and unhappy. When we're out of control, we are definitely not in our power. One early step toward being awakened is taking responsibility. When we can acknowledge that the world is a reflection of our thoughts and choices, we make huge strides in our growth, both personally and spiritually.

Even my printer declares its victim identity when it has a paper jam and says, "It's not my fault. Pay attention to the printer." The first time I heard that microchip emit those words, I was hysterical with laughter. Oh dear, my printer has a victim identity! Poor, pitiful printer! "It's not my fault." The world of technology can stimulate laughter in addition to frustration.

TV Time

We are the world—the microcosm of the macrocosm. People of the world hold mass consciousness and we hold individual consciousness. When enough of us feel inner strength and know who we are and live lives rooted in truth, when enough of us permeate peace, the scales will finally be tipped and our planet will demonstrate that state of grace. However, if the scale tips the other way, we have a theme that life is one of fear, reaction, and control.

Today as we tune into the media, however, we can readily see there's work to be done. Currently, mass consciousness is not creating a state of grace. Individual work must be done to reach that critical turning point.

In an article called "Should You Toss Your TV?" written by Kristen Laine for *Delicious Living Magazine*, October 2003, Emma and Jake Linde, social work therapists, talk about the influence of TV in their clients' lives. Watching TV he says, gives the illusion of recovery time. You can avoid problems, avoid physical activity, and avoid other people while in front of the boob tube.

In the same article, Kirsten Elin, ex-producer of television commercials in New York City, says, "TV is so much worse than it use to be. It's so much faster-paced. Although highly stimulated, the brain is left passive, which may hinder developing language and certain types of complex reasoning." She believes that she and her sons are better off for having fired the "electronic baby sitter."

I know of a woman who rents a room in a home of a television addict. She told me, "This man heavily relies on TV for entertainment. He has no social life, avoiding the emotional and social parts of his life. I've invited him to movies, dinner, and social outings numerous times and his response is always the same – "you know I don't go out." This man is not agoraphobic – he simply prefers the tube.

The Linde's conclude this topic with the results of an extensive survey that was taken over a quarter century. The survey showed a strong correlation between heavy TV-watching and physical malaise. And further, it indicated a heavy reliance on TV for entertainment, a powerful predictor of unhappiness.

Television might also be a contributor to children's stress: The average child spends twenty-five hours a week in front of the TV, viewing assorted shows with much violent behavior. Destructive computer games and television have almost wiped out children's playtime. Whatever happened to creative games like Concentration, Lincoln Logs, and erector sets? If we truly care about our children, we will show it in our behavior by providing an environment based on mindfulness.

Again, I would question how much television the parent watches. How much time is spent with the family playing board games and interacting?

Lisa McNee is the Director of NASA Ames Child Care Center in Mountain View, California, which serves children from six weeks to six years. "I have been an Early Childhood Educator, Parent Educator, and Advocate for children and families for over twenty-five years. I am also a trainer for Non-Violence in the Lives of Children Project whose mission is to ensure that every child is entitled to a fair, just, and safe life in the home, school and community."

"One of the first things I always ask parents at conferences is, 'What kind of person do you want your child to grow up to be?' The answers are all different and my response is always the same. 'How do you imagine you are going to get that? What do you think you need to do to bring up your child to be the person that you would like to see them become?'"

"It never ceases to amaze me at how parents miss the connection between their actions, reactions, and attitudes, in the present, to the actions, reactions, and attitudes of their children, in the future."

"Children are absorbing everything adults say, do, and think. It is what adults DON'T say that actually makes the difference, however. AND this is the part that is most missed by parents. We want to believe that as adults we are absolved from the responsibility and accountability of our actions where children are concerned. We want to believe that the philosophy of, 'Do as I say, not as I do' is the truth. It is not, however. In fact, nothing could be further from the truth; we adults get to know this when it is often too late."

"We get to look at our newly cultivated young adults (better known as teenagers) and say, 'How the hell did I get this kid?' Or, 'How did this happen?'"

"As part of being an educator of young children and an advocate for children and families, I get to help adults understand that children learn through demonstration – by modeling. Children learn by observation. When words and actions are incongruent children learn that adults do not mean what they say. They learn that the world is an unsafe place and that the people in it are not to be trusted."

His Holiness Says...

Moving to the opposite end of the pendulum, we have The Dalai Lama, whose instructions for life in the new Millennium include responsibility. He says to follow the three R's – Respect for self, Respect for others, Responsibility for all actions:

- When you realize you've made a mistake, take immediate steps to correct it.
- Remember that silence is sometimes the best answer.
- In disagreements with loved ones, deal only with the current situation. Don't bring up the past.
- Be gentle with the Earth.

Parents, be the best possible example. Teach compassion by living it. Don't send your child to the soup kitchen to volunteer–go with her. Be tolerant, patient, and try to understand children's growth process. The more you make yourself a pure channel, the more love and light is available to flow through you. Be responsible for your own actions. Even from very early on, your child observes everything. Take it even further and be responsible for your thoughts and feelings, as your child will also respond to them. Live your life with integrity, make wise choices, and realize the consequences of each option. Discipline your child with boundaries and rules; that's what youngsters want. It takes courage to be strong and consistent.

The Seriousness of Toys

Not too many years ago, parents spent hours deciding which gifts to give their children. Perhaps a child desperately wanted a BB gun. The decision to give it as a gift was generally not taken lightly. Age appropriateness and level of responsibility were taken into consideration; and if a child was given such a gift, along with it came lessons on proper use and care, and a long list of strictly enforced rules around acceptable, responsible ownership of a BB gun. An example of a primary rule was to NEVER, EVER point a BB gun at anything living. Owning a BB gun was almost a rite of passage for many kids, indicating they were old enough, responsible enough, and mature enough to possess and wisely use such a toy.

Today, the pressure from our kids to purchase inappropriate gifts begins at a younger age, and the gifts we're asked to give them often aren't even appropriate for adults. Yet, with enough nagging, it seems many of us fold under the pressure to buy the item in question rather than using our good judgment. Such was the case of an eleven-year-old child who begged his mother for the video, "Grand Theft Auto Vice City," until she felt she had to give it to him.

AOL took a poll on this subject; 67% of those polled said they would buy the video and felt it was harmless; 33% said they wouldn't buy it because of the violence. And, when asked if it was a negative influence on society, 70% said no – that people can distinguish between reality and fantasy; 30% said yes – that it glorifies violence.

What's the video all about? Without getting into details, the game is focused on drugs, drug dealing, gangsters, prostitution, turf wars, destruction, gangs, and much, much more. At the time of this writing, there is a lawsuit being filed linking a murder by two boys to the game's content. Harmless? I think not.

Approximately four million copies of the video were sold in the 2002 holiday. And, out of that four million, you can bet many of them wind up in the hands of our children.

So who's responsible? As parents, we are. It's difficult to believe that the jury is still out on the long-term impact of violent video contact on today's youth, but regardless of the outcome, as parents we have to ask ourselves why we would succumb to purchasing anything for our kids with as many violent and mixed messages as the above video describes.

I asked my friend, Molly, a single mom, her opinion of who chooses for our kids? "Parents do! Just because our kids want something doesn't mean they should have it. If your ten-year-old daughter asks you for a shot of whiskey, do you let her have it? If your son wants his tongue pierced at age twelve, do you say yes? Our schools are currently working as fast as they can to introduce character-rich programs for our children. Organizations across the country are encouraging our kids to 'make a difference' in their communities, homes, and schools, by recognizing their work in volunteer programs to help enrich the lives of others. The list of constructive efforts on behalf of our kids is endless." What a wise mama.

All efforts we make for the betterment of our children come together in the outcome. If parents make poor choices by giving their children "toys" of the type mentioned above, how can they expect their children to make constructive, life-affirming choices in the future? If parents truly want to see their children grow up with a solid character foundation, capable of being honest, trustworthy, generous, respectful, responsible – AND good citizens – in what way will a violent video game support this end?

What to Teach

As a parent, the earlier you teach responsibility, the better. For example, here are some age-appropriate tasks for growing children adapted from lists compiled by the University of Arizona and Tucson Public Schools.

Ages 2-3: Put away toys, dress with help, make food choices, use toilet, brush teeth and hair, put dirty clothes in hamper

Ages 4-5: Set table, feed pet, share toys, make bed, dust, choose clothes and dress, answer phone

Ages 6-7: Fix lunch, walk dog, rake leaves, tie shoes, sweep patio, run errands near home, wipe dishes

Age 8-9: Help food preparation, mop floors, sew on buttons, paint fence, vacuum rugs

Age 10-11: Change sheets, operate washer and dryer, transport self by bike, earn money, pack own suitcase

Age 12-13: Mow lawn, deliver papers, cook easy meals, shovel snow, bring in wood, help with garbage

Teens: Earn money at job, use own checking account, help decide curfew, drive self to activities

Regularly assigned chores are good for children. It helps them develop responsibility. As a part of the family, they want to be included and learn self-reliance.

Self-reliance is teaching our children to communicate their feelings, the art of listening, to control their minds, how to deal with fearful thoughts and feelings, teaching them to reason, teaching them they have free will — choice, teaching them to take action, and teaching them about the wisdom and guidance from their intuition. We each want and need to know we make a difference. These lessons will help a child eventually know they make a difference.

Making a difference begins with the way we talk to others around our children, as well as through our behavior and our deeds. Children will mirror us. As parents, we have an awesome responsibility because we are our children's first teachers. The question is, what are we teaching? What do we want them to learn? Do we teach children to experience themselves as source of their reality? Do we teach them to be responsible? Do we teach them what we've resisted in our own childhood? Maybe we are teaching them beliefs that have been acquired over generations that don't work in our lives. Are we willing to examine our beliefs about parenting, about education, values, money, God, sex, success, power, relationships–about life? As the bumper sticker says, "Dare to explore and question authority." We can each be the parent we would want to have if we were still a child. With intention, we can be the change we want to see in our community to improve it for our children as well as others. That includes our global community as well.

Being responsible means keeping our agreements. It means living with integrity and doing what we say we're going to do. If something happens and we can't make that appointment or show up, communicate. Own our mistake rather than making excuses works better. If our lives are not working, we must first stop looking to blame life or other people. That action causes a shift. Then, we can be the person that can be depended on, that can be trusted and relied on.

The shift becomes complete when we believe excuses are lame and that they indicate weakness and lack of responsibility. The ego has an investment in you being right. This shift happens when you educate yourself through wisdom to know you are not your ego. Get off that position and everything that feeds it. Claim your birthright to freedom and everlasting joy! Just get off it! Notice the changes when you are willing to take control of your ego.

We are all responsible for knowing our needs and taking action to get them met. Self-expression is a function of responsibility. What could you do to achieve this more effectively? Instead of expecting others to read your mind and come to the rescue when you feel down, you can learn to tune into yourself, assess your needs, and communicate from your heart. Are you doing this?

352

We don't have to do this for anybody! We don't even have to do it. It is strictly a matter of choice. What brings happiness to your life and what doesn't? Just look! We are all unconditionally loved by the Universe, anyhow. If we choose to make changes, we are the only ones that can do it.

Reflection Time:

1. Do you know anybody who makes excuses?
2. What would you do if you just broke something while visiting a friend's home?
3. Do you allow fear to overrule your sense of responsibility?
4. Create a time line of your life: indicate events that brought joy, confidence, challenge, regret, responsibility, victim, sorrow. This can be an illuminating exercise. Have fun with it.
5. What is your definition of responsibility?
6. Do you consider responsibility a burden?
7. Do you resent taking having to take responsibility?
8. Everyone has needs; do you believe you do?
9. If you do, is it natural for you to express your needs? Do you feel deserving of having them met?
10. Do you recognize the needs of your child? Your partner? Your parent?

"It is not the strongest species that survives, nor the most intelligent, but the one most responsive to change."
Charles Darwin

S is for feeling... Sensitive

Definition: gentleness, sensorial, perceptive, caring, sympathetic
Opposite: unfeeling, insensitive, numb

To feel sensitive is to care, to feel connected, and to be aware. When we feel sensitive, we are capable of putting ourselves in someone else's shoes, to understand, and feel compassion. To feel sensitive is to be responsive to external conditions, emotions, and circumstances.

Did you know that a nervous system can be sensitive? Research, and our own experience, has proven that all animals, including humans, are sensitive. Here, I'm talking about energy, as in the phrase "picking up on the vibes." Why would this be unusual? We're a whirling mass of light; we're actually atoms and molecules held together by light. Of course we're sensitive. To experience this on your own, to feel energy move and feel your senses, I invite you to bring your palms together about three or four inches apart. If you want, you can close your eyes and just tune in. What do you feel?

The Power of Touch

When my niece and goddaughter, Eileen, was studying to be a holistic nurse practitioner, she forwarded some great information to me:

- A piece of skin the size of a quarter contains more than 3,000,000 cells, twelve feet of nerves, 100 sweat glands, fifty nerve endings, and three feet of blood vessels.
- It is estimated that we have approximately fifty sensory receptors per 100 square centimeters, a total of 900,000 receptors.

We would have to work at NOT being sensitive. We are feeling, caring, and sensitive beings on a physiological and biological level.

My friend, Willy McCarty, gave me some fascinating facts about the skin. Part of his marketing material as a fitness trainer, advocates dry skin brushing. He says that skin is "...the largest organ of the body, and comes in a variety of beautiful colors, textures, and personally unique patterns. It breathes, is waterproof, self-mending, self-cleaning, flexible, and will last over a hundred years. A square inch of this organ has approximately 200 blood and lymph vessels, more than 100 oil glands, over 650 sweat glands, twenty-eight motor nerves, thirteen sensors for cold, seventy-five for heat, 1,300 touch sensors, sixty-five hairs, plus millions of independent cells. It weighs about five pounds and covers an area of twenty square feet." Look at your skin right now. Appreciate what is happening in each quarter inch of it. Ask yourself if it is a source of prejudice in your life, and be honest with yourself.

When someone touches our skin, we can feel caring from that person that can benefit both parties. For example, the Touch Research Institute from the University of Miami School of Medicine's Winter of 1999 newsletter, "Touchpoints" (www.miami.edu/touch-research) says that in the case of "hospitalized children and infants in shelters...we are employing volunteer grandparent therapists. After a month of giving massages, the grandparent volunteers are less depressed, sleeping better, and making fewer visits to their physicians." It's a win/win for both generations. However, it is sad that our society frowns upon touch in schools. From the Winter of 1996 newsletter, "Touchpoints," "teachers were touching the zero to five-year-olds less than 12% of the time." Unfortunately, because of the child abuse cases, teachers are reluctant to touch children. Children are now taught good and bad touch. Bumper stickers like "Have you hugged your child today?" are being ignored. The first emotional bonds are built from physical contact, laying down the foundation for both emotional and intellectual development.

The Infant Massage Newsletter also shared a case where a patient claimed the reason for escaping and walking home from a local hospital in his pajamas and hospital wristband was, "fifteen days in a hospital without touch."

Is It Okay to be Sensitive?

Are we raising sensitive children? Is it okay to be sensitive? Based on this next tale, it's obviously NOT. An adolescent boy inflicted pain on himself in Sunday school while the priest talked about hell and damnation and how we are all sinners and how we have to "deserve" God's love. The little boy was so sensitive to what the priest said that he wanted to cry. The boy's experience told him that what the priest was saying wasn't true, and his sensitive nature was damaged. This boy had caring and kind, and he knew God to be loving. The priest's words were like bullets piercing the boy's reality. Because he wouldn't allow himself to cry or express those feelings because it would be unacceptable in church, he physically hurt himself so that he could have a reason to cry! His tears would then be acceptable but not because he was sensitive. IS it okay to be sensitive? Not according to this young boy.

Just Listen

Being sensitive to what someone is sharing with you is a skill from which we could all benefit. It's one of the indicators for being a good listener. When the queen of interviewers, Barbara Walters, was asked her advice about talking to people, she replied, "Recognize that all people have the same emotions and try to find points in common. Share a little bit and then listen – listen more than you talk." To listen well is to be sensitive.

Recall your last date, meeting, or dinner appointment. Who did most of the talking? Were you "interested" in your date, or did you talk in attempt to be "interesting?"

Judy Blume, popular author and confidante to thousands of young people, said the way to survive children's adolescent years is to "stay aware, listen carefully, and yell for help if you need it." The thousands of letters she receives in response to her books demonstrate the need young people have for their feelings to be acknowledged and their wish for unconditional love. "They wish their parents would make more time for them," Ms. Blume says. "They are desperate for someone to listen."

A client shared a comment made by his six-year-old daughter in response to his honesty. "I feel frustrated when you don't pick up your room," the father proclaimed. "Well," she said, "I feel frustrated when you don't listen to me when I talk to you."

I had a five-year-old client who told me what he was taught by a school counselor about listening. "What did you learn?" I asked. "Well, first of all, you have to look into the person's eyes. This is important, because you want to get their attention. Then you have to stop talking." "Yes?" I said, waiting for more guidelines. "Then, you just listen."

Piece of cake, right? Not really. This formula actually takes work. For one thing, it has been determined that humans speak at approximately 120 to 180 words per minute and think four or five times that rate. We spend 80% of our waking hours communicating and of that time 45% is spent listening, but only 25% is devoted to effective listening, which amounts to seven minutes per hour! Apparently we do need to make more of an effort.

A prerequisite to improve our listening skills is to have the intention to communicate effectively. We must take responsibility for our conversations through intention to deliver and receive words, then reach understanding with clarity.

Accepting

A major obstacle to listening is judgment and a lack of sensitivity. If we entertain judgmental thoughts, our mind is so occupied with this form of mental activity that we can't pay attention to the content of the conversation. If we express the judgments, we alienate others. Usually, their defenses rise, which leads to a break down of all communication channels. It takes energy to judge and evaluate. It truly keeps us from being present. Until we become aware enough, it also takes energy not to judge and evaluate. Notice your own way of conversing.

- Acceptance empowers people
- Acceptance opens people up rather than shuts them down.
- Acceptance frees others to share their feelings and problems.
- Acceptance is the basis for unconditional love.

Demonstrations of acceptance can produce startling results. How do we learn to accept others? The answer is simply to learn to accept ourselves!

We start to accept ourselves when we become open to our feelings, in lieu of numbing out through drugs and alcohol. Caroline Knapp, author of *Pack of Two, The Intricate Bond Between People and Dogs*, shared her personal story in the book. "One thing I've noticed since I quit drinking is that a person usually has two or three sets of impulses scratching away at some internal door at any given time. If you're sober – if you're alert, and paying attention to those impulses and not yielding to the instinct to anesthetize them – you can receive a lot of guidance about where to go, what to do next in life." In other words, one is more sensitive to their inner world when they are clear and receptive.

Acceptance doesn't necessarily mean agreement. We each have our own way of seeing the world. For example, a friend's grandson looked at a formation in a cloud and saw a dog. His big brother gazed at the same cloud then ruthlessly questioned his sibling's perception. The wisdom of the younger boy was expressed when he so honestly replied, "How do you know what I see with my eyes?" We each have our own reality and deserve the respect to have our perceptions heard.

Just as we've learned to cook, play golf, or use a computer, we can learn to become more sensitive, less judgmental, and a good listener. The more we practice using our sensitivities, the more they improve. We can acquire the skill of a well-trained, caring therapist and by doing so, directly influence the quality of our lives. Here are some questions to ask yourself to find out if you are a good listener:

- Have you ever recognized that you could hardly wait until the other person was finished talking, so you could share **your** experience? What's the result when this happens?
- Are you generally interested in what the other person is saying?
- Assume nothing. Your intuition will alert you if you're sensing that the listener is not listening. If this is the case, just stop talking.
- If you have a meaningful communication to deliver to your partner, do you preface it by stating that you want to talk and that it is important, then ask if this is a good time, and if not, what time would be preferable?
- To test your listening skills, you might ask, "What I hear you saying is _____. Is this accurate?"
- Give yourself time in nature; the silence will improve your ability to listen and broaden your sensitivity. Do it often. Take time-outs of silence for yourself, the longer the better. The mind will eventually quiet down and you can feel the joy of just being present in the moment.
- Learn to breathe deeply. Shallow breathing keeps us in our head, deep breathing takes us to our heart, to our feelings and to the moment.
- Are you truthful? Do you mention when your mind has strayed? This is how communication becomes an art form. It's remarkable where relationships can move by telling the truth.
- Is it easier to connect when the speaker shares heart-expressed feelings?
- What happens to your listening ability when someone is talking to you "from the head," versus sharing from their heart? Are you sensitive to where that person is coming from? Do you feel a difference in the presence of this type of person? Can you do anything to open this person's heart?

How many of these important life skills are taught in our schools? How many are taught in our homes?

Kids Know

Sensitive children have a deep empathy and compassion in life. For example, a four-year-old girl went up to her father while he was yelling at her mother and said, "Daddy. Don't yell at Mommy and call her names. It makes me sad when you do that. Be kind to her."

Children are so deeply sensitive. A ten-year-old girl's sensitivity to animals spurred her to initiate a program that provides bulletproof vests for police dogs. After reading an article in *Time Magazine* For Kids about police dogs that are killed in the line of duty, Stacey Hillman decided to do something to protect Florida's K-9s. Since the inception of her charity, Stacey has raised more than 80,000 dollars, enough to outfit 115 police dogs. www.psjournal.com

One study found that teenagers who were sensitive to the plight of other people or animals, and who were involved in helping others, felt very positive about their own lives and had high hopes for their own futures.

Danny Seo, author of *Heaven on Earth…15-Minute Miracles to Change the World*, wrote about an organization he founded with ten dollars when he was only twelve years old. "Ever since I was a young child, I've always believed I had a very specific mission in life. That mission was to show others that they can do extraordinary things if they allow themselves to reach their fullest potential." Read his inspiring book to learn how he was invited on Oprah's show to discuss how he raised 30,000 dollars in less than thirty days to pay for the construction of a Habitat for Humanity home. Danny's sensitivity as a child and his early success allowed him to carry on that wonderful quality as an adult.

Children are naturally caring. Studies are now finding that children can show signs of compassion and concern at a very early age. Researchers observed children whose parents were hurt somehow. What they saw were children who reacted with concern and wanted to make things better. Compassion and comfort were offered.

Parents and teachers: let's reward children for their acts of kindness. We're often quick to condemn and hold back on much deserved praise. It's important to be sensitive.

Reflection Time:

1. Would you qualify yourself as being a "sensitive" person?
2. If you judge this quality, is it negatively or favorably?
3. Do you make excuses for feeling sensitive?
4. Did you have sensitive experiences as a child and were criticized?
5. Describe through a sensitive child's eyes their world?
6. What three miracles occurred in your life in the last six hours?
7. Experiment with inhaling the many blessings in your life and exhaling old negative judgments. Feel, let go, feel, let go, feel, let go.
8. What are the five things that keep recurring in your life even though you don't want them to?
9. Is your sensitivity a quality for which you would like to be remembered?
10. Finish these sentences:

    *My sensitivity could change the world if I _____.
    *My greatest contribution to my family is _____.
    *My greatest wish for humanity is _____.

"You are the baker of the bread you eat."
Gurumayi Chidvilasananda, Siddha Yoga Foundation

S is for feeling... Separate

Definition: divided, detached, disconnected
Opposite: connect, attach, united

Our feelings of separateness encompass so many of the feelings we wish we didn't have: righteousness, desperation to survive, judgment, self-pity, dread, depression, defensiveness, jealousy, being victimized by our past and future, unhappiness, to name a few. When we feel separate, we may feel a huge sense of incompleteness, or of not being whole. We make choices out of fear, which are not in our best interests. We strive after the things we think will make us whole: THE perfect relationship, money, position, education, power, cars, homes, wardrobe, status, body perfection, a prestigious job. Can we recognize our ego?

To feel separate is to feel isolated, distant, or removed. Separateness means to experience a lack of connectedness to our purpose, our mate, to meaning, to life, or to Self. Probably something wounded us and we pulled away, distanced ourselves–first from one and then others. We feel detached and removed. Nobody cares, nobody understands, nobody needs us. If our ego steps in and takes charge, our glorious spirit becomes clouded over like a foggy day concealed by the sun.

It seems we are taught to separate from our pain. Do any of these phrases seem familiar? "Be a good little girl – don't interfere and don't make waves. Keep those feelings of concern, worry, and fear to yourself when you hear your mommy and daddy fighting. Put on a smile. Don't frown. Don't honor your body. Move further from your truth and from peace and from being a healthy adult, pleasing others so you'll be liked."

Sanskrit is the oldest language on the planet, and in it, there is no word for "exclusive." What if we were to eliminate that word from the English language? How would our lives be different? Exclusiveness and separation have become an addiction in our society. We have exclusive country clubs, neighborhoods with gates and guards, and even preschools have become exclusive! What if those walls were torn down?

Who's Better?

Hitler looked upon the Jewish people as being less than. They were forced to wear armbands marked with the Star of David to indicate their faith. They were spat upon, degraded, and murdered just because they were Jewish.

When people separate themselves from others, it is usually because they are experiencing some kind of fear. Fear is the root of racism and prejudice. We are all different! We have different shoe sizes, different handwritings, different religious beliefs, different eye color, different hair color, and different skin color. So much suffering has been attributed to the mere color of the skin!

So Alone

When we feel separate, ask what preceded those feelings? What happened prior to the awareness of feeling separate? When did it happen? Track it. We may be feeling like a lone piece of a puzzle, haphazardly tossed into a box just off the manufacturer's production line: detached, isolated, alone, removed. The truth is we may feel separate and alone, but these feelings have followed a thought. The thought is based in the past or future. It's impossible to feel separate in each present moment of now.

When we realize that each puzzle piece fits together to make up the whole, and we realize we're responsible for our thoughts, feelings, and behavior, we will then understand that without our perfect piece, which is our own uniqueness, the puzzle isn't complete.

Einstein said it beautifully. "A human being is a part of the whole called, by us, universe. A part limited in time and space. He experiences himself as thoughts and feelings as something separate from the rest. This is kind of an optical delusion of his consciousness. And this delusion is a kind of prison, restricting us to our personal desires, and to affection for a few persons nearest to us. Our task must be to free ourselves from this prison by widening our circle of compassion to embrace all living creatures and the whole of nature and its beauty."

This may be one of the moments to "stretch" your thinking, but in truth, your perception of the world is a reflection of your consciousness. We are not separate from our reality. Quantum physics has proven that the researcher who conducts an experiment cannot be separate from the observed phenomena —from the results. There is a connectedness between the observer and the observed–oneness. To feel separate is an illusion because we are all connected.

Staying Connected

Geese obviously know the importance of staying connected. One of the benefits from conferences is gathering marvelous handouts. Milton Olson gives us an insight in his piece, "Lessons from Geese." He recognizes the correlation between a flock of geese flying in a V-formation and the importance in being involved in community. The "V" creates an "uplift," he says, so that it is much easier for the geese to fly in a group rather than alone. Also, when the lead goose gets tired, it goes to the back of the formation and lets another take the front position. Olson even mentions that if one of the geese gets injured, a couple of others will drop out of the formation to help or protect it. What can we, as humans, learn from flying geese? When we work together, we go further with less effort. When we are tired, we could let someone else take the lead. And in difficult times, we could reach out to others.

One of the reasons I choose to live where I do is because of my connection to the community. There is a central thread of gratitude amongst those living in this incredibly beautiful environment, and sincere caring from most people who have demonstrated willingness to support me on my journey. It is also mutual. Connections run deep. It was like I had known some of the people before. We knew each other at a heart level. This is the kind of experience my friend, Joyce Friedman, achieves through her mentoring.

"I volunteered because I wanted to reach out to others. What I did not expect was that while helping others, I would grow so much from the experience. When deciding to volunteer, I remembered the difficult times I went through in my twenties and thirties. During that time, having a person in my life that was willing to spend time with me to listen to whatever was on my mind made a dramatic difference in me. Meeting with someone whom I felt truly cared, helped me to change negative perspectives to positive actions – even if just for that day."

"I knew I wanted to pass on that experience. I wanted to help women in crisis by providing a safe, caring, and supportive friendship, a relationship in which the women could share thoughts in an environment without judgment or unwanted suggestions. I hoped I could create a 'space' that fostered feelings of worthiness, self-respect, and acknowledgement."

"Through my encounters with the wonderful women I met through volunteering, I learned and grew, too. I learned to let my patience lead a discussion and not to allow my expectations to get in the way of giving unconditional support. I learned that each woman with whom I worked wanted to share a medley of her life's experiences – from joyful to frightening – as we developed trust within our relationship. I just needed to be there to listen, to touch her shoulder, and to be 'in the present' during our time together."

"And in the process of offering unconditional friendship, I found I was beginning to see and understand people and the world around me in ways I had not considered before. I was less confined by the limiting social and economic boundaries of my world. In time, I realized that volunteering helps everyone involved. There is not a giver and a receiver in the endeavor, but rather each person involved both gives and receives."

Joyce is offering service to something bigger than herself. It's a bigger picture that allows us to transcend our problems when we feel so stuck. To commit our lives to something bigger than our own, prevents us from feeling separate.

While connected, we can still express our individuality, not necessarily feeling separate, but yet honoring our uniqueness within the whole. The logo of my promotional brochure says – Connecting the Pieces Creates Wholeness. The following story used on a previous brochure of mine illustrates this idea:

"Once upon a time there was a father who needed to accomplish an important task in his office at home. His young son wanted his father's attention and continually interrupted his work. In an attempt to occupy the boy's time, he tore out a page from a magazine with a picture of the world on it, then tore it into many small pieces and suggested the boy go to his room and put them together like a puzzle. Much to the father's amazement, his son returned rather quickly. 'Back so soon?' the father said. 'It didn't take me long,' said the boy, 'because while you were tearing the picture of the world out of the magazine, I saw a picture of a man on the back of the page. I just put the man back together and the world came together.'"

When we feel connected to others, to life, to ourselves, we tend to give from our heart, want to be helpful, live in the now, feel compassion, passion, joy, and appreciation. When we see beauty in life, we are honest and live with integrity. We feel enthusiasm and inspiration. Life is a wondrous adventure where we are co-creators and we trust the process. We have a sense we are whole, total, and complete where we are right now.

Reflection Time:

1. Make a list of things that you think make you feel separate. Examine each one carefully and with introspection.

2. How could you shift your perception?

3. Are you willing to?

4. What would you have to give up to do so?

5. What are the human traits that you fear, dislike, and criticize in yourself and/or in others that perpetuate feeling separate?

6. Are you holding a grudge towards someone? If so, with whom? Why? How does it serve you? Do you want to heal the wound? How would you do that? Are you willing to take that action? If not, why not?

7. How do you feel during those moments of feeling connected? Separate? Which is empowering? Choose.

8. What are your beliefs about this subject? Start a list and kee writing until you have an "aha" (insight) experience.

9. How does feeling separate keep you safe?

10. Does the color of someone's skin distance you?

"We seem to have grasped the notion that it takes a village to raise a healthy child. An emerging new insight is that it takes an engaged, creative community to support the adults who create that village."

Michael Mendizza, Optimum Learning Relationships for
Children & Adults Newsletter

S is for feeling...Supported

Definition: safe, upheld, maintained, preserved
Opposite: ignored, abandoned, broken, disregarded

To feel supported is to feel like there are people out there who believe in you. We all need to feel supported in our endeavors whether we think we can do it all alone or not. Whether it's a friend, an acquaintance, a spouse, or an entire community, to feel supported keeps us high on our path, motivated, and reassured that everything's going to be okay.

More than once in my career of self-development, I've heard that it takes only one person to believe in you, to keep you going. Just one person who says, "Yes, I believe in you. Yes, I know you can do it!" Just like a support beam in a house is instrumental for the support of the structure, our lives are more fully lived when we feel supported by family, by friends, and by colleagues. I would say there is a desire in all of us to feel supported in our endeavors, our projects, and our goals. Although this may not always be the case, I believe it's crucial.

A professional friend and gifted healer of our community felt supported when friends organized a fund-raiser to help defray expenses for travel and treatment for his threatening rare type of cancer. The oversold, quite successful event must have brought tremendous validation to him. I'm sure it was a great comfort as he made peace within himself during the last few months of his life. Unfortunately, his remarkable attitude wasn't enough to pull him through his ordeal, but his attitude made a difference in how he endured his trials and through it we were all inspired to examine our own attitudes and values.

I recall watching on CNN the story of the nine miners who were rescued after being trapped for seventy-seven hours in a mine in Somerset, Pennsylvania in July 2002. "Everybody had strong moments at any certain times. Maybe when one guy got down, and then the rest pulled together and then that guy would get back up and maybe someone else would feel a little weak. But it was a team effort. That's the only way it could've been." Team effort is the key. None of us have to do it alone.

Running Support

Two good friends of mine appear to have a mutual support system going in their twenty-five-year marriage. Barbara completed her spiritual education by participating in a three-year course of study to become a Minister in the Church of Religious Science. This commitment involved her traveling out of state quite frequently to do her work. Bob, also a Religious Science minister, travels to Russia every summer to pursue his mission to bring the Religious Science principles to the many inhabitants who hunger for the message.

Bob gave me an amazing summary of his supportive relationship with his wife: "One of the many times when I felt support from Barbara was when I realized they don't shorten the 26.2 miles of a marathon just because you are sixty years of age. Running had been a cherished activity of mine beginning in my late forties. Virtually all runners dream of doing at least one marathon, and by my sixtieth birthday, I decided it was now or never. One becomes relatively mono-directional in training to that level of commitment – large blocks of running time, changed eating habits, more sleep, less time for social and other activities, etc. This requires a great deal of accommodation from your mate. Barbara adapted to my changed needs and was instrumental in my getting through that period and the big event itself. It was the fulfillment of a major dream, and we agreed afterwards that once was quite enough!"

"The reciprocal part of our mutual support system began early in our relationship when Barbara decided to enter law school. Fifteen years later, when I decided to enroll in ministerial school in Los Angeles, a three-year course, Barbara stayed in Idaho to maintain our home and business. A few years after my graduation, Barbara also decided to enter ministerial school. The requirements had changed to a somewhat more demanding master's degree program, and Barbara chose to do it through a weekend program so she wouldn't have to move from Idaho. That meant flying twice monthly to St. Louis for two years, so this time I kept the home fires burning! And now her accumulated frequent flyer miles support my global ministry, allowing me to travel to Russia and the Ukraine annually."

"Truthfully, the most important support area is the spiritual and mental support that we share. From the days when we played competitive tennis, we have always participated in life as a team, knowing that we together are infinitely more effective together than we are individually.

We consult on letters, proposals, projects, investments, and virtually all segments of our lives. We have grown a lot from it, and it has been wonderfully rewarding."

The Idaho Women's Celebration, a five-kilometer race, walk, run, or stroll for women and children for the purpose of educating women about a healthy lifestyle is a yearly event where 19,000+ women gather in Boise, Idaho to support this cause. Danielle, my daughter, and I were at the starting line together. It was quite thrilling! After the event, there was an acknowledgement dinner and because Danielle was a volunteer staff member, we also attended. There was a young girl who was racing in a wheelchair that tipped over. Her father spoke at the dinner, stating that they were shy two hundred dollars and weren't able to get her a new racing wheelchair. Danielle and I looked at each other and we had the same thought – synergy occurred. "Let's grab the baskets on the table that hold the flowers and pass them around and see what we can raise." She went to one side of the room, and I to the other. We knelt down to the attendees while speeches were continuing. People generously looked into their wallets and pockets and quickly wrote checks and dropped in bills. In less than twenty minutes, we raised the extra money that was needed to buy her that chair! Once again, evidence of the human spirit! The mind had nothing to do with this. It was all spontaneous and intuitive, and we took action. Support comes from the heart.

Rabbi Martin Levy wrote in the Wood River Jewish Community newsletter, October 2003: "The human heart that responds to the sounds of other hearts in the world is the truest index of a person's humanity."

My friend Marcia Mode-Stavros, who also ran a marathon, shares her inspiring and uplifting experience about support and love:

"It started with an email from an acquaintance, who asked if I would ever consider running a marathon. She had a doable training program and thought we could achieve the goal over the course of the next several months. I read the email at my desk, where I spend long days. Having passed the half-century mark, and carrying twenty extra pounds, I knew I needed a goal and timidly agreed. Ten months later, I crossed the finish line of the Honolulu Marathon. It took me hours and hours and hours. However, for me, it wasn't about the race or the time or the event itself. I wrote in my journal afterward that what meant the most was the support I'd received from my beloved husband, family, and friends. Emails, letters, good-luck packages, good thoughts, and prayers added to the feeling of a joyful celebration. This encouraging support from others carried me through long training runs, moments of self-doubt, times of decreased motivation and butterflies as the date approached. The last

Sunday prior to departing for Hawaii, I attended my favorite spiritual center. My plan was to run home. The entire congregation gathered round and gave me a heartfelt send-off. I later wrote that I felt like I ran with the wind that day. My friends' support empowered me and I felt I could do anything! When the long-anticipated morning of the marathon arrived, I got up early and reread all the good wishes. When my husband asked if I was nervous, I said softly, 'No, when I look at these messages of support from friends, and reflect on the past months, this day is simply the icing on the cake.'"

I Do

One of the keys to a healthy and enduring marriage is to support and feel supported. My husband, Gene, has been a support to me throughout our marriage. He's my P. R. agent and biggest fan. Our forty years of marriage have not exactly been like living in Camelot. Do you know anyone who lives there? Princess Di certainly wasn't happy. What about all the pain Jackie O went through? Life is full of "situations" that require attention and action, and it's lovely to have support while we are facing those challenging times. Our children are grown adults now, and make their own decisions but they know we are always there to support them in their journey.

My daughter, Danielle, and her husband, Michael, have lived together in holy matrimony for two years at the time of this writing. They chose to be one of one hundred couples who experienced a "couples weekend" offered by her alma mater, University of Santa Monica.

Although their marriage is and was in good shape, they wanted to support it more and grow closer through acquiring skills to communicate feelings, to learn the art of listening, and to enhance what their current ability. It's not to say their young marriage didn't have challenges, because it did.

As the spiritual minister at the wedding, I invited them to repeat the following vows on December 16, 2001:

"I choose you for who you are and who you may become, to be sensitive to your needs, expressing understanding and compassion. I choose to cherish you and honor your process – to be there for you in sickness and in health, in sorrow and in joy. I choose you as my partner on this path to live life to the fullest with unconditional love."

They took these words seriously. Each moment has not been as romantic and thrilling as their fairytale wedding night in Sun Valley, Idaho, with a backdrop of glistening moonlit, snow-laden mountains, twinkle lights, and magic in the air. The following year, filled with uncertainty about Michael's livelihood, was a roller coaster of emotions–heartache, trust, frustration, joy, worry, and surrender, all of which led them to a deeper and more intimate relationship.

The words from the ceremony continued with, "When you embrace commitment in marriage, you invoke a force that is always there for you, to help overcome anything. This force is as close as your breath."

Michael's intention in the USM experience was to learn some of the tools Danielle, a USM graduate school alumni, already had, like "soul-centered listening." What he said after the workshop was powerful, "Rather than defending myself, I'm coming from a more loving and understanding place. A conscious course of action is required now, but as anything else, with practice, it will become easier and natural. The need to defend and self-criticize is replaced with self-awareness and kindness."

Supporting our Youth

Sometimes, to give space to someone is to support that person. Rather than hovering, asking questions, or being in the way, which may look like support, it might actually be lack of support for the other person. Instead, you could simply hold that person in a vision of light and love and know whatever she is going through is absolutely perfect and that you trust it will work out. You let the person know that you are there for them if they should want to reach out to you. This is what it means to give space as a means of support.

Parents are expected to support their children. Real support does not include agreeing with everything they say, or with allowing them to do whatever they desire, or satisfying any whim they may express. The greatest support we can offer our children is through giving them our time, our attention, our caring, and our unconditional love.

Unfortunately, too many young people move through life without support and understanding. Instead they harm themselves and others because they lack or have lacked enough positive role models from which to learn to live a happy life. Too few adults live with integrity, honesty, and a healthy self-esteem in order to make a difference in a child's life. What kind of company are you keeping? Are your friends actually supportive or competitive? I like this quote from Louise Beal: "Love thy neighbor as thyself, but choose your neighborhood." Choice is empowering. If you don't feel supported, express yourself, and make choices.

Neediness, loneliness, lack of faith, feeling hopeless, helpless and unsupported are too frequently the feelings of our young people, the future of the world. Many kids have no significant connection to healthy adults. They turn to drugs, alcohol, crime, food, or starvation, largely due to lack of recognition of feelings and then an inability to communicate them. Wouldn't it be a comfort to have an adult to turn to when we're being teased or bullied? Researchers have found that teachers do relatively little to put a stop to bullying behavior. A study done by Educational Equity Concepts and the Wellesley College Center for Research on Women on grades kindergarten through third showed that although present at all times, teachers and/or adults were uninvolved, or ignored 71% of the observed incidents. Where was the support for these young people?

A friend and colleague of mine, Lea Flocchini, is the founder of a non-profit organization called "Council Circle Foundation." Her purpose is to provide a safe setting for individuals of all ages to meet weekly for a given period of time and share what is in their hearts and on their minds. A talking piece is used by the person speaking while the others listen without judgment. The piece is passed like a baton to each member of the circle. This program fosters respectful communication and emotional intelligence through compassionate listening and healthy expression of thoughts and feelings. The participants experience tremendous support through this empowering procedure.

I would say for all of us, there are times when we don't feel supported. We can ask for it. We can reach out and say, "I am looking for your support right now." It gives us an opportunity to evaluate if we have been supportive to others. Often we need to look within ourselves for support. That gentle, inner support seems to come to us with quiet time, with watching our breath, and through wise words from books or recorded materials. Pay attention to where your thoughts are sourced. Are you coming from the heart or the mind? From love or from fear? From obligation or service? From resistance or support? It's your call.

Reflection Time:

1. How do you support your body? How much water do you drink a day? What's your typical menu? Is it nutritionally healthy? What are the proportions of proteins to carbohydrates and sugars?

2. Do your thoughts support you? Are they uplifting or negative?

3. What influences your thoughts?

4. Do you allow your emotions to support or discourage you?

5. If you have a spiritual path, how would you describe it?

6. Are you expressing your creativity and passion for life?

7. Is there at least one person who believes in you and believes that there isn't anything you can't do?

8. If you don't have that one person, what would have to happen for you to create that person in your reality?

9. Are you supportive to others? Do you have a space for them to say and be who they are? Do you truly listen to them without judgment or criticism?

10. Who is on your support team and why? Can you count on them?

"Children today are tyrants. They terrorize their parents, gobble their food, and tyrannize their teachers."
Socrates (470-399 BC)

T is for feeling...Tolerant

Definition: liberal, patient, accepting, moderate, receptive, broad-minded

Opposite: biased, unfair, bigoted, narrow,

To feel tolerant is to not let the situation or person get the best of you. There are times for tolerance and there are times to put one's foot down and say, "Enough." Sometimes, in order to feel tolerant, one has to take on the role of the "bigger person."

For example: you may feel tolerant of the person who pulls in front of you on the highway; tolerant of the fact that you misplaced a twenty dollar bill; maybe you forgot to turn the heat off on the rice that was cooking, and that beautiful wild rice that you were anticipating is now more than a bit crunchy, but you feel tolerant about it, and make the best of it by adding delicate greens to enhance your main course. Although initially annoyed that a river-drenched dog jumps on you, you can feel tolerant, understanding his eagerness to see you by his wagging tail. These types of situations are tolerable because they rank as the small stuff.

Some people can't tolerate the gray, wet weather of Seattle during the winter and others are very tolerant of it. Some feel tolerant of the humidity in the South, while others cannot endure it. What makes one more tolerant of a situation than another? Our uniqueness is the answer to that. Mary has accepted a promotion in her work, which involves moving to the Northeast. Both she and her husband have spent their married life in a warm, dry climate. They both agree to make the move and to be tolerant of their new environment.

"Those" People

Yet tolerance can be taken to another level. I have several friends whose children are gay/lesbian. In every situation, they have chosen to be tolerant, to accept what is, to love their child unconditionally, and to trust the process. To be tolerant of another's religious and spiritual beliefs is to be broad-minded and to know that we are all unique, living in a diverse culture. To be tolerant means to embrace, honor, respect, and invite that exact situation into your life the way it is.

Intolerance of people's acceptance to diversity is a major issue in our society. Do you recall the movie *Guess Who's Coming to Dinner?* with Sidney Poitier and Katharine Hepburn? Weren't both parents shocked when their daughter invited a black man to dinner?

I heard Reverend Ronald Matheney speak as part of the 'Season for Non-Violence' series offered by Light On The Mountains Spiritual Center. SNV was proclaimed by the United Nations as a time to come together and connect in unity to examine issues of violence and what might be done to create a world of non-violence. The first day of the series is the anniversary of Gandhi's assassination on January 30, and ends with Martin Luther King's commemoration on April 4.

Rev. Matheney was born on the same day as Martin Luther King. He said that King was the greatest influence in his life. Matheney grew up in a small town in the South, yet he was somewhat shielded from racism and violence because he was an outstanding athlete recognized throughout the state. As long as he ran the football and signed autographs, it was great. But because of severe injuries, he stopped playing and didn't go pro, and his world changed.

"No longer was I received as a star. No longer was anybody asking for my autograph. In the South, as an African American, you develop a mentality you never outgrow – one of cautiousness, no matter how nice people are."

"A memory that hurt me as a second grader happened one morning while walking to the [almost] all-white school [which I attended] through an all-white neighborhood. The schools were just being integrated at the time. I had been sick but was feeling better, and my mother told me I had to walk to school. My home was only about ten blocks from school, and I was still feeling sick, when a dog came out of this house and attacked me. As I looked to the house, there in the window was a lady laughing. It validated all the negative things I'd heard as a child – 'Don't trust certain people.'"

"But somehow, the Creator gave me a heart that loves people, no matter who they are (as the Creator has given us all). Hearing Martin Luther King helped me to understand that healing and wholeness can take place, and that racial and religious barriers can be broken. 'I'm an African-American, and we've experienced terrorism all our lives.'"

If you want to hear an inspiring speaker and visit a beautiful place on the planet, check out the Chapel in the Valley, in Swan Valley, Idaho where he is pastor. Rev. Matheney is a beautiful individual who is making a difference. Talk to him about issues you might have about trust. He said, "My colleagues have asked me, 'What is a black man doing in Idaho?' I'll tell you what, because I make a difference, that's why."

How boring if we were all the same; we can learn so much about ourselves through our differences. What prevents us from living our life in tolerance is our ego and the need to control and be right. A sad state of affairs indeed, as it keeps us from our joy.

Who Makes the Rules?

To feel tolerant of a leader that makes decisions without regard for the environment is quite challenging. (It's certainly my area in which to grow.) At the time of this writing, the United States aggressively invaded Iraq. Many people in this great country who love and value their homeland were intolerant of this action. Tremendous numbers of individuals and groups protested through petitions, demonstrations, letter-writing campaigns, and electronic mail.

I met one such group at the American Counseling Association (ACA) Conference, in Anaheim, CA in March 2003. Counselors for Social Justice, a community of counselors and other professionals, who recognize that many of the issues and concerns they address in their work result from societal injustice and oppression, were exhibitors at the conference. Their booths displayed peace flags, balloons, a variety of trading pins; one displayed Einstein's picture in the center surrounded by the words, "You cannot simultaneously prevent and prepare for war." Another pin stated the words of Gandhi: "It is possible to live in peace." The backdrop of their booth was a large sign stating, "No War on Iraq." Their tables were covered with bumper stickers that read:

"God is too big for one religion."

"I support our illegitimate president."

"Real men don't use violence."

"Revenge will not heal our grief."

"End the cycle of violence."

"Never have so few taken so much from so many for so long."

To feel tolerant of something you don't believe in would be denying your true feelings. We all have our levels of tolerance. Like cookie dough, which can be rolled out only so thin, or a rope when stretched too hard for too long, we too have a breaking point.

Do we tolerate our youth coming to school with weapons? Do we say, "Oh this is fine, I'll just tolerate it"? I performed an Internet search for the article about a young boy who killed the principal of his school, in addition to himself, typing in the three words "boy kills principal." I expected to tap into three or four links, but the results produced 6,310 references! I was shocked to read one after another of the absence of tolerance of societal rules and the laws of the universe.

- Student kills two, wounds six at Kentucky School
- Student kills two classmates, wounds thirteen near San Diego
- Seventeen-year-old shoots and wounds assistant principal in New Mexico
- A sixteen-year-old boy takes a shotgun to school in Alaska
- Kyoto kid kills self in front of class
- Arizona six-year-old kills self
- Ten-year-old apologizes for poor grades and then hangs himself

The list goes on. The violence that is taking place on our planet, that most of us don't even know about, is something we cannot and should not tolerate. What's going on inside of these young minds? Where is the charismatic adult to positively influence them in their lives? Could it be you?

More Results of Intolerance

If you want to talk about the opposite of tolerant, check out the video, *The Laramie Project*. It depicts the story of intolerance, bigotry, negativity, hatred, and discrimination. In 1986, Matthew Shepard was strapped to a fence and beaten to death because his sexuality preference was being gay. This twenty-seven year old, kind, young man was described as being "polite, clean, and quiet" and apparently not one to provoke.

I watched the television broadcasts of when the father of Matthew Shepard spoke at the court hearing. "He was not alone. There were his lifelong friends with him. Friends he grew up with. You're probably wondering who they were. They were the beautiful night sky and the stars and moon we used to see through a telescope. Then the daylight and sun to shine on him. Through it all, breathing in the scent of the pine trees from the snowy range. He heard the wind, the ever-present Wyoming wind for the last time. Most of all, he had one friend, he had God." (This story is now available on DVD, *Journey to a Hate-Free Millennium*, available through New Light Media), **www.newlightmedia.org**.

Judy Shepard's comments the morning of October 12, 1998, when her son died were, "Go home and hug your kids – tell them you love them. Don't let a day go by without telling them you love them."

Charismatic Adult

In many cases it is obvious that the child's mind becomes like the cookie dough and is intolerant and causes him/her to react emotionally and violently. These children are so out of touch with their true beauty, their innocence, their desire to be cherished, and their inability to feel, to have the vocabulary to share those feelings and then communicate from their heart. They deserve so much more. They deserve to be taught from an early age a vocabulary for feelings. In order to teach it, their adult model must also embrace it. How did we get to be a culture so out of touch, in denial, and judgmental of our emotions?

Dr. Robert Brooks, co-author of *Raising Resilient Children* and member of the Harvard Medical School faculty, is one of today's leading speakers and authors on the themes of resilience, self-esteem, and motivation of family relationships. Dr. Brooks defines the term 'charismatic adult' as a person who demonstrates unconditional love for a child. This kind of adult doesn't deny any problems a child might have, yet focuses on a child's strengths. The term, 'charismatic adult,' was coined by the late Julius Segal as, ". . .someone from whom a child or adolescent gathers strength." Dr. Brooks says, "Even as adults, we need charismatic adults in our lives and we must play that role for others." **www.drrobertbrooks.com**

So how do we teach a child tolerance? From another of my yellowed articles from *Knight-Ridder* newspaper, dated November 19, 1996, Kathleen Curry suggests that teaching tolerance starts in the home. In the book entitled *Teaching Tolerance, Raising Open-minded, Apathetic Children*, author Sarah Bollard, offers tips for families.

- Look in the mirror. Teach by example. If you are intolerant, your child will most likely be.
- Don't go it alone. Include children in making the rules to achieve equality even in the home.
- Lay down the law simply. Rules are made to make us better people.
- No penalty box. Use consequences instead.
- Encourage empathy. Talk to your children about their favorite and least favorite moment in their day.

In order for someone to feel tolerant, one may also need to cope with certain situations that have a nagging annoyance associated with them. "Okay," Jane says, "I'll deal with you wanting to watch every sporting event on television, but I won't be happy about it." In other words, she is saying, "I'll tolerate it. I'll put up with it. And it will still bug me." From that point of view, being tolerant is not an enhanced character. To me, it sounds more like a victim and that she might use that at another time as revenge. Jane is bitter about it and unwilling to communicate how she truly feels, with the intention of a win-win. If our hearts are not open, clear, and clean, the grievances of the past will present themselves and take over the quality of our lives. Jane may say, "I need you to hear what I am feeling about the sports watching issue that seems to be prevalent in our home." If Jane experienced tolerance with the sports issue, she would be more open-minded, understanding, and be willing to share her feelings about it from a tolerant point of view. She might say, "I've been feeling that the sports events have become a priority to our time together. I understand and can appreciate that you really enjoy sports. I'm feeling ignored, left out, and unappreciated. Watch your sports programs and enjoy them, but just don't shut me out of your life. I need to know if there is a reason why you are watching so much television."

Do you see the difference in how Jane relates to the situation? If she puts up with something, chances are she has developed some hidden agenda and harbors some resentment. In the other scenario, where she came from heart-centered communication and wanted to be heard, she resolved the situation without conflict. Communication is always the key.

Reflection Time:

1. Would you consider yourself a charismatic adult?

2. As a young person, do you have a charismatic adult in your life?

3. What are you putting up with, being tolerant of, and being bitter about?

4. Are you tolerating your job, your stepmother, your car, the promotion your colleague got instead of you, your new neighbors that have a different colored skin? Make your list, and make a choice.

5. What are the human traits that you fear, dislike and criticize in yourself and/or in others?

6. Can you accept and appreciate the many parts of yourself that you don't like?

7. Did your parents demonstrate patience, tolerance and understanding?

8. Do you want to change anything about yourself with regard to your level of feeling tolerant?

9. Is there someone who has affected your life profoundly when you explore the feeling of tolerant?

10. As a teen, are your parents tolerant of your moods, friends, behavior, beliefs, approach to life? The same question is posed to the adult.

T is for feeling...Trapped

Definition: cornered, in a jam, stuck, no way out

Opposite: free, unshackled, loose

To feel trapped is to feel confined. There is no way out, no choice, and no options. To feel trapped can mean feeling isolated and alone. One may experience his or her body going through anxiety or trauma when feeling trapped. Breathing may increase. The body may even feel condensed, strained, or restricted. Blood pressure may go up because we don't know what to do. We feel trapped!

Consider a woman who was being evaluated for possible admittance to the hospital. Initially her blood pressure was 130, but when they decided to admit her, it went up to 200. Once she knew she was going in to the hospital, she felt trapped and fear kicked in. Panic is a response that restricts the blood vessels and is a disease in itself.

During one of our "Color Your Feelings" contests, we had a submission from a second grader who drew a picture of a boy with a scowling look on his face behind bars. The picture was entitled "Trapped," and drew a clear vision of what "trapped" looked like.

A Butterfly's Cage

I was curious to see the construction progress being made on a friend's new home, so I dropped by for the grand tour. Nobody was there, and I conducted my own tour, guessing one room from another. Then I heard something that drew my attention. I followed the sound to discover a beautiful butterfly that struggled against heavy plastic. It desperately yearned to be free. I spoke compassionately to my new winged friend, "All you need to do is descend only a few inches and freedom is yours." I sensed a state of panic in her as she flailed her gentle body again and again towards the obscured light. I combed the lumber pile and found a piece of wood to assist her in her life-threatening dilemma. She was trapped but not lost hopelessly. Eventually, I ushered her down the rafter, then off she flew. Free at last! I felt that place of joy within myself and tears welled in my eyes. We all seek freedom!

Here Comes the Bride

During the early years of my marriage in 1964, I recall a time when I attempted to remove my diamond wedding ring in order to clean it, and was unable to do so. I put my fingers under cold water, used soap and oil, as the panic within me mounted. I couldn't get this beautiful diamond ring off my finger. All that it represented: marital bliss, holy matrimony, walking off into the sunset as we aged together, being surrounded by grandchildren, all of these fantasy images, were preventing me from breathing at the moment. I couldn't breathe! I could NOT get it off! I did what any normal neurotic newlywed would do. I drove myself to the nearest jewelry store and proceeded to have them saw it off. Can you believe it?! We all have our own form of craziness.

The ring was an outward manifestation of the feelings I was experiencing in being trapped. Not being able to take off this ring represented not being able to get out my marriage. It's not that I was even unhappy, because I wasn't. I am such a free spirit that when this drama occurred, I must have been feeling I no longer had choices, that my freedom was inhibited, and that marriage put me in a category of dependency.

Now I have a latch on my wedding ring so that it is easily removable. The option is always there, however, after forty years of marriage (February 2004), I'm sticking with the winner of a husband through thick and thin.

Unresolved Issues

As parents, I believe we sometimes feel trapped. We feel victimized by our own past and therefore react to our children, rather than respond. Dr. T. Berry Brazelton is a tremendous source for good advice to new and seasoned parents. A pediatrician for more than forty years, having more than 25,000 children passing through his care, he states, "The lesson is the need to become aware. Once you get in touch with your past, you're ready to deal rationally with your child's situation instead of burdening it with unresolved issues from your childhood." Hooray, Dr. Brazelton!

On peer pressure, Dr. Brazelton responded to questions about variables that would determine whether children would succeed in life or end up desolate. He was able to determine, through the study, which children would not end up desolate. Those were the musicians or athletes or had some other burning interest of their own, or they were in families that had been through a crisis and had all faced it together. "They felt they were a part of the solution." (Family Circle 9/1/98) It sounds to me like these young people had a passion and didn't feel trapped by a poor attitude and limited beliefs.

We hear so often about young people who feel peer pressure to smoke, to wear designer clothes, to compete, to have lots of friends, to fit in, to be cool, to be accepted, to be liked. This is feeling trapped. Often this goes against what the intuition is saying. Kids feel they have to go along or they'll be outcast. Trapped! Sometimes it screams within. Sometimes our young people don't hear it and can only react to that invisible something as a result.

The list of pressures is often long when we're young, for example, to practice an instrument, clean our room, do the dishes, get good grades, be happy, or even do drugs. It can be overwhelming. We can actually feel heaviness on our chest or elsewhere in the body. That wall of heaviness represents a feeling of being trapped.

A young man by the name of Charles Andy Williams was humiliated by teachers, smoked pot daily, was bullied by friends, called names, abandoned by his mother at age three, and felt like a "leftover." He felt like no one cared for him and pleaded to his mother to come back. He said he felt trapped. When you feel trapped, you feel like no one cares, as 'Andy' did. Feeling this way can lead to choices that are not in your highest good. The more insecure, the poorer the choices. Fifteen-year-old Andy ended up killing two people and wounded fifteen at Santana High School in San Diego, California. He will be eligible for parole in fifty years.

One twelve-year-old boy told me that sometimes he feels so pressured he wants to leave his home. These are thoughts that just flash through his mind, "Fear, fear, fear. Will I do the right thing? Will I make the right choices?" When we feel pressured and trapped, we can't think clearly.

Pressure can be a negative or a positive in life. Teens are not the only group to experience excessive pressure. It's a condition of life. Self-imposed pressure motivates me to accomplish a project. I'll set up that deadline, then go for it, sometimes I even feel trapped by my own goal. Pressure and stress are synonymous; they can activate the feeling of trapped.

Imagine

How often do we feel trapped in life, with our job, our relationship, or our thoughts? We seek combinations that will bring us a measure of happiness and joy. Frustration comes easily as we look for solutions to take us out of the quagmire of life. The "no pain, no gain" concept has been so deeply ingrained in our consciousness that life appears to be synonymous with struggle.

Pain doesn't have to be our only teacher. In our society, a new opportunity may emerge which embraces a new paradigm to view the world. If we would hold a higher vision of ourselves and realize we deserve to have what we want, we can transform the quality of every moment. We all have active imaginations, which can be used as a bridge to free us from our self-imposed limitations. "Imagination is more important than knowledge," said Albert Einstein, a genius who contributed massively to human evolution. This paradigm is open to those who are willing to take total – this means 100%, not 50% – responsibility for their lives. In return for this inner shift of perspective, our rewards are joy and freedom–not when we retire, not when we acquire a new mate, not when the kids are on their own–but now.

When we learn to connect with our feelings, with others, and with that higher place within, we will become free, no longer feel trapped. That freedom means we communicate our truth, stand up for what we believe in and for who we are. We don't have to be the victim of feeling trapped. The choice we have is to give ourselves freedom! To give up the struggle, stop complaining about what doesn't work and consciously and actively create what does. (See the "F is for feeling...Free" chapter.)

Victor Frankl, author of *Man's Search for Meaning*, was a psychiatrist and prisoner who transformed years of suffering in Nazi concentration camps into insights for his life-long study of man's quest for meaning. He said, "Everything can be taken from us but one thing, the last of the human freedoms, to choose one's attitude in any given set of circumstances. There is nothing in the world I would venture to say that would so effectively help someone to survive, even the worst conditions, as the knowledge that there is a meaning to one's life." There is no security outside of ourselves, he theorized. These were extremely profound words from a man who undoubtedly felt trapped.

I met a man on a plane (sound familiar?) by the name of Carl Nomura who share with me such an inspiring story about how he overcame the feeling of trapped. A book entitled, *Organic Chemistry*, was the stimulus for a fabulous conversation and a new friendship. Carl told me how his algebra teacher gave him advice that helped him decide to grasp more from life than simple survival. Before that, he felt that he was destined for a life of farming or truck driving. In his own words he said, "She told me I was a person of very limited ability and that I should not take geometry and take the place of a more deserving person. She suggested

I should take auto and workshop and two hours of study hall. I decided I couldn't let her think that I was an idiot. I went from an 'F' student to an 'A' in Algebra and eventually a Ph.D. in Physics."

Carl's teacher's words could have trapped him into a limited lifestyle if he had believed the lie she projected about him! What an insult! What an arrogant position this teacher imposed on young Carl, who was an impressionable young man who wanted to respect his elders.

He went on to tackle advanced Algebra, Trigonometry, Solid Geometry, and Latin. He said, "I could have accepted the teacher's appraisal, but I didn't. I thought I'd fight this and in the process I learned the joys of excelling at everything." And he did. He went on to become a significant executive in Honeywell, Inc., and in 1988, he was honored by the University of Minnesota, his Alma Mater, with the highest award, "The Distinguished Graduate Outstanding Achievement Award." Carl Nomura is someone who didn't succumb to the pressure of his teacher to be mediocre. Instead, he used that to motivate himself to excellence. Hurray for Carl! You're my kind of guy! The last holiday greeting I got from Carl, concluded with, "Although I met you only once, you seem like an old friend."

Freedom is the nature of the soul. Our nature is expansive, limitless, and infinite. So once again, we can replace ignorance with understanding and wisdom. With a change of attitude, along with a new set of beliefs, we could find ourselves changed and happier.

Reflection Time:

1. Recall a time when you felt trapped. Did you feel like you were in prison?
2. Is there an issue you're struggling with currently that makes you feel trapped?
3. What are the walls? Where are the locks? Who has the key?
4. What can you do about this feeling?
5. Have you given your power away?
6. Are you feeling pressured to make a decision?
7. Are you willing to take responsibility for what is happening?
8. Does inner peace evade you? What can you do to bring more joy into your life?
9. How do you communicate to the person who you believe is controlling your life?
10. Do you have support in your life to choose a new reality?

"Trust is the final stage in humankind's evolutionary process toward wholeness"

Paul Brenner, M.D., *Seeing Your Life Through New Eyes*

T is for feeling... Trustful

Definition: accepting, confidant, believing

Opposite: skeptical, doubtful, cynical, dubious

Trust is having faith that things are going to work out. There is a level of confidence that we come to within ourselves that allows us to surrender to the moment when we're feeling trustful. We may be trusting of our partner, a total stranger, or the Universe at large. Whatever the circumstances, we are letting go of control, and we are relying on someone or something else instead of ourselves.

Things don't always turn out the way we want, but if we develop and adopt an attitude of understanding, knowing there was some reason it didn't work out, we can know there is a gift there for us. We simply need to relax and trust, once again, the guidance and be open to receive it.

I have developed trust over the years as a result of pursuing spirituality. I trust life to turn out perfectly, as it does every day and every moment. The more I learned of the Laws of Nature and the perfect timing of the Universe, the more I trusted. The more I learned of the precisely designed digestive system, and the more I was astounded by how the human body operates, the more I trusted. The more I reviewed my past in relationship to the present, the more I trusted. The more I learned to surrender my will and control to the Greater Power, the more I trusted. I grew to trust my intuition and follow its advice, knowing that it was a gift I was given at birth. I learned to trust that the experiences of my life were there to serve me and awaken my Truth. The words, "Trust the process," became a mantra ingrained in my brain. Repeatedly I chose trust instead of fear. Of course, there were times when the choices I made were not in my best interest. But when you trust, times like those are to be respected, honored, and reviewed, knowing they happen for a reason, learning the lesson, and moving on – trusting Life.

Unconscious Trust

While driving the car, I noticed the subconscious trust I had that the drivers on the other side of the street would travel on that side of the street and not mine! I just trusted without thinking about it!

The full moon becomes full at a very precise time. I trust that it will show up when it does! I have no control over when it does; I simply trust that it does.

As I let go of the way I think something should look or how an event should turn out or how people should be, I trust that the perfection unfolds, regardless of the pictures in my mind. I trust that the events of my life, and yours, and your neighbor down the street, are all working perfectly, each circumstance unraveling perfectly. Trust invites you to become a buddy with Creative Intelligence. Trust is based in the present, which is all there is. The power comes from living more in your heart, rather than in your head, being willing to feel each moment, and letting it go. Introspection, then being guided by that receptive wisdom. These are the forces that support a trusting attitude.

Control Freaks

To teach a child to be trusting may start with basic respect for the simplicities of life. A mother told me of her child's school that schedules bathroom and water fountain breaks for first graders. If a child has the need to visit the bathroom, it must be postponed or ignored until the scheduled time. That's absolutely absurd; trust can't be validated that way. Rather than teaching a child to trust his or her body and natural instincts, a child must learn to deny the body's message, to not trust it, and to wait.

People who need to control have difficulty feeling trustful. They need to be in control even when they can't, and that gets scary. The person who needs to be in control has little time to relax, because they're too busy worrying. This trait starts in childhood, which should be no big shock to you by now. We learn to control and manipulate in order to survive. It comes from the mind and the ego, not the heart or the soul. It comes from fear, from being wounded, from deep hurt. Fear goes with doubt like peanut butter and jelly. Love goes with trust like bagel and cream cheese. The choice, once again, is always yours.

Look at our many reasons for mistrust. We may be disappointed in the outcome of some circumstance. We may trust God to care for our child, and something unpleasant occurs. A major break of trust. Maybe someone didn't show up for the support we had counted on. We might have trusted that a parcel would come based on when it was sent, and days later, we discovered it was not sent at all. We trusted and we were let down. Maybe communication was out or maybe we heard something we wanted to hear. The big question is, how did you respond to the outcome?

The Trust Circle

Do you project a feeling of trust? I often led encounter groups during an internship at a teenage drop-in center. Those groups involved discussions, but often we had revealing interactive evenings. The "Trust Circle" was one of our favorite exercises. We all gathered in a tight circle with one person standing in the center. That person then closed his or her eyes in complete trust and fell into the circle, allowing her body to just surrender and trust that he or she would be caught. It was very interesting to observe how each individual responded to this exercise. Some were actually scared to death of letting go. Many were so frightened nobody would catch them they laughed and carried on until they were in tears. What became the foundation for this experience, was the feeling of being alone and with nobody to trust during their yearly years on the planet.

Every child needs at least one adult in his or her life that he or she can count on for a long period of time. How does a child develop trust without this? When a father walks out on his young child's life, it is challenging for the child to build trust as he or she grows into adulthood. My research indicates the wound is quite deep, and it takes work to free oneself of the feelings of low self-esteem, being unlovable, feeling guilt ("what did I do wrong?"), and resentment. There is work to be done, and being a responsible parent and adult can circumvent the poor results if the wound remains.

How do we commit if we can't learn and develop trust? If someone continually lets us down, it's time to look at our relationship with that person. Discuss what is happening and be unwilling to settle for anything other than feeling complete about it. No matter what the results might be, keep going, until there is closure.

Possessed

Have you ever been the object of a possessive friend, lover, or employer? Perhaps that person was suspicious or watchful. Being possessive is the opposite of feeling trustful.

Often when we are possessive, we may feel protective in an attempt to keep someone from harm, attack, or injury of some kind. We may have a deep fear that something will happen, and we worry. Out of fear, we may become obsessed and possessive, and the one we feel possessive over, may feel trapped.

A young man, age thirteen, told me he felt very angry because his parents were so possessive. He understood their concern and their worry for his well-being, but he felt trapped. He felt they didn't trust him to be responsible. He openly and honestly stated, "They have to give me some breathing room to try things on my own and reach out. I'm growing up, and I'm maturing. They have to understand." He is indeed a mature young man and has a command of communicating his feelings. I was impressed with his heart-felt sharing. He was in touch with his feelings and had the vocabulary to express them.

When we are feeling possessive, we want to protect our need to stay in control. We don't trust the soul's journey. We feel a need to stay in charge. Of course, we feel we know best. In relationships, when we struggle to maintain control, the one who feels possessed may scream because they feel trapped like a prisoner in their own home. Jealousy is a feeling related to possessiveness. Some men feel possessive with their women, and if things look threatening, watch out–she could end up in the home for abused women. The thought that "you are mine, and I can do whatever I want with you" often accompanies this feeling.

Unfortunately, too many parents feel possessive over their children, as if they are pawns that can be moved and manipulated. "Our children come through us," as Kahil Gibran's *The Prophet* says. "They are the children of the Universe."

Another good saying is, "There are two things you give your children. One is roots and the other is wings." Give security and consistency, yet give them permission to grow and unfold according to their spirit, their mission, and their purpose.

Letting Go of Fear

Ultimately, the trust of ourselves is what we're all looking for, because that's where trust begins. Trust our body–listen to it. When somebody says something that we react to, notice the body sensations. What emotions do we feel? What is our attitude about it? Our state of mind? How do we explore and trust our findings? Begin to develop intuition and learn to trust your sixth sense.

The opposite of trust is fear, called "The Great Attractor," by Neale Donald Walsh, author of the *Conversations with God* books. "It brings to us precisely what it is that we hope to avoid. The strength of an emotion is what produces or attracts results in one's life." Walsh's suggestion on how to step away from fear is "simply not to acknowledge it as real, and move immediately into gratitude." Because fear is one of the strongest human emotions next to love, Walsh created this affirmation to assist people in moving through fear. It is as follows:

"All that I once feared, I now embrace and heal. All negative human experience which may come to me in my life, I now see as a gift and a blessing – a treasure to behold – and a glorious opportunity for me to declare and to announce, to be and to decide, to express and fulfill Who I Really Am."

Paramahansa Yogananda speaks about fear in a little book called *Laws of Success*. "Fear exhausts life energy. It is one of the greatest enemies of dynamic willpower. Fear causes the life force that ordinarily flows steadily through the nerves to be squeezed out and the nerves themselves to become as though paralyzed. The vitality of the whole body is lowered. Fear doesn't help you to get away from the object of fear. It only weakens your willpower. Fear causes the brain to send an inhibiting message to all bodily organs. It constricts the heart, checks the digestive functions, and causes many other physical disturbances."

Yogananda suggests we overcome fear with courage and trust. As we learn to trust ourselves, we can grow more trusting of others and of the universal laws, for they keep us humble, and they keep us at peace.

Confidence and trust in your self affects everything. It comes from giving up your personal agenda to allow the highest to manifest. You set up that intention, while you give up your expectation, and then you trust. If you believe in yourself and know you're in partnership with Life, you're going to create joy in your relationships, in parenting, in your community, and in everything you undertake. Life becomes a blast!

Reflection Time:

1. What is the level of trust in your life?

2. If it's not very high, is there some action you can take to influence that level?

3. Parents, do you spend quality time with your children discussing moral and ethical issues?

4. Are you, the adult, being a role model for trust?

5. Are you, as the young person, learning trust?

6. Who do you trust and who do you not trust?

7. How would you describe your character? Your mother's? Your father's? Your child's?

8. What part does fear play in your life? Can you recognize it as the opposite of trust?

9. Would you identify yourself as a control freak? (Be honest now.)

10. What would be the worst thing to happen if you let go?

U is for feeling... Unique

Definition: special, one of a kind, unequaled, unparalleled,

Opposite: ordinary, common, normal

Whether we're small, tall, short, round, dark, light, funny, serious, left-brained, right-brained, athletic, artistic, gay, straight, whatever – we're unique! How wonderful!

No one else in the whole world has your fingerprint. Think about that! Isn't that an awesome statement and realization? How special you are! How very special!

Nobody else in the world would want my penmanship. My unique writing has withstood the criticism of my friends and family for years. Although they have all been eager for me to use my computer for correspondence, they have the opportunity to be tolerant of my unique handwriting.

Aaaah-choo!

Have you ever noticed how unique people's sneezes are? If taken off guard, my husband's sneeze sends a jolt through me that makes me jump. Some people sneeze so quietly you hardly know they are sneezing and others sneeze many times in a row, short and rapid. Sneezes are as unique as we are.

You are You and I am I

We each have our own unique way of growing to the light, which we will all do eventually. One way is not better than another. Again, I say, how boring it would be if we were all the same! What stops us from accepting people's uniqueness, their skin color, their religious preference, and their sexual preferences? What stops us is our ignorance, our limited thinking, our smallness, and pettiness.

Even if interests are the same, they can be expressed differently because of our uniqueness. When my graduate school mentor suggested

I write a book, I recall saying, "Oh yeah – right! Just what we need – another self-help book on the shelves." She replied, "But this one would be written through your unique style, your energy, and your experiences." That statement indeed caused me to pause and think...and now you hold the product of that new thought in your hands!

When our first grandchild, Alissa, was born, my daughter-in-law, Linda, gave me a very special gift. It's called a Giving Ball. The idea is to place something of meaning inside the decorative ball, which opens and has a latch, then periodically exchange it back and forth, being the giver and then the receiver. What a unique gift! We have traded back and forth several times in the last three years of Alissa's life. The most recent was a hand-painted glass paperweight. Linda said Alissa chose it for me. "I think YiaYia would like this." Now it's my turn to select something to put in the Giving Ball for her. A lovely ritual has been started between granddaughter and grandmother, thanks to a special and thoughtful daughter-in-law.

While hiking Bald Mountain with my friend, Bobbie, it became apparent to us, that we each take different trails and proceed in a variety of different ways, but eventually, we get to the same destination. A gentleman greeted us in a chipper manner as he walked past us while we ascended the switchbacks to the top. We chuckled when we saw him descending prior to our reaching the peak. Another person was climbing the face of Baldy with two poles in hand, walking straight up. Yet another was jogging the face of the mountain. We each have our own style, our own agenda, and our own pace. Let's remind each other of this as we embrace our day.

Do you know that there are even those unique people who have formed an Armadillo Club? They have a unique but similar interest. There's another group of people who meet in Washington yearly, and their commonality is that they all have a space in the middle of their front teeth. Hey, whatever goes! We're all unique and it's all wonderful!

The late cellist, Pablo Casals reminds us to tell our children how unique they are. "You are a marvel...In all the world there is no other child exactly like you. And look at your body; what a wonder it is! Your arms, your cunning fingers, the way you move. You may become a Shakespeare, a Michelangelo, a Beethoven; you have the capacity for anything. And when you grow up, can you then harm another who is like you – a marvel? You must cherish one another." Casals encourages us all to work to make this world worthy of its children.

Sandra Brown Turner, M.A., an assistant professor in Memphis, Tennessee talks about the "children's souls" and how and why caregivers should nurture them in the article "Caretaking of Children's Souls" in Young Children Magazine, January 2000. She says, "In using the term 'children's souls,' my reference is not limited by traditional religious training...I refer to the essence of uniqueness, the spark of fire in each human person. It is beyond the concept of physical being and into the eternal realm....The toughest test of respect is being mindful that each child who comes to us is on his or her own journey. When we take a stand, with quiet courage or impassioned fire, against violations of the human spirit, we affect their future."

There is an old Hasidic tale in which a Jewish Rabbi says, "When you die and go to heaven and meet your Maker, your Maker is not going to ask you why didn't you discover the cure for such and such. Why weren't you a leader? Why weren't you successful? Why didn't you become more? The only question that will be asked of you is, why didn't you become you? Why didn't you stay true to yourself? Why didn't you feel good about yourself? Why did you pretend to be something or someone you weren't? Why weren't you proud of who I made you to be? Why didn't you ever get to know who you really are? Why didn't you listen to me, with your soul? Why were you afraid to step out? Why didn't you become you?"

The Tale of Four Daughters

When I was a child, I had a belief that nobody wanted a fourth daughter. Wow, did I buy into that! VICTIM with capital letters. Poor me. That's how I see it now, but at the time I felt unwanted, unappreciated, and unimportant for who I was. I didn't recognize my own uniqueness until I matured. Throughout my childhood and adolescence, I tried to be like my big sisters, but always failed miserably, because I wasn't being me! All the while, I didn't value my own uniqueness.

The four Delis girls have certainly had our differences over the years because we are all so unique; we have unique and shared interests, physical characteristics, eating habits, exercise patterns, and very different beliefs, but we always individually held the value of what is highly important. After our mother passed away in 1972, we took Daddy back to Greece to visit Lala, the humble little village in the mountains above Olympia where he was born. From there we went into Athens for laughs, dancing, and a steady intake of scrumptious food. The last night there, Daddy said a final farewell to Uncle George, his ninety-six-year-old brother. In Greek, they sang a tune they'd sung many times as boys. The next morning, over tea at "Syndigma," or Constitution Square, with tear-filled eyes and after much prodding, he told us the song was about two brothers who would break through the mountain to be together. "This is how I want you girls to be no matter what happens." This message left an indelible mark on each one of us.

After all, who else shares the same history of our life if not our family? Who else can laugh and cry with us over the experiences of childhood? I have fond memories of swimming with my sisters from dawn to dusk in Lake Erie and helping Mom braid her classic homemade egg bread. (I got to top the loaves with egg yolk and sesame seeds.) ...taking turns having our hair braided... running through the freshly washed sheets that were hung on the clothes lines... using the summer breezes to dry them, in lieu of the Sears dryer... walking to the local park's outdoor ice skating pond with my skates on, ankles buckling at every step.

A client said, "But the history was too painful – the feelings weren't good – who wants to remember it anyway, or be reminded? My parents fought and argued so much, I would anticipate the next fight. These are not pleasant or nurturing moments." Granted, they are distressing memories, but nonetheless, they were part of what brought her to my office. "Your past, exactly as it was, made you who you are today," I told her. "You can choose your life today, while processing the memories that don't serve your highest good. When you come home from a vacation, you don't keep the dirty clothes in the suitcase, do you? Clear up your past and create what you prefer in this moment of your life script."

We've all had our degree of suffering, and it has made us who we are today, unique in many ways because of our choices. I've had clients who haven't spoken with siblings for years, still carrying the old baggage around and dragging it with them everyday. After a NPR session with me, each is willing to forgive, release the past, and accept others for who they are. Forgiveness of oneself is monumentally freeing. We don't have to hold on; we just need to feel, honor, let go, and replace. It's only a myth that it's so hard. It's all choice.

In the book, *Growing Up and Feeling Good*, author Ellen Rosenberg writes about a woman who feels that certain friends have become like sisters. "There is nothing we wouldn't have given up if we needed each other. That's dedication, a feeling of true loyalty, a feeling that if your hand is out, you know you can count on each other. But my own brother and sister never gave me that feeling." She and her friends are closer and more trusting than she ever was with her real sister and brother. Her friends have become her family. Hey, whatever works. Nobody gives you a desired feeling; you have to create it through your intention to communicate and close the annals of the painful past.

A family closeness can be felt through a biological family, through a created family in marriage or through a group of supportive, like-minded people who may not be related through blood. I would say Jane Goodall believes the chimpanzees are very much her family. Through family, there are incredible opportunities for self-discovery, to learn acceptance, forgiveness, respect, trust, honesty, and for unconditional love.

In his book, *The Isaiah Effect*, Gregg Braden, author and guide to sacred sites, states, "...each person is a unique, individualized expression of a single, unified awareness. Within this oneness, the choices and actions of each person affect all others to some degree. In a field of unified consciousness, each choice that we make and every act we perform in each moment of each day must affect every other person in this world. Some actions produce a greater effect and some a lesser one. Still, the effect is there."

Again, I ask you dear reader, are you making choices that serve your own highest good as well as all of humankind? Do you believe you are here to be a conduit for Love and Light? Do you realize you can actually co-create a peaceful and joyful experience on the planet? You are an important piece of the puzzle. Do you get it?

You are the Perfect Gift

A child knows. A child picks up on everything. A child feels intensely before they can talk. This was evident as I talked with a young couple who had stopped at my conference exhibitor table about the ABC Feelings audiotape. I played a portion of it, six-year-old Julia singing, "I Love You, No Matter What You Do." Their fourteen-month-old son turned his head in the direction of the music. His eyes were open wide and barely blinked as he sat in his stroller, tapping his little foot to the rhythm. It was obvious to all that this child was relating to something very special – maybe the sounds of Julia's voice, maybe the words of love, or maybe he aligned with a feeling called love.

Children want the gift of our unique laughter, of our joy and acceptance. This doesn't mean we can't give a gift as a symbol to celebrate the bond that is shared. In your gift giving, keep things in perspective and be aware of where you choose to place your focus. What they really want is to feel respected and honored, and allowed to be free to be themselves. Adults want the same thing.

Like Michelangelo's David, we are all originals. He chipped away at what didn't belong. The David was already in the stone. We've not been cloned. We're not mass-produced like a microwave or stereo player. We are unique! Although we are the same, we are different, and it is through that difference that we contribute our gift. How can a gift be a gift if it's not shared? The gift is you!

Reflection Time:

1. Do you have unfinished business with your family?
2. Do you accept each member's uniqueness?
3. Do you carry grudges?
4. Would you like closure on an aspect of your past?
5. What needs to be said or done for this to happen?
6. Who will be there for you as you stretch out your hand?
7. Whose hand will you reach out to grab when support is needed?
8. What are you doing to create "family" with your children and provide them with rich memories?
9. As a child, what was your most cherished gift? What was the most fun to give? To receive? What would you like to receive from someone special?
10. Find the labels that best describe your own unique qualities.

"Most of what we know, even 'scientific fact,' is based on our cultural viewpoint. We're usually unaware of this because our basic assumptions about the world are learned at such an early age and embedded so deeply within us that we take them for granted. But looking from a different perspective, we can see how our beliefs about the way the world works make us cling to illogical ideas and ignore evidence that points in another direction."

Marc S. Micozzi, M.D., Ph.D., *Many Paths to Healing*

U is for feeling...Unloved

Definition: unwanted, unresponded to, low self-esteem, worthless
Opposite: loved, cherished, respected, wanted

Feeling unloved is the root of the distressing feelings mentioned in this book. When one feels unloved, one feels worthless, inadequate and empty, which often is expressed through anger, upset, and frustration. To feel unloved, is to feel like the world is a cold, cruel place. Hope is lost. Despair sets in. Keep in mind, it is the feeling that we're talking about. A parent may have loved their child the best they could, however, it's the experience the child has that is important. We want to experience feeling loved, unconditionally, and if we don't, it becomes the breeding ground for dysfunction. Examples are lashing out at defenseless creatures such as the 62 animals poisoned to death at the San Paulo Zoo in Brazil, or the nine children killed in Fresno, California. When and how are the wounds to be healed?

The common thread in most of my client sessions is the feeling of unloved. As usual, the feeling stems from childhood and has become absorbed into the cellular structure. A seven-year-old client acquired beliefs already about her self-worth and how to survive in the world of, "It's all my fault," and "It's a scary world." We acquire these beliefs through our environment, and they become a self-fulfilling prophecy for our life.

The following list of beliefs is an important one to read and contemplate. Better yet, put a check next to the ones you take clam to. These are very common beliefs, held by a huge populous:

❏ "It's not okay to be who I am."

❏ "I have to please people to earn their love."

❏ "I'm not enough the way I am."

❏ "If I were a male, I'd receive more attention and love."

❏ "Others aren't capable of caring for themselves, so I have to."

❏ "It's not safe to be alone."

❏ "I'm not important enough for you to come to my school programs."

❏ "I choose to be alone out of self-protection."

❏ "I avoid risk, in fear of being rejected."

❏ "My body is disgusting and gross."

❏ "If Dad doesn't have time for me, who would?"

❏ "I'm not good enough to deserve love."

❏ "Mom always favored my brother."

❏ "I'm fearful of being left."

❏ "If I avoid conflict, I'll be loved."

❏ "Just being me is bad."

❏ "My birth was a mistake."

❏ "I am an injured person."

❏ "My mother always squashed my dreams."

❏ "No matter how hard I try, there's no way to win."

❏ "I'm destined to always be #2."

❏ "I'm a loser."

❏ "It's hopeless, so why try?"

❏ "I don't trust that people will be there for me."

❏ "Love will never be part of my future."

❏ "I'm incapable of being loved."

❏ "Just being me is unlovable and not enough."

❏ "If I learn about people intimately, I'll know their needs and attempt to fill them, which will guarantee me love."

❏ "I'm terrified to give love, because it won't come back."

❏ "I'm not comfortable being a woman."

❏ "I'm not worthy of being accepted."

❏ "I try to be perfect to be loved."

❏ "I have to be a good girl to please others.

❏ "I cover my hurt, buried feelings with laughter."

❏ "Why start something, I won't finish it anyhow."

If a parent has high expectations and a child doesn't live up to them, she may feel she has let her parent down and see herself as a failure, and unloved.

During a session with a client, I will ask for the earliest experience they can recall that relates to the issue that causes the suffering. Invariably, the client will share a time in early childhood when they were abandoned, either physically or emotionally. Feelings that include, "I'm not good enough to have my parents stay" are accompanied by feelings of worthlessness, not being wanted, and actually feeling responsible for the behavior of the negligent parent. "If only I had been better, Daddy would not have left." "If only I had not cried as much." "If only I had not upset him."

The energy of being the unloved child remains through adolescence and adulthood when it manifests itself in a myriad of ways. Whining, nagging, and demanding are examples. Someone said whining is anger coming through a small hole. The inner child is looking for attention, reassurance, and security.

As adults, some clients have compensated quite beautifully, and still carry the energy of this unloved child in their electromagnetic field. Good quality, short-term counseling can be very beneficial. Quality is the word I stress here.

In Dr. Robert Brooks and Sam Goldstein's book, *Nurturing Resilient Children*, they define mindset as, "a set of ideas, beliefs, attitudes, skills, and assumptions, all of which guide our behavior." Dr. Brooks went on to tell me, "Often we may not even be aware that we have these assumptions. In our book, *Raising Resilient Children*, we describe the mindset of resilient children in the following way:

- Resilient youngsters feel special and appreciated.
- They have learned to set realistic goals and expectations for themselves.
- They have developed the ability to solve problems and make decisions and thus are more likely to view mistakes, hardships, and obstacles as challenges to confront rather than as stressors to avoid.
- They rely on productive coping strategies that are growth–fostering rather than self-defeating.
- They are aware of their weaknesses and vulnerabilities, but they also recognize their strong points and talents.
- Their self-concept is filled with images of strength and competence.

- They have developed effective interpersonal skills with peers and adults who can provide the support they need.
- They are able to define the aspects of their lives over which they have control and to focus their energy and attention on these rather than on factors over which they have little, of any, influence."

This is tremendous information from Brooks and Goldstein, which they also apply to adults in their new book, *The Power of Resilience*. All of their books are so important for parents, as well as those who care about children. As I see it, feeling unloved as a way of life, is not part of the mindset of a resilient child, or adult.

Teach by Example - Teach Through Experience

I am a supportive parent. I am a supportive partner. I am content and fulfilled. I welcome change. I embrace self-improvement. I make a difference. I love my job.

Let the child figure out the lesson. Be patient, persevere. How easy is it for you to say you're sorry? One of the best things a father can do for his child is to love that child's mother, and vice versa. Gentleness and boundaries mean we love you. You can't suppress a child's will by being a domineering parent. Children must be hugged, touched, and cuddled. They all need to be reassured that they are loved, and that they don't have to earn it. Beliefs: "I have to live up to my parent's expectations, or I may not be loved." They have to FEEL they are loved. They have to EXPERIENCE they are loved. Putting a child down with words or with laughter is abuse. Deal with the situation, not the person.

It's not what happens to us that matters, but what we make of ourselves because of it. Whatever happens, accept it, embrace it, and invite it in. It means you're acknowledging the truth; you're acknowledging what is. It is a way of honoring the universe. Get busy and weed the garden of your life.

Who am I? What am I? How am I?

When I believe I am anything other than my soul, I have invested in the world, my five senses, and ego consciousness. That's the package, and that's okay. Just be aware of your choices.

Am I my job? Another recollection is of a man who left a job after many long dedicated years to his employer. Being the breadwinner of the family with little ones to provide for, Joe was the type of person who was not comfortable seeing problems as opportunities and in grasping the adage that one door may close but another will open. His self-image diminished and negative emotions flooded his mind. Thwarting them became his greatest challenge. The myth that he would have one job throughout his life was shattered and now it was necessary to form a new belief about earning a livelihood. Our work is an expression of us; it is NOT who we are. It is healthy and wise to experience the uneasiness of the transition time and complete any undelivered communications. However, knowing there are no accidents and having faith in the process of life, we can embrace the unexpected and listen for the wisdom to empower us to move forward.

Am I my bank account? Turning to history and the stock market crash of the thirties, there were many that lived their lives thinking they **were** their money. When it was gone, they chose to die, feeling no desire or purpose for life. Family members suffered at the loss of their loved ones, as well as their security. Many marriages are not resilient enough to sustain these kinds of changes, and some are. I'm reminded of a couple who recently endured very hard times after enjoying the pleasures of a rather lucrative income. Because they both mutually agreed this would strengthen their marriage, they were able to look at options, design a new budget, and make changes, to move through and endure a painful time in their lives. They came out of it on the positive side. It takes diligence.

Am I my body? I once knew a woman whose relationship meant everything. Virginia cared so much for this man that there wasn't anything she wouldn't do to please him, and her obsession with her body was obvious to all who knew her. She was continually on a diet, compulsive about exercise, and face and body lotions filled her shelves. Firm buns, washboard abs, muscle definition. This is what many people are after, and what they won't do to get it! Virginia struggled to maintain a body her boyfriend would approve of. However, still unsatisfied with what she saw in the mirror, even after an exercise schedule that matched an Olympic athlete's, she had surgery. Eventually, her idol called it quits and, you guessed it, she was devastated. Is Virginia her body? Our body is to be cared for and respected, fed nutritious food, bathed, accepted, AND used as a conduit to allow wisdom and love to flow through it. It is constantly changing and will serve you well, if you love and respect it for what it is, a vehicle to function in the physical world.

Am I my relationship? A young couple met, connected, and then started to share a new and stimulating friendship. Mary and Fred were quite different. She was a reflection of her mother—outgoing and vivacious. He, also a product of his home environment, was somewhat unexpressive and hesitant about life. Days, months, and years passed with frequent disagreements, periodic separations, and mounting inner strife for both. "I can't be who you want me to be," Fred declared. In this case, Mary did not disintegrate. They mutually agreed to take a time out as they individually explored what makes them tick and the issues they bring to a relationship. As she felt her sadness and anger, she was also open to life and allowed new ideas to flow. A long-awaited trip was planned and life goes on. Mary is NOT her relationship. Her dependence is NOT with Fred but with herself.

Commonalities

Here are even more of the most commonly shared attitudes and beliefs from my clients:

❑ "I'm unworthy and undeserving to be loved, to love, to be happy, to have dreams."

❑ "I don't have what it takes."

❑ "I'm inadequate."

❑ "Life is a struggle."

❑ "I'm not good enough."

"I'm afraid to trust again."

❑ "If I don't do it, it won't get done right."

❑ "Suppressing feelings will help me survive."

❑ "I'm not accepted for who I am."

❑ "Being vulnerable is painful and scary."

❑ "If I please, be good, cooperate, I'll be loved."

❑ "I'll do anything to get attention."

❑ "My needs are not important."

Here is a list of the type of people who would have the above beliefs:

❑ Someone with low self-esteem and no confidence.

❑ Someone who efforts.

❑ Someone who is angry.

❑ Someone who is controlling and untrusting.

❑ Someone who denies and stuffs feelings.

❑ Someone who is fearful and guarded.

❑ Someone who is a good little girl and a caregiver.

❑ Someone who is desperate and needy.

❐ Someone who has been abandoned.

❐ Someone who is a victim and getting a payoff for it.

Here is a list of supportive beliefs to replace the old, self-sabotaging ones:

❐ I deserve to be loved and manifest my dreams.

❐ My thoughts are supportive and positive.

❐ Expressing my needs is taking care of myself.

❐ Everything always works out for my highest good.

❐ I believe things happen for a reason to help me learn the lesson.

❐ I have within me all I need to produce a fulfilling and joyful life.

❐ I am enough.

❐ My life functions with ease and grace.

Overcoming the feeling of unloved has to do with getting in touch with and nurturing the inner child. Loving yourself is the only cure to feeling unloved. You will experience this as you get in touch with and nurture your inner child.

Reflection Time:

1. Make a list with three columns: Child, Adolescent, Adult, and write beliefs about feeling unloved from each point of view.

2. Now, take it one step further and sit in three different chairs for each identity, assuming the posture, attitude, and energy of that personality.

3. Make a list of the characteristics that you aspire to today.

4. How does feeling unloved prevent you from manifesting your dreams?

5. What words are synonymous with feeling unloved – free associate (as you say the word unloved, allow any word that comes to you to be written down on paper without thinking).

6. Push the rewind button on your life tape and discover the first time you felt unloved.

7. Draw a picture of how you feel feeling unloved. Now, draw, paint, dance, or sing an expression of the opposite.

8. Are you willing to talk to your parents about feeling unloved? Or anyone?

9. What would have to happen for your to FEEL loved?

10. What would you have to give up to feel loved?

"The behavior of the worried, upset, or unhappy person reacts on those around him, sometimes more destructively than an infectious disease."

Laura Archera Huxley, *You Are Not the Target*

U is for feeling... Upset

Definition: disturbed, distressed, victimized

Opposite: peaceful, content, detached

The word "upset" literally means "to overturn or capsize." If we think about it in this way, feeling upset could mean that one's balance or equilibrium has been turned upside-down! To feel upset is to feel distressed about something. What upsets you?

Here's a list of a few things that come to mind that manage to push my buttons, especially when I'm feeling off:

- When I'm trying to get through to Fed-Ex or some other large company and after punching in a series of numbers, an automated voice comes on, acting like a human, saying, "Okay, let's start again. I didn't get that."

- When I'm just trying to put an ink cartridge in my printer, and I have to fight through layers and layers of tough, wasteful plastic and cardboard to get to the product. Excess packaging gets the best of me!

- I went to order a car from Dollar Rent-a-Car and, in a pleasant, cheerful voice, the computerized voice said, "Hi. Where are you coming from and where are you going...Now what date are you coming in?" I said, "Agent." I could feel the voice's smile when she said, "Sorry I didn't get that. Could you repeat the city again?"

- People who don't leave their phone numbers on my answering machine tend to upset me, especially when I so kindly ask them to do so on my outgoing message.

The Life Drama

We all have our own unique dramas, all happening at the same time. Someone's getting brain surgery, another is considering bankruptcy, a car breaks down, a grandmother is visiting her toddler grandchild, a hundred-year-old tree is cut down in a neighborhood, a young man is desperate and courageous in a search for a job, and a software company folds. The moments of life still continue to click on. We don't know what's around the corner or what message will be on the other end of the phone when it rings. Life is pleasure and pain. Life is duality. Life is the ebb and flow, like it or not. Sure, you can resist what is; you have free will. But does your resistance bring you joy, fulfillment, and happiness? I would venture to say that it brings you more suffering. So, consider changing your attitude and the beliefs associated with that resistance, and STILL speak up, but with a wise detachment.

You think you're upset with your problem?! Imagine if you were this man: After going into the hospital for surgery for bladder cancer, he was shocked and mad when his wife told him that yes, indeed, they had removed the cancer, but they had removed his penis as well! He filed a negligence lawsuit as this horrible result was never discussed with his doctors before, nor after the surgery. To add insult to injury, the examined slides revealed there was no penile cancer evident. Try dealing with that!

The Missing Child

Margot Thornton experienced an array of feelings during the two-year period her daughter was missing. I spoke with her many times during this emotional time in her life. Yes, she was upset, deeply concerned, weary, confused, angry, and persistent, but because of her attitude and belief system, she was able to keep perspective on this traumatic situation and seek productive ways to live. She had the belief that adversity comes, but you have the choice on how to handle it. (Similar to Victor Frankl's outlook.) Margot and Lily were eventually united after their life-altering ordeal. Lily is thriving back home, while mom pursues the law school, with a burning desire to give back. Right on Margot!

Unfulfilled

Brilliant theorist and psychiatrist, Carl Jung, said, "There is nothing that affects a child's life more than the unfulfilled life of the parent." What a powerful statement! Many parents raise children feeling upset about their own childhood, their own inadequacies, their own unfulfilled dreams.

Maybe we didn't fulfill our parents' expectations and that makes us feel upset. For example, a colleague told me about the time when he had taken a test with 50,000 other students in England and came in with the top five. When he gave the good news to his mother, she wanted to know why he didn't come in number one. I'd say that was a potential cause for upset.

Upset brings a lot of opportunity to look within and explore. Gary Zukav, author of *The Seat of the Soul* once said, "It is not the anger that causes consequences, it's the action of the anger."

A Course in Miracles says, "I am never upset for the reasons I think…" What does that mean? "There are no small upsets; they are equally disturbing to my peace of mind." Upset can be a form of anger, resentment, jealousy, or depression, but the Course states that these are all feelings that represent some sort of fear. Further, the Course says, "We have a choice…" Does that sound familiar? We can experience either love or fear. When we choose love, the fear dispels, and we need not feel fear for any reason. This is certainly great food for thought!

Take a look at the following examples of "upsetting" scenarios:

- Let's say you're upset because the stock market goes down. What you're really upset about is the fear you will lose your investment. SURVIVAL.

- You're upset because you have lost your job. You may be fearful you won't be able to pay your bills, your mortgage, nor your airline tickets to Hawaii that you just confirmed. SURVIVAL.

- Your child's grades are dropping – possibly under the upset is fear that she'll be kept a grade behind, or he'll flunk out of his freshman year at college. That's a reflection of parenting, perhaps the concern is what will people say. SURVIVAL.

- You've just been notified that you didn't make the first string on the football team, and you have a huge upset. The fear behind it might be low self-esteem, not being good enough, you don't have what it takes, or fear of being excluded. SURVIVAL.

- As a fifth grader you're upset because you missed the school bus. Your mom and dad have already left for work. Underlying the upset could be, how do I get to school; I'm going to get in trouble; I didn't manage my time well, and I'll miss the test in first period. SURVIVAL.

- You're on the playground and the bully pushes you, and you're feeling upset. Just below the surface of that upset could be fear that your friends have witnessed this, and they will call you a sissy. Nobody will believe your story. Your new jeans are now stained, and you are really upset. SURVIVAL.

Alzheimer's

Take any upsetting scenario and I venture to say fear will be at the crux of it. However, my friend, Joanne, has not masked her anger and has found that being true to herself has brought her trust as well as peace of mind. Joanne is a woman in her sixties who feels that life is full of lemons but loves to make lemonade. She feels her feelings. For thirteen years, Joanne has been caring for and administering to her husband who was diagnosed with Alzheimer's at the age of fifty-eight. Joanne was fifty-one. She was very angry with Mark, because she knew he had begun to abandon her.

"The beauty of our twenty-year marriage was how we grew simultaneously. I realized he wasn't climbing the tree at the same rate I was, and I didn't know why. He became psychotic, feeling like I was stealing from him. He'd walk off, and I would hope he'd get hit by a car. I saw the relationship begin to fade. We weren't the same people anymore. I had to come to the realization that this was an actualization. I couldn't be in denial anymore, so I chose to drop my anger. It wasn't getting me any place. It wasn't helping anybody. By letting go of anger, I could see the beauty of growth and the journey taking a different road – different than I'd ever anticipated. There was a conscious choice to give up anger, get out of denial, and say I'm going to learn a new trade. I'm going to be the best I can be. Being the best I can be, I will have a positive affect on others."

Their son, Steven, was nineteen years old at the time and cared for his father at home. "Steven was the one with the patience and love. He made his father feel important and helped him to not lose his dignity."

"I had to take over the reins, financially and emotionally. I had to learn everything possible in order to make life the best it could be. In doing so, I learned to be more compassionate. I had a choice – to be miserable or ecstatic. My choice led me to learning to love myself more than I ever thought was possible. By loving myself I have the ability to touch people in a way that's deeper. I can't put it into words. It's a soul connection. It's beyond a personality level, all the garbage, and all the feelings. It's a place that makes a difference, so then they can pass it on. I see these last thirteen years as a positive experience. I've acquired an attitude of honor – I feel fortunate to have this experience. My life has run the gamut of emotions. God has given me the ability to access the depth of my mind and heart and soul. Today, I feel complete."

At the time of this writing, Joanne continues to love, cherish, and care for her mate. I've known Joanne since the sixties when she married one of my husband's best friends. She has touched my life knowing what she has been through – health, financial, and family challenges for starters. Joanne is the personification of someone who has demonstrated the power of choice. She's chosen a new and supportive attitude as well as a set of beliefs that work for her today and she endures her path. Congratulations to you, my fellow Capricorn friend.

When we're upset, no doubt we're experiencing any one of the following feelings: irritation, anger, jealousy, annoyance, frustration, resentment, distress, anxiety, violence, rage, vulnerability, fear, intolerance, trouble, confusion, tension, threat – are there more? You betcha. Any one of these emotions affects our immune systems and cellular structure. Any one of these can do damage to our hearts.

While we are feeling upset for any reason, true or not, the world rotates at the rate of 1000 miles per hour. Its annual revolution around the sun travels at twenty miles per second. The solar system is moving within the local star system at thirteen miles per second. The local star system moves within the Milky Way at two hundred miles per second. The whole Milky Way drifts in all different directions in relation to the remote galaxies at one hundred miles per second. All this is going on while we are feeling upset.

Roger Sperry, Ph.D. and Nobel Prize winner for brain research provided this insight: "Better than 90% of the energy output of the brain is used in relating to the physical body in its gravitational field. The more mechanically distorted, the less energy is available for thinking, metabolizing and healing. Being upset would be considered a distortion." How much energy are you exerting with your upsets?

Reflection Time:

1. Reflect on something you feel upset about. Take a peak and determine if fear is underneath it.

2. Is there some action you could take that might cause positive consequences and dispel the upset you experience?

3. Take a moment and think of the last time you felt upset about towards someone.

4. What happened to your peace of mind?

5. How did your body respond?

6. Did people want to be around you?

7. Did your self-esteem soar or plummet?

8. How about your immune system, how did it react to your upset?

9. What did you do with your upset?

10. What was that person doing with his or her life while you were upset?

"I believe the children are our future, teach them well and let them lead the way. Show them all the beauty they possess inside. Give them a sense of pride to make it easier. Oh let the children's laughter remind us how we used to be...I decided long ago never to walk in anyone's shadow. If I fail, if I succeed, at least I live as I believe...I found the greatest love of all inside of me..."

"The Greatest Love of All," written by Michael Maser,
sung by Whitney Houston

V is for feeling...Valued

Definition: honored, highly regarded, respected, trusted
Opposite: lack of confidence, low self-esteem, worthless

When we say something has "value," we mean that it has importance and is worth something to us, whether it be sentimentally, financially or emotionally. If something is valuable, we either display it with pride, or protect it by putting it away in a safe place. Whatever we choose to do with our valued object, we take the best care of it that we possibly can, for we are proud of it.

When we feel valued, we feel worthy. Perhaps someone is proud of us. Perhaps we have just won an award or received a raise at work. Whatever it may be, feeling valued has to do with self-esteem, whether it comes from outside of us, or from within. When we feel confident of our choices and our direction, we generally have a healthy self-esteem. When we feel valued, we feel as though we are important in this world, and we know it. We all want to be able to say, "Who I am is important."

Feeling valued means to feel deserving, worthy, and good about ourselves. Knowing who we are and knowing what we have to say is important. With confidence training, we make ourselves feel self-reliant, self-respectful, and self-loving. We all make a difference. Feeling valued begins at birth and builds from there.

Here's a funny and touching email I received that pertains to how we value our mothers:

4 years old: My Mommy can do anything!

8 years old: My Mom knows a lot! A whole lot!

12 years old: My Mother doesn't really know quite everything.

14 years old: Naturally, Mother doesn't know that, either.

16 years old: Mother? She's hopelessly old-fashioned.

18 years old: That old woman? She's way out of date!

25 years old: Well, she might know a little bit about it.

35 years old: Before we decide, let's get Mom's opinion.

45 years old: I wonder what Mom would have thought about it?

65 years old: I wish I could talk it over with Mom.

Treasures on Tape

People's lives are worth recording. While raising our family on the edge of the continent in Malibu, California, I thoroughly enjoyed my business called Treasures on Tape. TOT was an audio-taped, professional interview of one's life, lasting approximately two hours, retracing the steps of the past and taking a "talk" down memory lane. Over many years, I interviewed people of all ages. I received requests from the elderly as an ethical will, on Father's Day as a unique gift from his children, and from grown children who wanted to capture the unique lives of their parents or grandparents. Once, I was hired by the family of their terminally-ill daughter, who wanted her philosophies and memories as a lasting memento. Another client, Gigi, was inspiring, alive, and playful, even at a century old!

I recently completed a Treasures on Tape interview with Mimi Feldman, a long-time friend of my sister-in-law. Her concluding remarks focused on a music school she and her two brothers, Herb and David, had built in the valley in Jerusalem. There, Arab and Jewish children play instruments side by side. Mimi said, "Visiting the Louis and Tillie Alpert Music Center was a thrill. It was dedicated in 1979. Thirty members of her family attended this dedication. It's a warm feeling to know that this is going on over there." Teachers from the Israeli Symphony offer their talent to approximately eighty students that study at the center.

Mimi's gentle manner, creative nature, and positive attitude make her quite the lady. She took those qualities and applied them to her late husband's cable business, Victor Wire and Cable Corp. After his passing, she chose to transform the business by remodeling the building with paint, new carpet, and art on the walls. The employees were so impressed by her interest that they wanted to know what they could do to be of help. The business took a new turn, as she became one of the few women in this type of business to assume the position of President. *The Wire Journal* did a feature article on her. This humanitarian is making a difference in the world of music, business, and human relations. Congratulations, Mimi; you are a valued and inspirational soul.

Everybody's life is of value and deserves being preserved. Children and adults of the next generations can learn through listening to the story of how their relative became who they are. My mother-in-law spoke on her TOT on how she wore the same brown dress to the dances. My daughter, a young, impressionable adolescent at the time she heard it, said, "Grandma had only one dress?!"

One of the testimonials I received was the expression of how this experience was "...like an open book. I've relived my life. It's important to me for my family to know where their traditions and values began." Ali Macgraw, a fellow yoga enthusiast while I was living in Malibu, told me "The taped interview of my son has meant so much to me. It is a treasure and I am so grateful to have it." Do you value your life enough to record it on tape? Have you recorded your life for your children and grandchildren? And do they know your values?

Values

Valuing someone is letting them know they are important. Values, on the other hand, are principles and standards which you believe are important. What do you consider valuable? In other words, what are your values? There are seemingly a few different meanings to the word "value," yet upon closer look, there is a link. Are your inner values reflecting what you are valuing? For example, if your values include helping others, are you treating others with worth? If your values include looking presentable, are you valuing the clothes you wear and the work that went into creating that particular outfit? Values are important. They shape who we are. When comparing your values to what you are valuing in your life, do they match up, or is there a gap? Recognizing this promotes awareness.

When we have morals and values strong enough to withstand the traumas and temptations of life, we are rooted in what is real and solid, the basis for lasting happiness. Yogananda says, "To stand unshaken amidst the crashing worlds..."

Values must be instilled at an early age – very early. A child of two years can be shown at the end of the day to put books and toys away and dirty clothes in the hamper. In the morning, she could tidy up her bed before she starts her day. This teaches the virtue of cleanliness, responsibility, orderliness, respectfulness, self-discipline, and confidence, to name a few. The earlier the better; teach values that develop character.

How much more research needs to be done to verify that parents play the central role in instilling values and self-confidence in their children? Optimize the adult, and the child will be just fine. They will only have their own karma to work out in this lifetime. Put the parent in the scenario, with all of mom and dad's baggage, plus the grandparents', and you've got a mulligan stew!

The seeds of worthiness and self-esteem are planted during the very earliest years. What kind of programming are we giving our children? What kind of programming have we had in our childhood? Joy, love, beauty, wisdom, and worthiness are qualities that are all part of our birthright. To believe we are not worthy is a false belief. Being worthy does not suggest we won't have our challenges in life; we will. Being worthy does not relate to ideas that we can't handle or the support we might need with them. We will need support, and we will have those challenges. It's sort of like the pig's tail. You know if you try to straighten it out, it'll always curl right back up again. Well, problems are a part of life. How do we react to them? How do we resolve them? How do we understand them and respond to them?

Each parent automatically becomes the most important role model, and a child's first teacher. Although this responsibility may sound rather awesome, it doesn't have to be overwhelming. During those precious and vital years of child-rearing, parenthood is an opportunity for us to examine our own spiritual values and determine how they can be taught to our children.

During challenging moments of raising children, one of the profound truths sometimes forgotten is that there are no accidents! I believe a family is formed by divine order, to learn vital lessons from each other about life. Each beautiful child has come through the set of parents, on loan and entrusted by God, to teach and nurture this soul, to assist the child in realizing his or her true nature and purpose here on Earth. The child is not a possession or someone through whom to live our unfulfilled desires. As Gibran says in *The Prophet*, "They are the sons and daughters of Life's longing for itself." A parent's job is to allow that perfect blueprint to unfold and express. The more a parent can observe a child's behavior, interests, and characteristics, the more equipped they are to guide and fulfill their role as teachers.

From an early age, it is crucial to teach children spiritual values. During those fresh years, toddlers are a captive audience. Consistent exposure to love, joy, laughter, and peace reminds them of their true home. There is an abundance of spiritual lessons to teach a child to support self-esteem and feelings of value. I put together a list that can't help but enhance a young one's life immeasurably.

415

Instilling Values

1. The child is more than what we see. We are holistic beings, composed of body, mind, and soul. We have a body, but we are not our body. Our body is a vehicle to house our soul as it learns its lessons here on Earth. The body is to be cared for like a loved pet and respected; it knows its true function. To correlate this idea, imagine water in a corked bottle floating in the sea. The bottle represents the body, the water inside is the soul, and the cork is the ego, and of course, the vast sea is our true nature.

2. The young child's ability for natural knowing is to be honored, nurtured, and revered. Trust them when they share something that may sound peculiar. Be open to their words and wisdom. Validate this by teaching them that in addition to our five senses (hearing, sight, sound, touch and taste), we also possess an intuitive sense. Given to us at birth, our sixth sense allows us to have a direct line of communication with the Great Spirit. Perfect guidance and direction speaks to us about the best course to follow. We all need to teach children to listen to that perfect voice and to trust it.

3. Teach the child the value of meditation and quiet time. If only for a few minutes every morning, we can all start forming the habit of making an appointment with ourselves. In India, this is recognized and taught at an early age and becomes a part of life. Initially, the child can learn to imitate the animals, stretching and energizing the body, preparing it subtly for quiet time. Then teach them to watch their breath, imagining the breath entering the body and energizing the cells. Guided imagery is a marvelous tool to free the creative imagination. These are all beginning steps to a committed lifestyle of meditation, morning and night. Just as the securely attached boat in the harbor does not break from its anchor when a storm comes, the child will also be centered in self.

4. The grooves of attitude and beliefs are created early in life. Teach the child to think high, positive, and loving thoughts. Teach them that they can do anything supported by their heart and mind. Through the quality of the thousands and thousands of thoughts in the mind each day, children need to know they are responsible for their reality. This empowers them and encourages unlimited, expansive thinking.

5. Allow them free time to daydream, gazing into space at a cloud formation or closely at the intricate design of a tiny flower.

Daydreaming is generally unacceptable behavior in the adult world. Avoid the tendency to cram the child's day with a myriad of extracurricular activities. Like adults, children need and require time to just be, rather than do. All sorts of wonderful things can happen. Teachers have observed an expansion of vocabulary, profound writing, and greater self-confidence in students when they're given the freedom to daydream.

6. The perfection and beauty of the Universe is especially manifest in Nature. Teaching a child the Laws of Nature is relevant to personal and spiritual growth. Her mysterious ways are indeed challenging for the young child to understand and assimilate. How do the whales know when and where to migrate to birth their calves? Why are trees referred to as the lungs of the planet? What is the significance of the relationship between a bee and a flower? As a part of Nature, how do we, as holistic beings, fit into the grand scheme? The Indians have tried to teach us a deep reverence for the land and sky; they respect the Earth as our Mother, the giver of life. Children learn through imitation. Teach them the importance of a clean and pure environment in which to live and be a positive role model for this learned behavior.

7. Each one of us is a unique and special child of an abundant Universe. We all have our own journey and methods of learning the Truth. To teach a child to respect others and their process is an important lesson. When faced with trying circumstances with other individuals, a child can learn to ponder the question, "How would I feel if I were in their shoes?" Judge not is lesson number seven.

8. How to recognize, honor, and communicate emotions is of great spiritual value to the child. It is beneficial for a child to learn about anger, frustration, and sadness as emotions that are based in the personality, but also know that the soul can never be hurt or rejected. This truth can be transforming.

9. A child needs to know her true identity. She is a soul, and she has a personality. Characteristics of the soul include unconditional love, peace, bliss, truth, joy, and beauty. The soul is immortal. From the Bhagavad Gita, the Hindu Bible, "No weapon can pierce the soul, no fire can burn it, no water can moisten it, and no wind can wither it." Teach your children to know the truth about who they are. They will be empowered by it, and will learn at a young age not to fear death, knowing that the body only

417

changes its form of energy.

10. Encourage children to develop and use a strong will. It is a most admirable trait to achieve. Developing the capacity to control oneself in any situation is an art. What a beautiful world we would live in if we each could be the master of the moments in our life. When a child is exposed to this way of being, he knows not the meaning of victim. He or she only knows what it means to take full responsibility for their thoughts, words, and actions.

The list goes on.

- Teach your children at an early age to create order. Order in their outer world supports a calm and peaceful inner world.
- Ask for and respect their opinions. Let them know their opinions are valuable and deserve to be considered as an option.
- Process your impatience so your child doesn't have to be affected by it.
- Read books together that are inspiring.
- Set forth examples of character traits that you would want your child to emulate.
- Be a role model.
- Do not live your life through your child. You had your own childhood. Let your child have his or hers.
- If you don't feel like a confident parent, do what it takes to be one.

Am I Important?

A former client came into the office determined to eliminate anything that might prevent her from being the best parent she could to her adopted Chinese two-year-old daughter. The baby was abandoned, and found in the midst of cantaloupes in a vegetable market. She was taken to an orphanage–all within her first twenty-four hours of life. My client and her husband are enamored with this little girl. However, in the first years of adoption, my client had symptoms of canker sores lining both sides of her tongue. She would wake up in the middle of the night in rage, hugging the opposite edge of the bed from her husband. We explored her past. Her father held a high office in government and was rarely home and rarely had time for her. She recalled climbing underneath the constant parade of newspapers he'd hold and read, to get to his lap, only to experience him pushing her away. "What is more important in those papers than I am?" After her third attempt, she would giggle and leave the room. She could hear the rustling of the papers and the smell of the newsprint, and all they represented, as she processed this experience. Two hours into the session, she relived the pain of the inner child, feeling the feelings of being unloved, unwanted, and insignificant, which was the worst pain of all. Then reprogrammed her cells to beliefs and a life she deserves today.

The protocol works. It's quite remarkable. Her husband told her the following night at dinner that she looked different. And she felt different—even on the physical level. She felt more connected to herself, the Earth, her daughter, and her husband. She's sleeping better and when she wakes in the middle of the night, there is no panic or anxiety. "I'm happy and now reach out to my husband to touch him, rather than rolling the other way," she says. "I knew what needed to be done intellectually, but nothing happened. I just couldn't get to it. I even felt myself drifting from my beloved daughter."

The investment that my client made in this brief interlude with me cleared her of the cobwebs and sabotaging beliefs that kept her from being truly present in her life today. That night, her daughter held her mother's face in her hands, looked deep into her eyes, and repeated, "Mama. Mama." Her soul knew her Mama had finally shown up. She equates this experience to magic.

The more a parent realizes the vitally important role they play in a child's upbringing, the more attention the job will be given, thereby accepting it as a priority in life.

Paramahansa Yogananda said, "The echo in God's love is drowned out when harshness of speech, unkindness, wrath, selfishness, and distrust vibrate in the body temple." Parents should base their relationship with each child on love and fill their hearts with true unselfish love. To listen and trust their own inner guidance will produce the best instructions on how to raise the child. Then, what values to teach will always be as close as the next breath. Those critical early years will be smooth, as they'll be fueled from personal self-confidence and the flow of Infinite Intelligence—a truly brilliant partnership.

Abraham Maslow, one of the foremost spokesmen of the humanistic, or "Third-Force" psychology, was an optimist and philosopher of science. He wrote, "The ultimate disease of our time is valuelessness, and this state is more critically dangerous than ever before in our history. This state of valuelessness can be described as amorality, estrangement, rootlessness, separateness, alienation, emptiness, purposelessness, and meaninglessness. Wealth, prosperity, technological advance, widespread education, and democratic political forms have failed to produce peace, brotherhood, serenity, and happiness and have confronted us even more nakedly and unavoidably with the profundities that mankind has been avoiding by its business with the superficial."

Maslow's acclaimed "Hierarchy of Needs" chart proposed two general need systems: physiological, or "basic" needs such as safety, belongingness, and love, and "meta" needs which include cognitive, aesthetic, and at the pinnacle, Self-Actualization.

Perusing my notes from graduate school, I found a list of personality strengths of a "Self-Actualizer." The qualities of this person would be one who:

❏ depends on own resources for growth
❏ possesses spontaneity, simplicity, naturalness
❏ prefers solitude
❏ appreciates over and over again the basic goods of life with awe and wonder.
❏ is satisfied with self and others
❏ has values which are often in opposition to mainstream culture
❏ is creative
❏ has a philosophical sense of humor
❏ focuses on problems and tasks outside of self
❏ has feelings of great ecstasy, or peak experiences
❏ possesses a desire to help the human race
❏ has more profound interpersonal relationships than others
❏ is friendly, regardless of class, education, race, color, or political beliefs

The "peak experiences" Maslow refers to are described in Maslow's The Farthest Reaches of Human Nature, as a "generalization of the best moments of the human being, for the happiest moments of life, for experiences of ecstasy, rapture, bliss, of the greatest joy."

Obviously, this Self-Actualizer has to feel valued and deserving of peak experiences as well. This feeling of value, or self-worth, blossoms from the seed which is nurtured while in the womb. How do we give that to our unborn child, if we don't have it? It is our responsibility as a parent to instill this in our child.

Our little ones deserve to be told the truth of their nature. They need to hear they are loved. They need to feel cherished, valued, adored, and special. Make yourself and your loved ones at the top of your list of values, and find out what value truly means.

Reflection Time:
1. How strong are your values?
2. Which ones could possibly be swayed?
3. Are you ever tempted to abandon your values? What are the circumstances?
4. Do you experience feeling valued? If so, in what ways and by whom?
5. If not, what critical voices live on within you, like old tape recordings, making you feel less valued?
6. What loving and nurturing messages could you replace them with to achieve feeling more valued?
7. How many can you check off on the personality trails of a Self Actualizer list?
8. What would you add to the list?
9. Imagine you have just landed on a new planet. How would you set up the structure? With what values?
10. What is of value to you?

V is for feeling...Venturesome

Definition: risky, speculative, adventurous, courageous
Opposite: cautious, uncertain, apprehensive, timid

The dictionary defines "venturesome" as "inclined to venture or to take risks." "Venture," in turn, means "to brave the dangers of." When we feel venturesome, we are something of the explorer who goes where no one else has gone before. To feel venturesome includes an adventure of some sort where a risk is undertaken.

Being venturesome is both risky and tremendously gratifying; it produces growth in both instances. It encourages you to stretch, be present, and certainly observe your behavior when in new circumstances. It helps you to know yourself, and how you relate to your world. We can acquire an equivalent to college credit courses through travel by being exposed to a diversity of cultures and beliefs.

Feeling venturesome can also apply to starting a new business or embarking on a specific course of new learning we have always dreamed of, such as "How to Build a Boat." Feeling venturesome can mean stretching your usual boundaries, or "pushing the envelope," as they say. It takes courage to do what many will judge and label as "crazy," and it may require us to go beyond our self-imposed limitations,

Kayaking

I had never been kayaking before – especially not in the cold waters of the Beardsley Islands in Alaska, but what an adventure! Our adolescent children were up for anything, as we told them of our plan to spend three weeks of summer vacation exploring Alaska.

We kayaked with a guide, meandering through the waters to a group of islands where we spent the night. Campfire conversation and dinner on the beach were followed by a good night's sleep in my cozy sleeping bag. The next morning our guide gave us instructions on exactly how to leave the island before the tide came in. "We must paddle out in a specific direction in order to avoid getting caught in the current." Danielle and I were in a kayak together and got a poor start, which required us to work diligently against the tide to prevent being left behind....forever and ever and ever. She was about ten years of age at the time, but she held her own. "You can do it," I repeated as she expressed being tired from paddling against the current. Sure enough, this mother and daughter team survived a rather risky situation. Today, we recall our venture with hearty laughter and fun.

Feeling venturesome could mean being spontaneous or feeling alive inside and wanting to try new things without always having a plan or a map. Spontaneity means going with the flow and discovering what the universe has in store. It relates to synchronicity! It involves having deep trust in the process, trusting your intuition, being open to life, and being totally in the present moment.

Sherwin-William's Paints

When I was young, I would often ramble on to my mother about things I wanted to do and places I wanted to visit. I had no shortage of adventures I wanted to undertake, to the point that my mother used to say, "You can't cover the world like Sherwin-Williams paints." We've laughed about that one over the years.

If I wore the hat of a travel agent like my big sister Clara used to wear, I'm sure I would have covered this world several times by now! Clara's suitcase was out of the closet more than it was in. She and Georgia, another big sister, have traveled to the far corners of the world being venturesome.

Clara shares that, "In every part of the world I profited most by talking to the local people. I learned so much this way, about the culture and the people. When in the mountains of Nepal, or the ruins of Machu Picchu in Peru, or the plains of Africa, or the jungles of Borneo, the very old cultures have not changed. Their colorful arts and customs were striking, as well as their facial expression – especially the sparkle in their eyes. It was the worship of God that created phenomenal monuments like the Pyramids of Egypt. In China, the fear of warring neighbors, even in such a huge country, led to the building of the Great Wall. China's history soon becomes mind-boggling. When we were in Australia, the Aborigines, who live like nomads in their own country, dug up grubs and roasted them for us to sample. 'Nice and fresh,' they said as they passed the tray around. I managed to avoid their delectable offer – fresh or not. Every country, every place, whether I was in the mountains, at the oceans, or in the desert, I now remember only the best, and the uniqueness of each location. As a travel agent, I never realized I would be given such opportunities. My 'job' was not sitting at a desk recommending places for others to go. Quite the contrary – I took people with me, and we saw a world that will live in my heart, to my last breath."

Greg's Vision

Greg Mortenson, Executive Director of Central Asia Institute, had no idea how his life would change after his failed attempt to scale the summit of Pakistan's famed K2. Forced to abandon the mission by physical exhaustion, Mortenson was nursed back to health by Islamic mountain dwellers in Korphe, a remote outpost in the unforgiving terrain. To repay the villagers' kindness, he asked what he could do. He learned that one of every three infants in the region dies before reaching its first birthday. The literacy rate is less than 3%; among women, it is one-tenth of one percent. He chose to take on a mission of setting up schools for young Muslims – mainly girls – all from the basement of his home in Montana! Greg reached out to the wealthy and famous, but regrettably received only one check. So, Greg tried other venues.

He got his real start from a boy by the name of Jeffrey, at Westside Elementary school in River Falls, Wisconsin, where his mother was the principal. After hearing Greg's presentation, Jeffrey said, "I have a penny and I'd like to give it to the children for the school." His heartfelt gesture was the impetus for a campaign that raised 62,300 pennies. Jars were filled from the pennies brought in by the students during the school year. Six-hundred-twenty-three dollars goes a long way in Pakistan – enough, in fact, to buy materials to build a school.

As of January 2004, there are thirty-eight schools in Pakistan and Afghanistan that are all successful. The program director of CAI told me that Greg is a "revered figure" in the village. People drop what they are doing and walk for five days to see him. These are village people, self-sustaining from remote villages. "It's more than the project; it's about relationship and that he keeps coming back." And that he has. Greg has been coming back for ten years.

Remember Greg through his venturesome energy and Jeffrey through his pure and sincere innocence.

The person who is open to whatever emerges has the characteristics of a wise leader. From *The Tao of Leadership*, author John Heider says, "Being open and attentive is more effective than being judgmental. Perhaps the leader seems naïve and childlike in this uncritical openness to whatever emerges...but openness is simply more potent than any system of judgments ever devised."

The Family That Ventures

Attitude is crucial to raising children. It is important as a parent to share your passions with your children, as two local residents of Sun Valley have done with theirs. Melissa Boley, a colleague, has quite a history of adventuring and living a venturesome life. Her two boys, Tate, age eleven, and Trevor, age thirteen, are products of their parents' love of the outdoors. They also embrace challenge through rock climbing. Tom is the Director of Outdoor Education at the Community School in Sun Valley, Idaho. Together they decided to embark on a six-and-a-half month sabbatical around the world.

Following are some of their thoughts that may stimulate ideas for you and your family. I asked Melissa if she would advise a family to take such a trip. "We would absolutely suggest it! We decided to go around the world in order to see several countries and get a 'feel' for the different cultures. We also wanted to do adventure-based activities that would bring us together while experiencing beautiful places and people. Part of our purpose of the trip was to return to places we had hiked and climbed in the past, like the Alps, and share the majesty of those magical spots with our children. We tacked on the fall semester to their summer vacation so they wouldn't miss that much school."

"However, the main reason for the trip was because we felt our lives were already getting complicated. Between sports, school, work, and friends, our family was missing more and more time together. Due to our extensive time and experiences with Mother Nature, we know She has a way of simplifying things and bringing people together. The trip would give us a 'time out' from the normal stresses of life, and hopefully, teach the boys confidence, humbleness, and initiative. The trip started in Europe and ended in Fiji. When we stayed with a family in New Zealand, we got involved in a discussion about parenting. They asked, 'Who is in charge of your families in the U.S.?' Our response to them was our observation and opinion of how parenting has swung from autocratic to more collaborative styles, and parents are trying too hard to be friends. We feel kids are given too much power in decision-making. Both parents working has taken away active time with our kids. We don't have as much family time and that unfortunately erodes away bonds as well. The trip concluded in a most unique Christmas holiday in Bali – one that will be long remembered by each family member."

Upon returning to their home in the States, their work and school, Melissa and Tom had concern they'd lose this incredible bond they'd all created through this indelible experience. "We changed our lifestyle quite a bit and cut out several activities that were taking away from us being together," Tom said. "Wherever we could simplify things we did." The Boley family continues to travel in search of new adventures and family bonding, the most recent trip being to Peru, as Melissa and Tom have instilled a venturesome attitude in their children as well.

Paula, The Dog Goddess

To feel venturesome is not better than to not feel venturesome. There are people who haven't left their corner of the globe, their state, or their community. They don't have a desire to visit other cultures and that's okay. If that is our category, maybe we feel venturesome in other ways. We can dare to create a new recipe when guests come, sew drapes for our windows, plant a vegetable garden, or even be willing to open up a can of worms and talk about what's been on our minds for some time.

Paula is a truly beautiful person who cares for Max, our dog, when I am away on trips. He LOVES going to Doggy Day Care because he loves Paula so much, and April, Cody, Mars, Luna, Halo, Mollie, and all his other four-legged friends. I feel responsible for Max's activity and when I am at home and deeply engrossed in a project with a deadline, I don't always give him the exercise he needs and deserves. This is when I call Paula. Paula's world exists on her two splendid acres of property where her yard is designed to accommodate the many dogs she boards. She expresses her passion in her chosen work and her wisdom is profound. The following quote is an example. "Beyond traveling the globe, we've now conquered outer space and added debris and trash to the moon! It appears we're getting further and further away from ourselves." I am oh-so-grateful for Paula in my life.

I have another friend who has no desire to travel the world. His challenge is conquering his inner world. He plays the piano to earn a living in the outer world, but the true song he sings is within, as he has made meditation and Self-realization the priority in his life. His feelings of venturesome are an inward journey.

The most challenging, meaningful, and rewarding venture is truly the one inside–the exploration of inner space. Who am I? Where did I come from? What am I doing here? Where am I going? Now, that's a risk I dare you to undertake!

Reflection Time:

1. Are you living vicariously through your children?

2. Are you willing to go beyond limited thinking to embrace feeling venturesome in some area of your life?

3. Do you have the inner courage to go beyond your mind and live from your heart.

4. Is there some place you'd like to visit? Maybe there's a dreamspot you'd like to explore.

5. Is there a business you'd like to start? It could fail you know – and it could succeed.

6. Is there something you 'must' do in this lifetime?

7. What has to happen in order for you to do it?

8. Could you ever imagine yourself doing what Greg Mortensen did?

9. As a parent, do you place value on the Boley expedition?

10. Do you consider raising a family venturesome?

"Should you shield the canyons from the windstorms, you would never see the beauty of their carvings."
  Elizabeth Kubler-Ross, M.D.

V is for feeling... Vulnerable

Definition: exposed, unprotected, unguarded, defenseless
Opposite: open, trusting, reflective, nothing to protect

To feel vulnerable means being open with your feelings and expressing yourself no matter how embarrassed you may be or how challenging it may appear. Being vulnerable means stepping up to 'who' you are and sharing, even though it may feel awkward and uncomfortable. Risk-taking is involved. Being vulnerable is showing your humanness and not being afraid to express who you are–ALL of who you are. Vulnerability doesn't have to be such a bad thing if you're comfortable with yourself and willing to risk opening and sharing your deepest emotions and thoughts.

Often, I don't wear my garden gloves when I work in the garden, and invariably, I'll get poked by a raspberry plant. When dirt gets into that wound, it stings. The cut is vulnerable. So I must wash, bandage, and protect it from pain. When I open myself to express my feelings, my sadness, embarrassment, or my pain, I also feel very vulnerable. We always have the choice to share it or bury it.

Our Inner Psyches

Duality is a part of life. We don't know small unless we know large – birth/death – hot/cold – attraction/repulsion. At times we have mean, nasty thoughts and at other times, our thoughts are radiant and loving. The former would fit into the description of our "shadow." Carl Jung, author of *Man and His Symbols*, describes the shadow as the repressed or neglected part of ourselves that settle into the unconscious with unaccountable consequences. He says, "Many well-meaning people are understandably afraid of the unconscious and incidentally of psychology." We may not always be ready to see certain parts of ourselves, especially those parts that are dark, embarrassing, mean, and rude. The healing comes from being willing to embrace this part of ourselves and recognize it as a key to our sacred exploration. What darkness lies in you? Where is your passive violence based?

The shadow is the dark side that lives in the deepest part of our being, like in the *Phantom of the Opera*. Shadow slips through in our dreams and brings us messages that benefit our growth and help us understand our nature. When we look into our dreams, shadow elements can make us vulnerable because we may not like what we discover. The information may wrinkle the patina of confidence and charisma we wear as our most current mask. Dreams support us and warn us. They are also messengers of recurring patterns of behavior and unexpressed feelings. Dreams can help to correct imbalances in our life and they can speak for the unacknowledged parts of ourselves. What a gift our psyche gives us if we're prepared to receive it.

Psychotherapist Sandra Hyde conducts the dream group I participate in on Monday evenings when I'm in town and not inundated with a project. Our dream group is valuable and fun. Sandy says, "Dreams also get us in touch with our inner self, Higher Purpose, and inner counselor. Dream work is soul work – an opportunity for curiosity, creativity, and play." Many people tend to ignore their dreams for one reason or another. Either they're too hard to figure out, don't make sense, or they can only remember bits and pieces. There are so many ways of working with our dreams. We can recognize them as important messages from deep parts within us, or we can ignore them. Once again, we have choices.

One method of learning about dreams, I learned years ago in a dream class, was to write out the dream and highlight the significant words. Using free association, write down four or five words, without thinking about them, that come to mind that relate to the highlighted words. Then reread the dream using those new words. It's really fun and quite fascinating.

Ouch!

I was harboring some feelings about a dear friend, and when I had to confront myself with my truth, I felt embarrassed about my behavior; I felt vulnerable. What will she think when I open myself to her and share my heart? Once I realized the shadow had emerged, I was determined to honor and work with it, which brought me freedom from it. I was actually eager to call and express the parts of me that weren't very kind. Once I knew I was at the point of no return–sort of like going to Hawaii from the West Coast and the pilot announces, "We're now at the point of no return," I knew there was no going back for me. I felt enlivened and energetic. I noticed my reality had shifted once I chose to go forward with my honesty. It was incredible in fact. I knew those beliefs had surfaced to serve my highest self and that I would grow, expand, and vibrate at a higher frequency. We are electromagnetic forms, pure energy. We are meant to soar higher and higher, experiencing freedom in the knowing of our true nature – light, joy, love, peace, wisdom, beauty.

Don't take my word for it. Experiment on yourself. Be aware of when you feel vulnerable. Dive into it. Be brave. Be courageous and willing to risk. Dance on the edge and experience the consequences.

Superman?

My friend, Ed, had been home only a few days after hip replacement surgery when I called to inquire about his healing progress. He was aware of how long he'd lived with the pain and how it had become somewhat normal; it was so much a part of him. It wasn't until after the surgery that he realized how good he felt to be free of that old pain. It made a huge difference in his awareness; he had to become vulnerable and go through surgery in order to experience this new state.

We do similar things with emotional pain. We get so used to feeling blocked, distant, and out-of-balance, that we think it's normal. When we're willing to be vulnerable and peel through the layers of old beliefs that hold us back, then we begin to feel the levity and lightness of our being. I have the privilege to see this lightness every time I work with a client who is willing to go for it.

Sheltered

As well-intended parents, we may try to shield our children from life. It doesn't work, folks, so give it up. Children have to learn their lessons too; they are not exempt. Life isn't always fair, we can't protect them. Pain and pleasure are all part of the duality. What we can teach them is that their true nature is holistic and that they have many diverse aspects. Teach them about the law of cause and effect. Every action generates a force of energy that returns to us in the like kind. What we sow is what we reap.

Acquire the book by Dr. Deepak Chopra called *Seven Spiritual Laws for Parents*. Chopra teaches us that:

- Everything is possible
- If you want to get something, give it.
- When you make a choice, you change the future.

This is a life-skills book for any age, for any role in life. It's packed with great and helpful material. Unfortunately, many of us grew up with

430

parents who did not have the tools offered in books like Dr. Chopra's. The following case history speaks of this:

"When I came to Dr. Alexandra, I had just broken up with my boyfriend. It was evident I needed to work on some things because I couldn't justify my behavior anymore. I was over-reactive and frustrated. I would rage, only to have discovered fear beneath it. As I cleared the fear, there was joy in my life!"

"In my first session I learned that 'I was my mother.' Alexandra tested me through kinesiology. All of those attributes I could attribute to my wonderful and strong-willed mother were in me. But I didn't want to be her. I didn't want her fear or anger. I wanted to be me. I was identified with my mother and took on her attitudes and beliefs unknowingly and subconsciously and adopted them as my own. I put myself on the 'back burner,' as Alexandra said. If it sounds a little weird, I felt that way too, but I knew it was so. I was not living my life fully. I would actually feel like her when she lashed out in anger and frustration. I questioned a lot of my spontaneous behavior. I could trace my behavior to unwanted patterns. I had always said I didn't want to be like my mother. The resistance created an attachment and manifested those same qualities. Absolutely amazing to me!"

"I couldn't talk about my vulnerability without attacking. For example: if I felt slighted or unappreciated, I'd usually be passive aggressive and it would come out with hostility. I couldn't express myself without hurting and blaming. My mother taught me how to use the power of words to intimidate and overwhelm others by using volume and choice of words, and how you look when you say them. It all came from fear. I was taught by example. I remember when I was in the sixth grade after I had really laid into a boy who had hurt my feelings. I ripped into him and could see how he cringed. I remember making a promise to myself that I'd never do that again. I was a good student, and my mother was a good teacher. I had no other tools and that is how I dealt with things. I saw people who were assertive without being aggressive, but apparently, it was so unconscious, I couldn't be that way. I didn't know how to do that behavior."

"I found myself unhappy and without the kind of intimate relationship I wanted. Following the first session, I started feeling better immediately. Initially the anger went. There were fewer knee-jerk reactions. I became more conscious and could see I had choices in stressful situations. Later on I was able to deal with the underlying fear that gave rise to the anger as we identified the different belief systems."

"When there is no need to blame others, the victim identity falls away.

431

You have to blame someone to be a victim. Taking responsibility for what I create in my life and my relationships is the place of power and freedom. You can't have freedom if you feel others are affecting your life and your joy. No more will I give my power away."

"I did realize in the middle of the session, I'd been expecting my partner to know how I felt without speaking my heart and my truth. Of course that never works. The biggest shift after letting go of major fears was then being able to be in touch with my true heart and to be able to express it without blame. To own my truth. This was huge."

"That is what has set me free. Being able to trust my feelings and express them without anger and fear. Instead of being reactive with negative behavior I'd use offensively, I am able now to let myself know what it is, trust myself, and express my feelings appropriately."

"My relationships work. I have tremendous harmony in all of them. Walls have come down, and I can now feel present with people. My work as an acupuncturist has deepened. I share with my clients an intimacy that was never there before. This past birthday was the best one I've ever had because I am free and happy. I'm happy from within myself – that's what makes the difference."

"I can communicate clearly and know my feelings while honoring others and their feelings. I was aware my behavior was ruining my life and relationships, but there was so much unconsciousness that caused these outbursts. The defensive and offensive behavior would happen so fast, I just couldn't control it."

"I had an unconscious belief system, but once I uncovered and neutralized these old beliefs, I made better choices. I can now say 'I am so angry,' and I don't have to lash out anymore. If I do, it's brief, I catch myself, and it's not dramatized. In the past, I was unaware of the power of my behavior and my words. I was only aware of my pain."

"Everyday I speak with the intention of respecting others feelings and my own. I empower, rather then dis-empower. What a difference this has made to every moment! There is such joy in empowering people. Thank you, my friend. I will send every patient to you who is willing to face his or her pain and be vulnerable because I know they will benefit from working with you and your healing energy."

When others share deeply with me, being vulnerable and intimately opening their hearts, I feel profoundly connected with them. I have more compassion. My mission is to convey understanding and support for their awareness and a commitment to integrity and truth. I feel endeared toward my clients and others who share with me. I deeply respect people for being real.

We can't protect ourselves from everything. Well, I guess we can. I guess it all depends on the results we want. I'm committed to growth, introspection, and expansion, and will do whatever it takes to know myself. How about you?

Drugged

There is another way to view "vulnerable," and that's when we have to play the role of protector for those who are vulnerable. Again, I'm speaking of children here.

"Just say No" isn't working. ALERT magazine, Fall 2003 writes, "According to a national household survey conducted by The Substance Abuse and Mental Health Services Administration, of the eleven million people estimated to have used prescription drugs non-medically in 2001, nearly half were younger than twenty-five. According to the survey, nearly three million adolescents age twelve to seventeen used prescriptions drugs for recreational purposes or other non-medical reasons at least once..." Why are so many people numbing themselves? The most significant aspect of drug abuse is the lack of awareness that goes along with it. Teens are popping pills without knowing what it is or where it came from. OxyContin is a painkiller that, when abused, can be lethal. Kids aren't educated on this kind of thing. A strong message about a crucial topic. Educate yourself.

Gender speaking, boys are losing ground academically. Instead of pursuing sound solutions, many educators advocate prescribing more attention-focusing Ritalin for the boys, who receive the drug four to eight times the rate of girls. Boys and girls learn differently. Education researchers need to explore more effective strategies for teaching boys. Let's educate instead of medicate. Today's education system fails many of our young boys.

There are alternatives to Ritalin. Flax oil, for example, helps to boost children's IQ, as well as improves behavior. The oil is extracted from a small seed that contains the rich Omega-3 and six fatty acids, which have been credited to reduce the risk of asthma and protect against ADHD. This material is taken from a newsletter entitled "Essential Foods for Life," sent out as supportive documentation from Barlean's Organic Oils, and it is an option to Ritalin worth looking into.

Say Good Bye to ADD and ADHA by Dr. Devi S. Nambudripad, D.C. might be fascinating reading material for anyone associated with this malady. "There is now ongoing research on allergens crossing the blood brain barrier and thus causing the symptoms of ADD/ADHA," says Mary Crouch, co-founder of Health Dynamics with regard to her quest for

433

Ritalin alternatives.

Homeopathy is safe, natural, and lacks the side effects of conventional medicine, treating the whole person. Francine Kanter, CCH, a homeopath in Hawaii, discussed this topic in "Inspiration: A Journal for the Mind, Body and Spirit" in the October 2003 issue. She says, "ADHD children are calmer, have more friends, sleep better, have less anxiety, and feel better about themselves. All this without taking Ritalin." She adds that, "Not only do learning and behavioral problems improve, so do most or all of the other physical, mental, and emotional complaints." Again, another option, folks.

I, for one, am concerned about the vulnerability of children. It is our duty as parents and adults to protect them and speak out for them when need be. I am incensed by how freely medication is given to children. Medication is often given as a Band-aid to the so-called symptoms, and the cause never really gets attention through caring investigation. In the year 2000, public concern was voiced about the numbers of children being given drugs like Ritalin, Prozac, and other psychotropic drugs. According to a study reported in the Journal of American Medical Association, approximately one percent of children aged two to four are using Ritalin or Ritalin-like drugs. At the time of the study, the FDA had not approved the use of these drugs in children under age six! Is this protecting our children? How do we know the effects these drugs may have on them later in life?

Dr. Peter R. Breggin is on a mission to save children. He wrote books entitled *Talking Back to Prozac* and *Talking Back to Ritalin*. He states that we are a society of adults at risk of hurting our children. As we identify ourselves as the problem, it is more likely that we can find ways to eliminate the problem. Ignorant parents and dysfunctional families as well as impatient doctors and well-meaning but harmful teachers are all part of this equation. He recommends "time-in" instead of "time-out." "Whenever a child misbehaves, he or she is subject to time-in with an adult at the school, discussing the problem from every angle, lasting until a mutually-agreed-upon solution is determined." Dr. Breggin, I am climbing on your bandwagon! ("Making a Difference" Newsletter, Vol.2, Issue 8, March 2001)

So find the line on the "vulnerable scale" that you'd like to be on, and that you'd like to put your children on. Protect them without smothering them. Tell the truth and be willing to hear it. Learn from vulnerability rather than pushing it aside as "feeling weak." Within every vulnerable moment is a gift waiting to be opened.

Reflection Time:

1. Is there some form of protection shielding you?

2. Are you willing to be vulnerable in order to experience the best this life has to offer?

3. If there is more weight on your body than you'd prefer, I invite you to ask yourself what you are protecting.

4. Each negative self-concept must be dealt with. What negative self-talk keeps you held back?

5. I feel weak or vulnerable when _____. Complete that sentence as many times as you like, focusing on the states of body and mind.

6. When is the last time you did service work? What were the results?

7. Take baby steps in experimenting with feeling vulnerable. Take risks, put yourself out there, and trust. Did you survive?

8. What is the single most important lesson you learned about yourself from this experiment?

9. Strengthen that aspect of yourself. Acknowledge your inner vigor. Live your life coming from this core place of potentiality, possibilities, and purpose.

10. Observe the process, the next time you have an open cut or wound.

> *"I live with the memory and the spirit of my son and his death each day, and each day I wake up surprised, once again, that this is now the path I walk. I do not dwell in dark, shadowed corners. I have learned from him that my secrets can kill me."*
> **Judy Collins,** *Sanity & Grace*

W is for feeling... Wise

Definition: intelligent, judicious, insightful, reasonable
Opposite: foolish, ignorant, dumb

Imagine this. Within you, within me, and within us all, are deep, rich wells of wisdom. Sure, words of wisdom can be given to us in the form of advice, but to be truly wise, we must tap into our truest of selves, into our wells. Only then, can wisdom really burst forth.

How do we tap into this intuitive wisdom? If the full moon is reflecting on a lake stirred with ripples and waves, the reflection will be distorted. However, when the lake is calm, there is a perfect reflection of the moon. When our minds are calm, we will receive infinite wisdom of our truth.

Through that inner voice, we can arrive at the wisdom that we are not our mind, our body, our job, our car, our bank account, or our relationship. When any one of those fail, we may then choose to shift our perspective so those outer accoutrements, which are content in our lives, will only be the context around our lives.

Another memorable one-liner from my rich files suggests we become the "fruit bowl of life rather than the fruit." In other words, we're bigger than the stuff that happens in our lives. The events are all merely situations. Through our intuition we learn the wisdom within us is the place of good, lasting, quality happiness. Happiness cannot be found in the world with its temporary and sensory pleasures. There is nothing wrong with pleasure if you realize that it is part of duality and the other side of it is pain. We look into our reality and believe it's all so real. After all, it's solid, or so it appears to our senses.

Let's go back again to attitude. How true are you to yourself? How true are you to your beliefs and values? Do you speak and live your inner truth? For example, you may be stuck in a job that causes illness, inner turmoil, and breakdown of your family, yet you may continue punching the time clock due to fear of the unknown. What will I have if I don't have this? Be still, seek solitude, turn the searchlight inward. Inside, in your hidden chamber, you will find the strength and wisdom to pursue your calling.

To the Teepee

Our Native American brothers and sisters demonstrated their wisdom by sending their misbehaved children to spend time in the grandparent's teepee to benefit from the wisdom of their years. There were no old age homes for these Native Americans; the wisdom of the elders was respected.

That reminds me of a story my father used to tell when we were kids. One day the wife spoke to her husband and said, "I think it's time your aged father should go out and live in the shed." Her husband questioned her, yet reluctantly approached his father and said, "Dad, you're getting old, and we both feel it's time for you to go live in the shed." As they both walked out the door, the son grabbed a blanket, then handed it to his father at the entrance to the shed. "Here, Dad, is a blanket to keep you warm." The father replied, "Son, you keep it. You'll need it when your son brings you here."

This story is a demonstration of ignorance in lieu of wisdom. No doubt, similar stories are taking place everyday. Our elderly are regularly being sent off to the "shed."

A friend of mine, attended the Science and Consciousness Conference where Gregg Braden, scientist and author, spoke. She shared her tapes from the conference with me, and we all benefited from them. The subject was "Living As If Earth Is Our Home, And People Are Our Family." Gregg Braden tells us, "Our chain of knowledge, the lineage of wisdom, that links us with our past has been broken on a number of occasions. We know that information was lost because we are beginning to find it again. Now that we're finding it, what does it say to us?"

He goes on to say, "There are universal themes that we find in these ancient texts. One of the themes says that humankind, our species, is unique in the universe. There is something about us that doesn't exist anywhere else. Through our uniqueness, we are given the power of life, peace, death, and healing both in the present and in the future perhaps in ways that we are only beginning to understand. They say that power comes to us through ancient secrets."

Gregg leads groups to sacred sites around the globe and delves into the wisdom of those who have preceded us. "Almost universally the ancient, indigenous people, the shamanic traditions, in those monasteries, in the old temples, in the old text, are all saying that somehow you and

I are all related to our world and what we become and hear is mirrored back in the world around us." As quantum physics emerged in the nineties, the Western world started to take notice that maybe we're all saying the same thing. The suggestion that "we are bathed in the field of intelligent energy and that this field is described as being everywhere all the time. Not out there somewhere – it is here right now. We're part of it; it is the stuff that fills the nothing. It's in between every atom, in between you and me and in between every cell of our bodies. It's been here from the moment; from the beginning of time." Gregg Braden is making an enormous contribution to our awareness.

The Wise Yogi

Yoga has been around a long time but has only recently came to the West with such acceptance and participation. Yoga classes are now in demand, with teacher trainings gaining tremendous popularity. Yoga appears to be offering a large percentage of the population what they are searching for, a form of exercise while aspiring to a peaceful inner world. People desire a more peaceful inner world and are searching for ways to accomplish it. As each one of us makes this a priority, mass consciousness benefits.

I've had the blessing to know and study with Ryan Redman, a wise twenty-five-year-old yoga teacher who follows his heart as he shares his path with his students. I asked Ryan to share some ideas about yoga, wisdom, and the practice. This is what he had to say:

"It is interesting to look at the practice of yoga itself and how it has been accepted in our country. There is more attention on the 'asanas,' or 'postures.' That part of it is indeed valuable as we are an action-oriented culture."

"Underlying the container of asana, is being in 'union,' which is the meaning of 'yoga' – in harmony with ourselves – with life. This deeper level of yoga can help us resolve conflicts, as well as observe how we act and what to act. Once we start to be at peace with our choices, the practice then becomes a clear reflection of our state of consciousness – like clear water. I may be pushing myself to go beyond my limits, and bend further to touch my toes, because that is what the person next to me is doing. I can see this action as a kind of disease within myself, of not being content with where I am comfortable in my stretch, or I can step back in one moment, not push further, and in doing so, can change the whole pattern of the day. Through the practice of yoga, we can re-sculpt our patterns and habits to truly reflect who we really are."

"There are different paths you can take in yoga and in your life.

438

One would be the path of 'citta,' which is 'the individual sprouted consciousness' and how we create a direct relationship with the external world. For most, this is done by gratifying the senses, and being driven by sensual gratification. It is the motion of moving outward. Many associate with this path and do so because it is right for them."

"When we still the citta, we find "cit" – the unaltered witness or observer of consciousness – which is more reflective of our inner being. Its purpose is to connect with the soul (atma), where there is no sensory gratification, and the senses and mind are still, giving us access into our own wisdom. This experience is feeling-oriented or heart-oriented, rather than something in which you talk about. It is circular rather then linear. It is self-fulfilling, and its purpose is to align with the higher self, where all wisdom is found."

"Following one path is not better then the other. It is unfair to judge another's path because it is their path, and they are following their truth. Just be compassionate and observe yourself. We are all divine in our own respect and we must trust that everything is perfect the way it is supposed to be, for each of us, to attain what we need to further our evolution."

"If you can look at the universe with a sense of acceptance and imagine that everything is food for you – there for you to digest – you get exactly what you need, when you need it. It may not feel like it at the time, but the more and more you hold this attitude the easier life becomes – less struggle, less frustration."

"I've noticed in my classes that at first people do the practice, then gradually, they start to be the practice. They become more present, aware, and accepting. It's quite inspiring to observe. They become more trusting of life and less controlling of how everything must go. They feel more content and live their life with greater serenity."

"One of my first teachers told me it wouldn't come from the outside, and that 'everything you need to know is already there inside of you.' Stay in observation of yourself and everything will be revealed to you. As spoken by one of the ancient yogis – reaching for a flower is more difficult than enlightenment because you have to reach out for the flower, while enlightenment is already within you."

Ryan is such a wise soul, and I absolutely treasure the yoga experience I have with him. He is one of the many blessings in my life that I am grateful for every day. "Inhale and expand. Expand and ground. Inhale the warmth of the sun. Exhale the coolness of the moon. Our life is a lot like a Hollywood movie set. It seems too real. When you walk behind that set, it's not what you thought was on the surface." Although he is in

439

India now, at the time of this printing, I can hear his profound words and loving message in my heart.

Across from Ryan's yoga studio was a market called Paul's. It was being torn down to be replaced by a series of businesses. Ryan told us that Paul's had been there since he was a kid. "There it is, the Law of Impermanence, being shown to us as the bulldozers take away a part of my childhood memories." Nothing is permanent.

Ryan continues: "'Ahimsa' means 'non-violence.'" In the practice of yoga, we can empower ourselves by applying non-violence to self and by being kind and compassionate to self. Use the practice as a mirror – am I being non-violent to myself? If we create violence on the mat, we take it outside through our thoughts, words, and action. 'I'm really bad at this pose. Look at _____. She can do it so much better than I can. I've been doing it longer than she has.' This is creating violence to the self."

"Some poses are quite beautiful, like the tree, for example. It reflects balance and concentration, while peacock and eagle develop resilience. Stay mindful when you see change coming in your life. Build poise and don't collapse into the world. Acceptance softens the tissue. Awareness expands it."

"To have a good attitude, it is so important to open your heart each day and feel what is already there. As we move closer to the experience of the heart, we can feel our way into our inner wisdom, which can help us preserve a positive attitude in our daily lives."

I noticed during my practice that when I look to observe how another is working with an asana, my attention is not on my own breath and process, but is outside of myself. I return to being centered and work on myself, observing my acceptance, at times only being able to stretch so far in a pose, as well as other times when I'm feeling more flexible and supple. Can you understand how practicing yoga does not conclude when class is over? It can be applied to every moment of life.

One suggestion Ryan offers us is to close our eyes while we are standing, and imagine ourselves on top of a flagpole, 200 feet about the ground. On this flagpole, we have heightened awareness, we feel secure, even if we sway a bit, finding our balance.

Legislative Yogis?

If only our legislative sessions would start with a brief yoga class. How about it Ryan? Legislators have demanded that educators pump our children full of as much of the three R's (reading, "'riting," and "'rithmetic") as humanly possible within a certain amount of time. Authorities, in an

440

attempt to prepare children for life, often ignore the wisdom of some of our great thinkers. For example, Ralph Waldo Emerson's quote, "It's not what's outside of us, it's what's within us that matters." Do we teach our children that they have the power to rely on their inner world to achieve true wisdom? Must we learn through our own experience or can we benefit and grow through the experience of others? Do we teach our children that there is a valuable voice within them called their intuition? That sixth sense, our intuition, can guide us to making wise choices.

I have a formula to support you in making wise choices. Here is the example:

My attitude: I'm irritated because there is a lack of customer service.

My belief: There is never anyone to help me.

My choices: Lash out, be rude and make the other person wrong.

OR

Get frustrated and leave without my product.

OR

Recognize my irritation for what it is; breathe, feel it, let go, and take responsibility for my reality. Be kind while expressing myself.

You can apply this with any life situation. Remembering it's just a situation—it's neutral. Take the time to go inward and evaluate the moment. Will you be consumed by this incident, or will you own and honor it, as part of your reality? Your choice – pleasure or pain?

I was given a most unusual business card by David R. Mead. In lieu of the typical business details, it read, "Surveyor of sunrises/sunsets, clouds and storms; Inspector of untamed paths, ridge tops, and meadows; Sharer in the passing parade." What wise words! What part are you playing in the "passing parade"? Will it be a positive influence on the spectators and the fellow participants? And how does this part affect you?

Reflection Time:

1. Consider doing a vision quest.
2. Consider participating in a sweat lodge.
3. Consider learning a meditation technique.
4. Consider being aware of your intuitive voice on a daily basis.
5. Consider taking a yoga class.
6. Consider exploring your intuition, imagination, and creativity. Make sense out of the messages from your higher self. Value and be true to the voices of wisdom within you.
7. Consider communicating with intention? Do you know what that would look like?
8. Consider pondering the expression, "wise beyond her or his years."
9. Consider if you would describe your parents as wise?
10. Consider knowing the source of your wisdom?

"There is fire in water. There is an invisible flame, hidden in water that creates not heat but life. And in this bewildering age, no matter how dark or glib some humans work to make it, wild salmon still climb rivers and mountain ranges in absolute earnest, solely to make contact with that flame.

David James Duncan, *"A Prayer for the Salmon's Second Coming"* from *My Story as Told by Water*

W is for Feeling ... Wondrous

Definition: miraculous, extraordinary, astounding
Opposite: bored, complacent, jaded, dull

The sun sinking in the Pacific was always a wondrous sight to me. I always thought it was absolutely miraculous, and maybe even equal to the first rays of sunlight on the Sawtooth Mountains. The miracle of seeing a lunar eclipse, which emphasizes the brilliance of light emanating from a full moon, is astounding. Nature provides extraordinary entertainment for us every moment of life. Just think of the awesome exchange of oxygen to carbon dioxide in our bodies.

The Wondrous Order in Life

There is an infinite organizing power in Nature that operates on precise timing. We are part of this wondrous truth. I recall a time when I had garbanzo beans boiling on the stove. Because of the intense heat, a scum appeared on the top of the water. I walked away for a moment and when I returned there was a definite pattern to the scum similar to a snowflake. This was such a wondrous experience that I called our daughter, Danielle, to tell her of this awareness. There is order in chaos.

We would often take our kids down to the beach when the tide was low to explore nature. I liked the wondrous lesson I learned from the anemones. When I touched them in their vulnerable state, they would instantly close up, demonstrating to me a behavior so familiar with so many people, at times when we're feeling guarded or self-protective. It also reminded me how we can react with a knee-jerk reaction, like the anemone does, in lieu of responding from the heart. We are the human species and have choice. Unlike the anemones, we can choose our responses.

A relationship can be wondrous. Richard Bach, author of *Bridge*

Across Forever, describes "A soul mate is someone who has locks that fit our keys and keys to fit our locks. When we feel safe enough to open the locks, our truest selves step out and we can be completely and honestly who we are with that one person... we are safe in our own paradise...our soul mate is the one who makes life come to life."

It is wondrous to me that at six weeks a fetus is half-inch long, at eight weeks its joints are formed, at ten weeks, it is two inches long, at fourteen weeks, it sucks its thumb, and at sixteen weeks, it turns fully formed. An acquaintance of mine, a pediatrician, delivered his granddaughter. It was a deeply sacred experience when they looked in each other's eyes, (the first ones to see in the physical realm) as he truly acknowledged that they knew each other.

One of the late Erma Bombeck's quips about living life over, fits perfectly for feeling wondrous. "Instead of wishing away nine months of pregnancy, I'd have cherished every moment, realizing that the wonderment growing inside of me was the only chance in life to assist God in a miracle." Whew! Takes my breath away.

Salmon

The spawning of the salmon is a most wondrous event. Anadromous fish are ones that return to fresh water from the ocean to lay their eggs. They travel in hardship and risk to reach their spawning grounds relentlessly day and night, without stopping to rest or eat. There intention is set to reach the shallow riffles where they were born to commit their eggs and sperm. They tirelessly fight upstream currents for more than 800 miles, climb to an elevation of 6,000 feet above sea level, and arrive exhausted. When nests (redds) are created by the female; she lays her eggs, then the male fertilizes them. Their life is over at this point. In the winter, the eggs hatch and during their first year of growth, tens of thousands of "fry" leave their birthplace for the sea. At this stage they are called "smolt." If this isn't wondrous, I don't know what is. How all this happens so orderly and so predictably is a mystery. And, what have humans done with our brilliance and free will? We've built dams that prevent this sacred journey. Total ignorance!

I continue to trust the process. I trust the fish who come back upstream to their birthplace will be the ones who survive the dams and man's interference. They will be the perfect ones to survive, while the ones that didn't make it, didn't make it for a reason. It doesn't mean that we don't continue to protest those disastrous, cement, manmade obstacles. We must if we believe they should come down! We do the work and make our protest known, stand up for our beliefs, AND we trust the process, letting go of the way we think it should look like. We can learn to protest from a most positive approach. For example: "I'm protesting against the Snake River Dams" (old approach) to "I'm in favor of freedom for the salmon to return to their birthplace." Another example, but different category of protest: rather than protesting domestic violence, be in support of families living in harmony. We could shift from protesting war to favoring peace. Get the idea? One view is filled with vengeance and the other is coming from the heart. This new approach is a more wondrous way in which to live life.

Julia "Butterfly" Hill is a wondrous human being who has dedicated her life to preserving our wondrous planet. She climbed into a Redwood tree named Luna and did not set foot on the ground for two entire years in an attempt to save it and other old growth trees from being cut down. Her passion for the Redwood trees and Mother Nature at large is such an inspiration. Her book, entitled The Legacy of Luna, was written while in the tree and documents the experience.

If we could all see the wonders of the world the entire universe would benefit. So, recapture your wonder if you may have lost it. Climb a tree, as Julia did, and see the world from a more wondrous point of view.

Reflection Time:

1. Examine your life and be frank with yourself. Is your reality one of astonishment and awe or gloom and despair?
2. Make a point of finding something wondrous each day.
3. Where are you missing the mark to view life as wondrous?
4. If you could write a prescription for yourself to experience a wondrous moment, what would it be?
5. Do you find the digestive process wondrous?
6. At what point did you realize you were taking life and maybe people for granted?
7. Can you let go of control long enough to experience the wondrous experience of a moment?
8. Suggestion: Start a group called "The Wondrous Ones," meeting regularly to share your miracles.
9. Do others tend to live more wondrous lives than you? Why do you suppose?
10. Take a moment to focus on anything. Imagine what your eyes have just done upon your command.

"The rays of the sun are many through refraction. But they have the same source. I cannot, therefore, detach myself from the wickedest soul (nor may I be denied identity with the most virtuous)."

Gandhi

W is for feeling...Worried

Definition: anxiety-ridden, upset, distressed, fearful
Opposite: trusting, content, settled, peaceful

Have you ever heard the saying, "Worrying is like a rocking chair. It gives you something to do, but it doesn't get you anywhere." Feeling worried means feeling uneasy or troubled about someone or some situation. When we feel worried, we feel out of control, burdened, and fearful.

Our puppy occasionally demonstrated some unacceptable behavior when he cruised our old neighborhood with his Dalmatian friend. They would be gone for several hours at a time. I worried even though I believed he was protected and would return. I proceeded with my work, but there was an underlying concern about Max while I wondered where he was.

Wisdom reveals that most of what we worry about never manifests. What a waste of time and energy worrying is! Worrying can keep us stuck and prevent us from growing or moving on. We cannot be totally present. We're definitely not being in the flow. There are some people who worry about everything, and I do mean everything. Those folks use worry almost as an addiction. This can cause a lot of stress and disease. Do you have anyone in mind?

I once tried to thread a needle when I was worried and upset about something. I had no success whatsoever. I couldn't concentrate on the job at hand, and because concentration is such a powerful tool, mine went to my worry. Try it the next time you're worried, angry, or fearful.

So if you want more worry in your life, then worry. If you want to experience a life filled with trust, then be trusting.

Children often feel worried, but have not been exposed to the word to describe their feelings, so they act out for attention to camouflage their unidentified worry. "Most people are as clueless about why they have certain feelings as they are about how their lungs work," quotes Dr.

Wayne Drevels of the National Institute of Mental Health.

One young client's distress was as innocent as, "Are we going to leave on our vacation Friday morning or Monday morning?" She wasn't aware of the feeling of worry until I suggested it to her. Once she heard it and its definition, she recognized that she indeed had worry, concern, and questions about her vacation plans. She wanted to be included in knowing the arrangements.

Many of us lack a "feelings vocabulary" – parents, teachers, surgeons, welfare recipients, pilots, lifeguards, drillers, anyone who hasn't been raised with a vocabulary for his or her feelings most likely relate to feelings as a foreign language.. Many people need to be taught the skills to communicate. Once worry is identified as a feeling, we can choose whether to worry or not.

Worry creates anxiety, and both have the same symptoms as fear. Anxiety lingers, often associated with panic attacks, and even depression. Prolonged worry creates stress in the body, mind and spirit.

My son-in-law Michael, started a business he felt confident would succeed, prior to proposing to our daughter, Danielle. The first year of marriage was a definite challenge for both Michael and Danielle. He was feeling determined to make this business work and provide an income, as he had been raised to believe it was his responsibility. However, life showed him something different and it didn't turn out according to his plans. Worry, effort, struggle, frustration, despair, were all words he felt and knew oh-too-well. His business was eventually dissolved. You've no doubt heard that old proverb, "One door closes and another opens." Today, Michael has his Emergency Medical Training credential under his belt. While working in a hospital setting, he passed, with flying colors, the tests to qualify as a Certified Nurses Assistant, and now the next step, nursing school. From driller to nurse. Who says we can't change careers? It's so inspiring to see what a natural he is in the helping profession. He's a deeply sensitive, compassionate man and a grand addition to our family.

Flawless?

In a *Self-Realization* article (Summer 2001), entitled "Flawless", Dr. Lewis Tariaglia, says the ten most common flaws are:

- Addicted to being right
- Raging indignation
- Blame
- Worry and fear

- Intolerance
- Poor me
- Self-regard (me, me, me)
- Excuse for everything
- Fault-finders
- Chronic dishonesty

He then gives suggestions on what to do about them:

- Surrender – a mark of greatness
- Honesty – a mark of realism
- Forgiveness
- Humility
- Confidence
- Faith
- Peacefulness
- Wisdom
- Self-service
- Love

People tend to be self-absorbed. Someone may be gabbing on and on about him or herself, not letting you get a word in. Me, me, me, me, me. They pause and then say, "Enough about me. Now tell me what you think of me."

Dr. Tariaglia's book is another that can transform your life. I share the universal wisdom I heard so much as a child from my father: "You can take a horse to water, but you can't make him drink." There are thousands of self-help books on the shelves, maybe more. It's what you do with what you read that makes the difference.

One client discovered she had the belief that the more you worry about someone, the more you love them. I believe sometimes people carry guilt, fear, or worry with them, because it was passed down through the generations. This client happens to have been raised in the Jewish faith. The Jewish people were persecuted for their identity. They were made to feel wrong simply because they were born into the Jewish faith. If this is not understood on a conscious level, it can be passed on from generation to generation. In other words, my client was driven by the belief that she must worry, simply because she is Jewish. Worry and love are not the same thing. We don't have to do anything to love or be loved.

Worry Plus

Worry can manifest in panic disorders or unexpected attacks of acute anxiety that reoccur periodically, OCD - obsessive-compulsive disorders, or PTSD - post-traumatic stress disorder, which is mentally reliving a traumatic event. These disorders demonstrate beliefs such as:

- "I'm too tall."
- "I'm too short."
- "I can't leave the house until I check the burners on the stove."
- "I never walk on a street that has no sidewalks."
- "People always stare at me."
- "I'll be hurt again if I go on a horse."
- "People who say they're my friends will betray me."
- "I'll never trust anyone to care for my animal."

Money Worry

All anxiety, stress, and worries are based in fear. We have worry when life is not going the way we want it to. We also have worry when life IS going the way we want it to. Financial stress is an enormous source of worry in people's lives. I once heard money referred to as "pictures of dead presidents on paper bark." Money is also a series of beeps. For example, when I transfer money from one account to another, I simply press the appropriate numbers on the keypad–those become a series of beeps.

We can teach children to worry about money, or by example, we can pass along wisdom about how they can manage their money. The Credit Union National Association, (CUNA) says, "Pre-school is not too early to teach children about handling money." CUNA says, "Teens spend more than eighty billion dollars a year, yet fewer than half know the basics about credit, checking, savings accounts, or auto insurance." You could start this education with a piggy bank and advance to a weekly allowance.

If we worry about what we are eating, our children will worry about what they eat. If we worry about not having enough, our children will learn scarcity. We set the pace and those young ones simply pick it us.

Many people have felt worried about the loss of their money when the stock market took a dive in 2002. I know of an individual who lost her retirement money. Was she worried? No, because she chose to have a perspective about the experience that was healthy to her peace of mind.

It's so important to know how your partner feels about money before a serious relationship forms. Money attitudes are products of their environment. Suze Orman, financial guru and author of *The Road to Wealth*, says, "Talk openly about your respective attitudes towards spending, debt, and savings...ask each other ...about how well you share, how much you intend to spend, and on how much you save, how much you invest, and what your long term financial goals are." She continues to say, "If you don't start thinking and talking about these issues now, they are likely to become more complicated and difficult to discuss as time goes on. Your relationship will be stronger for having talked through some of your similarities, differences, and concerns." That is wise advice from an expert on the subject.

Help! A few solutions to the worry habit are:

- Notice your thinking and how much time you spend in the present moment;

- Observe your breathing – is it shallow or deep? Examine beliefs around that issue;

- Develop options for alternative perspectives. Why did you choose what you have chosen?

Why spend time in worry mode when we have other choices? It is a choice to worry. It dampens our spirit and outlook on life. It can be the impetus for positive change, if we know we are in charge of our thoughts. Yes, it can be challenging, but that is part of life. Going forward, acquiring necessary information, asking for support, and taking action. You can do it.

Reflection Time:

1. Worry exercise: Find something that you worry about. Now really worry about it. Worry about it even more. Intend to worry about it. Feel it in your body. Worry about it like you've never worried about it before. Feel it even more deeply. Let pictures surface about the worry. Feel a color associated with the feeling of worry. Feel shapes, or anything else associated with the feeling of worry. Now, really feel it. Keep allowing and intending yourself to feel worried. It will disappear if it hasn't already.

2. Where there is worry, there is a struggle for control. What are you trying to control?

3. Complete this sentence: I struggle to be in control because _____.

4. Exercise: Practice several deep breaths, being aware of the in and out flow. Choose a relationship that is challenging. Be aware of the nature of it. Now, write down how you are currently responding to it. Think about it. Feel it.

5. Now make a list of all the possibilities there are in each category. Next, simply review the list and choose the ones that will serve you the best. Be empowered.

6. Did you have a parent who was a worrier? If so, what did you learn about life because of your exposure to this behavior?

7. What percentage of the time do you think about the past? The future?

8. Did you ever worry that you'd be left?

9. What does worrying do for you? Serve you?

10. Do you have friends who are worriers? What could you do to assist them with a new perspective?

451

"Ninety-five percent of the beliefs we've stored in our mind are nothing but lies we suffer, because we believe these lies."
don Miguel Ruiz, *The Four Agreements*

X is for feeling... Xenophobic

Definition: fearful of what is foreign

Opposite: gregarious, outgoing, friendly, trusting

It's not easy coming up with a feeling word that starts with "X" but I found one! The classical definition of a phobic disorder is an "irrational, persistent fear of a person, or some particular activity or situation." The American Psychiatric Association subdivides phobic disorders into:

Agoraphobia - fear and avoidance of open spaces

Social phobia - fear of and avoidance of ridicule

Simple phobia - fear of and avoidance of simple objects

There are also life cycle phobias: completing school, growing old, getting married, puberty, dating/divorce, raising children, or losing children. The Stress Management Center/Phobia Institute was started by Dr. Donald Dossey to treat these disorders. He defines phobia as "Any behavior or feeling that is unacceptable and uncomfortable which results in the past or projected pictures of the future."

The Phobia Institute says that the seven steps to mastering stress and phobias are:

1. Controlling your mind
2. Controlling your feelings
3. Controlling your actions
4. Relaxation techniques
5. Physical activity for fun
6. Power foods and stress-diminishing supplements
7. Predictable communication strategies to decrease tension.

Fears or phobias are addictions that control one's mind and feelings. The following is a partial list of current fears and phobias:

- Technophobia - technology or computers, breakdown/ making mistakes/breaking machines
- Phobophobia - fear

- Kakorraphiaphobia - failure
- Halophobia - speaking
- Arachibutyrophobia - peanut butter sticking to the roof of mouth
- Giraffeophobia - fear of sticking your neck out

As you can see, they've come up with a word for just about any kind of fear! Isn't it amazing what a human being can be afraid of? Although some of you may get a chuckle from one or two of the above examples, these fears are very real to some.

A solution to these fears and all fears would be to learn to control the mind, body, and actions. We can learn to live more in the present moment rather than in reflection about the past or projection into the future. A way to process the fear is to feel the event that triggered the fear (NPR protocol) along with the resisted emotions associated with it.

However, in this section, I'm going to focus on a very particular phobia: xenophobia. Feeling xenophobic is the fear of what is foreign or fear of a stranger. It seems to me that we live in a society that separates us from others, whether it be cooped up in our cars day to day, or in our houses with their gates and locks and more gates. I recall from the classic Greek text, The Odyssey, the importance of welcoming strangers, and/or foreigners into one's home, a ritual my Aunt Alexandra followed in her Greek village. The legend had it that one should offer hospitality to anyone asking it, because that person just may be the powerful Greek goddess, Athena, in disguise. Do we practice this tradition today? I would venture to say we do the opposite!

After September 11th, widespread fears developed alarmingly. One fear in particular was xenophobia. Many people feared anyone who might be a terrorist because of the color of their eyes and skin. How sad to judge and criticize others for their heritage!

The Golden Rule across the Globe

How foreign are we to each other anyway? Are we really so different? Yes, we eat different foods, have different daily rituals, wear different clothes, speak different languages, and believe in a "different" God – or do we? I came across several different variations of The Golden Rule, and guess what–it exists in all of the so-called "different" religions of the world.

- Buddhism: Hurt not others in ways that you yourself would find hurtful.
- Judaism: What is hateful to you, do not to your fellow man.

453

That is the entire Law; all the rest is commentary.

- Christianity: Do unto others as you would have them do unto you.
- Baha'i Faith: Blessed is he who prefers his brother before himself.
- Islam: No one of you is a believer until he desires for his brother that which he desires for himself.
- Hinduism: This is the sum of duty: do not to others which if done to thee would cause thee pain.
- Zoroastrianism: That nature only is good when it shall not do unto another whatever is not good for its own self.

If we could embrace the notion that others aren't so foreign after all, maybe xenophobia would cease to exist.

Strangers as Gifts

In the book *Simple Abundance*, author Sarah Ban Breathnach wrote a chapter entitled "The Kindness of Strangers." She suggests we think of kindness as a positive exchange of comfort and compassion in the Circle of Life. After all, aren't we all connected, like a string of beads held together by the thread of life and love? Breathnach suggests we become consciously aware of encounters with strangers. Of course, use discrimination, but keep in mind we learn from each other through our differences. Strangers can really be exceptional gifts to us.

There is a fine line between strangers and the "strangers" we warn our children about. This is an art to teach our children. We can teach them in a way so fear doesn't run them. They need to learn discernment, but they also need to feel free to express their natural curiosity without feeling judged or fearful of the consequences.

In all of my travels, I have met many people who started out to be strangers and ended up being my friends. One such occasion happened on a flight from New York to Salt Lake City. I sat next to a man from Malaysia. It was my intention, I thought, to curl up as best as possible in an airline seat, comforted by a blanket and pillow, and rest my weary body after quite an exciting New York adventure. However, one simple comment to that stranger started a four and a half-hour conversation. Paul Lewis is the director of EdgeWalks, an experiential education program. We shared much in common including our love of nature. We discussed our mutual beliefs that nature allowed us to expand personally and spiritually. Paul was associated as an instructor with the North Carolina Outward Bound School for twenty years and now has his own company, EdgeWalks.

Our communication became sensitive, heart-centered, deep, and profound. He asked me two questions that endeared me to him even more: 1) If you could have dinner with anybody, who would it be? 2) What event in your life impacted you the most?

Paul holds these thoughts about the feeling of xenophobic: "The unknown is where most dreams are realized or unrealized. It all starts with our dreams, or thoughts, our unknowns, our action or inaction. Think about your greatest learning. Most likely it involved risks and moving into the unknown. Most of my journeys with the students at the North Carolina Outward Bound School were taken with people who want to move forward with simple steps from where they are now and take the risk of moving into the unknown for self-discovery and purposeful living. The philosophy of the school demands that students act on their feelings, their dreams, their thoughts, and celebrate their lives, their accomplishments, and their humanness."

As we bid adieu with a warm embrace and a heart connection, I invited Paul to come visit me and spend a few days. He did come, as he loves snow-skiing, and we have created a lovely friendship that we both value.

The Aloha Spirit

As the winter lingers and spring doesn't feel like it's "just around the corner," the lure of the Hawaiian Islands is indeed powerful. One trip in particular opened me to many wonderful "strangers." I decided that Hawaii was a perfect spot for my work-play as a motivational speaker and transformational trainer. After all, where else does one receive a glorious flower lei as part of the introduction when speaking to an audience? The Hawaiian experience definitely makes up for the challenge of trying to read and pronounce the street signs, like the Kalanianole Highway. Sometimes, in fact, I felt like I was in a foreign country. Each day I learned more and more about Asian people, a prevalent population in the islands, and more specifically, about their relationship to feelings, a topic dear to my heart.

A portion of my work-play time in the islands was spent interviewing young people, ages nine to seventeen. One of my interviewees was a delightful thirteen-year-old girl whose ethnic background is Hawaiian, Chinese, and Spanish. She has a condition called alopecia, which is the loss of hair. It has progressed from small bare patches to almost her entire head. To this brave young girl, who believes laughter is the best cure for anything, the alopecia has been her biggest challenge. "It's no

455

excuse to do poorly," she told me, "but actually a reason to do better." During the entire interview, her speech was eloquent and mannerisms endearing. Wow, what an inspiration!

Another subject for my book was an eleven-year-old girl of Asian descent, who was diagnosed early with hip cancer. She had an ostectomy, or the removal of bone. In other words, her leg was removed. A crutch replaced her left leg as well as a portion of her pelvis. I was awed at her ability to deal with the circumstances. "I haven't changed. I'm still the same person," she declared. "I just wish people wouldn't treat me like I was so different." As I drove back to town along the shores of the crashing Pacific, I felt humbled to have been allowed into her world, even for only a brief period. Her courage had a lasting and powerful impact on me.

My journey back to the mainland also involved deep connections with people who began as "strangers." As we know, air travel notoriously provides passengers the opportunity to open up communication and divulge their life story. The wife of a commercial pilot occupied one of the last few seats left on the flight, next to mine. During lunch we exchanged stories about our grown children and how blessed we both felt in having them as our friends. I soon learned that one of her three sons was killed at age fourteen in an accident. She shared with me how the family dealt with the death. She grieved at the time, and then eventually co-founded a Compassionate Friends chapter in her area.

Her husband, however, dealt with the death quite differently, mostly through denial of his feelings as he exuded strength. After many years, his feelings needed confrontation. His wife felt more adept to assist him then because of her own healing. We each have our own way and our own time.

Back on the continent, I needed to board another flight home, to a different kind of beauty and magnificence. I had a long layover and couldn't resist a linguine special at the airport restaurant. I chose to dine with another fellow traveler that opened her heart and told me she had never realized how much her eight-year marriage meant to her until she came close to losing it. The intensity of her feelings was new and cumbersome, yet she believed they would teach her more about herself. Once again, I interacted with another person who was willing to be vulnerable and expose her feelings.

Most likely, I'll never be reunited with any of those who shared their hearts with me. Maybe that's what made it so easy for them to talk openly, but maybe not. Perhaps they each recognized in their own way the indescribable benefit of "bearing one's soul" to another.

Maybe some have more of a knack than others for being outgoing and gregarious. Others may prefer to be more private. There is no right or wrong. Just what is. Once again, diversity is good, and it's natural to be different. Being naturally reserved is okay too. However, when fear comes into the picture, we want to question and examine. Not everyone has to be sociable and jovial to be all right, nor as gregarious as I am. Did I have a hardy laugh when I heard a line from a television movie that reminded me too much of myself. The son endearingly spoke about his elderly father; "He speaks to anyone with a pulse."

Anyhow, the message of this chapter is just to open your heart. You then feel more connected to people and to life. We are all the same, and we're different.

The greeting in India is called "Namaste" which translates to "I bow to the Divine in you." When we bow to the Divine in each other, we see no fear. We see the Divine. So, Namaste, dear reader. Namaste.

Reflection Time:

1. How do you teach the lesson of discernment to your children?
2. If it was taught to you as a child, how so?
3. Can you see the divine in others?
4. Would you ever consider talking to "strangers"?
5. If so, how would you conduct yourself?
6. Do you express your needs to others?
7. If not, why not?
8. Each night, take a few minutes before you sleep and review your day. Were you open to strangers? Were you shut off to new experiences? Would your action today be something others would want to emulate?
9. As a child, were you ever frightened by a stranger?
10. Did your parents ever invite strangers to your home? Regardless of your answer, how did it affect you?

Y is for feeling... Yearning

Definition: longing, craving, desire, want, wish
Opposite: satisfied, complete, whole

To yearn is to have a strong desire or longing, or to feel a deep pity, sympathy, or tenderness. We all have feelings of yearning from time to time. What was it you felt you were missing? What did you want or yearn for? Having a yearning feeling indicates lack in an area of your life. Perhaps you yearn for someone to love, or someone to love you; maybe a yearning to go home after being gone for weeks, or visit your family. Maybe you yearn for a child, or a trip to some exotic country.

We can yearn for something passionately–for business to be successful, for relationship to flourish, or to be understood! God how we yearn to be understood! We yearn to live on a peaceful planet. We yearn for tolerance, patience, and understanding.

When we don't have health, we yearn to be healthy. When we don't have wealth, we yearn to be wealthy. Many yearn to recall their youth as well as those who yearn to be accomplished. Yearning really isn't being in the present. You're so concentrated on what you want, that it keeps you from being present.

Our yearning can be so strong when we want to share our joys with those who may not on this planet anymore. How many times I've wished for my folks to have known Alissa and Corianna, our granddaughters. I met a woman who approached my booth at a conference, and after a heart-to-heart conversation, she told me how she yearned to hold her son again. He had made his transition at the age of eighteen.

If we've spent an extended period of time in a foreign country, we may have begun to yearn for the familiar. For example, in some countries I've visited it is difficult to find fresh vegetables and I'd begin to yearn for my organic veggies. We might yearn for our own customs, our own bed, our familiar magnets on the refrigerator door. Now that I live in the mountains, I no longer yearn for pure fresh air nor do I have a deep desire to see blue skies and white fluffy clouds because I have them! That yearning created my reality.

Are You a Sourpuss?

I believe we all yearn to be with people who are positive and supportive. Gary Crow and Marissa Crow, who wrote *The Friend Factory*, teach seven to ten-year-old children about making friends. It's a delightful book. I've extracted a few definitions about positive people:

"Positive people are the opposite of sourpusses. It's easy to have fun when positive people are around."

"Positive people get upset sometimes, but they get over it quickly. They don't pout or call people names. They don't yell at people either. They get angry sometimes but don't stay angry very long. If they get into an argument, they say what they think and then stop arguing."

"Positive people are fun to be around. They don't make fun of anyone. They follow this rule, 'If I don't have something nice to say about someone, I'll keep quiet.'"

Are you yearning for a good friend? If you don't have one, ask yourself if you are a sourpuss.

Grandmotherly Love

There are times when I yearn to see Alissa and Corianna, our granddaughters. I have recorded Alissa's voice since she was three weeks old. I know if I play the tape, I will yearn for her even more. My heart aches at times because I want to be near her and take her to children's hour at the library or to explore a new flower garden. Although I've made it a point to not go longer than six or seven weeks without seeing her, I still yearn for more of an involvement in her everyday life.

I often heard of the yearning to be a grandparent, but never totally related to it. I can understand those feelings now that I have that identity.

Long before I was a grandmother, I had been a member of Grandmothers for Peace. Now my membership has more meaning to me. GFP was formed in 1982 at the height of the Cold War. The late Barbara Weidner became aware of 150 nuclear weapons at Mather Air Force Base, fifteen minutes from her home in Sacramento, California. She realized that if things didn't change, her precious grandchildren could be part of the last generation on Earth. "The thought catapulted me out of my kitchen to join others at the gates of Mather in protest of the nuclear arms race." In 1982, Weidner was arrested for an act of non-violent civil disobedience. During her five days in jail, she realized that grandmothers have a very powerful and important role to play in the struggle to eliminate nuclear weapons from the face of the Earth. "I decided to form Grandmothers for Peace, and in May, eleven women gathered in my living room to declare ourselves just that – Grandmothers for Peace. **www.grandmothersforpeace.org.**

In the latest newsletter, November 2003, the "Grannies" took on the Iraq Infant Care Project. "This project was perfect for us because GMP has no borders. Children are the same all over the world. We can say we did our small part to help, but nothing is small if done from the heart." Grannies rule!!!!!

From the book called *Grandloving*, authors Sue Johnson and Julie Carson write, "Toss aside your embarrassment about how you look playing in the sandbox or giving your special bear hug at the nursery school door and revel in knowing that your grandchild only has eyes for the wonderful person you are inside. That's the magic of the love between grandchild and grandparent." Amen.

Sometimes the grandparent will take over responsibility of raising the grandchild. AARP (American Association of Retired Persons) **www.aarp.org** states in a 1995 U.S. Census that 3.9 million children are raised in grandparent households. Out of those children 1.5 million, or 38.5% are raised by a grandparent in households in which neither parent is present. I'll be eager to see the results of the 2004 census. Have our parents become more or less responsible? What's your vote?

Getting Back to Ourselves

One of my beliefs is that we all yearn to get back to our highest nature, our spiritual side. All the things we try to accomplish are really efforts to get in touch with a vague feeling, a sense of self we've lost over time in our Earthly walk. As we establish a philosophy or belief in life about our highest purpose and potential, we begin to move toward a SELF where we feel most at home. We begin to move toward truth. From that point, we develop character traits that honor rather than compromise, and we tend to yearn less for what we don't have in life. With this movement, perhaps we yearn even more for the reconnection with our soul. We begin to see who we really are, is all we need for a satisfying life. Knowing there is rightness in all things, we become content to be almost anywhere. We are less in conflict with our identity, more aware of our interconnectedness with all of life, and more accepting of our being-ness. Do you have beliefs of this type?

Is yearning a negative feeling? I would say definitely NOT! If yearning moves us to a feeling of completion, then it isn't negative at all. If we choose to stay in the feeling of yearning and fail to recognize the message or move in the direction we are guided, it can become an obsession, always wanting–never fulfilled. No one consciously desires to live in a state of WANT all of the time, but to continually experience dissatisfaction is a choice like all others. Yearning can be used to inspire and direct, if we tune in and listen.

A client told me that one of her most lucid times of day is early in the morning. "When my eyes first open I have a clear sense of how I'm 'feeling' that day – not looking at my bones or my body – but my feelings. This is a good time to contemplate and discover any yearnings or unfulfilled desires I might have."

You might want to try it. Use it for exploration and possible resolution to find any sense of yearning you might have. Tomorrow morning when you wake up, give yourself time to lie there. Close your eyes and concentrate on your heart. What do you feel? What are you thinking? Do you have excitement about the day? Are you experiencing apprehension? Is there something you would like to have different in your life? Are you missing someone? Do you feel fulfilled and satisfied that your purpose in life is being completed? Do a scan of the moment and see what's there.

If you feel wonderful, that's fantastic! Count your many blessings and breathe a breath of gratitude into the universe. But, if you're missing something, someone, or a way of being, if you are yearning for something, remind yourself that today is a whole new day and you and only you choose what to do with it and how to feel.

Annie's Yearning

Some people long to find their purpose in life. Examples of yearning are experiences of a feeling, desire, want, or a longing. When you are yearning, you can't be fully satisfied with how things are right now, and you can't be fully present in any task you begin.

Annie, a client who found her life purpose in teaching preschool, had the following to say: "Even though I worked with therapy in the past, Alexandra's method helped me to feel deeply, which allowed me to process the pain of my childhood, leading to my healing. With each session I came closer to my Self, which has allowed me to be more present for each child. I found my authentic Self. I had prayed to find out what I was meant to do on this planet, and that prayer was answered. I have since found my life work, and as a bonus, it doesn't feel like work at all. To reach my authentic Self, there had to be an unveiling of a mask. Alexandra was the only one who made me feel, and feel fully, in order to process things to get the wonderful results."

"I now feel better equipped to understand what a child is going through. I offer them support and always remind them of their choices."

"I've observed when a child gets tired, he or she really wants boundaries. For example, a child grabbed a lid off a Lego box container and started to make a banging sound. I asked him if he was feeling tired, and his reply was, 'yes.' He repeated it, then ran to me, and gave me a huge hug. He felt heard and validated. Children act out when they need something and are not heard. They need to be given tools to understand their feelings and as we work together we all create a peaceful community in our school. A child will walk into the school and say to me that they don't think (another child) likes them anymore. When those times happen, we sit in a circle and the child asks the other child, 'Do you love me?' The other child always answers, 'yes. I still love you.' There is an immediate shift in the feelings of the child who had the issue. I help them bring their feelings to the forefront."

"I believe we do in life what we need to do most, because I learn every day from these children. I continue to feel blessed for my new life. Thank you Alexandra."

Annie reminds us to choose to use our sense of desire to change something in our life. Her desire was to find her authentic Self and meaningful work. It doesn't have to be monumental in the beginning – even the Taj Mahal was a pile of rubble prior to being built! Each morning add to your list of personal changes until you begin to see the magnificent story of your life unfolding in front of you. Know that in a way, you are the Taj Mahal, complete and perfect without a need in the world.

As I look at the word "yearn," I see the word "earn." We feel we have to earn love and kindness, and that makes us yearn for it. We yearn and crave for the rewards, the acknowledgement, and the recognition. If we perform our duties with a cheerful heart, with selfless service, doing the now, we can come to a place in ourselves where we are free from yearning for anything, other than feeling the peace of being in the present moment. Then we are filled full, free of the chains of the past and torments of the future. Quiet, pensive, and reflective time is required however, to become aware, insightful, and honest with self. This course of action will give you what you truly yearn for–peace of mind, acceptance, respect, and to be loved unconditionally.

Reflection Time:

1. Experiment with looking into the heart of your desires, every morning for a few minutes, every day for a week. Then expand it to a few more minutes. How does it feel? What have you discovered?

2. Is there something you are yearning to do to make the world a better place, like grandmother Barbara Weidner did? What might be holding you back?

3. What does the bright side of life look like to you?

4. What changes do you need to get there?

5. Is there something you are yearning to do, accomplish, be, or acquire?

6. Experiment with the inner child exercise. Write down a question to your inner child, and then answer it with your non-dominant hand. The questions could be very simple, such as: How old are you? How are you feeling right now? Do you have something to tell me? Once again, have fun with it.

7. Write a list of sixteen ideas, goals, or desires you'd like to achieve. Then look at them in groups of four. Out of the four, which would you want to do the most? So now, you'll have only a list of four. Out of those four, which one has the strongest pull? Do it!

8. Is your control mode on?

9. Are you okay with falling on your face after trying something new?

10. Is your life fulfilled holistically?

Y is for feeling... Youthful

Definition: childlike, young, immature, juvenile

Opposite: elderly, senile, old, aged, seasoned

Young, fresh, or in an early stage of development–that's youthful! We all recognize the attitudes, behaviors, and the glow of youth, but what is a youthful feeling once we're out of childhood and into maturity? Being youthful isn't just how old a person is; it's a feeling!

To feel young is a process. Why not create the belief that age is only a number? Feeling youthful is a reflection of the quality of life we choose to live.

I came across this amazing passage written by Frenchman Stanley Olman in the fifteenth century. "Youth is not a time of life; it is a state of mind. It is a matter of will, a quality of imagination, of vigor, of emotions. It is the freshness of the deep spring of life. Youth means the predominance of courage over timidity, of adventure over the love of ease. We grow old by deserting our ideals. Years may wrinkle the skin but to give up enthusiasm wrinkles the soul. Worry, doubt, self-distrust, fear, and despair – these bow the heart and turn the spirit back to dust. Whether sixty or sixteen, there is in every human being's heart the love of wonder, the sweet amazement of the stars and the star-like things, the undaunted challenge of events. The unfailing childlike appetite for 'what next?' And the joy in the game of living. You are as young as your faith, as old as your doubt, as young as your self-confidence, as old as your fear, as young as your hope, as old as your despair." That says it all, if you ask me!

When we're young, anything is an adventure. Every new experience beckons to be tried. We feel enthusiastic, willing, hopeful, and at times, apprehensive, but the point is, we DO feel. Feeling youthful indicates we are open to new experiences, new thoughts, new encounters, and new lessons. We can enter into each new arena without worry based on experiences. We can truly enjoy the moment.

Kids Say the Darndest Things

There's a cute story about a young child who gently touches the wrinkled face of her aged grandpa. "Did God make you?" she inquired. "Yes," he replied, "a long time ago. And he made you too." She removed her small hand from his face and placed it on her own. Caressing her skin she said, "He's getting better."

My sister Georgia was in the hospital and Ryan, her grandson, inquired why. To her simplistic answer, he added, "You must be old." How does a child learn that being old is associated with being in a hospital?

Here are some hilarious responses, thanks to email, that some children gave on some "adult" topics.

Q: When is it okay to kiss someone?

A: You should never kiss a girl unless you have enough bucks to buy her a big ring and her own VCR, 'cause she'll want to have videos of the wedding. (Jim, 10)

A: It's never okay to kiss a boy. They always slobber all over you... that's why I stopped doing it. (Jean, 10)

A: Never kiss in front of other people. It's a big embarrassing thing if anybody sees you. But if nobody sees you, I might be willing to try it with a handsome boy, but just for a few hours. (Kally, 9)

Q: How does a person learn to kiss?

A: You learn it right on the spot, when the gooshy feeling gets the best of you. (Doug, 7)

A: It might help if you watched soap operas all day. (Carin, 9)

Q: Why do you think two people fall in love?

A: No one is sure why it happens, but I heard it has something to do with how you smell. That's why perfume and deodorant are so popular. (Jan, 9)

Q: How would you make a marriage work?

A: Tell your wife that she looks pretty even if she looks a like a truck. (Ricky, 10)

And, finally, Kenny, age seven, when asked if it was better to be single or married said, "It gives me a headache to think about that stuff. I'm just a kid. I don't need that kind of trouble."

How interesting romance would be if we approached it with the attitude of the little ones!

Forever Young

I read an article about a woman who went mountain climbing when she was eighty-nine. That's inspiring, wouldn't you say? How are you going to be when you're eighty-nine? We really get to create that right here and now.

My dear friend, Bobbie, has a license plate that reads YNG4EVR. Her son and daughter gave her the license plate as a Christmas gift because they had heard many of her friends tell her how young she looked. Her words of wisdom on the subject are worth sharing: "At that time, I was still young, but the 'image' has managed to stay with me to this day. I'm looooonnnggg past my twenties, but I'm told I still look young. If I believe and think I'm young, I am. The reminder on my license plates helps a lot. Staying young is a strong belief system of mine, but it's also a lifestyle. I think young, and I have a very active and balanced lifestyle, physically, mentally, and spiritually. I work at keeping my body in good shape by regular exercises and healthy food choices, and I keep my mind in shape by a positive and receptive outlook. I really think our minds are our most powerful asset and thinking young is something we can do at any age. I just never intend to get old; and I intend to keep this license plate forever."

The National Council on Aging says that there were 50,545 centenarians in 2000, a 35% increase from 1990. This number is expected to increase to 324,000 by 2030 and to 834,000 in 2050!

Through email, Comedian George Carlin gives us suggestions on how to stay young:

- Throw out nonessential numbers – age, weight, height.
- Keep only cheerful friends. The grouches will pull you down.
- Keep learning – never let the brain idle.
- Enjoy the simple things.
- Laugh often, loud and long.
- Tears happen. The only person who is with us our entire life is ourselves.
- Be ALIVE while you are alive.
- Surround yourself with what you love – family, pets, hobbies, music, whatever.

- Cherish your health; if it is good, preserve it. If it is unstable, improve it. If it's beyond what you can improve, get help.
- Don't take guilt trips – go to the mall, or a foreign country, but not to

  where the guilt is.
- Tell the people you love, that you love them at every opportunity.

Fresh Look, Fresh Perspective

Here's a funny example of breaking an old belief in order to feel youthful. I have a friend whose mother said women should never wear red because it makes them look big. To this day, every time she puts on something red, she thinks of her mother. She didn't wear red for years because she thought it would make her look fat. However, she liked the color occasionally and decided she'd give it a try. No bad things befell her even though she wore red! In other words, she chose to honor herself rather than the silly belief that women shouldn't wear red, which she had been taught. This is an example that demonstrates how easily we can learn and unlearn beliefs that don't serve us.

What does wearing red have to do with feeling youthful? Well, the example demonstrates just one little filter. One little belief clouds the youthful feeling of living in the NOW. Some beliefs can lead to far more devastating effects in our lives than wearing or not wearing red! Take that one filter off, and voila, you can experience red in your life again! It might sound silly, but add thousands of filters to your views on life and take another look around. Just because we believe something does not make it true!

I use a variety of sunglasses to demonstrate this idea at workshops. The audience calls out a sabotaging belief; I put on one of the sunglasses, representing a filter that colors the way something is seen. I eventually have seven or eight sunglasses on my face, which obviously distorts my vision. It's quite effective in making the point that we don't see things as they truly are, but instead see them through our beliefs.

I invite you to try it. How can you possibly feel youthful if every new experience is being clouded over by your beliefs about aging? How can you even see the moment for what it is through all the darkness? How can you make fresh choices, unless you are willing to remove the sunglasses?

Do you have a red sweater hidden in the back of your closet you've always loved but won't wear? Trust me...wear it!

If you are curious about someone's age, rather than asking how old they are, ask how young they are. It sets up a whole different feeling. I understand that in China the women brag about their age. The older, the better. And, over there, red is the good luck color. Brides even wear it on their wedding day!

As I gracefully age, I feel young inside. Yes, I attempt to look my best when I present myself in public. I peruse my closet to select the best-matching ensemble. I fuss with my hair, and I apply some make-up to enhance my eyes. And all the while, I know it's not who I am. And it doesn't necessarily match with what I see in the mirror. So, where am I going to place my emphasis? On my inner world, or outer world? I have taken on the belief of Peace Pilgrim, "I have radiant energy, and I am ageless."

State of Mind

So getting old is a state of mind. You are as old as your attitude, your belief system, and the choices you make.

These wise suggestions from the late Audrey Hepburn came to me through email:

"For attractive lips, speak words of kindness.

For lovely eyes, seek out the good in people.

For a slim figure, share your food with the hungry.

For beautiful hair, let a child run his/her fingers through it once a day.

For poise, walk with the knowledge that you never walk alone.

People, even more than things, have to be restored, renewed,

revived, reclaimed, and redeemed; never throw out anyone.

Remember, if you ever need a helping hand, you will find one at the end of each of your arms.

As you grow older, you will discover that you have two hands; one for helping yourself, and the other for helping others."

Someone once said we can grow up without growing old. What can you add to the following list?

✓ Be sensitive to others' needs.

✓ Keep in touch with the child within. Be playful, be zany, be childlike.

✓ Put a spark in your life.

✓ Challenge yourself in every way.

✓ Never stop learning.

✓ Laugh often.

✓ Frequently check your attitudes and beliefs and be willing to change.

✓ Notice the reasons behind the choices you're making.

Reflection Time:

1. What is your perception of youth? Of age? Of old?

2. What makes you feel old?

3. What would make you feel young?

4. Who has been your role model for old or young feelings?

5. What would have to happen for you to adjust your attitude about age and feeling youthful?

6. Are you harboring guilt?

7. What are some ways you can peel the filters of your beliefs back to expose your new, fresh, youthful feelings?

8. Are you experiencing the same life you would be, without the negative filters? Do you think the filters of your beliefs protect you from something?

9. Are you nervous about exposing what hides beneath the filters?

10. Have you put some of those belief filters in place to gain the approval of others?

Y is for feeling... Yucky

Definition: gross, nasty, repulsive, out of sorts, off, queasy, squeamish, heebie-jeebies all over

Opposite: high, enthusiastic, peachy

Eeeew. Yuck! What a word to describe that certain feeling! All of us have felt yucky, and all of us may have different definitions of the word. One client used "shameful," "alienated," and "uncomfortable in her own skin," as ways to describe feeling yucky. Yucky connotes images of being "slimed on."

When I dropped an egg on the floor and had to maneuver a way to pick it up without it sliding through my fingers and back onto the floor, I learned about yucky. It's gooey, slimy, and uncomfortable.

I made a choice to say "yes" when I was invited to become an initiate in a non-affiliated high school club, called Y-Hi Sweaters. There were also the Echoes and Y-Hi Jackets. Well, the initiation into this special club has been embedded in my memory bank. I was blindfolded and before I knew it, a slithery, salty, slimy something was popped into my mouth. And then came another. I gagged and felt certain I'd throw up. Eauuuuu! But, compared to today's fraternity and sorority initiations, this was nothing. It was a piece of cake. (Actually, it was an oyster.) That was yucky! (Maybe it was this experience that founded my vegetarianism that has lasted approximately twenty-five years.)

Odors can also make you feel yucky. An overwhelming discomfort can be triggered through smell. The idea of parasites running around in the body could feel yucky as well as bacteria living on your teeth. Eewww. Sounds pretty yucky to me. But this is part of life, whether it's yucky or not. Each one of those bacteria is a whole world! There is order to be respected within each single microorganism.

What about the non-tangible kind of yucky, such as finding ourselves in a situation that isn't entirely comfortable and we're not really afraid, but we're not really confident either – yuck. Maybe we all have one thing or another that makes us feel yucky, but my yuckies relate to feeling out of balance in life.

When I select a pair of slacks to wear and they don't feel or look right, I feel overweight, and I feel yucky. When my nails look like I've been working on the railroad and my hair looks like I slept on a crocodile, I feel yucky. Then, of course everyone else looks like a shining star. I can slip into feeling disappointed, disgusted, judgmental, and oh-so-down on myself. "Wait a minute," my Self says to my ego, "Not so fast. This is just what's happening right now and it has nothing to do with your self-esteem. You are NOT your nails or your hair. What do you want to do about making different choices?"

Cleansing the Yuckies

Many people would label having a colonic a yucky experience, but it's simply emptying your trash, which we all do on a regular basis. A colonic is cleansing your colon. In my opinion, it is one of the healthiest things you can do for yourself.

Brenda Watson, colon therapist and President of the International Association of Colon Therapy says, "Constipation is a serious health issue that should not be ignored. The problems that result from constipation range from depression to fatigue to serious diseases of the colon." Good elimination requires hydrating the colon. It's rather amazing what is eliminated in a cleanse.

Brenda Watson is also the president of Renew Formulas, Inc. Their literature educates the reader about the body. For example, do you know that every six months the major organs in the body die off because the new cells are born? The entire skeleton replaces itself every two years. Everything dies off! There is birth and death in every moment! What you may think of as yucky can be seen as freeing yourself of muck. Detoxifying the body is one of the best things you can do for yourself. But it has to be done properly.

Lotus Lessons

We can use yucky to express the things that are hard to describe, like being in mud, or feeling dense, in the muck, out of balance, dark, and sludgy. Where is the diamond when it's covered with dirt and slime? It's always there and will surface again. Like the lotus flower that grows from the mud, muck, and the yucky soil, it rises above and blossoms. The Lotus is the ancient symbol of Yoga because it rises above muddy waters to bloom in great beauty. The flower is usually white or pink and has fifteen or more oval petals that spread open. It has been a symbol of spiritual enlightenment for thousands of years.

Sometimes we have to go through the muck to get to the joy of life. When we're feeling out of sorts, stuck, unclear, muddled, and yucky, it's okay. But is it okay with you? It may not portray that image of confidence, strength and control you identify with on a daily basis. And what we do to keep those in tack.

When we tracked the course of a client's sleepless patterns and low energy, we discovered she spent hours in the middle of the night, as a child, playing and being herself, because she had such an image to present during the day; it was the only time she could truly be herself. That behavior had prevented her from getting regular restful sleep, feeling yucky during the day because of lack of rest and low energy. Once discovered and eliminated, ahhhhh sleepless no more.

Reflection Time:

1. What does feeling yucky mean to you?
2. Examine the roots of your destructive patterns and confront your inner (yucky) demons.
3. Tell which situations or people trigger or cue you into playing a role you don't like.
4. How do you really feel inside when you're in that role?
5. Trip back into your high school days. What did you do that you would associate with the feeling of "yucky?"
6. Are you involved in a relationship that feels yucky? This can be a person, project, or situation.
7. Write a contract with yourself about this relationship.
8. What are you committed to renew, re-evaluate, or regurgitate with regard to this relationship?
9. Do a brief meditation, after breathing in and out for several minutes, being aware of your breath. Start consuming yourself with the feelings of yucky. Allow any images from the past to surface. Simply observe and feel. Notice the results. Then create feeling the opposite of what you dissolved. Live your life this way.
10. Be the lotus flower blooming in all its brilliance.

> *"Instead of seeing the rug being pulled out from under us, we can learn to dance on a shifting carpet."*
> **Thomas F. Crum, *The Magic of Conflict***

Z is for feeling... Zany

Definition: crazy, wacky, goofy, silly, nonsensical
Opposite: serious, solemn, grave, thoughtful

The dictionary tells me that the word "zany" refers to "a ludicrous, buffoonish character in old comedies who mimics ineptly the tricks of the clown." In other words, to feel zany is to feel crazy, silly, and outlandish, much like the clowns we have today! The word has evolved to simply mean "ludicrously comical" or "crazy." When was the last time you felt zany? Have you ever?

The Burn

My friend, Katie, attended the Burning Man Festival (**www.burningman. com**) in 2002, where there are plenty of zany characters, according to her. This is what she had to say about it:

"Whenever anyone asks me about the Burning Man Festival, I sum it up by saying 'It is a phenomenon on the planet Earth.' It truly is! I attended with my roommate, her brother, and about eight other acquaintances. We drove the thirteen hours from Los Angeles to Black Rock Desert, Nevada where the festival has been held for the past ten or so years. Nothing could have prepared me for the experience."

"For seven days, I knew we would be living under semi-primitive conditions and that we had to bring in all of our supplies, such as food, water, toiletries, etc, and that it was to be a 'freak show' of sorts. I had seen pictures of the people running around without clothes on, or dressed in wild, exotic, and zany costumes. I knew there was to be no money exchange – only trade, and that there would be music and fire-dancing and human-sized mazes and art projects of all sizes and shapes. I understood that there would be a seven story 'man' built out of wood in the center of everything and that on the last night of the festival, he would be burned, symbolizing 'letting go' of an old identity so that the new could be reborn. But no picture, sketch, story, or photograph could have compared to the actual experience itself."

"You wanna talk about zany? The first night I was there, I was somewhat overwhelmed with the strangeness of the whole event. I remember riding my bike around the 'playa' within the 'city's' six-mile circumference, looking at all the artwork and especially the people who wore costumes and lights and were just plain out of the ordinary. I said aloud, 'Great Spirit, I feel like I'm on some alien planet!' It took a day to adjust, but once I did, there was no holding me back! I dressed in whatever costume I could conjure up, let some artists paint some body art on me, explored the days away, and danced the nights away. I met people of all sorts and witnessed the infamous Dr. Thunderbolt. Imagine a man in a lightning-proof suit jumping on a mini-trampoline with a four-foot matchstick in his hand and igniting it on the electricity emitted from a giant Tessler coil spark, that has the same voltage as a bolt of lightning! As he jumped on the trampoline, the 'lightning' was transmitted through his voltage-proof suit and the sparks went through his feet to the Earth as visible little electric bolts! Crazy! Only someone who calls himself Dr. Thunderbolt would put himself through such a thing."

"The 'burn' itself would bring out the 'zany' in the dullest of folks. Hundreds of people in costumes and strange make-up and lit-up devices surrounded this giant 'man,' spinning fire, or merely waiting for the moment. Fire balls exploded into the moonlit sky. I turned to a new friend – 'It's a celebration of light!' I declared."

"I went back to LA a changed person, with a new set of eyes that didn't see buildings, signs, cars, and traffic lights, but saw art work in everything! I highly recommend getting in touch with your 'inner zaniness' and taking a trip to the annual Burning Man Festival. You might not be the same again!"

Masked

Costumes and parties are a great way to explore your inner zaniness. Halloween is a time for children to mask the body and face and fill bags with candy as they canvas neighborhoods in search of goblins and ghosts. Adults also scheme to devise the most clever, scary, or funny ensemble to wear to work or parties. This autumn holiday tends to stir the imagination to outrageousness where we don a new identity. The urge to portray a fantasy of someone far removed from our lifestyle is tempting and often carried out. One year my sister and brother-in-law hosted a gathering at their home and stepped into the parts of Scarlet O'Hara and Rhett Butler. They had a ball getting into the characters of the stars from *Gone with the Wind*.

When we lived near the beach, one Halloween my husband and I dressed up in our sons' wet suits. We went down to the beach just before the party and filled buckets up with seaweed. We walked into the party covered with the seaweed, complete with our goggles and flippers. Can you imagine what we looked like? We were zany, we were a little outrageous, and we had so much fun.

Another fun party we attended required we come prepared to perform a skit. I dressed up as the late Chef Julia Childs. I made a turkey outfit out of brown felt material, for Gene that had a variety of colored felt pieces glued on it as feathers. Our daughter's red knee sock served as the waddle. My demonstration was how to prepare this turkey for Thanksgiving dinner. It was hysterical. Did I have fun with that baster!

Sometimes craziness and outlandish behavior goes along with being youthful, doesn't it? That youthful child in us and those crazy ideas don't really go away. They're still within us. It's fun to go back and remember those times when we were comical and nonsensical.

California Koo-koo's

We all know what they say about those California folks. Well, I'm proud to say I was one of the "those" for most of my life. My friend, another ex-California resident, sent me an email entitled, "You know you're in California when... '...you know which restaurant serves the freshest arugula.' (It's absolutely true.) '...both you and your dog have therapists.'" Zany—yes, but what would the world do without those Californians?

Many people are so concerned about what everybody else might say about them. I remember when my treasured friend Judy and I went out to lunch. We were being so outrageous, just having such a blast, laughing, and having the best time! Two women stopped by our table on the way out of the restaurant and suggested we should bottle our laughter; no doubt we could make a lot of money selling it. They said they had so much fun watching us that they wanted to come over and join our table.

Being totally zany is being outrageous; it's getting out of our head. Unfortunately, too many of us spend too much time far away from zany, in the serious, linear world. Zany is about doing something you haven't done in years, just on the spur of the moment. Let that playful child come out more often. It's our nature to be resilient, playful, in the moment, and uninhibited.

A Forest of Christmas Trees

My husband Gene, got in touch with his zaniness as a child when, after the Christmas holiday, he would parade through his neighborhood picking up Christmas trees that were put out for trash. What does a six-year-old do with discarded Christmas trees? Drag them to his back yard and create his own forest of course! Call this zany, creative, imaginative, or decorative; it's still pretty darn cute.

Feeling zany is feeling playful. Dr. Frances Vaughn, transpersonal psychologist and author of *Awakening Intuition*, told me during an interview for my dissertation, "Laughter is useful in breaking mental sets. It can present an alternative way of seeing things and also as a release of feeling, just as tears can be. Laughter is cathartic and is also contagious. It can provide a fresh perspective that breaks out of the ordinary way of seeing. The ability to laugh at our own foibles can be a powerful aid to self-healing."

Being playful and spontaneous takes a little practice. We should take some lessons from our kids. One day I was feeling giddy while walking from our car to a restaurant. I felt just like a kid; I had to touch everything and stay in constant motion. I was jumping on and off the curb, climbed over a water fountain, literally bounced off the walls. I made quick turns, ran forward then backward. It was exhausting. But I actually felt like a kid! Or a puppy! I felt zany. People were looking at me; my daughter was laughing hysterically, while my husband was trying to ignore me. I had a ball! You know it's never too late to start – start now! You just may get used to it.

Also from my dissertation interviews, Peter Alsop, (**www.peteralsop.com**), a musician who writes and sings some zany songs for children, told me, "If we could learn to value difference, to see the balance and beauty of things we are not, and to live with a little ambiguity instead of demanding that everything around us be similar and well-ordered, then we might not be as uncomfortable around each other or find it as hard to communicate. And we might not have the ghettos to separate us, or classes, or racism, and sexism. " One of his songs is entitled, "It's Only A WeeWee, So What's The Big Deal."

For my husband's fiftieth birthday, I made him a series of audiotapes that were very brief vignettes from people who have known him. When Gene re-listened to the tapes on his last birthday and heard again about the crazy tales of his youth, he laughed, and he cried. I reminded him that the zany part of him is still there.

When we urge those closest to us to remember to be silly like they used to be, then we give ourselves permission to be zany, too.

Reflection Time:

1. What percentage of your day do you feel comical or silly? What percentage of your life?
2. Are you ever outrageous and crazy? If not, what stops you?
3. What beliefs do you have about being zany?
4. If you could label the mask you wear, what would it be?
5. Through whose eyes are you perceiving your reality?
6. Is the source of your security outside of yourself?
7. Could you leave it or have it leave you and still be okay?
8. Do you have attachments that hold power over you?
9. What character are you playing in life? Is it really you?
10. Once you return the Halloween costume to the rental store, and the calendar rolls over to November, do you still wear the mask? The time might just be right to look in the mirror and ask yourself the question, "How do I present myself to the world?"

Z is for feeling... Zealous

Definition: enthusiastic, fervent, passionate
Opposite: indifferent cool, careless

To feel zealous is to be motivated, excited, and joyful. We can feel motivated and enthusiastic about anything that we choose – about our career, our love life, losing weight or even having a colonic! We can feel excited about life, no matter what is going on. If we're feeling zealous, we're enthusiastic, committed to the direction we're headed and ready to go! Beyond just kind-of interested, we're inspired; we feel good about what we're doing and will pursue it as long as the passionate feeling lasts! Remember the song "I'm So Excited" sung by the Pointer Sisters. "I'm so excited, and I just can't hide it. I'm about to lose control and I think I like it." The upbeat melody, and the lyrics convey the feeling of zeal perfectly. Can you allow yourself to lose control?

In what area of your life do you want to feel more zeal? You name it and feel zealous about it. If you want more love, give more love. If you want more money in your life, give it! Give it away. If you want more kindness in your life, feel zealous about giving kindness. We do live in an abundant universe. Anything you want more of–give it and watch what happens in your life!

After waiting a few minutes for an elevator in a hotel lobby, the doors opened and out bounced this little three-year-old girl announcing exuberantly to the circle of 'strangers,' "I'm going swimming!" This child was feeling zealous and free of any inhibitions. When and why do we learn to bury this in a dark, deep, deserted spot within us?

Wouldn't it be great if we pursued all things with zeal rather than approaching so many of life's challenges with dread or little enthusiasm? There are several things in my life that inspire me, and they're not always what others would consider necessary or even fun. For example, when I organize things in my life, my office or my home, I do it with complete zeal, and I don't stop until the job is complete! I feel zealous cleaning out and organizing drawers, cupboards, and shelves. It's one of my favorites things to do. I pull everything out and toss out what is no longer serving a purpose in my life. When I straighten up the appearance, I fill up with energy and move on to the next task! I love the way it feels and the intention behind it; I thoroughly embrace the completion!

New Deals

New Year's seems to spark feelings of zeal in many of us. With enthusiasm we commit to all sorts of fresh starts. It's different for each of us, but I like to start new projects after the first of a New Year, and I like to have all other projects completed. I like projects. I like to start them as well as complete them.

A friend said her grandfather was that way with Mondays. As an engineer, he would never commit to a new job on a Friday. All new projects had to begin on a Monday as he felt it set a tone of eagerness and success to the overall project. That might seem odd to some of us, but it gave him a feeling of 'rightness' in his pursuits.

Straight to the Heart

Here's some wisdom: There is a link between the experience of zeal and being connected with our true self. Having passion for what we do doesn't mean our energy is so high we can't sit still. It means we can easily become engrossed in what we're doing, feel passionate about it, and in that passion, there is a sense of connection and direction.

I was volunteering one night at an outdoor concert, when a woman in her wheelchair was going down a slope of the theatre with zeal. It looked like she was a little out of control, so I scurried over to help her. When I got there she simply said, "I'm okay. Besides, what's the worst thing that could happen?" Don't you just love that attitude?

Some Eastern philosophers suggest we do what we dread doing most until we find peace in the center of the activity. Recall in the movie *Karate Kid* when his teacher suggested he wipe wax on a car and wipe it off, over and over. He continued until he became immersed in the activity.

Most of us probably won't arrive at a state where we passionately apply wax to our cars, but we can be sure there is someone out there who does! Are there areas in your life where you procrastinate because you think the experience will be a bore rather than a potential moment of inspiration?

An old proverb says, "Go straight to the heart of the fire for there you will find safety." What does that mean to you? What it says to me is embrace the discomfort and feel. You will not only come through it, but

479

you will thrive as a result. We can experience unbelievable excitement in life if we only travel on the edge more often. Our old comfort zone will always be there, but why would you want it? Push the envelope — go beyond the boundaries.

What we are zealous about may not always be beneficial, but it will tell the story of our lives. Gibran suggested that nothing great was ever accomplished without zeal, but that same level of ardor has led to disastrous consequences.

Fanatics and Bores

Fanaticism is a type of mindless zeal, where what is pursued can have hurtful or harmful consequences. Truth and integrity pursued with zeal result in enlightenment, but other types of zeal have led many into the darkest woods. Be ever mindful because it is possible to be so overcome with enthusiasm that we fail to exercise common sense. This is often true when we're young. In the moment, it might have seemed so right! When we fail to listen to the voice of wisdom within, those pursuits disregard our common sense. Beware of the ignorance that overshadows natural knowing.

Zealots are those who are so intensely addicted to a cause that they are far removed from the center. Balance is key in our process, our journey. We don't know zealous, unless we know indifference, ho-hum, who cares, and whatever. When we connect with our passion, zeal in life, our attitude toward all people and things shifts. On the other hand, if we cling to some ideas with such zeal that we've become unapproachable on the topic, are we in balance?

Maybe the lack of passion and zealousness in your life is associated in some way with fear? If there is something you're yearning to do, I encourage you to examine why you're not doing it. Has your passion been squelched? What are your unique gifts the world is waiting for? Who told you it couldn't be done or you don't have what it takes? Who did you allow to rob you of your life? Who did you give your power to? When did you first believe you didn't matter? That you didn't make a difference?

From the book *I Will Not Die an Unlived Life*, author Dawna Markova says, "Fear is passion without breath. How do we mother our passion? To be fully alive, we have no choice but to finally move closer toward what we usually veer way from…What would it be like to open our hearts to our fear, to befriend it with wonder, as one would a deer in the forest? What if you could bring it right into the heart of your awareness instead of ignoring it?" Go for it!

Reflection Time:

1. Try to make some time for yourself to question whether you're truly living. What are your keenest thoughts and experiences? Are they just memories? Wouldn't you like to feel more intensely about some area in your life?

2. Sign up for the speech class you've dreaded taking all these years.

3. Tell a person in your life how important they are to you.

4. Volunteer to do something you know you're good at but have been afraid to declare to the group or world.

5. What do you enjoy doing? Do it!

6. What are some things that fire you up?

7. Take some time to consider the passion in your life. Even twenty minutes of contemplation about what you love to do and who you love to be with, can be a freeing experience.

8. Have you stayed connected with your enthusiastic side or have you given it up for the daily grind?

9. Do you know someone who seems to approach all she does with zeal?

10. What steps, if any, are you willing to take to get in touch with the zealous side of yourself?

"Psychiatrists tell us that one out of every four Americans is mentally ill. Check your friends. If three seem all right, you're it."

Unknown

Z is for feeling... Zonked

Definition: weary, exhausted, glazed over, tired out, worn out

Opposite: wired, energetic, set to go, turned on

Feeling zonked isn't the most pleasant feeling a human can have. It means to feel stupefied or stunned. Zonked also describes a state of being senseless or intoxicated from drugs or alcohol.

I don't think it takes either drugs or alcohol to experience the feeling of being zonked. Have you ever worked so hard or gone through such an emotional period that you felt "zonked" when it was over? Did your mind feel sharp? Probably not!

My research hasn't uncovered many people who can be quoted to describe the word "zonked." Perhaps that's because if you're zonked, you can't think of anything to say OR because no one wants to be known throughout history as the one person who had something profound to say about being zonked!

In short, when we're zonked, we're not connected, not energized, not inspired, and maybe not very happy. I know I've been there. In those moments, it is time for me to regroup, spend some time with myself, rest, and rebalance. It is time to recommit to Self.

The more we stay connected with our inner self and purpose, the less likely it is that we will ever experience the physically and emotionally draining sensations of being zonked. Feeling empty and depleted could also describe this feeling, maybe like a zombie (whatever that feels like).

Life can throw some startling, stunning events our way, but, if we stay focused on what we know to be true, and take care of ourselves along the way, we can lessen the impact of the challenges we receive in life. We can let zonked get the best of us, or we can endure. There are times to take care of ourselves and times to keep charging ahead. Your inner self will let you know.

Sleepytime

I can honestly say I know the meaning of "zonked." After putting in long hours on this book and going to bed at one a.m., I was ready for a good night's sleep after a cup of Sleepytime Tea. I was in bed no longer than five minutes when the smoke alarm started beeping every few minutes. Max does not like high-pitched sounds like smoke alarms, fireworks, or sirens. Before I knew it, he was at the head of our bed, on my pillow, curling up closer and closer, pawing his way into the covers. This went on for several hours until we decided to move into the guest room and sleep, away from the sound. However, Max's ears could still pick up the beeping, and again he took up residency at the top of my head on my pillow, pawing his way miserably at the covers. This was one unhappy dog and two unhappy parents. Gene was getting frustrated, and I was working at compassion. Thank God morning came after maybe thirty minutes of sleep!

I woke up with bags under my eyes that could be filled with treasures galore. I felt completely zonked. I didn't come to life until after my morning shower.

The day clipped along at my normal pace, quickly and steadily, until my client at 2:30 P.M., a seven-year-old girl. She explained to me that "disappointed" meant "if someone does something mean to you, you're disappointed," and told me of a girl who threw snow in her face that day. I asked this beautiful child, here only seven years on the planet, what she said to her. "True friends don't do that. I'm going to find a new true friend." She then shared with me how her mom gets grumpy and yells. I asked how she could respond to her. "Mom, could you please not scream so much? It makes me sad; it hurts my ears." I gave the little girl a magic wand and asked, 'if you could have your life be however you wanted it to be, how would you have it?' She said, "My sisters would be nice to me." I asked what would have to happen for her sisters be nice to her. Her heartfelt response was, "If I was nice to them, then maybe they would be nice to me." Brilliant insight. She said she would also want her mom not to scream and her dad not to work on the computer so much. This young child expressed her innate wisdom. We can nurture this in a child or we can let it fade and become dormant.

We left each other with heart-warming hugs and Eskimo kisses. What happened to my feeling of "zonked?" It was absorbed into the space of pure love–that's what! Children deserve kindness, caring, and time. They deserve to be cherished and made a priority in our lives. Not to just speak the words, but to take action like we truly mean it; our children deserve the best. How many adults are equipped to give it to them?

We can change our attitudes and beliefs on the spot and make choices that enhance the lives of others which will eventually make for peace on Earth.

The Long Dance

When I participated in a Native American event called the Long Dance, I certainly could have let the feeling of zonked get me down. The weekend experience was held in the mountains of Boulder, Colorado on wild, privately-owned forested property. Friday night, the eighty or so participants spoke about and displayed their uniquely hand-crafted banners that we created as part of the ritual. These banners depicted where we came from, where we were, and where we were going symbolically. Each one was a magnificent work of art representing one's lifetime. We hung our banners high on a line that served as a boundary for a large irregular shaped track in which we would take our Long Dance.

All day Saturday was spent in introspection and silence without food, only water. At dusk, we were called to the circle to commence in the Long Dance. A Native American man called Beautiful Painted Arrow started the dance with the sound of a drum that continued to sound throughout the night without stopping. This drum was large enough for four people to play it. We were instructed to continue walking to the beat of the drum, resting if we chose for brief periods, without sleeping. Halfway through the night, the drum stopped momentarily as we changed directions. In the tradition of my Capricorn, goat-like determination, I continued to walk without stopping, not even once. I felt the energy of my Native American brothers and sisters who, years ago, were evicted from their land and homes. I felt the despair of the Jewish people walking the concentration camp encampment. I felt the pain and suffering of convicts who are allowed brief moments in the yards of their prison for exercise. My heart was heavy as I walked one step after another for eight hours and ten minutes. There were short moments when I skipped feeling the energy of a joyful, magical child, then side-stepped as I replicated the energy of a serpent, as well as hop scotched my way through the dawn, as I watched Venus rise in the eastern sky.

Eight hours and ten minutes! I wasn't zonked. I was in bliss. My heart exploded with incredible gratitude and zeal for life, loving myself for who I am, saying "yes!" to this experience, embracing each step and moment with passion.

Each of the eighty had their own experience, perfect for each soul. After juice and delectables we gathered to share our personal experiences.

The electromagnetic energy that makes up my physical body was not the same as before. I was different. I had changed.

Returning to my home and family, the most profound lesson from the Long Dance was how important each moment is. Each step in the Great Mystery is a choice in which we determine the quality of our lives which is expressed through our attitude which grows from our beliefs. Appreciation for every moment is a resounding mantra for me. I invite you to be open to receive your own Long Dance.

Reflection Time:

1. Have you experienced the feeling of being zonked?
2. What thoughts and feelings do you conjure up when you think about that time?
3. Were there steps you could have taken to prevent it?
4. What is your relationship to recreational drugs?
5. When have you stretched the rubber band in participating in an activity, project, event?
6. Do you criticize others when they feel "zonked?"
7. If so, notice if you were made to feel guilty when you wanted to be lazy.
8. Do you have a strategy for moving through laziness, or feelings of being zonked?
9. When feeling zonked, have you ever also felt inspired or passion?
10. In what ways do you take care of yourself when you do feel zonked?

101 Attitude Shifts That Will Improve Your Life

From Ego Consciousness	To Soul Consciousness:
1. Control and holding on	Release and Surrender
2. Confusion and scattered thinking	Intention, focus and clarity
3. Fear	Love
4. Doubt	Trust
5. Victim consciousness	Personal empowerment
6. Blame	Personal responsibility
7. Needy and controlling relationships	Spiritual partnerships
8. Bored and unenthusiastic	Alive and vital
9. Worry and conflict	Peace of mind
10. Rigid and narrow thinking	Expansive, unlimited thinking
11. Closed to change	Flexible and open to change
12. Living in the past and future	Living in the now
13. Holding grudges and bitterness	Forgiveness
14. Being righteous	Being happy
15. Judgment and criticism	Acceptance, tolerance, introspection
16. Denying feelings	Honoring feelings
17. Resisting life	Allowing and flowing with life
18. Cluttered	Organized
19. I can do it myself thinking	Reaching out
20. Oblivious	Self-aware
21. Day by day existence	Purpose and meaning
22. Doing, doing, doing	Being and doing
23. Separate, splintered	Connected, wholeness
24. Identified with Ego	Identified with essence
25. Waste	Recycle
26. Greed	Simple abundance
27. Children as possessions	Children as teachers
28. Taking for granted	Grateful and acknowledging
29. Arrogant, ego attached, cocky, know it all	Humble

From Ego Consciousness	To Soul Consciousness:
30. Weak	Self-empowered
31. Low self-esteem	Self-confident
32. Negativity	Optimism
33. Self-absorbed	Interested and caring
34. Five sensory beings	Multi-sensory beings
35. Ignorance	Wisdom
36. Lack of self trust	Living by your intuition
37. Needing to change others	Acceptance
38. Constant activity	Retreat, rest, quiet time, restore
39. Playing it safe	Willing to risk
40. Why me? mentality	Trusting in a greater plan
41. Numbing out	Feeling life
42. Over medicating	Exploring the cause
43. "I don't need anybody"	It takes a village
44. Fast food	Conscious meals
45. Disrespectful of nature	Respectful of nature
46. Uncaring	Compassionate
47. Fear of looking within beliefs	Exploring and examining
48. Routine	Creative planning and living
49. Stuck	Changing your thinking and your life
50. Wavering, uncertain and indecisive	Ability to commit
51. Life sucks	All is well and in order
52. Greedy	Giving, sharing, helpful
53. Scarcity and lack	Abundance
54. Serious nature	Playful
55. Untrusting and skeptical	Discernment and trust
56. Living small	Enthusiastic and open
57. Defeated, given up	Determined
58. The world is out to get me	The world is a friendly place
59. Victim of self-pity; Nothing ever goes my way, but it does for others.	Accountability/Observer in appreciation

From Ego Consciousness	To Soul Consciousness:
60. Incapable and inadequate accomplish	There isn't anything I can't
61. Martyr: I'd rather do it myself, know it will get done – RIGHT.	Appreciative for support and I assistance
62. Need for attention	Self acceptance
63. Belligerent and irritable	Willing to chill and be aware
64. Aggressive	Assertive
65. My way or the highway perspectives	Honoring individual
66. Unhappiness	Joyful living
67. Reactive	Responsive
68. Rough, heartless and cruel	Gentle and kind
69. Abusive	Non-violent
70. Cynical	Friendly, open, and trustful
71. Envious and jealous	Happy for others and yourself
72. Undeserving	Deserving
73. Fault finding	Seeing the good in all
74. Loser	Winner
75. Harsh	Gentle
76. Abandoned	One with all life
77. Disappointed	Seeing the bigger picture
78. Intolerant	Tolerant / understanding
79. Despairing and discouraged anything	Hopeful and optimistic / is possible
80. Being a people pleaser	Honoring who you are
81. Doing just enough to get by	Doing your best
82. Attack	Understanding
83. Irritable / moody	Patient, even-tempered
84. Removed / distant	Engaged
85. Selfish	Selfless
86. Competition	Cooperation
87. Pessimistic	Optimistic
88. Powerless	Self-Mastery
89. Personal power	Authentic power

From Ego Consciousness	To Soul Consciousness:
90. Angry	Peaceful and insightful
91. Defensive / Guarded	Open
92. Neediness – better/less than	Equality
93. War mentality	Peaceful-win/win
94. Controlled by habits and subconscious	Conscious choice
95. Impatient	Patient
96. Procrastination	Self-discipline
97. Needing to prove self	Self-acceptance
98. Intimidating	Welcoming and open
99. Lonely	Content with self
100.Gossip and complaining	Direct contact and self responsibility
101.Worry / anxiety	Faith, trusting the process

Additional Resources from "The Attitude Doc"

Unlimited Vision
A 5-Day Program to Revitalize Your Potential

Recharge Your Life Script in 5 Days!
Open the world of possibilities as you open your mind. Break through stagnant patterns to find new avenues to happiness. Challenge your mind to let go...and expand your immeasurable potential.

Unlimited Vision will help you SEE, FEEL, HEAR, TOUCH, and BELIEVE in your life's purpose. **Unlimited Vision** will bring to light the role of resistance in your life, the principal of energy and thought, and the value of taking responsibility. In just five days you will have the opportunity to receive the blessing of forgiveness.

So get ready, and Set Your Intention to Recharge Your Life Script. In a world absolutely ruled by dynamic energy (that means change) nothing in your life is set in stone, if you do not wish it so. The rules however, do require you to make choices and achieve a new level of self-respect. Are you ready? Let's do it!

Conscious Choice – Conscious Creation
A 21-Day Program for Personal Transformation

You're in Charge! Your Life is Your Choice!
Conscious Choice – Conscious Creation offers daily words of wisdom, in-depth lessons, activities and affirmations to guide you toward the life you CHOOSE to live. Conscious Choice – Conscious Creation takes an in-depth look at YOU with lessons about personal power, communication, abundance, love and manifesting the life and relationships you desire.

Success is an elusive concept. What does it require? Are you in charge of your own potential? Who holds the measuring stick? Who made the measuring stick, anyway? Are you the one responsible?

You Can Choose:
   Happiness - Fulfillment - Satisfaction - Success - Peace - Love - Joy

Go to www.theattitudedoc.com to purchase
Unlimited Vision or **Conscious Choice** – Conscious Creation.

While visiting us online, check out the free articles and the teleclass schedule.

Bibliography, Part I: Books

Albom, Mitch. Tuesdays with Morrie. New York: Doubleday, 1997.

Angelou, Maya. Heart of a Woman. New York: Random House, 1981.

Bach, Richard. Bridge Across Forever. Thorndike, ME: Thorndike Press, 1985.

Bach, Richard. Illusions. New York: Delacorte Press, 1977.

Bach, Richard. Jonathan Livingston Seagull. New York: Macmillan Corp.,1970.

Barrentine, Pat edited by. When the Canary Stops Singing. San Francisco: Berrett-Koehler Publishing, 1993.

Bensen, Herbert and Klipper, Mariam Z. The Relaxation Response. Harper Torch, 1976.

Bokser, Ben Zion, translated by. The Talmud. New York: Paulist Press, 1989.

Braden, Gregg. The Isaiah Effect. New York: Harmony Books, 2000.

Breathnach, Sarah. Simply Abundance. New York:Time Warner Books, 1995.

Breggin, Dr. Peter. Talking Back to Prozac: What Doctors Aren't Telling You About Today's Most Controversial Drug, St. Martin's Press, Dept., 1995.

Brenner, Paul, M.D. Seeing Your Life Through New Eyes: Insights To Freedom From Your Past, Beyond Words Publ., Aug. 2000.

Bridges, Helice. Who I am Makes a Difference. Difference Makers Intl. 1977.

Brooks, Robert, M.D., Ph.D. and Goldstein, Sam, Ph.D. Nurturing Resilient Children. Chicago: Contemporary Books, 2002.

Brooks, Robert, M.D., Ph.D. and Goldstein, Sam, Ph.D. Raising Resilient Children. Lincolnwood, IL: Contemporary Books, 2001.

Buscaglia, Leo. Love. New York: Ballantine, 1972.

Bulland, Sarah, Teaching Tolerance. Main Street Books, Reprint edition, 1997.

Bushell, Linda Kay. Forever in our Hearts. Pittsburgh: Dorrance Publications, 2002.

Buzan, Tony. Use Both Sides of the Brain. New York: E. P. Dutton & Co., Inc., 1976.

Caldicott, Helen. If You Love This Planet. New York: W. W. Norton, 1992.

Cameron, Julia. The Artist's Way. New York: Putnam Publishing, 1992.

Campbell, Joseph. The Masks of God. New York: Viking Press, 1959.

Capacchione, Lucia. The Creative Journal. Athens, OH: Swallow Press, 1979.

Carlson, Julie and Johnson, Sue. *Grandloving*. Minneapolis: Fairview Press, 1996.

Chamberlain, David, Ph. D. *The Mind of your Newborn Baby*. Berkeley, CA: North Atlantic Books, 1998.

Chopra, Deepak, M.D. *The Seven Spiritual Laws for Parents*. New York: Harmony Books, 1997.

Chopra, Deepak, M.D., *Ageless Body, Timeless Mind*. New York: Crown Publishing, 1993

Choquette, Sonia. *The Wise Child: A Spiritual Guide to Nurturing Your Child's Intuition*. Three Rivers Press, 1st edition March, 1999.

Cousins, Norman. *The Anatomy of an Illness*. New York: Norton, 1979.

Crow, Gary and Crow, Melissa. *The Friend Factory*. Hamilton, MI: Koenisha Publications, 2002.

Crum, Thomas F. *The Magic of Conflict*. New York: Simon & Schuster, 1987.

Dale, Theresa, N.D., Ph. D. *Transform Your Emotional DNA*. Santa Barbara, CA: The Wellness Center for Research & Education, Inc., 1995.

Dantes, Ligia, *The Unmanifest Self*. Asian Publ., March. 1990.

Delis-Abrams, Alexandra, Ph. D. *The Feelings Dictionary*. Coeur d'Alene, ID: Adage Publishing, 1999.

Delis-Abrams, Alexandra, Ph. D. *The Feelings Storybook*. Coeur d'Alene, ID: Adage Publishing, 1998.

Donaldson, O. Fred, Ph. D. *Playing by Heart*. Deerfield Beach, FL: Health Communications, Inc., 1993.

Duncan, David James. *My Story as Told by Wate: Confessions, Druidic Rants, Reflections, Bird-Watchings, Fish Stalkings, Visions, Songs and Prayers Refracting Light, from Living Rivers, in the Age of Industrial Dark*. Sierra Club, 2003.

Emergy, Stewar. *The Owner's Manual for Your Life: The Book You Should Have Gotten at Birth, but Didn't*. Doubleday, Feb, 1982.

Forman, Linda. *Dreaming in Real Time*. Berkeley, CA: North Atlantic Books, 2003.

Foundation for Inner Peace. *A Course of Miracles*. New York: Viking Penguin, 1975.

Frankl, Victor. *Man's Search for Meaning*. Boston: Beacon Press, 1963.

Fuller, Buckminster. *Intuition*. Garden City, NY: Doubleday, 1972.

Gibran, Kahlil. *The Prophet*. New York, Alfred A. Knoff, Inc., 1923.

Goodall, Jane. *Reasons for Hope*. New York: Warner Books, 1999.

492

Grunwell, Erin. *The Freedom Writers Diary*. New York: Broadway Books, 1999.

Hample, Stuart and Marshall, Eric, compiled by. *Children's Letters to God*. New York: Workman Publishing, 1991.

Hartman, Thom. *The Last Hours of Ancient Sunlight*. Northfield, VT: Mythical Intelligence, Inc., 1998.

Hawkins, David R. *Power vs. Force*. Sedona, AZ: Veritas Publishing, 1998.

Heider, John. *The Tao of Leadership*. Atlanta, GA: Humanics Limited, 1985.

Hemingway, Mariel. *Finding My Balance*. New York: Simon & Schuster, 2003.

Hill, Julia Butterfly. *Legacy of Luna*. San Francisco: Harper San Francisco, 2000.

Hill, Napolean. *Think and Grow Rich*. North Hollywood, CA: Melvin Powers, Wilshire Book Co., 1966.

Hoff, Mark. *Wolves*. Andrews McNeel, 1997.

Holmes, Ernest. *Science of Mind*. New York: G. P. Putnams Sons, 1983.

Holmes, Ernest. *This Thing Called You*. New York: G.P. Putnams Sons, 1948.

Homer. *The Odyssey*. New York: Chelsea House, 1988.

Huber, Stephanie. *Life in the Canine*. Carlsborg, WA: Legacy by Mail, Inc., 1999.

Humphreys, James H. *Stress Management for Elementary Schools*. Charles C. Thomas Publ. Ltd, May, 1993.

Huxley, Laura Archera. *You Are Not the Target*. Ambassador Books, Ltd., 1963.

Jampolsky, Gerald G., M.D. *Love is Letting Go of Fear*. Millbrae, CA: Celestial Arts, 1979.

Johnson, Anthony Godby. *A Rock & a Hard Place*. New York: Crown Publishers, 1993.

Johnson, Robert A. *He*. New York: Harper & Row, 1974.

Jung, Carl. *Man and His Symbols*. New York: Dell Publishing Co., Inc., 1964.

Karr-Morse, Robin and Wiley, Meredith S. *Ghosts from the Nursery*. New York: The Atlantic Monthly Press, 1997.

Kaufman, Barry Neil. *Happiness is a Choice*. New York: Fawcett Columbine, 1991.

Kazantzakis, Nikos. *Zorba the Greek*. New York: Simon & Schuster, 1953.

Kiyosaki, Robert T. *Rich Dad, Poor Dad*. Paradise Valley, AZ: Tech Press, Inc., 1997.

Knapp, Caroline. *Pack of Two*. New York: Random House, 1995.

Lao Tzu with Mitchell, Stephen, translated by, *Tao Te Ching*. New York: Harper & Row, 1988.

Larsen, Laura. Facing the Final Mystery. 1st Books Library, 2000.

Liberman, O. D. Take Off Your Glasses and See. New York: Crown Publishers, Inc., 1995.

Lindbergh, Anne Morrow. Gifts from the Sea. New York: Pantheon Books, 1955.
Markova, Dawna. I Will Not Die an Unlived Life. Berkeley: Conari Press, 2000.

Martin, William. The Parents' Tao Te Ching. New York: Marlowe & Company, 1999.

Maslow, Abraham H. The Farther Reaches of Human Nature. New York: Viking Press, Inc.,1971.

McKibben, Bill. Enough: Staying Human in an Engineering Age. New York: Times Books, 2003.

Micozzi, Dr. Marc S. Many Paths to Healing. Eagle, CA: Sunn Publishing, 2000.

Miles, Elizabeth. Tune Your Brain: Using Music to Manage Your Mind, Body and Mood. 1997

Montessori, Maria. The Absorbent Mind. New York: Dell Publishing, 1967.

Moody, Raymond A. Jr. M.D. Laugh After Laugh. Jacksonville, FL: Headwaters Press, 1978.

Moorman, Chick. Parent Talk. Merrill, Michigan: Person Power Press, 1998.

Morgan, Marlo. Mutant Messages Down Under. New York: HarperCollins Publishers, 1994.

Nambudripad, Devi S., Say Goodbye to Illness. Buena Park, CA: Delta Publishing Co.,1999.

Nichols, Barbara. Beethoven Lives Upstairs. New York: Orchard Books, 1994.

Orman, Suze. The Road To Wealth. Riverhead Books, Revised and updated edition, Dec, 2003.

Paul, Anthea. girlosophy. St. Leonards, NSW, Australia: Allen & Unwin, 2000.

Peace Pilgrim. Friends of Peace Pilgrim. 1982.

Pearce, Joseph Chilton. Magical Child. New York: Bantam New Age Books, 1977.

Pearsall, Paul, Ph. D. Making Miracles. New York: Prentice Hall Press, 1991.

Pelzer, David J. A Child Called It. Deerfield Beach, Florida: Health Communications, Inc.,1995.

Pert, Dr. Candace. Molecules of Emotion. New York: Touchstone, 1997.

Paramahansa Yogananda. Autobiography of a Yogi. Los Angeles: Self-Realization Fellowship, 1969.

Paramahansa Yogananda. Bhagavad-Gita. Los Angeles: Self-Realization Fellowship, 1995.

Rahim, Shanto. Imagine Peace. Peace Pilgrim coloring book.

Ram Dass. Conscious Aging. Boulder, CO: Sounds True, 1992.

Reina, Dennis and Reina, Michelle R. Trust and Betrayal in the Workplace. San Francisco: Berrett-Koehler Publishers, Inc., 1999.

Robinson, Joe. Work to Live. The Guide to Getting A Life, Perigree, 2003.

Rogers, Fred and Barry Head, Mister Rogers Talks With Parents, Hal Leonard; Aug. 1993

Rosenberg, Ellen. Growing Up Feeling Good. New York, Beaufort Books, 1983.

Rosenberg, Marshall B. Non-violent Communication. Del Mar, CA: Puddle Dancer Press, 1999.

Rowling, J. K. Harry Potter and the Chamber of Secrets. New York: Arthur A. Levine Books, 1999.

Ruiz, don Miguel. The Four Agreements. San Rafael, CA: Amber-Allen Publishing, 1997.

Sacker, Dr. Ira and Zimmer, Marc A. Dying To Be Thin: Defeating Anorexia Nervosa & Bulimia, A Practical Life Saving Guide. New York: Warner Books, updated Aug., 1987.

Saphier, Ruthann. Fridge Notes for the Strung Out Mom and Dad. M & K Enterprises, Inc., 2000.

Schenk de Regniers, Beatrice. How Sam & Joe Got Together. New York: Parents Magazine Press, 1965.

Schloss, Eva with Kent, Evelyn Julia. Eva's Story. Great Britain: W. H. Allen & Co. Publications, 1988.

Seligman, Martin E. P. Learned Optimism. New York: Alfred A. Knopf, Inc., 1990.

Seo, Danny. Heaven on Earth. New York: Simon & Schuster, 1999.

Smotherman, Dr. Ron. Playball: The Miracle of Children. Context Publishing, reprint, 2001.

Steinbeck, John. East of Eden. New York: The Viking Press, Inc., 1952.

Stone, Hal and Sidra, Winkelman. Voice Dialogue: A Tool for Transformation. DeVorss & Co., June, 1987.

Suzuki, Shunryu. Zen Mind, Beginner's Mind. New York: Weatherhill, Inc., 1977.

Tariaglia, Louis A., M.D., and Les Brown. Flawless! The Ten Most Common Character Flaws and What You Can Do About Them. William Morrow, Feb., 1999.

Thich Nhat Hahn. *Anger.* New York: Berkley Publishing Group, 2001.

Thomas, Arthur G. *Abundance is Your Right.* Marina del Rey, California: DeVorss & Co., 1977.

Tolle, Eckhart. *The Power of Now.* Novato, CA: New World Library, 1999.

Vaughn, Frances E., Ph.D., *Awakening Intuition,* Anchor, Dec. 1978.

Walsh, Neale Donald. *Conversations with God.* Norfolk, VA: Hampton Roads Publishing Co., 1998.

Walsh, Neale Donald. *The Little Soul & the Sun.* Charlottesville, VA: Hampton Roads Publishing Co., 1998.

Warren, Peggy. *Gathering Peace.* Nederland, CO: Art After Five, 1996.

Webster's II Dictionary. The Riverside Publishing Company, 1984.

Weisel, Elie. *Night.* New York: Bantam Books, 1960.

Wilber, Ken. *Grace and Grit.* Boston: Shambhala Publication, Inc., 1991

Young, Robert O., Ph. D. and Young, Shelley Redford. *The pH Miracle.* New York: Warner Books, 2002.

Zukav, Gary. *Dancing Wu Li Masters.* New York: Morrow, 1979.

Zukav, Gary. *The Seat of the Soul.* New York: Simon & Schuster, 1989.

Bibliography, Part II: Articles/Newsletters/Journals/Periodicals

ABC News Study, "Mandatory Labeling of Genetically Engineered Foods," June, 2001.

Berenson, Gerald S., Bogalusa Heart Study, Tulane University, httpL///www.son.tulane.edu/cardiohealth/bog.htm, 1972-2005.

Breggin, Dr. Peter, Making A Difference Newsletter, Vol.2, Issue 8, "Reclaiming Our Children," March, 2001.

Browne Turner, Sandra, M.A., Young Child Magazine, " Caring for Children's Souls"

Buffington, P.W., Ph.D., "Harkin' These Words!", SKY magazine, May, 1982.

Curry, Kathleen, Knight-Ridge Newspaper, Tolerance Starts At Home, Desert Magazine, 1936, "Mr. Desert."

Dietrich, William, The Seattle Times Magazine, "Story of a Survivor," March 19, 2003.

Environmental Resource Center, "Eliminating Junkmail," Ketchum, Idaho, 2003.

Family Circle, Sept. 1, 1998.

Fideler, David, GNOSIS Newsletter, Fall, 2003.

Frawley-Holler, Janis, Hemispheres, "Personal Growth: Island Lessons," Nov., 2003.

Friends of Peace Pilgrim Newsletter Winter, 2003/04.

Properties of H2O and Coke Study, University of Washington, "H2O or Coke." Internet.

Hattam, Jennifer, Sierra Club, Nov/Dec, 2003.

Hooven, Carol, USA Weekend Sept 8-10,1995.

Kanter, Francine, Inspiration: Body, Mind, Spirit, "Drugs For Lunch? ADHD and Homeopathy," Sept/Oct., 2003.

Laine, Kristin, Delicious Magazine,   "Shall I Toss My TV?," Oct., 2003.

Croal, N'Gai, Sojnathan Alter, Sr. Editor Newsweek, "Mentoring Makes A Difference," Nov. 2, 1998.

Mundell, Gary/Fostaod,Rick, Cruising World, "Castaway," Sept., 1987.

Plaskin, Glenn, Family Circle, "Barbara Walters: How to Talk To People- and Get Them To Listen," Feb., 1988.

Quammen, David, National Geographic, "Jane In The Jungle," April, 2003.

Ryan, Michael, Parade Magazine, "They Call Their Boss A Hero," Sept. 8, 1996.

Sapolsky, Robert, Newsweek, "It's Not All In The Genes", April 10, 2000.

Resources

Adopt a Mountain Gorilla
The Dian Fossey Gorilla Fund
International
800 Cherokee Ave., SE
Atlanta, Georgia 30315-1440
800-851-0203
http://www.gorillafund.org/

American Institute of Stress
124 Park Avenue
Yonkers, New York 10703
(914) 963-1200
http://www.americaninstituteofstress.o
rg/

Ammachi
M.A. Center
P.O. Box 613
San Ramon, CA 94583 USA
510.537.9417
http://www.ammachi.org/

American Psychiatric Association
750 First Street, NE
Washington, DC 20002-4242
(800) 374-2721
http://www.apa.org/

American Association of Retired Persons
601 E. Street NW
Washington, DC 20049
888-OUR-AARP
http://www.aarp.org/

Antioch University
150 E. South College Street
Yellow Springs, OH 45387
937-769-1340
http://www.antioch.edu/

Banff Mountain Film Festival
Mountain Culture, The Banff Centre
Box 1020
107 Tunnel Mountain Drive
Banff, Alberta, Canada T1L 1H5
403-762-6675
http://www.banffmountainfestivals.ca/

Barlean's Organic Oils, L.L.C.
4936 Lake Terrell Rd.
Ferndale Washington 98248
360.384.0485
http://www.barleans.com/

California Literacy
133 N. Altadena Drive, Suite 410
Pasadena, CA 91107-2379
Ph: (626) 395-9989
http://www.caliteracy.org/

Center for Attitudinal Healing
Gerald G. Jampolsky, M.D.33 Buchanan
Drive
Sausalito, California 94965
415-331-6161
http://attitudinalhealing.org/

Central Asia Institute
Greg Mortenson
PO Box 7209
Bozeman, Montana 59771 USA
Tel: 877-585-7841(tollfree)
http://www.ikat.org/
CHARACTER COUNTS! National Office /
Josephson Institute of Ethics
9841 Airport Blvd., Suite 300
Los Angeles, CA 90045
(310) 846-4800
http://www.charactercounts.org/

Character Connection
Janie Hamilton & Marla Lowe
2566 Deerwood Way
Oakdale, CA
(209) 526-4459
http://www.characterconnectionprogra
m.com/

Daniella Chace, MS, CN, Nutritionist
P.O. Box 2032
Hailey, ID 83333
Credit Union National Association
P.O. Box 431
Madison, WI 53701-0431
(800) 356-9655
http://www.cuna.org/

Counselors for Social Justice
c/o ACA
5999 Stevenson Ave.
Alexandria, VA 22304
800-347-6647
http://www.counselorsforsocialjustice.org

Daily Blessing Foods, Inc.
(541) 372-2373
http://organic-meat.com/

Elderhostel
11 Avenue de Lafayette
Boston, MA 02111-1746
Call us toll-free at
1-877-426-8056
http://www.elderhostel.org/

Friends of Peace Pilgrim
Steps For Inner Peace
Imagine Peace Color Book
7350 Dorado Canyon Rd.
Somerset, CA 95684
 (530) 620-0333
http://www.peacepilgrim.org/
Gesundheit Institute
P.O. Box 3134
Hagerstown, MD
21741-3134
http://www.patchadams.org/

Grandmothers For Peace International
P.O. Box 580788
Elk Grove, CA 95758
(916) 685-1130
http://www.grandmothersforpeace.org/

Greenpeace International
Ottho Heldringstraat 5
1066 AZ Amsterdam
The Netherlands
Tel: +31 20 5148150
http://www.greenpeace.org/

Dr. Alan Hallada
Clinic Mesa Veterinary Hospital
323 W. Tefft. Str.
Nipomo, CA 93444

Health Dynamics
Mary Crouch
20449 SW TV Hwy. #345
Aloha, OR 97006
208.344.7553
http://www.myhealthdynamics.com

Idaho Women's Celebration
7224 Monroe Ave. Evansville, IN 47715
812-476-4365

Journey To A Hate Free Millennium
New Light Media
100 S. Sunrise Way, #276
Palm Springs, CA 92262
760-322-4455
http://www.newlightmedia.org/

Landmark Education
353 Sacramento St., Ste. 200
San Francisco, CA 94111
415-981-8850
 http://www.landmarkeducation.com/

Light On The Mountains Spiritual Center
Rev. John Moreland
P.O.Box 1195
Sun Valley, ID 83353

Mayo Clinic
"Childhood Obesity; A Big Problem"
Feb.8, 2002
www.mayoclinic.com

National Alliance for Mental Illness
(NAMI)
Colonial Place Three
2107 Wilson Blvd., Suite 300
Arlington, VA 22201-3042
(703) 524-7600
http://www.nami.org/

National Association of Mental Illness for
Youth
A division of NAMI
NAMI -- YOUTH

499

National Council on Aging
NCOA Headquarters
300 D Street, SW Suite 801
Washington, D.C. 20024
(202) 479-1200
http://www.ncoa.org/

National Institutes of Health
Bethesda, MD
http://www.nih.gov/

National Institute of Mental Health (NIMH)
6001 Executive Boulevard, Room 8184,
MSC 9663
Bethesda, MD 20892-9663
301-443-4513 or 1-866-615-NIMH (6464),
toll-free
http://www.nimh.nih.gov/

National Mental Health Association
2001 N. Beauregard Street, 12th Floor
Alexandria, Virginia 22311
(800) 969-NMHA (6642)
http://www.nmha.org/

The Chocolate Farm
http://www.chocolatefarm.com

The Compassionate Friends, Inc.
P. O. Box 3696
Oak Brook IL
60522-3696
630-990-0010
http://www.compassionatefriends.org/

The Jane Goodall Institute - USA
Headquarters
Roots and Shoots
8700 Georgia Ave Suite 500
Silver Spring, MD 20910
(240) 645-4000
http://www.janegoodall.org/

The Mentoring Center
1221 Preservation Parkway, Suite 200
Oakland, California 94612
(510) 891-0427
http://www.mentor.org/

The National Mentoring Partnership
(202) 729-4340
http://www.mentoring.org

Northwest Coalition for Alternative to
Pesticides
PO Box 1393
Eugene OR 97440-1393
541-344-5044
http://www.pesticide.org/

Option Institute
Barry Neil Kaufman
2080 S Undermountain Road Sheffield
MA 01257-9643
(413)229-2100
http://www.option.org/

Operation Respect
Peter Yarrow, Founder
2 Penn Plaza, 5th Floor
New York, New York 10121
212-904-5243
http://www.operationrespect.org/

The Quartus Foundation
Jan & John Price
PO BOX 1768
Boerne, TX 78006
http://www.quartus.org/

ReNew Life Formulas Inc.
2076 Sunnydale Blvd.
Clearwater, FL 33765
800-830-4778
http://www.renewlife.com/

Santa Rose & San Jacinto Mountain
National Park
51-5000 Highway 74
Palm Desert, CA 92260
760-862-9984

Self-Realization Fellowship
3880 San Rafael Avenue, Dept. 9W
Los Angeles, CA 90065-3298
Tel: (323) 225-2471
http://www.yogananda-srf.org/

Siddha Yoga
SYDA Foundation
P.O. Box 600
371 Brickman Road
South Fallsburg, New York 12779-0600
845-434-2000
http://www.siddhayoga.org/

Sierra Club National Headquarters
85 Second Street, 2nd Floor
San Francisco, CA 94105
415-977-5500
http://www.sierraclub.org/

Socrates Café
socratescafe@aol.com
http://www.philosopher.org/

Stone Education
Dr. Suki Stone
P O Box 500315
San Diego, CA 92150
www.reading-right.org

Stress Management Center/
Phobia Institute
Dr. Donald Dossey
75 Cambridge Rd.
Asheville, NC 258804
Phone/FAX 828-258-1001

Sunn Institute
Lisa Marie Goold, CEO
863 W. Quarter Drive
Eagle, ID 83655
http://www.sunnrooibos.com/

Teaching Tolerance
400 Washington Avenue
Montgomery, AL 36104
334.956.8200
http://www.tolerance.org/teach/

Tostan
Molly Melching
Melching@telecomplus.sn

Trinity Water
Corporate Office
200 S. Main / Box 8810
Ketchum, ID 83340
208.726.7734 tel.
www.trinitysprings.com

University of Santa Monica
22nd & Wilshire Blvd.
Santa Monica, CA
(310) 829-7402
http://www.gousm.edu/

Westin Hotels
http://www.starwood.com/westin/
index.htm

Who I Am Makes A Difference
Helice Bridges
Differences Makers International
P O Box 2115
Del Mar, CA 92014
ablueribbon@aol.com
http://www.blueribbons.com/

Wolf Education and Research Center
P O Box 217
Winchester, ID 83555
208-924-6960
http://www.wolfcenter.org/